What Is Mormonism?

What Is Mormonism? A Student's Introduction is an easy-to-read and informative overview of the religion founded by Joseph Smith in 1830. This short and lively book ›vers Mormonism's history, core beliefs, rituals, and devotional practices, as well as e impact on the daily lives of its followers. The book focuses on the Church of Jesus ›rist of Latter-day Saints, the Salt Lake City-based church that is the largest and t-known expression of Mormonism, whilst also exploring lesser-known churches t claim descent from Smith's original revelations.

signed for undergraduate religious studies and history students, *What Is Mormonism?* ›vides a reliable and easily digestible introduction to a steadily growing religion at continues to befuddle even learned observers of American religion and culture.

trick Q. Mason is Howard W. Hunter Chair of Mormon Studies and Dean of the hool of Arts and Humanities at Claremont Graduate University, USA.

PATRICK Q. MASON

What Is Mormonism?

A Student's Introduction

 Routledge
Taylor & Francis Group

LONDON AND NEW YORK

First published 2017
by Routledge
2 Park Square, Milton Park, Abingdon, Oxon OX14 4RN

and by Routledge
711 Third Avenue, New York, NY 10017

Routledge is an imprint of the Taylor & Francis Group, an informa business

British Library Cataloguing-in-Publication Data
A catalogue record for this book is available from the British Library

Library of Congress Cataloging-in-Publication Data
Names: Mason, Patrick Q., author.
Title: What is Mormonism? : a student's introduction / Patrick Q. Mason.
Description: New York, NY : Routledge, 2016.
Identifiers: LCCN 2016013310 | ISBN 9781138794580 (hardback) | ISBN
   9781138794603 (pbk.) | ISBN 9781315759135 (e-book)
Subjects: LCSH: Mormon Church. | Church of Jesus Christ of Latter-day
   Saints.
Classification: LCC BX8635.3 .M27 2016 | DDC 289.3—dc23
LC record available at http://lccn.loc.gov/2016013310

ISBN: 978-1-138-79458-0 (hbk)
ISBN: 978-1-138-79460-3 (pbk)
ISBN: 978-1-315-75913-5 (ebk)

Typeset in Berling
by Apex CoVantage, LLC

Printed and bound in Great Britain by
TJ International Ltd, Padstow, Cornwall

CONTENTS

CONTENTS

• FIGURES

ACKNOWLEDGMENTS

I am grateful for the many individuals and institutions that supported the completion of this book. I wrote most of the manuscript during a sabbatical leave granted by my institution, Claremont Graduate University, for which I am thankful. I conducted my Romanian interviews during my time as a Fulbright Scholar, and I am very grateful for the support of the U.S. Fulbright Commission, my host institution of the West University of Timişoara, and especially my interviewees for their willingness to share their experiences. I couldn't have done it without Lincoln Hale's willingness to travel with and translate for me – even if his language skills couldn't get me out of the speeding ticket. The manuscript was substantially improved by the people who offered helpful comments on portions or all of it. Thanks to the Mormon Studies reading group at Claremont Graduate University, including Redge Benheim, Bryan Cottle, Deidre Green, Taylor Kerby, and Ben Spackman. I owe a special debt of gratitude to Shelby Hamm, Courtney Rabada, Randy Powell, and especially John Turner and Dallin Lewis for their extensive feedback. And as always, my deepest thanks goes to my family, especially to my brilliant and forbearing wife Melissa, who thinks it's cool that her husband writes books.

Introduction

A clip from the irreverent Comedy Central animated sitcom *South Park* shows a large group of people standing against a fiery background that looks a lot like Mordor. Weeping and wailing, the crowd's attention is turned to a stage, where after a quick mic check, a bespectacled man introducing himself as the "Hell Director" greets the "newbies." As he starts to orient them to their new state of eternal damnation – "you are dead, and this is Hell, so abandon all hope, and yadda yadda yadda" – a man from the crowd protests, "Hey, wait a minute, I shouldn't be here! I was a totally strict and devout Protestant! I thought we went to heaven." Another speaks up, saying he was a "practicing Jehovah's Witness." Both are told by the director that, alas, they "picked the wrong religion." When people ask, "Well, who was right? Who gets into heaven?," the director replies, with emphasis, "I'm afraid it was the *Mormons*. Yes, the *Mormons* were the correct answer."[1]

It is a matter of individual faith whether or not Mormonism is in fact "the correct answer." Rather than adjudicating the religion's truth claims, this book is designed to help readers better understand Mormonism and its adherents. Propelled by millions of people who have accepted the religion as divinely inspired, Mormonism – most commonly associated with its largest institutional form, the Church of Jesus Christ of Latter-day Saints (or LDS Church) – has become a fixture in the American religious landscape and a growing presence in many parts of the world. Accordingly, this book is about Mormons as much as Mormonism, and how each shapes the other.

Mormonism has enjoyed a surge in public visibility in recent years, especially in the United States. The 2002 Winter Olympics in Salt Lake City, Utah, where the LDS Church is headquartered; the presidential campaigns of Mitt Romney in 2008 and 2012; the Broadway smash hit *The Book of Mormon* (written by the creators of *South Park*); the Pulitzer Prize-winning play *Angels in America*; ubiquitous online and social media ad campaigns; popular television shows about polygamy such as *Big Love* and *Sister Wives*; widespread media coverage; numerous sports heroes, business tycoons, and other celebrities – in short, Mormons and Mormonism have been more prominent in early-twenty-first America than at any time since mainstream Mormons abandoned polygamy more than a century ago. During his two campaigns for the presidency, Mitt Romney generally refrained from saying much about his religion, but that didn't stop the media from talking about it incessantly. Despite the fact that

Romney received about twice as much religion-related media attention as did Barack Obama, however, the extensive publicity did little to educate the public about the religion. A Pew Forum poll showed that 82% of Americans said they learned little to nothing about Mormonism during the course of the 2012 campaign, less than half could correctly answer the most basic questions about the religion, and about six in ten said that Mormonism is "very different" from their own faith.[2]

Frequently hailed by scholars and other outside observers as "the American religion," one of the Western Hemisphere's novel contributions to global spirituality, Mormonism's opponents have maligned it as having "borrowed the worst features of all religions, and all creeds, and woven them into a conglomerate but compact mass of incongruous absurdities."[3] Conflicting stereotypes abound: Mormons are hard-working, devout, patriotic, family-centered, and neighborly on the one hand; clannish, secretive, gullible, theocratic, and non- (or even anti-) Christian on the other. Founding prophet Joseph Smith originally sought inspiration from God to cut through the "war of words and tumult of opinions" within early nineteenth-century Protestant Christianity, but his own religion seems only to have produced more of the same.[4]

So what, exactly, is Mormonism? There are many answers to the question, but this book offers four possibilities as themes that will run as undercurrents throughout the chapters: 1) Mormonism is a historical religion; 2) Mormonism is a global tribe; 3) Mormonism is a proposed solution to existential human problems; and 4) Mormonism is a lived religion. Since these themes will appear repeatedly throughout the book, though often only implicitly, let me explain what I mean by each.

First, Mormonism is a historical religion. Like every other religion, Mormonism emerged from and continues to operate in the particularities of history, geography, and culture. Although Mormons make the theological claim that theirs is actually a modern, "restored" form of first-century Christianity, historically speaking Mormonism originated in the nineteenth-century United States. Scholars have noted the religion's consonance with the early American culture from whence it sprang. Some of those cultural similarities were particular to the nineteenth century and have since diminished, whereas others are as pronounced in contemporary Mormonism as they were almost two centuries ago.[5]

All religions come from somewhere, and that original somewhere is often deeply embedded in the religion's DNA. Even religions that establish a global presence and take on the flavor of diverse cultures – a process scholars call "enculturation" – cannot shake the cultural contexts that shaped their origins. Think, for instance, of Islam, which exhibits tremendous diversity in its communities around the world but nevertheless retains certain aspects of its seventh-century Arabian origins, most prominently the insistence on Arabic as the language of God and thus the only authentic language of the Holy Qur'an. Or Christianity, arguably the paradigmatic world religion, which still maintains much of its late classical Mediterranean heritage, such as the influence of Greek philosophy in the formulation of orthodox Christian theology.

Nobody is "merely" Christian, and every particular manifestation (Roman Catholic, Pentecostal, Russian Orthodox, non-denominational, etc.) is rooted in developments that occurred in a discrete historical context. Even people who identify with no religion at all, the "nones" – those who answer "none" when asked about their religious affiliation, comprising the fastest growing segment of the contemporary American religious landscape – are formed by an age of postmodern hyper-individualism and therapeutic spirituality.[6]

Identifying Mormonism as a historical religion allows us to appreciate its capacity to adapt in response to changing conditions. Though many believers are attracted to Mormonism because it provides them with a spiritual anchor in a rapidly shifting culture, the tradition has been evolving ever since its founding. Indeed, both the formation and maintenance of Mormonism required enormous creativity and generativity sustained over time. As we will see, Mormons look to their own history, which they generally understand to be providentially guided, as a source of inspiration, meaning, and authority. This book therefore offers an overview of key events in Mormon history because it is impossible to understand Mormon identity, theology, culture, and practice without at least a basic understanding of the religion's past.

Second, Mormonism is a global tribe. Like many other religions, Mormonism is both "tribal" and "global." On the one hand, even while assimilating new members, it maintains the boundaries of a strong collective, intergenerational identity. On the other, it creates a sense of community among worldwide members that transcends national and geopolitical boundaries.[7] Those who believed Joseph Smith's revelations quickly began to think of themselves less as simply another denomination cluttering the American religious marketplace and more in terms of biblical peoplehood. Mormons frequently quote the New Testament verse, "But ye are a chosen generation, a royal priesthood, an holy nation, a peculiar people."[8] Mormon peoplehood is asserted in both positive and negative terms – that is, who and what they are, and who and what they are not. They see themselves united by a common culture, history, tradition, and indeed kinship. These common traits transcend political boundaries and run deeper than mere theological affinities. Mormon peoplehood is visceral – felt and experienced, not merely abstractly conceived.

Within only a few decades of Joseph Smith's founding revelations, Mormons had already constructed a shared history, distinctive marital and family practices, a common religious language if not tongue, and an organic social, political, and economic vision for their ideal society. They constructed and sharpened these identity traits largely in opposition to their surrounding culture, namely Protestant America. Nineteenth-century Mormons and non-Mormons alike spoke of Mormonism as a new "race," though they differed on whether that was a good thing.[9] The emergent ethnicity of the Mormon people was most pronounced in the late nineteenth century but since then has been diffused as Mormons have pursued a path of accommodation, rather than stark opposition, to national norms. Furthermore, from the mid-twentieth century on, a globally successful missionary program has expanded the church far beyond its early American and North Atlantic roots. Despite early efforts to the contrary, Mormons have never fully separated themselves from their host cultures, and in the twentieth and twenty-first centuries, they have even acquired the reputation as ideal national citizens. Yet church leaders still insist that a distinctive yet not fully defined "gospel culture" should override any aspects of national, local, or ethnic culture that clash with Mormon doctrine or practice.[10]

No longer a parochial subculture located almost entirely in the American Intermountain West, now the LDS Church encourages its members to unify (some would say conform) around a prescribed set of norms and practices. Following an American corporate model, the church goes to great lengths to maintain brand integrity and product similarity throughout the world. You will often hear Mormons brag about the fact that "the church is the same no matter where you go in the world." While this statement masks a considerable amount of internal diversity, a program of centralized institutional authority called "correlation" streamlines decisions over everything from architecture to Sunday School curriculum. As a result, Mormon beliefs, worship style, dress and grooming standards, and marriage practices are often strikingly similar whether you are in Utah or Uganda. These commonalities create and reinforce the tremendous affinity that Mormons have for their "brothers and sisters" around the world. Church members will sometimes joke about using "Mo-dar" to spot a fellow Mormon in a crowd.[11] In reality and not just theory, a church member traveling to a different city or even country will immediately be welcomed when entering a Mormon congregation there and can strike up a conversation and even instant friendship based on shared values and common experiences. In short, Mormonism is not a race or ethnicity, but neither is it "merely" a church. To be born a Mormon or to become one through conversion is to be a part of the Mormon people – indeed, to be a member of the global Mormon tribe.

Third, Mormonism offers a proposed solution to existential human problems. Religion scholar Stephen Prothero argues, "Each of the great religions begins with a sense that something is rotten with the human condition. . . . For Christians the problem is sin. For Buddhists it is suffering. For Muslims it is pride or self-sufficiency."[12] Each religion then proposes a solution to the problem, whether salvation through Jesus Christ for Christians or submission to Allah for Muslims. Though Mormons share many notions of sin and salvation with other Christians, the religious system emanating from Joseph Smith's revelations was never concerned merely with getting individuals to heaven. Smith's early nineteenth-century world – and no less ours today – was an age of religious, political, social, and economic commotion. Karl Marx and other theorists have noted how modernity has brought rapid technological advances but also human estrangement and alienation. As Smith intuited, no aspect of the human condition was immune from deep fracture – God and humans were divided from one another, families were separated by geography and death, nations were at war both between and within themselves, an unregulated market economy sowed competition and inequality, and even God's revelation was hopelessly fractured into a multiplicity of religions, churches, and sects. Mormonism proposed that such fissures could be and were meant to be healed, and humanity made whole. Not only did Joseph Smith seek to close the gap between the human and divine, partly through priestly rituals designed to "seal" together the entire human family from Adam and Eve to the present day, but he initiated a political system intended to end partisan conflict and even international war, organized a communal economy aiming to eliminate socioeconomic class distinctions, and restored God's "only true and living church upon the face of the whole earth" that would unite all humanity in the common pursuit of exaltation.[13] As religion scholar Philip Barlow has perceptively observed, "Doctrines, policies, priesthoods, keys, revelations, and ordinances" – the particular and sometimes esoteric religious framework for Smith's overarching vision – "were ultimately in the service of restoring proper relations and order in time and eternity." Like every great religion that had previously proffered its respective problem and solution, Mormonism burst onto the scene delivering a penetrating diagnosis of the fractured human condition, then proposed a set of cures to make humanity, all creation, and indeed the entire cosmos whole again.[14]

This sweeping cosmic vision is at the heart of Mormonism, but it is admittedly not the stuff of everyday Mormon existence, or even how most churchgoing Mormons would articulate their faith, what attracts them to it, and what it means in their life. The fourth recurring theme in this book is that Mormonism is, above all, a lived religion. It is how millions of people across the world organize their lives and frame their conceptions of and experiences with the divine. Mormonism shapes families, social networks, and worldviews. No account of Mormonism would be complete without a discussion of Joseph Smith, priesthood hierarchies, and church institutions. But Joseph Smith was a prophet only because people believed he was, priesthood hierarchies only function when believers participate in and defer to them, and church institutions are hollow administrative shells without the people in the pews. In short, Mormonism is inseparable and indistinct from Mormons. The religion makes the people even as the people make the religion. Mormonism is formed, molded, preserved, passed on, and transformed through the daily acts of millions of worldwide adherents.

What Is Mormonism? thus commences not with Joseph Smith's early religious stirrings or with an explication of Mormon orthodoxy and orthopraxis – though we will get there. Rather, the first chapter offers a semi-fictional account of a week in the life of a "typical" Mormon family. Of course, there's no such thing – Mormon families come in all shapes and sizes, and individual Mormons have widely disparate relationships to and experiences within their religion. Nevertheless, to understand the religion, it's important to get a flavor of how Mormonism might affect the everyday lives of its adherents. In general, this book approaches Mormonism from the inside out. The presentation is not uncritical, but it examines the religion and its people on terms that insiders would basically recognize (though many adherents will not agree with all my interpretations).

Two brief caveats regarding taxonomy are in order. Throughout most of this book, I use "Mormonism" and "Mormons" to mean the Church of Jesus Christ of Latter-day Saints and its members. I do so as a convenient shorthand, fully acknowledging that the LDS Church is only one institutional manifestation within the broader family of churches that can be included in a more expansive definition of Mormonism, as will be considered in Chapter 10. Though size does not necessarily connote relative importance, it is true that the LDS Church is the largest and best-known expression of Mormonism by many orders of magnitude. Furthermore, many (though not all) members of other churches descending from Joseph Smith disclaim the label "Mormon" and are willing to concede it entirely to the LDS Church. The Church of Jesus Christ of Latter-day Saints by no means has a monopoly on the term "Mormon" – and even some of its own leaders are nervous about the church's nickname obscuring its actual name – but this book will focus primarily on the Latter-day Saint experience and will use "Mormon" and "Mormonism" accordingly. I will also refer to members of the LDS Church as "Latter-day Saints" or simply "Saints," as is the common convention.

In addition, this book will typically distinguish between "Mormons" (or "Mormonism") and "Christians" (or "Christianity"). Much polemical ink has been spilled on the question of whether or not Mormons are Christians, or whether they constitute a different and new religion altogether. I will take up that question in more detail in Chapter 7. In short, my position – shared by many but by no means all scholars – is that Mormonism constitutes a distinctive branch of Christianity alongside Roman Catholicism, Orthodoxy, Protestantism, and perhaps Pentecostalism (whether or not Pentecostals properly fit within Protestantism is the topic for another book). Mormonism displays significant continuities with the broader Christian tradition, but also enough discontinuities and innovations so as to be considered categorically new. Simply as a matter of convenience, then, I use "Christian" where others might use more specific designators such as "traditional Christianity," "historic Christianity," and "Nicene Christianity."

Finally, *What Is Mormonism?* seeks to introduce readers to Mormon history, scripture, theology, culture, institutions, and internal diversity, but as an introductory survey it necessarily cannot cover all these topics (and many others) in full detail. Those interested in learning more about a particular subject are invited to consult the book's footnotes. My goal is to help you understand Mormonism as a critically thinking observer of religion but also as a neighbor, coworker, family member, or friend. Whether or not you think Mormonism is "the correct answer," as *South Park*'s Hell Director posited, in a pluralistic world that remains "as furiously religious as it ever was," good citizenship is predicated at least in part on religious literacy and simply getting to know our neighbors.[15] This book is intended as part of that broader spirit and project of mutual understanding that is so crucial – yet frequently so elusive – in the twenty-first century.

• NOTES

1 "Abandon All Hope," *South Park*, Comedy Central, available at http://southpark. cc.com/clips/152270/abandon-all-hope (accessed November 10, 2015).

2 Pew Research Center, "Americans Learned Little about the Mormon Faith, but Some Attitudes Have Softened," December 14, 2012, available at http://www. pewforum.org/2012/12/14/attitudes-toward-mormon-faith/ (accessed November 10, 2015).

3 Edgar E. Folk, *The Mormon Monster – or, the Story of Mormonism* (Chicago: Fleming H. Revell, 1900), 273.

4 Joseph Smith-History 1:10, Pearl of Great Price.

5 For overviews of this period, with considerations for the broader milieu into which Mormonism was born, see Nathan O. Hatch, *The Democratization of American Christianity* (New Haven, CT: Yale University Press, 1989); Charles Sellers, *The Market Revolution: Jacksonian America, 1815–1846* (New York: Oxford University Press, 1991); Sean Wilentz, *The Rise of American Democracy: Jefferson to Lincoln* (New York: W.W. Norton, 2005); Daniel Walker Howe, *What God Hath Wrought: The Transformation of America, 1815–1848* (New York: Oxford University Press, 2009).

6 Pew Research Center, "U.S. Public Becoming Less Religious," November 3, 2015, available at http://www.pewforum.org/2015/11/03/u-s-public-becoming-less-religious/ (accessed November 10, 2015).

7 Amin Maalouf, *In the Name of Identity: Violence and the Need to Belong*, trans. Barbara Bray (New York: Penguin Books, 2000), 93.

8 1 Peter 2:9.

9 See W. Paul Reeve, *Religion of a Different Color: Race and the Mormon Struggle for Whiteness* (New York: Oxford University Press, 2015).

10 For analysis and critiques of the notion of "gospel culture," see Walter E.A. van Beek, "Church Unity and the Challenge of Cultural Diversity: A View from across the Sahara," 72–98; and Wilfried Decoo, "Expanding Research for the Expanding International Church," 99–131, both essays in *Directions for Mormon Studies in the Twenty-First Century*, ed. Patrick Q. Mason (Salt Lake City: University of Utah Press, 2016).

11 At least one study suggests that this phenomenon might be real. See Nicholas O. Rule, James V. Garrett, and Nalini Ambady, "On the Perception of Religious Group Membership from Faces," *PLoS ONE* 5:12 (2010): e14241, available at http://doi.org/10.1371/journal.pone.0014241.

12 Benyamin Cohen, "Questions for Stephen Prothero, Author of *God Is Not One*," *Huffington Post*, July 6, 2010, available at http://www.huffingtonpost.com/benyamin-cohen/questions-for-stephen-pro_b_564900.html; Stephen Prothero, *God Is Note One: The Eight Rival Religions that Run the World – and Why Their Differences Matter* (New York: HarperOne, 2010).

13 Doctrine and Covenants 1:30.

14 Philip L. Barlow, "To Mend a Fractured Reality: Joseph Smith's Project," *Journal of Mormon History* 38:3 (Summer 2012): 28–50, quote on 48.
15 Peter L. Berger, "The Desecularization of the World: A Global Overview," in *The Desecularization of the World: Resurgent Religion and World Politics*, ed. Peter L. Berger (Grand Rapids, MI: Eerdmans, 1999), 2; Stephen Prothero, *Religious Literacy: What Every American Needs to Know – and Doesn't* (New York: HarperCollins, 2007); Robert D. Putnam, *American Grace: How Religion Divides Us and Unites Us* (New York: Simon & Schuster, 2012).

1

A week in the life of a Mormon family

• MONDAY

The first alarm of the day goes off in sixteen-year-old Jacob's basement bedroom at 5:00 am. He groggily throws an arm in its direction to hit snooze. With long experience he has learned that he can do this twice and still make it on time. At 5:16 he rolls off the bed, takes a cursory shower, and heads upstairs to the kitchen for a quick breakfast of cereal and juice, which he wolfs down while reading – loosely defined – his Book of Mormon. By 5:47 he's out the door, and makes the twelve-minute drive to the church building for seminary. Class starts at 6:00; he strolls in at 6:03. Close enough.

Jacob is one of the tens of thousands of Mormon teenagers who repeat this ritual every weekday to attend "early morning seminary." Since Mormons don't have a professional clergy, seminary isn't aimed at those specifically preparing for a ministerial career. Instead, it's more like daily Bible study, and it's for all Mormon high school students. Jacob frequently bemoans the fact that if he lived in Utah or southeastern Idaho, like his cousins do, then rather than getting up at this ridiculous hour, he could use a period of released time to attend seminary in a building located just across the street from the school campus.

"Sister Anderson" – Mormon adults usually go by "Brother" or "Sister" in church settings – cheerily welcomes her dozen or so bleary-eyed students. Under her direction, they begin by singing a drowsy rendition of a hymn, and then she asks Jacob to offer the opening prayer for the class. Once he settles back into his seat, Sister Anderson launches into her lesson. This year they're studying the New Testament, as are all the other Mormon seminary students around the world, whether in Salt Lake City or South Dakota or Suriname. The lesson today is based on the Gospel of Matthew, chapter 16. When cued, the girl sitting next to Jacob reads aloud verse 19, where Jesus tells Peter: "And I will give unto thee the keys of the kingdom of heaven: and whatsoever thou shalt bind on earth shall be bound in heaven: and whatsoever thou shalt loose on earth shall be loosed in heaven." (Mormons use the King James Bible, and are accustomed to all the thees and thous and shalts.) Sister Anderson tells a story about how one of the Mormon prophets – Jacob didn't catch which one – went somewhere in Europe and saw a statue of Peter holding keys, and said that now he, as the church president, had the keys. She fervently emphasizes to her students that other churches are full of good people worshiping God the best way they know how, but that none of those churches have the keys of the priesthood, or the authority that God gave to Peter and the apostles. After being lost for nearly two thousand years, that authority was restored to Joseph Smith, and now resides in the current prophet and apostles of "the Church." (When Sister Anderson says "the Church," she definitely means the Church of Jesus Christ of Latter-day Saints.) "I bear my testimony," she concludes, with tears in her eyes, "that we have a modern prophet and apostles who lead and guide this church, and that God restored his priesthood authority through the Prophet Joseph Smith." After a closing prayer, the class has cupcakes that one of the students brought for her birthday.

Jacob drives to school, giving a ride to a couple of the other kids whose parents had dropped them off at the church. These are his "church friends," whom he has grown up with for years as fellow members of the same ward, or congregation, and they're three of exactly fourteen Mormon students at the entire high school. Once at school they go their separate ways into their respective cliques – jocks, video gamers, mathletes, thespians – but those distinctions mostly disappear when they're together at church.

Today's a pretty normal Monday for Jacob. He endures his classes, flirts with a few girls, and hangs out with his friends in the halls and at lunch. Religion never comes up. After school he has swimming practice. The locker room banter is, well, locker room banter – adolescent males strutting around half naked, bragging about their weekend exploits or plans for coming exploits. Jacob is fully part of the group, but he doesn't swear – "gosh dang it" is about the most his friends can get out of him – and his contributions are decidedly PG compared to his buddies' raunchier R-rated material.

He heads home, and starts on his homework. Family dinner is at 6:00, after his dad, Mike, gets home from work. In the Williams home, you don't miss family dinner. Mike asks ten-year-old Emma to offer the blessing on the food, which she does as each member of the family folds their arms, bows their heads, and closes their eyes: "Dear Heavenly Father, thank you for this day. Thank you for our family and all our many blessings. Please bless Madison on her mission, and please bless the prophet. Please bless that Ethan will stop teasing me. [Twelve-year-old Ethan smirks.] Thank you for this food, and please bless it and bless Mom for preparing it. In the name of Jesus Christ, amen." The family devours lasagna as they each review the events of the day.

"Remember, kids," Jennifer says, "it's Monday, so tonight is Family Home Evening." Jacob and Ethan groan. For nearly a hundred years, church leaders have encouraged Mormon families to set aside one night a week – traditionally Monday night – for

"Family Home Evening." There's no particular format, though for many families, like the Williams, it will resemble a mini-church service, with prayer, hymn singing (Ethan's glad he plays piano for the family so he doesn't have to sing), and a short lesson, often presented by one of the kids. Every once in a while they'll have an outing instead – miniature golfing, hiking, and minor league baseball games are family staples. Tonight it's Jacob's turn to give the lesson. He repurposes something he learned in seminary a few weeks back, a passage from the Sermon on the Mount about not judging. That results in Ethan and Emma arguing about who should stop judging the other one. Mike plays referee, then thanks Jacob for the lesson. Jennifer puts her hand on his shoulder and says warmly, "You'll be a great missionary in two years!" Sensing the end of formalities, Emma asks, "Can we have treats now?" The family piles back into the kitchen for homemade ice cream sundaes.

Jacob retreats to his room, finishes his homework, and texts a few friends. By 10:30 he's exhausted and ready for bed. As he brushes his teeth, he gazes at the scripture he's pasted on the mirror next to the picture of Jesus: "Therefore, O ye that embark in the service of God, see that ye serve him with all your heart, might, mind and strength, that ye may stand blameless before God at the last day." Jacob reads his scriptures in bed for fifteen minutes, then kneels by his bedside and mumbles a prayer. "Please bless me to be a good influence on the guys on the team. Please bless that I'll do well on my history test tomorrow . . . ."

• TUESDAY

By 8:00 am, it's quiet. Jennifer has successfully wrangled Ethan and Emma out of bed (Jacob had left for seminary before they woke up), fed and clothed them, and whisked them off to school. Mike left for work a half hour ago. Having seen everyone off, Jennifer closes the door in relief and heads to the dining room table. This is her daily time of solitude. She reads her scriptures while she eats breakfast, counting on that daily ritual for a bit of inspiration and to get her bearings for the day. If she's lucky, she can even get a little exercise in before the phone starts ringing.

Today she's not so lucky. At 8:30 her cell phone buzzes. It's Sister Johnson. "Good morning, Sister Williams, I'm sorry to call so early. But I needed to let you know that Sister Hawkins was rushed to the hospital late last night. I think it's her heart." Jennifer gets the details and promises to go visit as soon as possible. As she hangs up she realizes that she missed another call while she was talking. She checks her voicemail. "Hi Jen, it's Nicole. Just wanted to let you know that Sister Walker had her baby last night. It's three weeks early, but it sounds like everything went fine. Should we do dinners?" Jennifer calls Nicole back to get the details. Of course, the Walkers are at a different hospital than Sister Hawkins, on the other side of town. "Yes, let's provide dinners for the family tonight and for the rest of the week. I'll call Denise and ask her to coordinate everything." As she hangs up and is about to call Denise, the phone rings again. "Hi Sister Williams, it's the missionaries. You know Lisa, who came to church with us yesterday for the first time? We met with her last night, and she said she really liked it. The thing is, she's not working right now, and says that she's kind of short on food for her and her kids. Can we do anything about that?" Jennifer responds that she'll talk to the bishop about what to do about the food and get back to them.

Jennifer's "calling," or her assignment within the church's all-volunteer staff, is as the ward Relief Society president, or leader of the women's organization of the local congregation. This gives her "stewardship" over all the women in the ward – and by extension their families – and makes her the busiest and most essential person in the congregation along with the bishop, who is the lay priesthood leader who presides over the congregation. Nicole and Denise are her two counselors; Mormon leadership positions are almost always constituted as a triumvirate. Some weeks Jennifer will spend upwards of thirty hours giving church service, making it the near equivalent of a full-time job even though she "doesn't work." For all her efforts she isn't paid a cent – "I get blessings in heaven!" she recites when people ask how she does it.

Several phone calls later, Jennifer gets herself ready and heads out the door. In addition to her usual errands, she now has two hospital visits to make. Thankfully, Sister Hawkins will be just fine, and the Walker baby is healthy and adorable. She assures the father that the Relief Society will bring in dinners every night, and promises that women will help babysit his older kids if he needs to be at the hospital with his wife and newborn. Jennifer gets home only a few minutes before Emma and Ethan trot in the door. The next three hours are taken up with chauffeuring them to piano lessons, baseball practice, and gymnastics, then grabbing to-go pizzas on the way home. Just as the family is sitting down to dinner, the phone rings. She would ignore it, but it's the bishop. She goes to the other room while Ethan prays and the family begins eating. She fills in the bishop on the missionaries' request on behalf of Lisa. He asks her to go to Lisa's house and assess the situation before he approves a church food order. She replies that she can drop by on Friday morning, after she drives Sister Moore to her doctor's appointment.

After dishes, helping with homework, ten minutes on Facebook (mostly to see if she's forgetting any ward members' birthdays), more phone calls, and family scripture study and prayer, at 9:30 Jennifer collapses on the couch. She pulls up a recorded episode of *Modern Family*, asking herself whether she's two or three weeks behind. She feels mildly guilty for watching a show that so clearly promotes "non-traditional" families – Sister Hawkins would surely disapprove – but figures it's harmless in the end. And she could use a good laugh.

● WEDNESDAY

Mike wakes up around the time that Jacob is pulling out of the driveway on his way to seminary. He puts on his headphones and cues up a talk from the church's last

General Conference, which he listens to as he goes for his morning run. After showering and joining Ethan and Emma for a quick breakfast, he heads out the door for work.

When he went away to college, Mike wasn't quite sure what he wanted to do when he grew up. After serving his two-year mission in Chile, he flirted with the idea of becoming a full-time seminary teacher. That quickly passed, but what stayed with him was that he wanted a job that would provide a good standard of living but also reasonable hours so that he could spend time at home with the kids and serve in the church. After weighing some options, and talking to a few people he knew from his parents' ward, he decided to become a dentist. It wouldn't require quite as much school as medical doctors, the pay was good, and he could be flexible with his hours. It was never really about the dentistry, though he took pride in his work. After a few years in a large practice, he set up his own private practice, with a big aquarium and train set in the front lobby to emphasize that he was family friendly. A lot of his patients are fellow ward members or other people they referred to him. The Spanish he learned on his mission also helped him build up a Hispanic clientele, and once a month he does pro bono work for immigrants who couldn't otherwise afford to see a dentist.

Today Mike is feeling guilty. Not because of anything he has done wrong – everyone agrees that he's the dictionary's definition of a "nice guy" – but because of what he hasn't done. In church the previous Sunday one of the lessons was about how church members should "share the gospel" with their friends, neighbors, and coworkers – "every member a missionary," as one prophet quipped. Then the talk he listened to on his morning run was about the Great Commission, or Jesus's commandment to his disciples to "Go ye therefore, and teach all nations, baptizing them in the name of the Father, and of the Son, and of the Holy Ghost." Mike thought of how, as a missionary in Chile, he had often quoted one of Joseph Smith's revelations: "it becometh every man who hath been warned to warn his neighbor." Mike knew he was a "good example" to people, and assumed that they thought well of his religion because they thought well of him. But he also knew that he hadn't exactly been the world's greatest "member missionary"; in fact, he couldn't remember the last time he had given someone a Book of Mormon or brought a friend to church.

Now he resolves to do better. All morning while cleaning teeth and installing fillings, he silently brainstorms brilliant ideas of how he could share the gospel in and through his workplace. "I don't want to offend anyone with a frontal assault," he thinks, so he considers subtler methods. He could put a Book of Mormon, or at least a copy of the church magazine *Ensign*, on the tables in the lobby with all the other magazines. He could put up a little card holder with "pass-along cards" produced by the church, which has a phone number or website where people could request a Bible, Book of Mormon, or church video. He could invite his hygienist, who has worked with him for eight years, to come to church that Sunday when he would be ordaining Ethan to the priesthood, or ask if his receptionist wanted to send her son to the church's

Boy Scout troop, where he could meet all the Mormon kids and by extension his mom would meet the Mormon parents. Even better, he could find ways to talk to his patients about the church – after all, they trust him, and they are the ultimate captive audience. People know that his daughter Madison is on a church mission in France, so that provides a perfect conversation starter, especially when they find out that she gave up college, dating, and movies for a year and a half to be a missionary.

Energized with all his ideas, when the clock hits noon, Mike walks down the street to have lunch with one of his old college roommates. Back at work, he spends the afternoon filling cavities. Several mouths in, he has completely forgotten his morning's elaborate strategizing to be a better member missionary.

After dinner that night, Mike drives Jacob and Ethan to the church. Wednesday night is activity night for the ward's youth group, known as Young Men's and Young Women's. Mike is first counselor in the ward's Young Men's presidency, which means he helps plan the weekly activities and mentors the eight or ten boys who usually show up. Since Ethan just turned twelve the weekend before, this is his first time attending Wednesday night activities. But since he knows all the kids – and all the adults – from years in the church, he blends right in, and immediately is as loud and obnoxious as all the other boys. After an opening hymn and prayer, Ethan stays at the church with the twelve- and thirteen-year-old boys to learn how to tie knots, while Mike goes with Jacob and all the other fourteen- to eighteen-year olds to the Smiths' house for a swimming party. The evening is mostly uneventful – Mike eats brownies and talks about the Lakers with Brother Smith, the Young Men's president, while the kids swim. The evening's one minor scandal occurs when one of the fifteen-year-old girls shows up in a two-piece swimming suit that is promptly deemed to be "immodest" by the Young Women leaders, who whisk her aside before any of the young men can ogle her. Fortunately the Smiths, who have two teenage daughters of their own, have "modest" one-piece swimsuits to spare. Crisis averted.

• THURSDAY

Emma, who is one of two Mormons in her fifth-grade class, comes bounding home waving an envelope. "Look, Mom, Olivia invited me to her birthday party!" Jennifer opens the invitation, and feels a pit in her stomach. "I'm sorry, honey, but the party is on a Sunday. Do you think a swimming party is appropriate for the Sabbath?"

Emma knows that "Keep the Sabbath day holy" is one of the Ten Commandments, right up there with the prohibitions against murder, adultery, theft, and lying, but the concept of a day of rest and worship is still a little too abstract for a ten-year-old. At dinner that night, the family discusses "appropriate Sunday activities." Mike struggles to explain to crestfallen Emma why birthday cake around the table at home with family and friends is appropriate for a Sunday, but a birthday cake at the table at a pool party is not. Jacob chimes in that he has skipped swim meets on Sunday and feels blessed by God for doing so. In his heart Mike knows this is all a bit arbitrary – after all, other families in the ward have different Sabbath rules (some considerably more lenient, some even stricter), and he and Jennifer agree to disagree about whether watching NFL games is okay. (Mike figures that since he does it with the boys, it counts as quality family time.)

Mike extemporizes a mini-sermon for the occasion: "Joseph Smith once said, 'I teach my people correct principles and let them govern themselves.' God gives us certain commandments, but often doesn't spell everything out. He expects us to use our agency and to figure out the best way to do his will. As members of his church, we can rely on the gift of the Holy Ghost to help us decide what is right and wrong." Mike feels satisfied with his little discourse until he looks across the table and sees Emma in tears. She sobs, "But I really wanted to go to Olivia's party!"

Jennifer jumps up from the table, remembering the Relief Society activity starting in twenty minutes. "I'm going to be late!" Mike promises to take care of the dishes and put the kids to bed while Jennifer hurries out the door. Tonight's monthly activity is a cooking demonstration put on by Sister Jones, who spent two years in the Peace Corps in India and is going to teach the sisters how to make curry. Jennifer feels some pride in pulling this off, since Sister Jones hasn't been to church for years. "I grew up in the church and have nothing against it," she told Jennifer on the phone, "but I just feel like my spiritual path has taken me elsewhere. That, and I just don't get why women can't have the priesthood. It doesn't make any sense to me." Jennifer asked her to sideline the priesthood question – "lots of people in our ward feel lots of different ways about that" – and just come and get to know the other sisters. The evening is a smashing success. Thirty women turn out, and they all have a great time. That is, all except for Sister Hawkins, who was discharged from the hospital the day before and complains that the curry is too spicy.

When she gets home after cleaning up the church, Jennifer asks Mike, "So how's Emma feeling about the whole birthday party thing?" He answers that he knelt down with Emma for bedtime prayers, and suggested that she ask Heavenly Father about whether or not she should go to Olivia's party. "I'm crossing my fingers that God doesn't tell her to go," he jokes.

• FRIDAY

Friday is Jennifer's favorite day of the week. Not because it's the end of the school and work week, but because it's when she gets letters from her daughter Madison, who left home five months ago for her full-time missionary service in France. Serving a mission had customarily been seen in the church as primarily a man's duty – which is why Jennifer didn't go on a mission while Mike did. But in 2012 the prophet and president of the church, Thomas S. Monson, had announced that the minimum missionary age for women would be reduced from twenty-one to nineteen. (It was simultaneously lowered from nineteen to eighteen for men.) This meant that women could now serve a mission before fully committing themselves to school or work or getting married (Mormons traditionally marry young). Promptly after the policy change, a tidal wave of nineteen-year-old "sister missionaries," plus eighteen-year-old men, flooded into "the mission field," with the total number of full-time missionaries maxing out at nearly 90,000 worldwide. Madison had jumped out of her seat when President Monson made the announcement, and promptly announced that she would be going on a mission as soon as she turned nineteen. She proved good to her word.

Missionaries proselytize full time for six days a week – usually upwards of seventy hours – but they get one "P-day" (short for "preparation") when they do their laundry, go grocery shopping, write letters home, and go sightseeing or otherwise have a bit of fun. So as to remain focused on their work, missionaries are typically allowed to call home only twice a year, on Christmas and Mother's Day. (Now that he's a missionary dad, Mike is a little resentful at Father's Day not making the cut.) Although Madison could use e-mail to write her weekly letters home, she is a bit old-fashioned, and handwrites them instead. Jennifer waits impatiently until the mailman arrives early each Friday afternoon, then rushes to the mailbox to tear open the letter from her oldest daughter.

Today, the weekly ritual is delayed. As she promised, Jennifer drives eighty-five-year-old Sister Moore to the doctor. That turns into a trip to the pharmacy, and then a "quick" visit to the Social Security office. After that, Jennifer stops by to see Lisa, the woman who had asked the missionaries for help with food after attending church with them. The apartment is in one of the worst neighborhoods in the city, a place Jennifer had forbidden Jacob to go at night, even if he is giving the missionaries a ride. Several other families from the church, many of them "less active" (meaning they rarely if ever came to church on Sunday), live in the same area. Jennifer parks on the street, makes sure her car is locked, and wanders through the apartment complex's courtyard, thumping with heavy bass and lyrics she didn't even want to understand, until she finds the right number. A man answers the door – hadn't Lisa said she wasn't married? – and when Jennifer introduces herself, he shouts back toward the hallway, "some church lady is here to see you." While waiting, Jennifer looks inside the apartment, and sees what she has seen many times before: three children under the age of five, two in diapers, one screaming. One dingy couch in the entire front room, opposite a sizable flatscreen TV. The place reeks of various types of smoke, and liquor bottles are strewn on the kitchen counter.

Lisa comes to the door, apologizes for the mess, and invites Jennifer in, as the unidentified man retreats out of sight. They sit down on the couch and start to talk. "All my life I've believed in Jesus," Lisa begins. "I grew up with my grandma taking me to church. I know I've done some things I shouldn't, but I still believe. When those missionaries knocked on my door the other day, I just felt like I should let them in. I feel like it's time to get back into a good church and change my life." Jennifer nods. "The

FIGURE 1.1 LDS sister missionaries offer tours at Temple Square in Salt Lake City, Utah

Copyright: Jim West/Alamy

problem is," Lisa continues, in between shushing children, "that I lost my job, and I don't get child support, and I'm just a little short this month." Jennifer nods again, and says that she understands that times are tough. "I'll talk to the bishop, and see if we can't give you a little bit of help to get you through. In the meantime, keep coming to church and meeting with the missionaries. I know that the message they have for you will really help you and your family, and give you the joy and strength that you need to change your life." Jennifer asks if they can say a prayer together, which they do, then gives Lisa a hug before leaving. On her way back to her car, Jennifer texts the bishop that she thinks they should help. A few minutes later he texts back and authorizes her to take Lisa to buy some groceries with the ward welfare fund. Jennifer calls Lisa and sets up a time for the next day.

When she finally gets home, she immediately checks the mailbox and tosses aside the bills and ads until she discovers Madison's letter. She looks at her watch and sees that the other kids will be getting home from school soon, so she restrains herself and waits until they can all read it together. Once they arrive, they excitedly perch around the kitchen counter while Jennifer opens the letter and reads aloud:

Bonjour ma famille,

Comment allez-vous? (That means, "How are you?") Things are so awesome here. I just got transferred to a new area this week. I'm in a town outside Marseille. It's SO gorgeous here, I love it! I'm going to miss my last area and all the amazing people there, but I know this is where the Lord wants me right now. My new companion is Sister Stone from Australia. She has the cutest accent! She kind of has a reputation of being hard to get along with, but I know that if I pray for charity and just show her love, we'll work miracles together.

Unfortunately the work is kind of slow here. This branch hasn't had a baptism in something like two years. I met the members at church on Sunday, and I think they just need to be encouraged and reminded of how important missionary work is. I'll admit that talking with French people about the gospel is a little harder than I expected. I mean, obviously I'm still not fluent, so I guess that's a big part of it. But I just feel like people here don't care enough about God. No one wants to talk to us. They just don't know how awesome the gospel of Jesus Christ is! I was starting to get a little down, but I talked with the mission president this week and he said that I just need to stay positive and show everyone how much joy the gospel brings me. I know that if they would just give the gospel a chance, and read the Book of Mormon and pray about it, they would totally be converted.

On Friday we met a woman from Africa who immigrated here two years ago. We had an awesome discussion, and she really felt the Spirit. She seems really open to the gospel. She couldn't come to church on Sunday, but we'll go back this week and have another lesson with her.

I miss you all so much, but I know this is where I'm supposed to be. I love France and the people here, and I just want them to have the same knowledge that I do.

Jacob, did you ever ask out Emily? Ethan, how's baseball going? Emma, don't get too comfortable in my room! (j/k) Mom and Dad, I'm so grateful for your examples and testimonies. I know the church is true, and that God lives and that Jesus is my Savior. I love you all!

Love,
Maddy

• SATURDAY

The Williams family is up and out of the house by 8:30 for a community service project organized by the stake, which is a collection of several wards. Coordinating with city officials, the church members are cleaning up a stretch of highway – pulling weeds, picking up litter, repainting a fence. Two hundred people, from eight different congregations, have shown up. Each is given an assignment and a bright yellow "Mormon Helping Hands" T-shirt to wear. There are so many people that they're practically on top of each other, and the work is done in just over an hour.

In between Ethan's baseball game and Jacob's swim meet, Jennifer runs out to take Lisa grocery shopping, extracting a promise that she'll see her at church the next day. At 4:00, Mike and Jennifer leave for the monthly ward temple night. Their regular church building is less than fifteen minutes away, open to the public, and used for regular Sunday services and social activities throughout the week. But the temple – one of less than 150 worldwide – is more than an hour from their house, and reserved only for special rituals (called "ordinances") performed by those members who are "worthy," Mormon parlance for being fully active in the church and obedient to church standards. The Williams try to go to the temple once a month, though admittedly life sometimes overwhelms them and so they may go two or three months in between visits.

When Mike told his neighbor across the fence that he would be going to the temple that night – meaning he would have to record the BYU-Notre Dame game and watch it later – his neighbor asked what he did there. Mike answered, "It's a little hard to explain. The ordinances we perform in the temple are the most sacred parts of our religion, so we don't really talk about them outside the temple, even among ourselves. But basically, we learn about the creation of the earth, Adam and Eve, and most of all our relationship to God and Jesus Christ. We also make covenants, or promises that we will be obedient to God and do our best to follow Jesus." His neighbor nodded weakly, still mystified. "I know that's pretty abstract," Mike admitted. "I guess the most concrete thing is that Jen and I were married in the temple, and we believe that our marriage will last not just 'until death do you part,' but rather for all eternity. So the temple is an amazing place for us to reconnect with God and each other, and just to feel peace."

FIGURE 1.2 Salt Lake Temple and Temple Square, Salt Lake City, Utah

Copyright: Gary Whitton/Alamy

By the time they are done at the temple, grab dinner with some friends, and then make the drive back home, it's almost 10:30 when they pull into their driveway. Jennifer observes an empty spot on the side of the driveway: "Jacob's not here." Jacob just turned 16 and got his driver's license, which has made trying to parent him a lot more complicated. They knew he was going dancing with friends downtown, but the deal was that he had to be back by 10:00 unless previous arrangements had been made (which they had not been). Mike tries calling Jacob's cell. It goes straight to voicemail. He texts. No reply. The minutes turn into hours. With no response, Mike and Jennifer discuss whether to start calling hospitals or to go looking for him in the likely hangouts, when finally, just after 1:00 am, Jacob saunters through the door, beaming. Relieved that he is alive, and that he is so obviously thrilled with a fun evening and so clearly innocent and unaware that he didn't have clearance to be out this late – and shown the evidence of a cell phone with a dead battery – their fury is somewhat alleviated. After a quick talk about "next time," and "what's the point of giving you a cell phone if you don't charge the battery," Jacob heads to his bedroom. Mike turns to Jennifer and tiredly jokes, "Well, I don't smell pot, his car isn't crashed, and it doesn't sound like he got anyone pregnant. So all in all I'd say it's a successful night."

Jennifer smiles exhaustedly. Growing up in a heavily Mormon community in Utah, both she and Mike sat through countless church lessons on the dangers of dating before you were sixteen – with plenty of morality tales about girls who ended up pregnant (the moral burden and consequences usually fell heaviest on the girls in these stories). Still, appropriate boy-girl relationships remained pretty vague. Riding in the same car alone to a movie was clearly a prohibited "date," for example, but making out behind the junior high? No problem. (Whenever Jennifer brought this up, Mike reminded her that not *everyone* had been so lucky as to be making out behind the junior high.) As their own kids began shifting into teen years, the ironies of these dating theories from their own youth began to grow on the Williams, so they decided to take a different tack, emphasizing relationships rather than activities, and *why* it was important to avoid relationships progressing too quickly.

Fortunately, Madison and now Jacob seem to have taken this idea to heart. Even though he's reasonably handsome and athletic, Jacob long ago made it known that he wouldn't have any girlfriend before sixteen. When a cute girl from school asked him to go with her to prom a couple months before his sixteenth birthday, he told her, "I'd be happy to go with you as friends." (He was worried about the whole dating thing, but truth be told, he was more concerned about where he was going to get the $45 for his ticket.) Now that he is sixteen, he's gone out a few times with a girl from another ward – the "Emily" mentioned in Madison's letter – but both of them are too busy with school and extracurricular activities to spend a whole lot of time paired off. For her part, Jennifer is mostly relieved that Jacob's eye has fallen on a "good Mormon girl." Although she and Mike feel like prohibiting him from dating non-Mormons would be counterproductive, they both believe that dating someone "with the same standards" just makes things easier – and after all, as Jennifer frequently reminds her kids, "you end up marrying who you date." And marrying a non-Mormon, though not expressly forbidden by the church, isn't even discussed in the Williams home as a viable option.

• SUNDAY

Church services begin at 9:00 on Sunday morning. But for Jennifer and the rest of the ward leadership, the morning starts much earlier. The bishop and his counselors are there beginning at 6:30, and then about eight other people, representing the various organizations within the ward (for men, women, youth, children, Sunday School, and missionaries), show up at 7:30 for "ward council." They begin with prayer, then after the bishop invites Jennifer to share a favorite scripture and offer a brief reflection on it, the meeting begins in earnest. The hour is spent mostly in planning and coordination. The missionaries report on people they are currently teaching; Jennifer gives an update on the health and welfare of various families in the ward, including some of the visits she made during the week; and the other ward leaders do likewise. The bishop – whose day job is as a financial planner – mostly listens, though when he weighs in on any particular issue, he is clearly regarded as the first among equals.

Mike and the kids arrive a few minutes before 9:00, and the Williams take their usual pew on the side of the unadorned but clean chapel. Jacob sits with another boy at a table near the front of the chapel, where he will prepare and bless the bread and water that will be distributed to the congregation as "the sacrament," or communion. One of the bishop's counselors conducts the meeting, which begins with a congregational hymn and a prayer. Ethan is then called up to the front podium, where he is presented to the congregation as having turned twelve and thus becoming eligible to receive the priesthood and be ordained to the office of a deacon. The entire congregation raises their hands in "common consent," signaling universal approval. The bishop shakes his hand and whispers, "We'll take care of the ordination after church," then Ethan trudges back to his seat next to Jennifer, who proudly tussles his hair. She looks around the chapel trying to see Lisa, but no sign of her. "Maybe she's just running late," she thinks. After another hymn, the sacrament is passed to all members of the congregation by the deacons – a group of six teenage boys, all dressed in an unofficial uniform of white shirts, ties, and dark slacks. "That'll be you next week," Mike whispers to Ethan.

The rest of the meeting, which takes just over an hour, is taken up by talks from three members of the ward: a high school student, a retired widow, and an accountant. All have done this before, though none are particularly skilled or scintillating public speakers. During an especially dry spell in the last talk, which features the accountant reading (in monotone) four paragraphs from an address recently delivered by one of the church's apostles, Mike surreptitiously starts checking scores and highlights from yesterday's games – until he sees Jen giving him a dirty look. A few minutes later, the closing hymn and prayer finally provide some relief.

Decades ago, the LDS Church decided that one hour of church on Sunday just wasn't enough. So following sacrament meeting, the ward members all leave the chapel and divide into various Sunday School classes, with all the adults in one room and the youth and children divided by age. Jennifer had planned on accompanying Lisa to the class for "investigators," but she never showed up; Jennifer catches herself feeling resentful that she went to the trouble of helping her out and Lisa couldn't even make the effort to come to church. So instead she joins Mike in the adult Sunday School class, which is focused for the year on studying the Book of Mormon. Today's teacher – a retired judge – has the uncomfortable habit of calling on people and making them generally feel like they are on the witness stand. But he's smart, occasionally funny, and at least not boring, so he's generally accepted as a "good" teacher.

After an hour of Sunday School, everyone divides again for another set of classes. All the adult women, except those who are teaching classes for the children, go into Relief Society, where Jennifer busily greets as many people as she can. She conducts the meeting, announces the Walkers' new baby and thanks those who took over meals, expresses appreciation for everyone who helped with the Thursday night activity and community service project the day before, and sends around a signup sheet soliciting people to volunteer for a weekday shift at the church-owned food cannery near the temple. On the other side of the church, Mike and the boys attend priesthood meeting. They begin all together, with a hymn, prayer, and announcements, then separate as the teenagers go to their own classes and the adult men divide between "high priests" (usually for older men) and "elders quorum" (typically for men in their twenties to forties). As a counselor in the Young Men's presidency, Mike goes with the boys. Today it's his turn to teach the lesson, which is meant to encourage his students to obey the church's health code, called the Word of Wisdom. To keep the attention of a half dozen teenaged boys, he liberally sprinkles in references to sports and pop culture along with warning them against the evils of alcohol, tobacco, and drugs.

At noon, church is over. Families find each other from the various corners of the building. The Williams gather near the bishop's office for Ethan's ordination to the priesthood. After waiting for a few minutes, the bishop ushers them in, shaking Ethan's hand warmly. He offers a few thoughts on what a sacred gift it is that God entrusts his power – the priesthood – with boys as young as Ethan. He urges Ethan to always remember what a sacred duty it is to be a priesthood holder, and that he should always live worthy and be a good example to his friends. Ethan nods somberly. At the bishop's invitation, Ethan sits in a chair in the center of the room. All the men, including Mike and Jacob and Jennifer's dad (in town just for the occasion), circle around him, each laying their right hand on his head and their left hand on the shoulder of the man next to them. Mike, standing directly behind him, speaks for the group: "Ethan George Williams, in the name of Jesus Christ and by the authority of the Melchizedek Priesthood which I hold, we lay our hands upon your head and confer upon you the Aaronic Priesthood, and ordain you to the office of a deacon within the Church of Jesus Christ of Latter-day Saints." Mike goes on to offer words of blessing and encouragement to his son, then closes "in the name of Jesus Christ, amen." Ethan shakes the hand of the men in the circle, and gives big hugs to his dad and mom, who wipes happy tears from her eyes. "I'm so proud of you," she whispers.

The sacredness of the occasion doesn't fully carry over back at the house, where within a half hour of walking in the door Ethan is reprimanded for teasing his sister. While Emma is setting the table for a big lunch – using the nice dishes to celebrate the special occasion, and with Grandpa and Grandma there – she asks Jennifer, "So will I get the priesthood too when I turn twelve?"

Jennifer looks up from slicing fruit. "No, Emma, the priesthood is only for boys."

"Why?"

"Because that's the way Heavenly Father made it. Going all the way back in the Bible, only men had the priesthood."

Emma thinks for a moment. "So are boys more important than girls?"

"No, absolutely not, honey. Heavenly Father loves his sons and daughters equally. Boys and girls are just different, and have different jobs. Just like how only girls get to have babies."

"Yeah, but boys still get to be dads. It doesn't seem very fair to me. I mean, I was watching Jimmy pass the sacrament today, and he went the wrong direction and messed it all up. I could totally do a better job."

"You're probably right about that," Jennifer laughs. Then, more seriously, "This is something that's really hard for a lot of people to understand. To be honest, I'm not even sure I totally understand all the reasons why. All I can tell you is that I know that the priesthood is God's power, and that it gives your dad and brothers really amazing opportunities to serve other people. I really don't feel like that not having it takes away from me at all. I don't feel discriminated against in the church. And think about your sister who's on a mission, preaching the gospel just like the boys do. I know that God loves me and you and Madison just as much as he loves the boys, and that the church has given me all kinds of opportunities to grow and serve and lead, even without being ordained to the priesthood."

By the time Jennifer is done with her homily, Emma has finished setting the table. "Okay, Mom," is all she offers as she skips out of the room, leaving Jennifer to sigh and think about raising her daughters to be strong women in a church where certain positions – and especially the highest ones – can only be held by men. When she tells Mike about it that night, he quips, "If it's good enough for a billion Catholics. . . .." She punches him on the shoulder.

After the big family lunch, Mike and Jacob go "home teaching," which entails priesthood holders visiting other members of the ward to see how they're doing and share a spiritual message. (The counterpart for women is called "visiting teaching.") The people assigned to the Williams include a couple of "active" (churchgoing) families and a "less active" single mother with two young children. Today they visit the two active families, which is fairly easy duty because they're all longtime friends. It's slightly awkward for Jacob, though, because the Millers have a son his age – they used to play together all the time when they were younger – who fell in with a different group of friends, got into drugs, and now refuses to come to church. Sister Miller cries every time she sees Jacob, and says how much she wishes her son was "good like you." Not only does Jacob squirm at the extra attention, but he also realizes that she probably uses that same line – "Why can't you be more like Jacob?" – when lecturing her son.

After home teaching, it's back to the house to watch one half of football and grab a quick bite of dinner before Mike and the boys head to the bishop's house for a "fireside," which Jacob has learned is just a code word for another hour of church on a Sunday night. Tonight it's not so bad, though, as the speaker is Brother Johnson, who did two tours in Iraq. After telling about how body armor saved the life of one of his buddies when he got shot, he talks about the importance of "putting on the whole armor of God." When Mike asks him about it on the drive home, Ethan, for whom this is his first youth fireside, replies, "It was pretty cool, how that guy got shot and all. And the brownies were really good."

The Williams finish the day with their daily family scripture reading and prayer, before everyone retreats to their rooms. Jacob is asleep by 10:00, knowing that 5:00 am comes awfully early.

* * *

This portrayal of the fictional Williams family is based on a composite sketch of real Latter-day Saint families who recorded for me a week in their lives, with special emphasis on their religious practices and commitments. As such, it is highly stylized and indeed idealized. White American middle-class suburban domesticity has become the normative image of the Mormon family, both by insiders and outsiders, and in this portrayal I explore what that stereotypical image might actually look like from the inside. But the fact remains that no two Mormon families are exactly alike. I could have just as easily profiled a single mother and her children, or a childless married couple heavily involved in their early careers, or elderly empty-nesters, or a single gay man, or a family in Brazil or Nigeria or Japan with their own culturally informed family dynamics and structures. Most Mormons aren't like the Williams; even those who resemble them demographically might spend far less time in religious pursuits. Not to mention the more-than-half of those people on the membership rolls of the church who rarely if ever attend Sunday services and may not even self-identify as Mormon. Even with those disclaimers in mind, however, most devout Mormons would resonate with the broad contours sketched out here, even if the reality of their own lives doesn't correspond in every detail. And some – a minority that constitutes much of the core membership and leadership of the church in North America – would say that this more or less describes their actual lived experience of being Mormon on a day-to-day, week-to-week basis.

What do we make of a family like the Williams? Are they religious fanatics, or just average God-fearing Americans? Regardless of one's normative judgment, the descriptive reality is that for many if not most committed Mormons, religion suffuses their everyday life. Fully acculturated, they go to the same schools, work in the same offices, watch the same television shows and movies, play the same sports, listen to the same music, and share many of the same hopes and fears and aspirations as other people in their societies. They do not live a life apart in sealed-off religious enclaves. But religion is a central presence in the soundtrack of their lives – if not perpetually the main melody, then almost always a steadily recurrent theme. It is so embedded in the daily rhythms of their lives that many Mormons may not even consciously recognize how distinctive many of their daily habits actually are.

Scholars speak of a "Mormon culture region" that stretches from southeastern Idaho through Utah to patches of Arizona. Yet even beyond that area, for families like the Williams, being Mormon makes them a member of a distinctive subculture that shapes much of the contours of their social interactions, voluntary commitments, speech patterns, entertainment choices, sartorial norms, family structures, and political ideology. Subsequent chapters will demonstrate that there is plenty of genuine diversity within the ranks of contemporary Mormondom. Amid that diversity, however, there remain certain patterns and cues, some subtle and others explicit, that distinguish Mormon individuals and families and give them a collective sense of solidarity. Mormons who are perfect strangers often find upon their first encounter that they have more in common with one another, as members of the same tribe, than they do with many of their non-Mormon coworkers and next-door neighbors. They will share certain unique life experiences – such as going on a mission, or serving in time-intensive church callings, or navigating professional or social interactions without drinking coffee or alcohol – that are not replicated elsewhere in the general culture and thus can be fully appreciated only by fellow insiders.

Mormons care about doctrine – or orthodoxy – far more than even most other religious people today. Much of the considerable time they dedicate to religious education, whether on Sundays, in seminary, or at the three different campuses of Brigham Young University (in Utah, Idaho, and Hawaii), focuses on reifying doctrinal distinctiveness. When Mormons "bear testimony," to one another or to outsiders, they will almost invariably speak in terms of what they "know" – that God lives, that Jesus is the Son of God and Savior of all humanity, that Joseph Smith was a true prophet called by God, that the Book of Mormon is true scripture, that the church is currently led by a living prophet, that "the church is true." Yet as our week with the Williams family demonstrated, Mormonism resides not only in a set of beliefs but in a multitude of practices and habits. It is a lived religion that is enacted through the body in a thousand minor repetitions. Most Mormons would agree that Jacob attending seminary almost matters more than what he remembers from what he was taught there on any given morning.

In the next three chapters, we turn from a semi-fictional and contemporary account to the historical development of Mormonism from its beginnings in the early nineteenth century. As we will see, Mormonism has always been defined by the Mormons who inhabit and shape it, and who are shaped by it.

2

Visions

In the winter of 1838, Louisa Barnes Pratt opened her front door to a stranger asking if he and his wife could lodge overnight at her home in western New York. She said yes and invited him in, only to be surprised when he presented his wife Caroline, Louisa's sister whom she had not seen in four years. Jonathan and Caroline Crosby stayed with Louisa and her husband Addison for a month. Many of their nighttime conversations revolved around the Crosbys' newfound religion. "They had embraced the faith of the Latter Day Saints," Louisa wrote many years later in her autobiography, "and were on their way to Kirtland," a community of Mormon believers in northern Ohio. Louisa remembered fondly how her sister and brother-in-law

> taught us concerning the great and marvelous work which had been brought to pass in this our day, by a revelation from heaven! They told us how an angel had appeared to a young man by the name of Joseph Smith in the State of N[ew] York. All this was new and astonishing!

Louisa, already a sincere Christian, thought it "too good news to be true." She had previously heard of the Latter-day Saints, in particular their reputation for healing the sick, but had been turned off by some acquaintances who "called them imposters, deceivers, and everything but good." Addison was skeptical of the new doctrines Caroline and Jonathan discussed, but Louisa acknowledged that the principles they taught were in harmony with the Bible.[1]

The Crosbys finally continued on their journey, but not before leaving the Pratts with a copy of the Book of Mormon. Overwhelmed by the demands of running a farm and raising small children, Louisa only occasionally picked up the book. However, she mulled things over in her mind, and became increasingly convinced that Mormonism represented a restoration of biblical Christianity, just as the Crosbys and other early followers of Joseph Smith claimed. Louisa was attracted to Mormonism's fundamental principles and practices of "Baptism for the remission of sins, laying on of hands for the gift of the Holy Ghost, healing the sick by faith, casting out devils, speaking in tongues and prophesying." Her neighbors scorned her Mormon relations, but that only seemed to strengthen Louisa's resolve.[2]

Throughout the spring, Louisa read her Bible "by day and by night," finding in its pages prophecies that "a work would be brought to pass in the latter days." She

FIGURE 2.1 Portrait of Louisa Barnes Pratt (1802–1880)

Courtesy of the Church History Library, The Church of Jesus Christ of Latter-day Saints, Salt Lake City, Utah

determined to go to Kirtland and see the Latter-day Saints for herself. She did so, and while there met with Martin Harris, one of Joseph Smith's earliest support- ers. Though currently disenchanted with the church, Harris nevertheless provided to Louisa his strong testimony of the authenticity of the Book of Mormon. Louisa returned home to New York encouraged and believing. Addison now took his turn to visit Kirtland and returned, to his wife's delight, as a baptized member of the church. Louisa immediately followed suit, being baptized in nearby Lake Erie. She was fired with all the zeal of a new convert, writing letters to her family in the east that she had learned by revelation from God that he was establishing his kingdom on the earth through her new church. "I had called on Him in mighty prayer," she reminisced, "and the light had burst forth upon my soul, like the sun bursting suddenly forth from behind a dark cloud! From that time I had never a doubt."[3]

• FOUNDATIONS

Louisa Pratt's revelation from heaven was one in an outpouring of divine manifes- tations that defined the founding generation of Mormonism. Though we can trace its spiritual genealogy back to various strains in European and early American religion, the proximate beginnings of Mormonism came with a series of visions claimed to have been experienced by Joseph Smith Jr. in or near his family's home in Palmyra, New York, during the 1820s. Smith's parents, Joseph Smith Sr. and Lucy Mack Smith, both descended from families that had been New Englanders for generations. But overwhelming debts led them to heed the siren call of bountiful land and economic opportunity that drove many early Americans westward. Far away from the more established churches of the eastern seaboard, western New York's religious culture was a highly competitive marketplace of churches and preachers later called the "burned-over district" because of the fires of revival that so regularly swept the area.[4] In Palmyra and other similar towns, you could find crossroads where there was literally a different church on every corner.

In the spring of 1820 or thereabouts, the religious fervor of the area left Joseph Smith, an otherwise unremarkable fourteen-year-old boy, deeply concerned about the state of his soul and the spiritual state of the world. His extended family was split on religious matters – his father's side was skeptical toward organized religion and tended toward universalism, while his mother's side was more traditionally evangelical (Lucy and three of Joseph's siblings joined the local Presbyterian church). Living in a biblically saturated culture, it was only natural that Joseph Smith turned to the Bible for answers to his spiritual yearnings. He stumbled upon a verse in the New Testament's Epistle of James: "If any of you lack wisdom, let him ask of God, that giveth to all men liberally, and upbraideth not; and it shall be given him."[5] Smith decided to take James's advice literally, asking God directly what he should do rather than relying on the advice of Palmyra's ministers.

What transpired next is foundational to Mormonism – and historically contested. The basic narrative is clear. Inspired by the Bible, the young Joseph Smith went to a grove of trees near his home and prayed. In the canonical account, written nearly two decades after the fact, Smith attested that as he began praying he felt nearly overwhelmed by an evil presence, but then was rescued by a heavenly vision:

> I saw a pillar of light exactly over my head, above the brightness of the sun, which descended gradually until it fell upon me. It no sooner appeared than I found myself delivered form the enemy which held me bound. When the light rested upon me I saw two Personages, whose brightness and glory defy all description, standing above me in the air. One of them spake unto me, calling me by name and said, pointing to the other – *This is My Beloved Son. Hear Him!*

When Smith gathered his wits and asked which was the right church that he should join, the second person (presumably Jesus Christ) "answered that I must join none of them, for they were all wrong." Mormons have long used this divine indictment of Smith's religious contemporaries as proof of a general "apostasy" of Christianity that could only be solved by a "restoration" of the true gospel in the "latter days" before Christ's Second Coming. At the time, however, it seems that Smith's takeaway lesson from his vision was somewhat less grand. When he arrived home, drained of energy,

FIGURE 2.2 Joseph Smith (1805–1844), founding prophet of Mormonism

Courtesy of Intellectual Reserve, The Church of Jesus Christ of Latter-day Saints, Salt Lake City, Utah

his mother asked if he was feeling alright. He simply replied, "I have learned for myself that Presbyterianism is not true."[6]

Though this canonical version is the most widely cited, in fact there are nine distinct contemporary accounts of what Mormons call "the First Vision" (usually capitalized for emphasis): four firsthand accounts written by Smith himself or dictated to scribes, and five accounts recorded by contemporaries who heard Smith relate his narrative. Depending on one's perspective, the different versions are either basically consistent or wildly incongruous. They clearly disagree on specific details such as his age at the time of the vision (twelve or fourteen), how many divine persons he saw in his vision (one or two), whether or not angels and evil forces were present, and the precise content of the message delivered to him.[7]

Are these many differing accounts evidence that Joseph Smith was a fraud, as some have suggested? The majority of modern scholars, including those who are not

INCEPTION OF MORMONISM—JOSEPH SMITH'S FIRST VISION.

FIGURE 2.3 *Inception of Mormonism – Joseph Smith's First Vision*. Wood engraving of Joseph Smith's foundational vision of God and Jesus Christ near his family farm in Palmyra, New York, in 1820.

Copyright: Granger Historical Picture Archive/Alamy

Latter-day Saints, accept that Smith was himself convinced that he had had some kind of visionary experience. The reasoning is simple: in Smith's milieu, visions and other supernatural experiences were relatively commonplace. People read about visions in the Bible. His family received and trusted dreams and visions. Published accounts of heavenly encounters among otherwise ordinary people circulated widely. In short, Joseph Smith lived in a visionary culture in which men and women expected to have visions and trusted that others had them as well.[8] Adding a touch of authenticity is the fact that Smith's entire adult life was predicated upon the notion that he had legitimate and powerful experiences with the divine. Though he received various forms of psychological and to a lesser extent financial compensations for his status as a visionary and then prophet, the price of real persecution that he paid over the course of many years, culminating in his violent death in 1844, suggests a commitment to something more than a known lie. Of course, there have always been skeptics. Smith later reported that the first minister he told about his 1820 vision "treated my communication not only lightly, but with great contempt, saying it was all of the devil, that there were no such things as visions or revelations in these days."[9] Modern critical assessments have generally ranged from the pious fraud presented by his mid-twentieth-century biographer Fawn Brodie to the religious genius proposed by prominent literary critic Harold Bloom (both nonbelievers).[10] For his part, Smith wrote in his defense:

> I had actually seen a light, and in the midst of that light I saw two Personages, and they did in reality speak to me; and though I was hated and persecuted for saying that I had seen a vision, yet it was true. . . . I knew it, and I knew that God knew it, and I could not deny it.[11]

Faithful Latter-day Saints, of course, take Smith at his word and believe that both God the Father and Jesus Christ actually did appear and speak to him on that spring day in 1820. However, this is far more of an article of faith for modern Mormons than it was for Joseph Smith's contemporary followers. In fact, most Latter-day Saint converts during Smith's lifetime probably never heard of the First Vision, and its recounting rarely persuaded anyone to join the church. The story that early missionaries typically told interested listeners was of Smith's visions of the angel Moroni that began three years later, as detailed below. For instance, recall that even in retrospect, Louisa Barnes Pratt remembered that her sister and brother-in-law told her that "an angel had appeared to a young man by the name of Joseph Smith in the State of N[ew] York" – nothing about a visit from God and Jesus. It seems that Smith initially thought of his 1820 vision as a private experience, only later coming to realize and articulate how it fit within a broader narrative of the church's origins and history. Indeed, no reference to the First Vision existed in any published Mormon literature until 1840, some twenty years after its occurrence and only four years before Smith's death. Not until the late 1880s did the second generation of church leadership elevate the vision to its current status as the first event of the "restoration of the gospel" and a singular revelatory experience from which a range of church doctrines, including the Mormon concept of the nature of God, could be gleaned and therefore taught.[12]

THE ANGEL MORONI AND GOLD PLATES

Joseph Smith's initial vision seems to have had little immediate impact on his life, except that he heeded the heavenly admonition not to join any of the current churches. The next three-and-a-half years passed mostly uneventfully; he reported simply, "I continued to pursue my common vocations in life," mostly as labor on his family's farm. He admitted freely that his was the ordinary life of a typical teenager: "mingling with all kinds of society, I frequently fell into many foolish errors, and displayed the weakness of youth, and the foibles of human nature." He was not a seriously bad character, he would reassure his audience, but neither was he some kind of paragon of saintliness. Personally convicted of his "weakness and imperfections," on the evening of September 21, 1823, he engaged in earnest prayer to God "for forgiveness of all my sins and follies." As an experienced visionary, he reported, Smith "had full confidence in obtaining a divine manifestation, as I previously had one."[13]

While engaged in prayer, Smith "discovered a light appearing in my room, which continued to increase until the room was lighter than at noonday, when immediately a personage appeared at my bedside, standing in the air." Before him stood a man clothed only in a white robe, his entire being seeming to glow. The angel introduced himself as Moroni (pronounced moe-ROE-nigh). He told the astonished boy that God had a special work for him to do, which entailed retrieving a book written on gold plates that was deposited under a stone in a hill near Smith's home. Moroni said the book was "an account of the former inhabitants of this continent," and that it contained "the fulness of the everlasting Gospel . . . as delivered by the Savior to the ancient inhabitants." Accompanying the gold plates were "two stones in a silver bow . . . fastened to a breastplate," which together was called the "Urim and Thummim." The use of these stones would enable the boy to become a "seer" and fulfill his mission to translate the language on the gold plates into English. Moroni quoted several passages from the Bible referring to the restoration of the gospel in the last days, then gave Smith a vision in his mind's eye of exactly where the plates were buried. He vanished, but then reappeared twice more during the night and once again the next morning, each time repeating essentially the same material.[14]

Smith's first audience for his original vision in 1820 was his mother, who without hesitation affirmed his experience. This time he related his visitations from Moroni to his father, who had a series of visionary dreams earlier in his life and thus immediately believed his son and told him to do as the angel had said. So young Joseph Smith went directly to the nearby hill, called Cumorah, that Moroni had shown him in his vision; so clear was the vision that he said he "knew the place the instant I arrived there." He used a lever to move aside a large rock and found underneath a concrete box containing the gold plates, stones, and breastplate, just as the angel had said. He tried reaching in to retrieve the plates, but Moroni appeared and disallowed it, saying that he was not yet prepared. In some historical accounts, Smith admitted that upon seeing the gold plates for the first time he immediately thought of the impoverished circumstances of his family and what that amount of gold could do for them. When he tried to grab the plates, he felt something like an electric shock that stopped him. Moroni then reminded him, reprovingly, that he should have "no other object in view in getting the plates but to glorify God," that the gold plates were not a means to accrue financial wealth. The angel told the boy to come back every year on the same day for further instructions, and that he could finally retrieve the plates four years later.[15]

True to his word, Moroni allowed Smith to take the gold plates and the accompanying items on September 22, 1827, with the command to commence translation of the ancient American record. The translation process ensued slowly and occurred in fits and starts, often interrupted by daily necessities and harassment from curious and sometimes grasping locals. Smith dictated to scribes including his new wife Emma and early believers such as prosperous local farmer Martin Harris, members of the nearby Whitmer family, and especially a schoolteacher named Oliver Cowdery. The bulk of the translation occurred from April to June 1829, with Smith and Cowdery working furiously to finish the project. At the time he retrieved them, Smith was expressly commanded by Moroni not to allow anyone else to actually see the plates.

FIGURE 2.4 *The Hill Cumorah*, by C.C.A. Christensen. Depiction of Joseph Smith receiving the gold plates from the Angel Moroni at the hill near his family home in Palmyra, New York.

Thus, throughout the entire translation process, Smith kept the plates obscured from view, typically keeping them under a cloth while translating then storing them in a box made especially for that purpose. After the translation was completed, eleven other men were allowed to see the plates for themselves. Oliver Cowdery, Martin Harris, and David Whitmer attested that "an angel of God came down from heaven, and he brought and laid before our eyes, that we beheld and saw the plates." Eight others certified that Joseph Smith showed them the plates, that they touched them with their own hands, and "saw the engravings thereon, all of which has the appearance of ancient work." Smith added these respective Testimonies of the Three Witnesses and Eight Witnesses to the manuscript to corroborate the authenticity of the work. He employed a local printer to publish the book, which finally appeared in early 1830 as a 588-page tome entitled *The Book of Mormon*.

The actual content of the Book of Mormon will be discussed in Chapter 5, but here it is necessary to take up two major questions: Did Joseph Smith actually have gold plates delivered to him from an angel? And how exactly did a lightly schooled farm boy produce a nearly 600-page book considered by millions of people around the world to be scripture? Indeed, the gold plates and the resultant Book of Mormon have stimulated fierce debate from the first time they became public knowledge. Smith's story is fantastic, to be sure. Believers take his claims to be absolute historical fact; nonbelievers are understandably more skeptical. But Smith did believe it, and went to his grave with the conviction that he really had seen God and angels, and that he really did have tangible gold plates that he translated into the Book of Mormon.

Of course, it is impossible to either verify or falsify Smith's visions. Many people, even those who do not consider Joseph Smith a prophet of God, are willing to concede that he may well have seen something that he interpreted to be Jesus Christ or Moroni. After all, many people throughout history have had visionary experiences, and unless one is willing to dismiss them all as completely delusional, the possibility of Joseph Smith having a vision is as good as anyone else. But according to his own story, Smith didn't just see something in his mind's eye. He claimed that his visions produced something tangible and tactile – that he unearthed actual, physical gold plates from underneath an actual, physical rock on an actual, physical hill that people can still visit today.

So did Joseph Smith actually have gold plates in his possession? There are several theories to explain his insistence that he did. The first two possibilities are straightforward: yes he did, just as he said – the orthodox Mormon position; and no he did not, he was simply lying – the standard non-Mormon critique. The problem with the faithful answer is that it is unverifiable, especially since Smith claimed that Moroni took back the gold plates as soon as their translation was complete. In other words, the only possible hard evidence is gone (rather conveniently, some would say). On the other hand, the problem with flatly denying the existence of gold plates is that several people independently testified that they saw or held them – not only the eleven formal witnesses, but also Emma Smith and Mary Whitmer. Admittedly, all were associated with Joseph Smith at the time as family members, friends, or early believers; there is no truly "independent" testimony. But the striking thing about the witnesses' accounts is that several of them broke with the Mormon movement at some point but never denied their original testimony that they actually saw or handled the gold plates. Over time, historians have acceded that this is in fact strong testimony that must be taken seriously. As a kind of compromise position, some nonbelieving scholars have recently suggested that there probably were real tangible plates for people to hold, see, and feel, but that Joseph Smith must have manufactured them himself out of tin or some other cheap metal rather than receiving them from an angel.[16]

Even if critics do not believe in tales of angels and gold plates, they still have to reckon with the fact that Joseph Smith produced a rather unlikely 270,000-word book, especially given his limited education and minor social standing. Multiple theories have sprouted over the years to explain away the existence of the Book of Mormon. Many people have simply dismissed it as a hoax, Smith as an impostor, and his followers as dupes. But more serious critics, especially those who have taken the time to at least peruse the book, have had to find better explanations for the Book of Mormon's complexity and origins. For many years the most prominent theory was that Smith had not written the book at all, but rather that Sidney Rigdon, an unquestionably learned Campbellite preacher who converted to Mormonism, had plagiarized a manuscript by author Solomon Spaulding, added some religious content, and smuggled it undetected to Joseph Smith. Despite being repeatedly discredited, the Spaulding theory was widely circulated for more than a century and still pops up in various forms. In the twentieth century, scholars informed by new discoveries in psychology surmised that the book emerged from Smith's own subconscious as he sought to work out his own personal and family history against the backdrop of the various religious, political, economic, and cultural controversies of his time. Others less enamored with putting the dead Joseph Smith on the psychiatrist's couch have more generously attributed the book to Smith's own innate, and inexplicable, genius. They point to internal textual evidence that proves in their mind that the book is not an ancient history as it purports to be but rather an obviously nineteenth-century literary creation. Dismissing supernatural explanations of any kind, these scholars would put the Book of Mormon in the same class as the world's other scriptures and religious writings, which they presume emerge from and speak to something deep in the human imagination.[17]

Smith and his followers both then and now agree with the plagiarist school of thought on one point: there is no way that Smith himself could have written the book. Rather than looking to Sidney Rigdon and Solomon Spaulding for an explanation, however, they look to heaven. Whenever Joseph Smith was asked how he translated the Book of Mormon, he answered directly and almost formulaically, "by the gift and power of God."[18] Thanks to the accounts of other eyewitnesses who served as scribes for the translation, we have a few more details than Smith typically provided. At the end of her life, Emma Smith reminisced that, at the time, her husband "could neither write nor dictate a coherent and well-worded letter, let alone dictat[e] a book like the Book of Mormon."[19] Nevertheless, over the course of two years, and mostly during the period of intense translation activity in late spring 1829, Smith dictated the book in an uninterrupted stream, never asking his scribe where he left off or going back to make corrections. The book purports to be written in ancient "reformed Egyptian," which of course Smith could not read. So his translation into English was actually an extended form of revelatory dictation.[20] He accomplished it with the aid of "interpreters," first the Urim and Thummim that he found in the box with the plates, then a small, egg-shaped, chocolate-colored "seer stone" that he had previously discovered in the ground. Most eyewitness accounts agree that Joseph placed either one or both of the stones from the Urim and Thummim or his own seer stone into a hat, put his face into the hat to block out light, and then read out English words that appeared before his eyes.[21] Smith was not even looking at the text that he was translating, since the plates typically laid on the table wrapped in a cloth.

Looking at a stone in a hat seems a funny way to accomplish much of anything, let alone translate an ancient book of scripture. But by the time that he set out to translate the Book of Mormon, Joseph Smith was accomplished at seeing lost and hidden objects with the use of a seer stone. Throughout the 1820s, Joseph Smith Sr. and at least some of his sons were involved in the common local practice of treasure seeking or "money digging." Individuals or small groups would use a variety of methods, including divining rods and seer stones, to search for lost objects, with much of their energy devoted to the quest for buried treasure. Most searchers, of course, did not find any treasure, but they were convinced that the elusive troves were protected by guardian spirits that consistently outwitted them.[22] Some people, including Joseph Smith Jr., acquired a reputation as skilled "seers," were recruited to locate things such as runaway horses (which he did find), and sometimes hired to go on treasure-seeking expeditions. In fact, Smith was on one such job searching for a lost Spanish silver mine in northern Pennsylvania when he met and fell in love with his wife Emma Hale. Smith never denied his participation in treasure seeking, even admitting it in official church publications. In the May 1838 issue of the *Elders' Journal*, when asked, "Was not Jo Smith a money digger," he answered cheekily, "Yes, but it was never a very profitable job for him, as he only got fourteen dollars a month for it."[23]

Though money digging was relatively common among rural folk, it attracted unsavory characters and spawned rumors of sacrificed animals and demonic rituals, prompting numerous localities to outlaw the practice. For his participation in treasure seeking, Joseph Smith was hauled into court in 1826 on charges of being a "disorderly person." A man present at the trial later recorded the testimony of Joseph Smith Sr., who had accompanied his twenty-year-old son. Joseph Sr. told the court that

> both he and his son were mortified that this wonderful power which God had so miraculously given him should be used only in search of filthy lucre. . . . His constant prayer to his Heavenly Father was to manifest His will concerning this

marvelous power. He trusted that the Son of Righteousness would some day illumine the heart of the boy, and enable him to see His will concerning him.[24]

The following year, Joseph Jr. would finally receive the plates from Moroni and be allowed to apply his "marvelous power" of seership to the production of new scripture rather than the quest for Spanish silver. In the process, as historian Richard Bushman has written, Smith was transformed from village seer to prophet.[25]

Stories of visions and angels and ancient books written on gold plates buried in nearby hills stretch the modern imagination. Even in his own time, which had not yet encountered the deep skepticism of late modernity, Smith's narrative was simply too farfetched for most, a fact that was not lost on the prophet. He closed one of his most famous sermons, delivered less than three months before his death, by stating frankly, "I don't blame any one for not believing my history. If I had not experienced what I have, I could not have believed it myself."[26] Mormonism does not simply present another entry in the parade of denominational diversity; it poses a genuine epistemological dilemma. Mormons sometimes tell their own origin story so often that they forget how fantastic it is. This same can largely be said of the founding narratives involving Moses, Jesus, and Muhammad, but the distance of centuries has elevated those stories even for skeptics to the respectable level of myth. One simply cannot square the orthodox narrative of Mormonism's founding with modern notions of evidence-based inquiry and naturalistic rationalism. For the most part, the proximity of the history, the rich trove of historical documents, and perhaps most of all the claim of the plates' tangibility have all prevented the miraculous beginnings of Mormonism to being reduced (or elevated) to the status of myth. The Joseph Smith story thus confronts the modern hearer with an uncomfortable set of questions: Is there a world of possibilities beyond what we can apprehend with our natural senses, and if so, is there room in that world for a farm boy to see God, talk to angels, unearth gold plates, and produce new scripture? Mormonism is the product of people, first by the handful and eventually by the millions, answering yes to those questions. In the process, they stake a claim for a distinctively Mormon way of being modern.

• A LATTER-DAY CHURCH

Even before the Book of Mormon went to press, Joseph Smith had a small band of followers who trusted in his visions and his direct revelations from heaven. They believed that God had called Smith as a new prophet with a mission to restore Christianity to its primitive and pristine form. They lived in anticipation of Christ's Second Coming as prophesied in the Bible, and interpreted Moroni as the angel mentioned in the Book of Revelation who was sent to deliver the "everlasting gospel" to the earth in preparation for the end of time.[27] Originally composed of Smith's family and friends, the group of believers soon expanded as missionaries were called by revelation to go preach the gospel to all who would listen. Many receptive souls who joined the new church had been associated with other restorationist Christian groups who sought to recover the purity of the gospel as contained in the Bible. Others were seekers who bounced from church to church looking for a more direct experience with God, which they finally found in the fledgling Mormon movement. Most converts, like Louisa Barnes Pratt, were drawn to both doctrinal proofs that Mormonism was the restored fulfillment of primitive Christianity and to the outpouring of spiritual gifts on converts to the new faith, including visions, dreams, healings, and speaking in tongues. They rejoiced in a new era of open revelation from heaven through a prophet who communed with God and angels and produced new scripture for a new age. In their minds, Mormonism promised to be "the restoration of all things spoken by the mouth of all the holy prophets since the world began," the latter-day kingdom of God on the earth.[28]

Throughout and following the translation of the Book of Mormon, Smith reported that he continued to receive visitations and instructions from heavenly messengers, sometimes alone but often in the company of one or more of his fellow believers. Among the most significant of these visitations were the appearances of the New Testament luminaries John the Baptist and then Jesus's apostles Peter, James, and John, who bestowed on Joseph Smith and Oliver Cowdery the priesthood, or authority of God, that had presumably been lost through the apostasy of the early Christian church. With the priesthood restored, Smith believed he had authorization to organize what had been a loose band of followers into the restored Church of Christ. The formal organization of the church took place on April 6, 1830, at the Peter Whitmer farmhouse in Fayette, New York, originally with six official members to satisfy state law – though many more were baptized that same day following the meeting. The new church went by various names in the early years until an April 1838 revelation established the formal designation of the Church of Jesus Christ of Latter-day Saints. The name denoted continuity with the church that Mormons believed Jesus Christ had established during his lifetime while recognizing the distinction between the saints of the "former days" and those in the "latter days" before Christ's Second Coming.[29]

In the space of a decade, Joseph Smith Jr. transformed from being a farm boy with a simple religious question of which church to join into a visionary prophet, producer of sacred texts, and church founder. Even so, his name may have been forgotten like that of so many other visionaries and mystics throughout history if not for the movement that he inspired and the organization that he built. Joseph Smith's visions were indispensable for the emergence of Mormonism. They gained true significance, however, only after converts such as Louisa and Addison Pratt believed that they heralded the divine restoration of God's true church. Yes, the visionary Joseph Smith founded Mormonism, but it is equally true that Mormonism produced the Prophet Joseph Smith. The years following the establishment of the church would bring doctrinal innovation, institutionalization, and broad-based popular commitment. Mormonism was on the move.

• NOTES

1 Louisa Barnes Pratt, *The History of Louisa Barnes Pratt: Being the Autobiography of a Mormon Missionary Widow and Pioneer*, ed. S. George Ellsworth (Logan: Utah State University Press, 1998), 48, 54–55.

2 Ibid.

3 Ibid., 56, 385 n. 3.

4 Whitney R. Cross, *The Burned-Over District: The Social and Intellectual History of Enthusiastic Religion in Western New York, 1800–1850* (Ithaca, NY: Cornell University Press, 2009 [1950]). For a brief overview of early Mormonism's historical context, see Daniel Walker Howe, "Emergent Mormonism in Context," in *The Oxford Handbook of Mormonism*, eds. Terryl L. Givens and Philip L. Barlow (New York: Oxford University Press, 2015), 24–37.

5 James 1:5.

6 Joseph Smith-History 1:16–20, Pearl of Great Price.

7 For links to the nine accounts of Joseph Smith's First Vision recorded during his lifetime, see http://josephsmithpapers.org/site/accounts-of-the-first-vision (accessed January 18, 2016).

8 Richard Lyman Bushman, "The Visionary World of Joseph Smith," in *Believing History: Latter-day Saint Essays*, eds. Reid L. Neilson and Jed Woodworth (New York: Columbia University Press, 2004), 199–216; Douglas L. Winiarski, "Souls Filled with Ravishing Transport: Heavenly Visions and the Radical Awakening in New England," *William and Mary Quarterly* 61:1 (January 2004): 3–46; Ann Kirchner, " 'Tending to Edify, Astonish, and Instruct': Published Narratives of Spiritual Dreams and Visions in the Early Republic," *Early American Studies* 1 (2003): 198–229.

9 Joseph Smith-History 1:21.

10 Fawn M. Brodie, *No Man Knows My History: The Life of Joseph Smith, the Mormon Prophet*, 2nd ed., rev. and enl. (New York: Vintage Books, 1995 [1945]); Harold Bloom, *The American Religion: The Emergence of the Post-Christian Nation* (New York: Touchstone, 1992). For an insightful conversation about the First Vision between a believing historian and nonbelieving but sympathetic scholar, see Ann Taves and Steven C. Harper, "Joseph Smith's First Vision: New Methods for the Analysis of Experience-Related Texts," *Mormon Studies Review* 3 (2016): 53–84.

11 Joseph Smith-History 1:25, Pearl of Great Price.

12 James B. Allen, "The Significance of Joseph Smith's 'First Vision' in Mormon Thought," *Dialogue: A Journal of Mormon Thought* 1 (Autumn 1966): 29–45; James B. Allen, "Emergence of a Fundamental: The Expanding Role of Joseph Smith's First Vision in Mormon Religious Thought," *Journal of Mormon History* 7 (1980): 43–61; Kathleen Flake, *The Politics of American Religious Identity: The Seating of Senator Reed Smoot, Mormon Apostle* (Chapel Hill: University of North Carolina Press, 2004), chap. 5; Gregory A. Prince, "Joseph Smith's First Vision in Historical Context: How a Historical Narrative Became Theological," *Journal of Mormon History* 41:4 (October 2015): 74–94.

13 Joseph Smith-History 1:27–29.

14 Joseph Smith-History 1:30–49. Smith's official account of his encounter with Moroni and discovery and translation of the gold plates is also printed at the front of every copy of the Book of Mormon as the "Testimony of the Prophet Joseph Smith."

15 Joseph Smith-History 1:51–54; Richard Lyman Bushman, *Joseph Smith: Rough Stone Rolling* (New York: Alfred A. Knopf, 2005), 45.

16 The most intriguing and theoretically rich argument along these lines is Ann Taves, "History and the Claims of Revelation: Joseph Smith and the Materialization of the Golden Plates," *Numen* 61 (2014): 182–207. A less nuanced naturalistic explanation is Dan Vogel, *Joseph Smith: The Making of a Prophet* (Salt Lake City: Signature Books, 2004).

17 For a more detailed survey of various theories explaining the authorship of the Book of Mormon, see Bushman, *Joseph Smith*, 88–92; Terryl L. Givens, *By the Hand of Mormon: The American Scripture that Launched a World Religion* (New York: Oxford University Press, 2002), chap. 6; Paul C. Gutjahr, *The Book of Mormon: A Biography* (Princeton, NJ: Princeton University Press, 2012), chap. 2.

18 Preface to the 1830 edition of the Book of Mormon.

19 "Last Testimony of Sister Emma," *Saints' Herald* 26 (October 1, 1879), 290.

20 The idea of a "revelatory dictation" has been acknowledged even in materials published by church historians, which represents a subtle shift from traditional language about the Book of Mormon's "translation." See Michael Hubbard MacKay, Gerrit J. Dirkmaat, Grant Underwood, Robert J. Woodford, and William G. Hartley, eds. *Documents, vol. 1: July 1828–June 1831 [The Joseph Smith Papers]* (Salt Lake City: The Church Historian's Press, 2013), xxviii.

21 Eyewitness accounts can be found in John W. Welch, "The Miraculous Translation of the Book of Mormon," in *Opening the Heavens: Accounts of Divine Manifestations, 1820–1844*, ed. John W. Welch (Provo, UT, and Salt Lake City: Brigham Young University Press and Deseret Book, 2005), 76–213.

22 See Alan Taylor, "Rediscovering the Context of Joseph Smith's Treasure Seeking," *Dialogue: A Journal of Mormon Thought* 19:4 (1986): 18–28; Alan Taylor, "The Early Republic's Supernatural Economy: Treasure-Seeking in the American Northeast, 1780–1830," *American Quarterly* 28 (Spring 1986): 6–34; and Jon Butler, *Awash in a Sea of Faith: Christianizing the American People* (Cambridge, MA: Harvard University Press, 1990), 242–244.

23 (Far West, MO) *Elders' Journal* (July 1838): 43, available online at http://josephsmithpapers.org/paperSummary/elders-journal-july-1838?p=12#!/paperSummary/elders-journal-july-1838&p=11.

24 Quoted in Bushman, *Joseph Smith*, 52. For an extensive examination of the role of folk magic and the hermetic tradition in early Mormonism, see D. Michael Quinn, *Early Mormonism and the Magic World View*, rev. and enl. (Salt Lake City: Signature Books, 1998); and John L. Brooke, *The Refiner's Fire: The Making of Mormon Cosmology, 1644–1844* (New York: Cambridge University Press, 1996).

25 This is a major theme in Richard L. Bushman, *Joseph Smith and the Beginnings of Mormonism* (Urbana: University of Illinois Press, 1984).

26 Joseph Smith Jr., "Sermon Delivered April 7, 1844," in *American Sermons: The Pilgrims to Martin Luther King Jr.*, ed. Michael Warner (New York: The Library of America, 1999), 599.

27 Revelation 14:6–7.

28 Doctrine and Covenants 27:6.

29 Doctrine and Covenants 115:1–4.

3

Gatherings

One of the distinctive characteristics of early Mormonism was the commandment for converts to "gather to Zion." In the 1830s this required newly baptized Latter-day Saints from across the eastern United States and Canada and eventually England to emigrate to northern Ohio or the western borders of Missouri. Following their baptism into the new church, Addison and Louisa Pratt spent the summer and early fall of 1838 selling their property and otherwise settling their affairs, intending to join the Saints in Missouri – "the 'Far West,'" as Louisa called it, and indeed it was the western limits of the American nation at the time. They had traveled five hundred miles through snow and mud on their journey to "Zion" when they received word that the Mormons had been violently expelled from Missouri. The family's destination – and the overall fortunes of the entire Latter-day Saint movement – now uncertain, the Pratts planted themselves right where they were in rural Indiana. They built a prosperous homestead over the next two and a half years, meeting for worship with a small group of a dozen Mormons in the area. They tried preaching to their neighbors that "the priesthood and gifts of the gospel were again restored to men on earth," but their message fell on deaf ears.[1]

By 1841 the Latter-day Saints had built their own new city called Nauvoo on the banks of the Mississippi River in western Illinois. Though Addison was content with his thriving Indiana farm, Louisa longed to fulfill their original intention to gather with the Saints. She prevailed upon him, and in the fall of 1841 they rented out their farm and made the journey to Nauvoo. The family, now with four young daughters, was elated to be in the company of fellow Latter-day Saints and their prophet, Joseph Smith. "We could live comfortably and hear the Prophet preach every Sabbath day," Louisa recalled of that happy time. "My heart rejoiced all the day long." A year and a half of bliss was interrupted in May 1843, when Addison was called to serve a proselytizing mission for the church. It was common for faithful Mormon men to be called on missions and leave their families behind for a season. Most traveled a few hundred miles, often to relatives in the East or South or perhaps Canada. A few, including many of the church's twelve apostles, went to Great Britain, where they converted literally thousands to the new religion. Imagine the Pratts' shock when they learned that Addison had been assigned to go to the Society Islands (now Tahiti) in the South Pacific, in one of the church's first efforts beyond the North Atlantic. "Never had such a thought entered my mind that he would be sent to a foreign land," Louisa wrote. "My four children to be schooled and clothed, and no money would be left with me." Though devastated, Louisa accepted her husband's assignment as the will of God. As Addison's steamboat pulled away from the dock, his young daughters were inconsolable. The family would not be reunited for nearly five years, half a continent away.[2]

Louisa was now responsible for supporting herself and her four young daughters. As a frontier city, Nauvoo was booming, due in large part to the influx of converts like the Pratts. At its peak, Nauvoo rivaled Chicago in size, and with upwards of 15,000 residents by 1845, it was one of the largest cities in what was then the American West. However, only after the Mormons purchased the low-lying swampland on the banks of the Mississippi River did they realize that it was a prime breeding ground for mosquitoes carrying malaria and other diseases. Sickness ran rampant through the city, and the Pratts were not immune. With no reliable medical treatments, Louisa and her fellow Latter-day Saints relied on home remedies and ultimately providence. When eleven-year-old Ellen caught a fever, the family "called on the Lord in faith, believing in anointing with oil and laying on of hands. She was soon well." At one point her brother-in-law contracted smallpox, and her neighbors understandably dared not approach her house. Louisa's third daughter, Lois, came down with a fever and began showing "pimples." Louisa sent for the elders to bless the child, but "they were afraid to come." So the desperate mother took matters into her own hands, literally: "I then declared in the name of the Lord, that the terrible disease should not come under my roof. 'The devil,' said I, 'shall not have power thus to afflict me!' I then laid hands on my child, and rebuked the fever. . . . In a few days the fever was gone." Louisa believed her faith had given her the power to save her daughter from one of the deadly scourges of the American frontier.[3]

The threats to the Latter-day Saints in Nauvoo were not simply those borne by mosquitoes. Political conflict between the Mormons and their neighbors escalated until June 1844, when a mob shot and killed Joseph Smith and his brother Hyrum, who were jailed in the nearby county seat of Carthage presumably while under guard of the governor. The prophet's murder devastated Louisa and her fellow Saints. She believed, with many others – including those who killed the Smith brothers – that "the church was ruined forever." In the coming days, Mormon men made military preparations to defend the city and their families from what they were sure was an impending attack by the Illinoisans. Louisa recalled the trepidation of that week:

> My children clung to me with great fear. . . . The question arose, where could we hide them. A deep cellar was suggested, a trap door, and carpet overspread. They shuddered at the thought of being concealed in such a place. We concluded to take our chances together, and trust in the Lord.

The attack never came, but tensions escalated, and in 1845 the Mormons signed a treaty with their neighbors agreeing to vacate the city they had built from the swamp, with their homes and yet-to-be-completed temple, by early the next year. Many years later, Louisa still fumed at the "sectarian churches" and state of Illinois, which she blamed for her prophet's murder and the Saints' expulsion. In the ensuing months, desperate to perform the sacred ceremonies that could only be performed there, the Mormons rushed to finish the temple. Like many other Latter-day Saints, one of the last things Louisa did in Nauvoo was to "receive [her] blessings" in the temple.[4]

Through all these difficulties, Addison was still in Tahiti laboring to convert Pacific Islanders. When the time came for the Saints to evacuate Nauvoo in spring 1846, Louisa asked a church leader what she should do. "Sister Pratt," he answered, "[we] expect you to be smart enough to go yourself without help, and even to assist others." The plucky Louisa thought to herself, "Well, I will show them what I can do." Almost singlehandedly, she prepared a wagon team and joined the mass exodus of the Saints, her four daughters, ages five to fourteen, in tow.[5] The journey across Iowa was far more difficult than the Saints had expected. They were forced to stop on the western edge of the Missouri River, just beyond Iowa Territory in Nebraska, and hunker down for the winter, appropriately naming their makeshift settlement Winter Quarters.

Like many others, Louisa arrived in Winter Quarters sick, and remained sick for most of the year and a half she lived there. With scant lumber available, the Mormon refugees were forced to construct shelter out of whatever they could. Louisa paid a man a five dollar gold piece to construct for her what she called "a sod cave," with only a blanket for a door. Unfortunately, a cow belonging to a neighbor kept knocking down her chimney, and she was forced to move with her daughters into a "dugout," five feet underground. The cold and damp, compounded by the lack of nutrition, meant more illness, including a long bout of scurvy for Louisa that led to the loss of her front teeth. "I pined for vegetables till I could feel my flesh waste away from off my bones," she remembered. The Pratt family's situation was so pathetic that when they were visited by a camp leader, all he could do was sit down and weep.[6] The Latter-day Saints were nothing if not a community, however, and Louisa was cheered by other women, many of whom were not much better off than she was. Together they pooled whatever resources they had, including their spiritual power, to survive. Louisa remembered that when she was at her lowest, a number of women "assembled at my tent, prayed, anointed me with oil, and laid their hands upon me. Although I was not wholly restored, I was comforted, and enabled to bear more patiently my distress." Camp leaders did what they could to relieve the suffering of the poor and "to keep life and spirit among the people," including organizing occasional picnics, music, and dances. But the suffering continued – at least three hundred people died at Winter Quarters, many buried in unmarked graves.[7]

Finally, Louisa was well enough to join Brigham Young, who had succeeded Joseph Smith at the head of the LDS Church, on his second, return trip to the Salt Lake Valley, departing in spring 1848. (Young had led a vanguard party in 1847 and immediately came back to Winter Quarters to take more Saints the following year.) Hers was one of six hundred wagons traveling the lonely trail westward to the Great Basin.

As anyone who has ever driven across the midsection of the United States can appreciate, the pioneers "traveled hundreds of miles without seeing a single tree." When at last they did spy a lone cedar tree far off the trail, a number of them walked to it simply for the pleasure of standing for a few moments under its shade. Finally, on August 20, 1848, the pioneer company crested the Wasatch Mountains and looked down upon the Salt Lake Valley. Louisa wrote exultantly in her daybook, "Our hearts leap for joy!"[8]

Louisa's adventures didn't stop after she arrived in the Salt Lake Valley. Addison returned from his mission and rejoined his family in Utah, only to be called to return to Tahiti on a second mission. This time Louisa and her girls would follow him, but they trailed behind and were unable to find which island he was on, so Louisa spent nineteen months on the small island of Tubuai teaching English, math, health and sanitation, handicrafts, music, and of course Mormonism. Penniless after years of missionary service, the Pratts moved back to Gold Rush San Francisco, where they sold goods to miners. They helped establish the Mormon colony in San Bernardino in southern California, only to be called back to central Utah when the march of federal troops against the Mormons in 1857 led Brigham Young to consolidate outlying settlements. Addison, no doubt exhausted after years of repeated relocations in the service of the church, refused to follow the order, so Louisa went alone with her daughters. Addison and Louisa's separation was also precipitated by conflict over the doctrine of plural marriage, or polygamy, introduced publicly to the church in Utah while the Pratts were away on their mission. Louisa embraced the new teaching as inspired revelation; Addison, who on the islands had spent years teaching chastity as a prerequisite for baptism, rejected the innovation wholesale. Ironically, though committed to the principle of plural marriage, Louisa spent the last twenty-two years of her life without her husband. She was a model Mormon and pillar of the church in central Utah until her death in 1880.

While unique in many ways, the life of Louisa Barnes Pratt exemplifies many themes in early Mormon history. She exemplifies the zeal of the faith's new converts, and the spiritual power and purpose they drew from their affiliation with Mormonism. Indeed, the early Latter-day Saints lived in a religious world of ecstatic spiritual experiences and seeming miracles, including healings, visions, prophecies, and speaking in tongues – not just by the male priesthood leadership, but by "ordinary" women as well. Louisa persevered through the hardships of frontier life, exacerbated by the Latter-day Saints' recurrent conflicts with their neighbors and their ensuing expulsions and migrations. Far more than merely joining a different Christian denomination, to become a Latter-day Saint was to give one's entire life – spiritually, physically, economically, emotionally – to God and his prophets. To be a nineteenth-century Mormon was to gather with the Saints in their appointed Zion and dedicate one's life to the building of the kingdom of God. Louisa, and tens of thousands of early converts like her, responded to the call, and in the process gave birth to a religion.

• KIRTLAND

The Mormon story in the nineteenth century is a remarkable one of increasingly innovative teachings and social experiments, severe persecution, repeated relocations through several states, and recurring conflicts with neighbors as well as local, state, and federal governments. Mormons typically organize their early history around these fledgling settlements and the repeated expulsions the Saints suffered from them. After the brief period associated with the founding of the church in New York, the church settled for several years in Kirtland, Ohio (1831–1837). In the fall of 1830, Joseph Smith sent a small party of missionaries to "Indian Territory" to preach to Native Americans, whom the early Mormons believed to be descendants of the Israelite civilization called "Lamanites" described in the Book of Mormon. The missionaries preached the gospel and sold copies of the Book of Mormon along their way. When the party arrived in Kirtland, near Cleveland in northern Ohio, they encountered another region permeated by religious factions and experiments of all kinds. These included a large community of Campbellites – followers of Alexander Campbell, one of the most prominent biblical restorationists of the day – as well as a Christian communal farm and a number of Christians dabbling in charismatic enthusiasms. Upon reading the Book of Mormon, the pastor of the Campbellite community, Sidney Rigdon, converted and soon led a large portion of his flock into Mormonism with him. Isaac Morley, the founder of the Christian commune, brought in still more converts and also injected into Mormonism a strong ethos of communal and cooperative living that would resonate within the church through the present day.[9]

With these new converts, the Church of Christ suddenly doubled and tripled in size. Kirtland became the de facto center of Mormon membership and activity. In late 1830 Joseph Smith received a revelation that the young church "should assemble together at the Ohio," legitimizing the fledgling Mormon outpost there. Smith moved to Kirtland in early 1831 along with his family and most of the original converts who had joined in New York. The revelation was the first explicit statement of one of Mormonism's most distinctive doctrines, that of "the gathering." Evangelistic and millennialist, early Mormonism designed to move not only people's souls but also their bodies in anticipation of the coming of Christ. Many of Smith's early prophecies were shot through with apocalyptic fervor, describing a world caught in the culminating stages of an age-old conflict between good and evil, God and Satan. These revelations attested that as the devil tightened his grip on an unbelieving world, the worst was yet to come. It would be an age of wars, disasters, and calamities, with the entire earth in tumult before the return of Christ inaugurated a thousand-year reign of peace called simply the Millennium (hence the term "millennialism"). A series of revelations to Joseph Smith commanded the Latter-day Saints to flee the sinful world and gather to Zion – not just spiritually, but physically. Only in the gathered centers of the church would the righteous find peace and rest from the violent, wicked world beyond.[10] Missionaries encouraged their converts to gather with the main body of the church as quickly after baptism as possible, which created significant centers of strength but relatively weak outlying branches of the church. Thousands of converts such as Addison and Louisa Pratt sold their homes and farms, said goodbye to family and friends, and headed with all their worldly goods toward Ohio and Missouri in the 1830s, Illinois in the early 1840s, and Utah for the rest of the century.

The Latter-day Saint impulse of gathering to Zion was never at heart a pessimistic rejection of the world. As historian Matthew Bowman has observed, Joseph Smith "was not simply a doomsayer but a builder."[11] Although millenarianism played prominently in many of Smith's revelations, his vision was at once grander and more grounded. Over the next several years in Kirtland, Smith received dozens of revelations that would begin to flesh out his vision for Zion, with components ranging from the priestly to the political, evangelical to ethical. One such revelation introduced a new health code for the church, the Word of Wisdom (discussed in Chapter 8). Another notable innovation was the establishment of a communitarian economy in which surpluses from prosperous church members would be distributed to less fortunate others. Though this redistributive and cooperative economic system would never really succeed, and caused considerable internal tension in the attempt, it formed a centerpiece of the Mormon social ideal throughout the pioneer period.

The high point of the Kirtland period came in 1836, when the Saints completed a temple that they had been commanded by revelation to build, at great sacrifice for a community with such meager resources. Its dedication was accompanied by a proliferation of individual and collective visions, speaking in tongues, and other charismatic events that recalled the Day of Pentecost as described in the Book of Acts. The culminating moment of divine encounter came when Joseph Smith and Oliver Cowdery, in their account, experienced a series of heavenly visits in the temple, first from Jesus Christ and then in turn from Moses, Elias, and Elijah. Many Saints counted the spiritual outpouring experienced at the time of the dedication of the Kirtland Temple among the highlights of their lives.

The euphoria was not to last, however. Internal dissension and external conflict began to plague the church. Many early converts simply melted away when their original spiritual burnings died down or they came to disagree with some aspect of the evolving religion. Others became angry and railed against the church and especially its prophet, often complaining about what they saw as the authoritarianism and arbitrariness of Smith's revelations. Those who left the church fueled a growing chorus of outside critics. Eber Howe, a nearby newspaper editor, was at first bemused and then alarmed by the burgeoning Mormon community in Kirtland. In 1834 he published *Mormonism Unvailed* [sic], which was the first entry in what would become a prominent genre of anti-Mormon exposés. Howe's book offered a series of affidavits from former neighbors of the Smith family in New York testifying to their bad character, and advanced the Spaulding manuscript theory of Book of Mormon authorship. Local opposition to Mormonism, fueled in part by ex-Mormons, at times became violent. On the night of March 24, 1832, a mob seized Joseph Smith and

FIGURE 3.1 Kirtland Temple, Kirtland, Ohio. The Kirtland Temple was the first temple built by Mormons and the site of ecstatic spiritual experiences after its dedication in 1836.

Sidney Rigdon from their homes. The attackers dragged Rigdon with his head bumping against the frozen ground until he became unconscious. Others tore off Smith's clothes and poured hot tar over his body. One member of the mob tried to shove a vial of poison into Smith's mouth. Most tragically, one of Joseph and Emma Smith's newly adopted sons, already suffering from measles, died of exposure from the cold air let in as the mob broke through the door.

In the year after the temple dedication, the Mormon community in Kirtland fractured. Trying to shore up a fragile economy predicated artificially on speculative real estate sales and temple construction, church leaders established a banking society with its own printed currency when the state legislature refused them a charter for their own bank. A quixotic measure to begin with, the Kirtland Safety Society collapsed almost immediately in the wake of a national economic crisis called the Panic of 1837. In the wake of the banking scandal, a wave of defections, involving even some of Smith's closest associates, tore apart the community; some dissenters even seized the Kirtland Temple and for a time joined with outside persecutors. At the end of 1837, Smith and his family evacuated Kirtland and headed for western Missouri, where a large Mormon colony had already been established. The Kirtland Saints still loyal to Smith followed him there the following spring.

• MISSOURI

The Missouri period (1831–1838) mostly overlapped with the Kirtland period, since Joseph Smith had urged the Saints to settle in both locations. A June 1831 revelation had identified Missouri as "the land of your inheritance," and when Joseph Smith shortly thereafter visited Jackson County, on the western border of the state, he received another revelation identifying it as the land "consecrated for the gathering of the saints" and "the place for the city of Zion." The Mormons learned that Independence, Missouri, was the "center place" of Zion, where they would construct a temple, build the New Jerusalem prophesied in both the Bible and Book of Mormon, provide a home base for preaching to the Lamanites (Native Americans), and prepare for the return of Jesus Christ.[12] For several years, then, the church had two gathering places. While Kirtland enjoyed the presence of the prophet and eventually the temple, Missouri enjoyed privilege of place as the Saints' promised land. However, the growing presence of Mormons in Missouri proved to be even more unwelcome to the local non-Mormon citizenry as it was in Kirtland. Not only did the Missouri Mormons publicly announce that God had given them Jackson County as their divinely granted inheritance, but they were also cultivating relationships with the nearby Indians and seemed to be welcoming freed blacks into the church. None of this went over well with a Missouri population that had migrated there in large part from the slaveholding southern states.

As the Mormon population in Missouri grew exponentially, the local non-Mormons perceived them as a growing political threat and responded with increasingly virulent extralegal violence, first in Jackson County in 1833. Vigilantes destroyed the Mormon printing office, razed Mormon homes, and tarred and feathered the Mormon bishop. The Mormons fled from Jackson County north into the next county (Clay), where at first they were welcomed as refugees with the understanding that their stay would be only temporary. In 1834, Joseph Smith led a futile expedition called Zion's Camp intended to "redeem the land of Zion" for the Saints. The expedition was forced to turn back to Ohio when the Missouri governor indicated that he would not support the Mormon cause – and did not particularly appreciate the prospect of Smith's armed band marching across the state. Further appeals to the state government led to the creation of a new county (Caldwell) just for the Mormons.

As more Latter-day Saints migrated to Missouri, their settlements soon spread into adjacent counties. Conflict between Mormons and the locals escalated, leading to skirmishes between the two parties, each of which had formed their own militias. Both groups appealed to the state government for assistance, reporting the depredations of the other side. On July 4, 1838, Sidney Rigdon delivered a fiery oration which he intended to be the Saints' declaration of independence from persecution:

> From this hour, we will bear it no more, our rights shall no more be trampled on with impunity. The man or the set of men, who attempts it, does it at the expense of their lives. And that mob that comes on us to disturb us; it shall be between us and them a war of extermination; for we will follow them till the last drop of their blood is spilled, or else they will have to exterminate us: for we will carry the seat of war to their own houses, and their own families, and one party or the other shall be utterly destroyed.[13]

Predictably, Rigdon's words did not rest well with the locals, and his bellicose talk of a "war of extermination" would soon come back to haunt the Saints. Armed conflict climaxed in October 1838 during what is called the Mormon War or Missouri War. Both sides suffered and inflicted casualties and depredations, though the outnumbered Mormons, especially those in outlying and isolated settlements, received the brunt of the violence. The Missouri militia, acting more like a mob, pillaged Mormon homes and farms, and looted and destroyed Mormon property; the Mormon militia responded in kind, though to a lesser extent. Several church leaders, including Joseph Smith, were beaten, tarred and feathered, and imprisoned, narrowly escaping execution. Some Mormon women were raped. In the most appalling incident, a Missouri militia slaughtered at least seventeen men and boys in the Hawn's Mill Massacre. They showed no mercy, hacking an elderly man to death with a corn cutter, blowing off the top of a ten-year-old boy's head, mortally wounding another nine-year-old boy, and shooting a six-year-old in the hip. One militiaman justified the brutal attack on children by sneering, "Nits make lice."[14]

The "Mormon War" ended only when Governor Lilburn Boggs issued an official order that the Mormons, as a threat to the peace, were to be either expelled from the state or exterminated by the militia. Refugees once again, thousands of Saints fled to the hospitality offered them in Quincy, Illinois, some 250 miles eastward, led by one of the church's leading apostles named Brigham Young. The Mormons left behind their

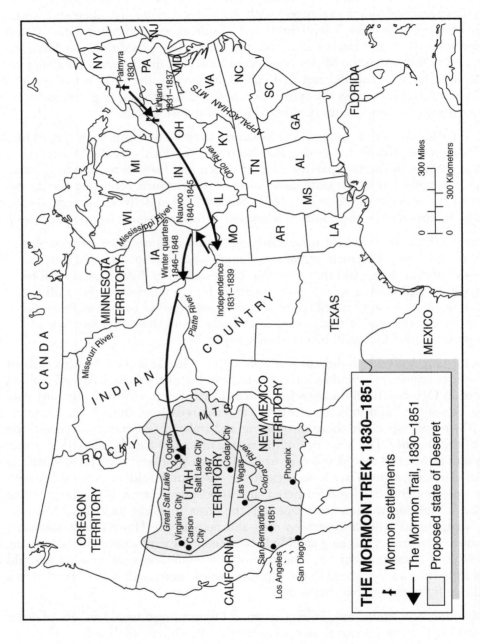

FIGURE 3.2 Early Mormon migrations

prophet, who with a few other church leaders suffered through a miserable winter in the ironically named Liberty Jail. Allowed to escape in early 1839, Smith rejoined his followers in Illinois as they began searching for yet another gathering place.

• NAUVOO

Mormonism was not yet ten years old in the winter of 1838–1839, but the Latter-day Saints had already been uprooted multiple times. Both their temple in Kirtland and their Zion in Missouri had been abandoned – violently, not voluntarily. Under Brigham Young's direction, the church's apostles who were not imprisoned or on missions spent the winter taking care of basic food and shelter needs but also looking for a new place to settle. They identified a large tract of land upriver around a town optimistically named Commerce. They began making land purchases in the spring, and the Mormons started constructing a city out of a swamp. In spite of the malaria that struck the new settlement, Smith channeled his native optimism in christening the place "Nauvoo," a transliteration of a Hebrew word meaning "beautiful." Before long, the Saints would informally call their new home on the Mississippi River the "City of Joseph." The Illinois legislature, still feeling generous toward the plight of the Mormon refugees and wanting to encourage immigration and development in the state, gave Nauvoo a generous charter that allowed it to function much like an independent Mormon city-state.[15]

With a new home, Smith renewed the call for the scattered Saints to gather. Those converts like Addison and Louisa Pratt who never quite made it to Missouri (probably for the best) now poured into Nauvoo, making it a hive of activity and one of the largest cities in the frontier state almost overnight. Much of the growth came from a wave of British immigrants who had converted to Mormonism during two spectacularly successful missions to England by several of the church's apostles in the late 1830s and early 1840s; over seventeen thousand British citizens joined the church by 1847, and several thousand of them made their way to Nauvoo. Wilford Woodruff famously converted an entire congregation, and Brigham Young earned both experience and widespread respect for his organizing efforts.

Mormonism became a mature and distinctive religion during the Nauvoo period (1839–1846), building upon but going well beyond the foundation laid in Ohio and Missouri. Joseph Smith was at the peak of his personal and ecclesiastical powers, leading to a series of confident, bold, but also brash innovations and developments. He presented novel doctrines with seemingly every sermon, and introduced a whole new set of rituals that required the building of a new temple to be properly performed (for more on temples, see Chapter 8). Placed on a prominent bluff overlooking the city and the river, construction of the temple would occupy an immense amount of the Saints' time, money, and labor. They never built a regular chapel in Nauvoo, preferring instead private worship services in homes. Public gatherings were held outdoors in a grove of trees on Sunday afternoons and twice a year for general church conferences.

One of the most significant developments in Nauvoo was the organization of a voluntary women's religious association called the Relief Society. Though women had always been baptized members of the church and had powerful spiritual experiences, for the first decade of Mormonism they had no formal role in the ecclesiastical organization. The revelations outlining the increasingly elaborate church hierarchy listed the specific duties of any number of priesthood offices, but they were all reserved exclusively for men. This gender distinction was common for the time, and reflected a general cultural belief in separate spheres with men serving public functions and women exercising authority in the private, domestic sphere.[16] When a number of leading women in Nauvoo came together to create a benevolent society, similar to other female reform groups across America, Smith intervened and said God had "something better for them." On March 17, 1842, Smith met with twenty women and said he would organize their society "after a pattern of the priesthood." Just like priesthood quorums, they would have a president (Joseph's wife Emma Hale Smith was elected unanimously) assisted by two counselors. The women chose the name Relief Society, denoting their mission to look after the needs of the poor as well as "correcting the morals and strengthening the virtues of the female community." The membership and scope of the society expanded quickly, as they not only organized charitable efforts but also became a place of female worship where they read scriptures, shared testimonies, spoke in tongues, and administered ritual blessings to one another.[17] Eventually the Relief Society would transition from an elective dues-paying membership to being the organization for all adult women in the church.

In Nauvoo the Mormons began to flesh out the revelations that referred to the church as the kingdom of God on earth. The Saints understood this to call for the establishment of an alternative priestly kingdom that would supplant the existing nations of the earth when Jesus triumphantly returned to earth as King of Kings. Their political aspirations were pragmatic as well. Wanting to prevent another Missouri disaster, the Mormons consolidated military and political power – for self-protection, they insisted, though their increasingly nervous neighbors were not so sure. With authority granted under the Nauvoo charter, the Saints formed a militia called the Nauvoo Legion, which at its peak numbered some five thousand men who regularly drilled and paraded through the city streets. (Compare this to the entire U.S. Army, which had fewer than 7,500 regulars in 1845.[18]) The legion elected Joseph Smith as commander and bestowed on him the rank of lieutenant general, higher than any other militia officer in the country.

Smith also became mayor of Nauvoo, with other senior church leaders serving in the city council. What the Saints came to describe as "theodemocracy," where God and the people ruled together, their opponents understood simply as a theocratic threat to American republican institutions.[19] It did not help that the Mormons played both sides of state politics, naively alternating their bloc vote between Whigs and then Democrats in exchange for promised favors. When both parties cried foul, the Saints found themselves politically isolated. As the 1844 presidential election approached, Smith was indignant that none of the presidential candidates would make promises of redress for the Saints' Missouri grievances. So he tossed his own hat in the ring as an independent candidate for the presidency. His quixotic campaign had almost no

FIGURE 3.3 John Hamer, *Last Public Address of Lieutenant-General Joseph Smith*, 1888. The combination of military, political, and religious power in Nauvoo made Joseph Smith a dangerous figure in his enemies' eyes.

practical chance of winning, and he was killed in June, months before the election occurred. Yet Smith's national political ambitions – inspired by either bold vision or unchecked hubris – demonstrated just how far he had come from his roots as a humble farmer only a decade and a half earlier.

Smith's actions in Nauvoo provoked not only political controversy but also moral scandal. The reason was his introduction, secretly and to a very limited group of close followers, of plural marriage, or polygamy, which the Saints would call "celestial marriage," "the new and everlasting covenant," or simply "the Principle." Since Mormonism was predicated on "the restoration of all things," it seemed logical to Smith that the ancient practice of polygamy, as practiced by Abraham and other biblical patriarchs, would be part of that restoration. In 1843 the prophet dictated a revelation that formalized both the doctrine of sealing, wherein a husband and wife could be joined together by priesthood authority for time and all eternity (not just "'til death do you part"), and the doctrine of plurality.[20] Both sealing and plural marriage indicated Smith's desire to gather people not just physically but also in large, ritually united familial networks across the generations and beyond death. Eternal marriage has been retained as one of Mormonism's most cherished doctrines, while plural marriage was central in nineteenth-century Mormonism and then abandoned by the twentieth-century church. Emma Smith hated polygamy, and except for a brief period of acquiescence, did all that she could to privately oppose it, including mobilizing the Relief Society to watch out for its spread.[21]

By the time Joseph dictated the revelation and Emma opposed it, however, he was already a much married man. His first plural wife was possibly a teenaged girl named Fanny Alger who lived and worked in the Smiths' home in Kirtland. Smith seems not to have pursued the practice for the next few years, until the Saints were safely ensconced in Illinois. He began taking plural wives in Nauvoo in April 1841, ultimately marrying at least thirty more women until his death in June 1844. By then, twenty-nine men and fifty women had been sealed plurally, a number that would climb steadily over the coming years until the doctrine was announced publicly in 1852. Because the practice was done in secret, historians have struggled to piece together the entire puzzle, with the number and names of Smith's wives a running debate. Most evidence is fragmentary, and much of it comes from questionably reliable sources such as anti-Mormon diatribes or highly politicized reminiscences produced years and even decades later. What we do know is that Smith was sealed to women ages fourteen to fifty-six. Some were single, others widowed, and a handful already married. The evidence suggests that at least some of these plural marriages were consummated sexually, although in other cases they were not and were understood to be "for eternity only." Contrary to the practice as it developed publicly in Utah, in Nauvoo husbands did not live with their plural wives or set up households for them; there seems to have been little or no economic aspect to the relationships.[22]

How do we explain plural marriage? Why did Smith introduce it, and why did anyone else go along with it? Critics have usually reduced Mormon polygamy to nothing more nor less than rapacious sexual desire gratified through the abuse of excessive power. Sex and power must certainly be accounted for, and may in the end be the best and simplest explanations. Yet the historical record complicates this simple explanation, as Joseph Smith appeared to sincerely believe he was fulfilling his religious duty, obeying a commandment of the Lord.[23] For Smith and many of his earlier followers, it was impossible to separate plural marriage from the revelation on eternal marriage in which it was textually and doctrinally embedded. As his biographer Richard Bushman observed, "Joseph did not marry women to form a warm, human companionship, but to create a network of related wives, children, and kinsmen that would endure into the eternities. . . . Like Abraham of old, Joseph yearned for familial plenitude. He did not lust for women so much as he lusted for kin."[24] When it comes to assessing the character of Joseph Smith, no other subject is either so ambiguous or so fraught as is his practice of polygamy. To reduce him to a puppet of the divine will on the one hand or an oversexed charlatan on the other simply fails to capture the complexity of the man.[25]

While Smith's followers often delighted in each new pearl of heavenly wisdom he revealed, even his most dedicated followers blanched when introduced to the idea of plural marriage. Smith's successor Brigham Young remarked, "It was the first time in my life that I had desired the grave, and I could hardly get over it for a long time." John Taylor, another apostle who later became the third president of the LDS Church, said learning about polygamy "made my flesh crawl."[26] Even Hyrum Smith, Joseph's older brother and perhaps most faithful disciple, rejected the doctrine at first and had to be persuaded by Brigham Young. What made these three, and the dozens of other men and women who accepted the principle in Nauvoo, come around? Consistently, they reported that an unmistakable spiritual confirmation from God told them that plural marriage, however difficult and unseemly, was a true principle that was required of them to show their faithfulness to God in all things. Lucy Walker, a sixteen-year-old girl who adamantly refused multiple proposals from Smith, was praying in anguish one night when she felt a heavenly presence "like the brilliant sunshine bursting through the darkest cloud." She was subsequently sealed to Smith, later becoming a plural wife of church leader Heber C. Kimball after Smith's death. "It was not a love matter," she wrote, "but simply the giving up of myself as a sacrifice to establish that grand and glorious principle that God had revealed to the world."[27] Mormonism was a religion that asked its followers to be willing to give everything to God, not just in terms of spirituality or even politics and economics, but also in the most intimate of human relationships.

In the end, all of it – polygamy, theocracy, the Nauvoo Legion, doctrinal and ritual innovations – was simply too much for some to bear. A group of prominent Mormons became reluctant dissenters and formed their own church that aimed to restore Mormonism to its pure form. They held to Smith's early revelations but believed that he had become a fallen prophet. In early June the reform movement published a newspaper called the *Nauvoo Expositor* that publicly exposed polygamy and called out

Joseph Smith for his departures from what they believed was the true faith. Smith lashed out. As mayor, he convened the city council, which passed an ordinance declaring the *Expositor* guilty of libel and a threat to public peace. Under Smith's orders, the city marshal and a hundred men marched on the *Expositor* office, destroyed the press, and burned the remaining copies of the newspaper in the street. The Mormons had howled when their press had been destroyed in Missouri; now they were guilty of the same.

The destruction of the *Expositor* was the last straw for Joseph Smith's enemies. Opponents in surrounding communities called for outright war. The situation was so enflamed that the state governor, Thomas Ford, rode immediately to the county seat of Carthage to try and preserve the peace. Illinoisans feared the Nauvoo Legion; the Mormons feared a repeat of Missouri. In the end, wishing to avoid civil war yet privately admitting he was going to his death, Joseph Smith surrendered himself to the state under the governor's promise of protection. That promise proved illusory. On June 27, 1844, a mob stormed the jail in Carthage where Joseph, his brother Hyrum, and two other Mormons were held. Following a futile attempt to defend themselves, the prisoners were overwhelmed. Joseph and Hyrum Smith were both shot to death – Joseph fell from the second-story window, his body riddled with bullets. The other two Mormons survived to tell the tale.[28]

Remembering the sorrow of the Latter-day Saints over their fallen prophet, Louisa Barnes Pratt wrote, "Such consternation was never known, since the rocks were rent and the sun darkened, when Christ the Lamb was slain!" Like many others, Mormon and otherwise, Louisa thought the church would die with its prophet.[29] Those who reveled at the prospect would ultimately be disappointed. In the ensuing weeks, a number of rival claimants offering to succeed Joseph Smith at the head of the church, though all were clear that they could never truly replace him. The leadership crisis unfolded because Smith had not left a clear plan for succession – or rather, he had privately left too many disparate plans. Sidney Rigdon offered to be the church's "guardian." The Smith family believed that the presidency should be hereditary, with Joseph's lone surviving brother William leading the church until his son, Joseph Smith III, came of age. A charismatic new convert named James Strang, who "appeared to be Joseph in miniature," complete with a seer stone, angelic visitations, and new revelations, attracted many.[30] Ultimately, however, the majority of the Latter-day Saints decided to follow the Quorum of the Twelve Apostles, with Brigham Young at the head. The apostles had shown their competence and earned the trust of the church members during the exodus from Missouri, and enjoyed the loyalty of the many thousands of converts they had gained on their missions in England. Furthermore, those who followed him believed Young when he said that only the apostles held the "keys" of the priesthood for the church, including the authority to conduct the sacred ceremonies of the temple. Having failed to capture the majority, Strang took his followers to Wisconsin, Rigdon moved to Pennsylvania, and the Smith family stayed in Nauvoo until Joseph III came of age and became president of the Reorganized Church of Jesus Christ of Latter Day Saints.

• PIONEER UTAH

Brigham Young and the Twelve Apostles were resolutely committed to remaining in Nauvoo to complete the temple that Smith's revelations had commanded them to build. However, circumstances became increasingly tenuous for the Latter-day Saints. In January 1845, seven months after Smith's death, the state legislature revoked Nauvoo's charter, stripping the city of most of its unique powers and protections. That fall, anti-Mormon vigilantes began attacking outlying Mormon settlements and positioned cannons around Nauvoo itself. Young brokered a deal with the vigilantes and the state that the Mormons would leave Illinois by the following spring if they would be unmolested in the meantime. The truce was accepted, and generally honored. That gave the Mormons time to complete their temple. Throughout the winter they conducted thousands of "endowment" ceremonies that they believed gave them the spiritual power necessary to face their next challenge, which might be their biggest yet: Brigham Young had announced that they were going to move to the valley of the Great Salt Lake in the Rocky Mountains. As Louisa Pratt's experience indicates, it was a bold move that produced both profound suffering and heroism. Most importantly, it put the Latter-day Saints beyond the reach of their antagonists, if only temporarily.

A number of religious groups were born or thrived in the aspiring, fluid openness of the nineteenth-century American West, but none more so than Mormonism. As a new phase of the Mormon gathering, their migration westward to Utah represented new opportunities for the Latter-day Saint movement. It also provided yet another crucible in which Mormon peoplehood and the Mormon character was forged. They understood their journey in parallel terms to the Hebrews' exodus from Egypt, with Brigham Young as their Moses and the Saints as a new Israel.

During the Mormon pioneers' journey across the plains, William Clayton, one of Joseph Smith's clerks, wrote lyrics for an English folk tune that became the anthem of the trail, and one of Mormonism's most cherished hymns ever since. The third verse reads:

We'll find the place which God for us prepared,
Far away in the West,
Where none shall come to hurt or make afraid;
There the Saints will be blessed.
We'll make the air with music ring,
Shout praises to our God and King;
Above the rest these words we'll tell –
All is well! All is well!
("Come, Come, Ye Saints," *Hymns* [Salt Lake City, UT: The Church of Jesus
    Christ of Latter-day Saints, 1985], 30.)

FIGURE 3.4 Brigham Young (1801–1877), second president of the Church of Jesus Christ of Latter-day Saints

Courtesy of the Church History Library, The Church of Jesus Christ of Latter-day Saints, Salt Lake City, Utah

Between 1847 and 1868, more than sixty thousand Latter-day Saints made the journey by foot across the continent along what came to be known as the Mormon Trail.
The majority of these were converts from Europe; during the peak year of 1855,
it is said that up to a third of all emigrants from the British Isles to America were
Mormons.[31] Wallace Stegner, who spent his youth in Salt Lake City and is sometimes
called the "Dean of Western Writers," incisively perceived the westward migration
as a great American saga of individual triumph and tragedy. Though most Mormon
pioneers traveled with wagon teams, the simultaneous heroism and pathos of the
poorer companies who pulled handcarts across the frontier has become iconic for
both Latter-day Saints and non-Mormon writers such as Stegner:

> In all its history, the American West never saw a more unlikely band of pio-
> neers than the 499 who were camped on the banks of the Iowa river at Iowa
> City in late May, 1856. They were not colorful – only improbable. Looking for
> the bronzed and resolute and weatherseasoned among them, you would have
> seen instead starved cheeks, pale skins, bad teeth, thin chests, all the stigmata
> of unhealthy work and bad diet. . . . There were many grey heads and white
> heads, many women. They looked more like the population of the poor farm on
> a picnic than like pioneers about to cross the plains. . . . Mainly Welshmen and
> Englishmen from the depressed collieries and mill towns, mainly the unsuccess-
> ful and poor, they were life's discards. But their intention was so imprudent it
> was almost sublime. Propertyless, ill equipped, untried and untrained, they were
> going to chance the Mormon Trail across 1400 miles of Indian country to the
> Mormon Zion in the Great Salt Lake City. And they were going to chance it on
> foot, hauling their belongings in handcarts.[32]

Brigham Young's vanguard company of Mormon pioneers first reached the Salt Lake
Valley in July 1847. Throughout the Mormon culture region, Latter-day Saints still
celebrate July 24 as Pioneer Day, the one distinctive Mormon holiday. There are
no special religious rites or rituals performed, and many if not most Mormons outside the intermountain West forget about the day altogether. But for those in Utah,
southeastern Idaho, and a few other Mormon communities, the day is full of church
and community breakfasts, family picnics and barbecues, rodeos, and fireworks. In
retrospect, Mormons and even historians have typically called the Salt Lake Valley
a desert, in large part because the pioneers often spoke of their settlement of the
region as fulfilling the biblical prophecy to make the desert "blossom as the rose."[33]
Yet in fact the valleys along the Wasatch Mountains made an ideal place for Mormon
settlement, with enough fresh water and timber to supply the rapidly growing population while still offering isolation from the "Gentile" society they left behind. To
be sure, the ecosystem was dramatically different from anything they had previously
experienced east of the Mississippi or in northern Europe, which forced the pioneers to adapt and innovate. They developed irrigation techniques that allowed them
to cultivate land in the Great Basin that previously had been resistant to sustained
agricultural production. After a few precarious years, and firm in the faith that they

had been providentially preserved, within a decade the Latter-day Saints were thriving. By the end of the century, they had established some five hundred settlements throughout the region, northward through eastern Idaho and western Wyoming, southward to San Bernardino, California, and Mesa, Arizona, and even with isolated outposts in northern Mexico and Alberta, Canada. Most of the settlements occurred within the "Mormon corridor" that begins in Cache Valley on the Utah-Idaho border then extends south-by-southwest through the length of Utah along modern-day Interstate-15.

Just as Nauvoo had provided a brief respite for the Saints in which Joseph Smith could introduce some of his most important religious innovations, Utah became a remote and secure laboratory for religion- and people-making. For Brigham Young, Utah was a godsend to the Latter-day Saints; he proclaimed it "a first-rate place to raise Saints."[34] Until the completion of the transcontinental railroad in 1869, Mormons dominated not only the religious landscape in Utah but also its economy, politics, and society.

Latter-day Saints had experimented with communitarian economics previously, but Utah allowed them to implement novel economic systems on a much grander scale. There was no single pattern, but the general principles of communitarianism and self-sufficiency were applied in dozens of towns throughout the Mormon corridor. One of these models was called the United Order, with one of the most rigorous and long-lasting implementations of which being accomplished in a settlement called, appropriately enough, Orderville. As historian Leonard Arrington wrote:

> They ate at a common table and wore clothes from the same bolt of cloth. The labor of all was directed by a Board of Management, and their life was regulated by a United Order bugler who signaled the community to rise, to eat, to attend to prayers, to go to work, to return from work, and so on. Put to the test of living like the ancient Christian Apostles, the members appear to have lived and worked together in remarkable harmony.[35]

However much Latter-day Saint communitarianism challenged American notions of individualism and the free market, even more unsettling were Mormon political practices. For Mormons, the kingdom of God established in the last days was literal, not just a metaphor. In pioneer Utah, Church leaders told members whom to vote for and often ran for office themselves. Brigham Young served simultaneously as president of the church and, from 1851–1858, as territorial governor. Mormons became (in)famous for their bloc voting, a trend that at least in presidential politics continues today, though not at the direct behest of church leaders.[36] Of course, plenty of other ethnic communities in nineteenth-century America voted as a bloc – think of the Irish role in building the Democratic Party machine in New York, Boston, and Chicago. But the fact that the Latter-day Saints were running, and electing, men whom they believed to be modern-day prophets and apostles was disconcerting to other Americans, who saw Mormon apostolic electioneering as the equivalent of the pope or a cardinal running for mayor or city council. Drawing on the concept of popular sovereignty regnant in antebellum America, Brigham Young defended the Mormons' right "to choose their own rulers," adding that it was only logical that a godly people would choose godly leaders.[37] Critics countered that citizens in the Mormon kingdom were free only insofar as they chose to submit to the rule of the prophet and other church hierarchs. The charge of theocracy – which was not entirely false – would eventually become one of the rallying cries for federal repression of Mormonism in the second half of the nineteenth century.

None of their innovative doctrinal beliefs, economic institutions, or political practices would set apart Mormons from the broader society more than did the practice of polygamy. Once safely ensconced in their mountain valleys, in 1852 the Latter-day Saints publicly announced plural marriage as a central feature of their religion that not only brought them closer to God but also instituted a higher type of family and social order. Mormons offered several arguments in polygamy's favor. They testified that it was commanded by God as revealed through his modern-day prophet Joseph Smith, and represented a restoration of the ancient order of marriage practiced by biblical patriarchs and prophets. Furthermore, they claimed polygamy would solve the rampant plague of prostitution by channeling what was widely believed to be a greater male sex drive into marriages. Plural marriage, they argued, provided economic protection and a place in families for widows and single women. Internally, they championed polygamy as an engine for population increase that would grow the church and kingdom of God more rapidly. Most dubiously, Mormons claimed polygamy created a new, elevated, and purer race of humanity. While outside critics considered polygamy morally retrograde, more in line with "barbaric" Asian or African societies than "enlightened" European and American civilization, Mormons always emphasized its moral components, insisting that their peculiar marriage system upheld rather than degraded the Victorian norm of sex being properly reserved only for the marriage bed. The difference, of course, was that Mormons simply added to the number of marriage beds that any one man could have. For women, the arrangement was similar to broader norms in that they could only have one husband – though the Mormon promise was that if a woman's husband had other sexual relationships they could be confident it was with another wife and not a mistress or prostitute.

Nauvoo polygamy had been shrouded in secrecy and practiced somewhat helter-skelter. In Utah, now that "the Principle" was out in the open, it was regularized and systematized. No man could receive a plural wife without approval from church priesthood leaders, which not only kept the practice firmly under church control but also attempted to protect women. For instance, a senior church leader said he turned down two applicants who requested plural wives, one because he was an alcoholic and the other because what the man needed more than a second wife was "sufficient brains to take care of one wife and one family."[38] Church leaders themselves typically had the most wives; Brigham Young set the bar with fifty-five. As much as political cartoonists loved portraying Young's considerable family as the Mormon norm, simple demographics meant that most Mormon men never became polygamists. In general only 20 to 30% of Mormons in Utah lived in polygamous families – though in some communities the number was significantly higher in the late 1850s, at the peak of the practice. Because wealthier men and church leaders were more likely to take on plural wives, polygamy represented a form of wealth redistribution among a larger subset of the population. The majority of polygamist men had only two wives at a time. Despite church leaders' consistent emphasis, the Mormon laity's participation in plural marriage dropped gradually over time. Nearly three-quarters of plural marriages occurred from 1847 to 1869, which meant that in one representative community, only about 10% of women marrying from 1870 to 1890 became plural wives.[39]

Polygamy created untold hardships for many women and children, as many husbands struggled to provide adequate financial and emotional care for their plural families. Even the institution's most ardent defenders admitted its difficulties. Yet Mormon men and women alike believed in and supported polygamy – though the percentages suggest that it was easier for the majority to believe in and support someone else's plural marriage. One of the features that made the system workable was a liberal divorce policy that functioned as a "safety valve." Though he generally encouraged couples to try and make things work, Brigham Young made it clear that women who wished to leave a plural marriage were free to do so; several of his own wives divorced him. He was less lenient on men, admonishing them to fulfill any extra family duties that they had willingly taken on but granting most divorce requests nevertheless.[40]

Perhaps the greatest surprise of nineteenth-century Mormon polygamy, which was an undoubtedly patriarchal system, is that it led to a remarkably strong female community, and even became the seedbed for Mormon feminism. The bonds of Mormon sisterhood grew deep in pioneer Utah. Plural wife Emmeline B. Wells wrote:

> The world says polygamy makes women inferior to men – we think differently. Polygamy gives women more time for thought, for mental culture, more freedom of action, a broader field of labor [and] leads women more directly to God, the fountain of all truth.[41]

Wells's claim to greater thought, mental culture, and freedom of action was by no means true for all women in plural marriages, but it was certainly true for some, especially those who had married wealthier men and already raised their children and thus had both time and resources at their disposal. The fact that they could not be helpless Victorian ladies entirely dependent on their husbands meant that plural wives had to learn to fend for themselves, either on their own or with other women. The Relief Society became the primary institutional outlet for women's public engagement. They raised their own funds to build meetinghouses and storehouses, and to support the poor. In 1882 the Relief Society in Salt Lake City opened a free medical clinic, staffed largely with female doctors and nurses whose medical education had been sponsored by the Society. Whereas some women preferred charitable works, others leaned toward political activism. From 1877 to 1914, the above-quoted

Emmeline Wells edited a newspaper called the *Women's Exponent* that sounded a clarion call for women's suffrage and property rights; the masthead read, "The Rights of the Women of Zion, and the Rights of the Women of All Nations." Wells and other Mormon women leaders allied themselves with leading feminists such as Susan B. Anthony and Elizabeth Cady Stanton, and traveled the country not only defending Mormon women's reputations but also stumping for the vote. In one of American history's great ironies, Mormon women in Utah – supposedly enslaved by their patriarchal polygamous husbands – were the first women in the United States to exercise the vote when they went to the ballot box in 1870.[42]

The Mormons' distinctive economic, political, and social arrangements meant that pioneer Utah never quite fit the general characterization of western settlement being about the heroic lone individual. From the beginning, Mormons prized community and cooperation. Unlike most Euro-American settlers in the American West, Mormons came as entire families. Wallace Stegner opined that Mormons "were the most systematic, organized, disciplined, and successful pioneers in [American] history."[43] When they arrived in Utah, they donated money and goods to assist others coming along behind them. Pioneer Utah had its fair share of conflicts, but in general Mormon communities displayed a remarkable degree of order and harmony that was legendarily lacking in most of the Wild West. This mixture of community and frontier living impressed Franklin Buck, a non-Mormon miner working in rough-and-tumble Nevada, who visited several southern Utah Mormon towns in 1871. "The Mormons are the Christians and we are the Heathens," he wrote. "In Pioche [Nevada] we have two courts, any number of sheriffs and police officers and a jail to force people to do what is right. There is a fight every day and a man killed about every week." In contrast, the Mormon towns had "no courts, no prisons. . . . All difficulties between each other are settled by the Elders and the Bishop. Instead of every man trying to hang his neighbor," Buck concluded, "they all pull together."[44] As Brigham Young had foreseen, Utah successfully became the gathering place where a distinctive and powerfully coherent Mormon identity and community was forged.

• CONFLICT AND RESOLUTION

Franklin Buck's sanguine observations notwithstanding, the Mormon Zion was not all peace, love, and understanding. Mormon identity throughout the last half of the nineteenth century continued to be forged in the furnace of conflict, typically with outside groups but internally as well. The pioneers' arrival in the Great Salt Lake Valley, rarely visited and never previously settled by Euro-Americans, sparked conflict with the native peoples in the region. The Salt Lake Valley itself was fairly uninhabited by native tribes, but as the pioneers kept streaming in, they needed new places to settle and began moving into areas occupied by Indians. Brigham Young's vision for colonizing the entire Great Basin expanded accordingly. Because nineteenth-century Mormons believed that Native Americans were the descendants of the Lamanite civilization, which the Book of Mormon prophesied would play an important role prior to Jesus Christ's Second Coming, it was possible that the Latter-day Saints could have deployed their unique theological resources toward a radically different set of relationships with their new neighbors than had been the white American norm. But as historian Jared Farmer has demonstrated, there was a profound "tension in Mormon thought between Indian-as-brother and Indian-as-other; between sympathy and contempt, belief and doubt. Pioneer leaders sincerely meant to *try* to redeem the Lamanites. But first things came first."[45]

The relative generosity of Mormon theology was overwhelmed by self-preservation, culturally bred instincts about Indian backwardness and savagery, and the desire for land and resources. Violent conflict between Mormons and Native Americans began during the settlement of Utah Valley, where the LDS Church's flagship school Brigham Young University now stands. Having led his people out of Missouri because of the governor's extermination order just over a decade earlier, in 1850 Young issued his own order for a war of extermination against the Utes: "I say go and kill them." Within a few years, having successfully initiated the steady removal of Indians as a real threat to Mormon settlement, Young's views became more lenient. He adopted a new policy, determining "it is cheaper to feed the Indians than to fight them." He even encouraged some Mormon missionaries to intermarry with Native American women (but never for Mormon women to marry Indian men), so as to expedite the process of "Lamanite redemption." The real solution to the "Indian problem," however, was removal. Within two decades of Mormon settlement, Latter-day Saints and Indians had developed a stable and often friendly relationship, predicated on native tribes vacating the land that Mormon settlers desired.[46]

The Latter-day Saints also maintained an often tense relationship with the nation they presumably had left behind. When they went to the Salt Lake Valley in 1847, Mormons had officially left the United States and entered Mexican territory. Yet in the following year's Treaty of Guadalupe-Hidalgo, which ended the Mexican-American War, Mexico ceded all its northern territories to the United States, thus bringing the Great Basin – and the Mormons – into the American fold. In 1850 the Mormons' short-lived independent State of Deseret became Utah Territory, which meant according to the Constitution that it would be supervised by Congress rather than enjoying local control as a state would. Thus began decades of recurring conflict between Mormons and Washington. Although Brigham Young was appointed territorial governor, Congress sent a number of appointed federal officials who clashed with the Mormons. Based on exaggerated claims by disenchanted federal appointees, in 1857 newly elected president James Buchanan decided to send a major army expedition to Utah to quell an alleged Mormon rebellion against the United States. The Utah Expedition, later dubbed by the Eastern press "Buchanan's Blunder," failed to reach the Salt Lake Valley before winter set in. Fearing mass violence but refusing to give in, Brigham Young moved virtually the entire Mormon population of Salt Lake to Utah Valley fifty miles south, and threatened to burn Salt Lake City to the ground rather than have it be taken by force. In the end, the "Utah War" of 1857–1858 was mediated and resolved nonviolently. One result of the Utah War was that it diminished the reach and resources of the LDS Church. In preparation for the army's invasion, Young had recalled all Mormons from outlying settlements such as San Bernardino, California, and Carson City, Nevada. These outposts were never resettled by Mormons.

In the year prior to receiving word of the advancing military expedition, Utah was already aflame in a period of religious purification and rededication called the Mormon Reformation. Brigham Young believed that the people had become too complacent in their new home, so he initiated a series of reforms, including requiring the rebaptism of all church members and suspending the sacrament (or communion) until the people showed sufficient contrition. Young and other church leaders went on preaching tours throughout the territory, condemning sin in terms that were often bellicose, overheated, and even violent. Some Mormon leaders, including Young, preached the doctrine of "blood atonement" – namely, that certain sins could only be forgiven through the voluntary shedding of the sinner's own blood. This fire-and-brimstone approach did in fact reinvigorate religious worship and led to a spike in plural marriages. At the same time, it alienated a number of church members and precipitated a wave of emigration from Utah Territory by many discontented Mormons and non-Mormons. A rash of violence against dissenters and "Gentiles," including a handful of extralegal murders, was probably an unintended but nevertheless grim consequence of the short-lived Reformation.

The greatest tragedy related to the Reformation and the Utah War, and indeed the single darkest day in Mormon history, occurred on September 11, 1857, in what is known as the Mountain Meadows Massacre. The massacre occurred at the tail end of the Reformation and in the tense period when the Mormons had received word of the U.S. Army's impeding invasion. Brigham Young declared martial law throughout the territory and told the Mormons to stop trading with emigrant wagon trains passing through Utah. As a California-bound emigrant company from Arkansas reached Cedar City, local Mormon leaders Isaac Haight and John D. Lee saw a chance to seize the travelers' supplies. They devised a plan to attack the company, with the hopes of laying blame on their local Paiute Indian allies. The emigrants repelled the first surprise attack, then the two sides dug in for what became a weeklong siege. To end the standoff, local Mormon leaders hatched a devious plan. On the morning of September 11, under a white flag of truce, Lee met with the emigrants and told them that that local Mormon militia would accompany them to safety provided they give up their arms. With supplies running out, the company had no choice. Upon a pre-arranged signal, the Mormons and Paiutes attacked the unarmed emigrants, brutally slaughtering some 120 men, women, and children. They spared only seventeen children whom they considered too young to testify against the attackers; the surviving children were placed temporarily in foster homes until finally being sent to relatives in the East. Though Brigham Young did not order the massacre, his martial rhetoric was an important background factor, and he did help orchestrate a cover-up after the fact in order to save the reputation of the church. John D. Lee was the only man convicted and executed for his involvement in the massacre.[47] For decades Mormons denied involvement and blamed the Paiutes; only in recent years have LDS Church leaders fully accepted Mormon responsibility for the massacre and expressed sincere regret for the horrific actions of the Mormon settlers.

By far the greatest cause of tension between Mormons and the broader culture in the late nineteenth century was polygamy.[48] After the doctrine's public announcement in 1852, anti-Mormonism was transformed from a local to national phenomenon. In 1856 the newly formed Republican Party listed polygamy alongside slavery on its platform against the "twin relics of barbarism." The Lincoln administration passed the Morrill Anti-Bigamy Act of 1862, but the government was preoccupied with fighting a war to save the Union and thus left the Mormons alone. Renewed attention came as federal Reconstruction of the South wound down. New anti-polygamy legislation and increased enforcement brought heightened resistance from the Mormons, who asserted their constitutional right to practice plural marriage as part of their religion. The Supreme Court denied that claim when it decided against the LDS Church in *Reynolds v. U.S.* (1879), the first case in which the court ruled on the free exercise clause of the First Amendment. *Reynolds* looms large in First Amendment jurisprudence as establishing the "belief-action distinction," namely that citizens can believe what they like but not necessarily practice it, and that the Constitution does not protect religious practices that directly counter federal law.[49]

Anti-Mormonism became an increasingly bipartisan and national affair, with all branches of government and all regions of the country weighing in. In his annual message to Congress in 1879, President Rutherford B. Hayes recommended stripping Mormons of their American citizenship if necessary to force them to abide by the law. The Hayes administration also made anti-Mormonism a plank of its foreign policy, sending a letter to various European governments asking them to prevent Mormon converts from emigrating to the United States – a request the Europeans politely declined. Hayes's pleading helped set the stage for the 1882 Edmunds Act, which along with the *Reynolds* case marked the real beginning of the end for Mormon plural marriage. The Edmunds Act declared polygamy a felony, enhanced prosecution, disenfranchised convicted polygamists, and pronounced them ineligible for jury duty or public office. In what Mormons called "the Raid," federal marshals began hounding polygamists throughout Utah Territory, forcing much of the LDS leadership (including church president John Taylor) underground. Successive presidents James Garfield, Chester Arthur, and Grover Cleveland picked up where Hayes left off, consistently listing Mormonism as a dangerous threat to the nation in their annual messages to Congress. The decisive blow against polygamy was the 1887 Edmunds-Tucker Act, which disincorporated the Church of Jesus Christ of Latter-day Saints, seized all church property in excess of $50,000 (including temples), and established the harshest methods and punishments yet for prosecuting polygamists. By the 1880s, Mormonism had gone beyond mere heresy or falsehood and entered the realm of the

FIGURE 3.5 William Jarman, "Startling Revelations for Saints and Sinners, Hell Upon Earth!," printed by H. Leducs Steam Printing Works, Exeter, England, 1884. Anti-Mormon cartoons such as this, often portraying Mormon men as lecherous polygamists preying on poor immigrant women and children, were common in the late nineteenth century.

criminal, with concerted actions taken against it by the federal executive, legislative, and judicial branches as well as numerous state governments.

Political and legal anti-Mormonism both fed and was inspired by a wave of literary, religious, and cultural anti-Mormonism, which in turn sometimes devolved into extralegal violence. In the postbellum South, vigilantes whipped, kidnapped, forcibly expelled, and on a few occasions even murdered Mormon missionaries and converts.[50] This violence was fed and in some ways justified by a host of anti-Mormon articles and books published throughout the United States and Europe in the second half of the nineteenth century, ranging from theological disputes to dime novels with Mormons – generally violent, lecherous, polygamist patriarchs – serving as stock villains.[51] Indeed, Sir Arthur Conan Doyle's breakthrough novel, *A Study in Scarlet*, has Sherlock Holmes tracking down murderous Mormons! Authors outdid themselves in attempting to describe just how fraudulent and base Mormonism was. Consider, for instance, prominent Southern Baptist preacher and editor Edgar Folk's estimation of the religion in his book *The Mormon Monster*. Mormonism, he wrote:

> is a travesty upon the name of religion, a stench in the nostrils of decency, a constantly running sore, an immense octopus reaching out its slimy tentacles and seeking to seize hold upon our religious, social and political institutions, an ugly and misshapen monster.[52]

It didn't matter that Doyle, Folk, and the hundreds of other anti-Mormon authors usually didn't have their facts straight. What they communicated, both individually and collectively, were the limits of acceptable religion in late nineteenth-century Anglo-America. Religion ceased to be religion when it was (in their eyes) coercive, theocratic, polygamous, and violent.[53] The irony was hardly lost on the Latter-day Saints that their opponents used all available levers of power to stamp out nineteenth-century Mormonism's core beliefs and practices, and even the entire religion if need be, all in the name of religious and civic freedom.

LDS leaders boldly proclaimed throughout the 1880s that they would never give into pressure and abandon their most cherished beliefs and practices. Yet in the clash of wills between Mormons and America, the imbalance of power was simply too great, and the Mormons blinked first. When Wilford Woodruff, who had been in the church's leadership since its first decade, became president of the church in 1890, he said he saw in vision what would happen to the church if it continued to fight against the nation. The Supreme Court had just ruled the harsh provisions of the Edmunds-Tucker Act to be constitutional, and hostile forces were pressing on the church from seemingly every side. Woodruff in particular was concerned with the government's impending seizure of the church's temples, which would not only defile the religion's holiest places but also make its most sacred rituals unavailable to its members. That prospect was more than he could bear. In September 1890 Woodruff issued a "Manifesto" in which he admitted that even true religion had to concede to the power of the nation, and thereby declared his "intention" to submit to the law and "use my influence with the members of the Church over which I preside to have them do likewise."[54]

The Manifesto did not rescind the doctrine of plural marriage, which remains enshrined in Mormon scripture today. Neither did it actually end the practice, as that generation of Mormons, having received presidential amnesty, continued to live in and provide for their polygamous families. More controversially, for another decade and a half after the Manifesto, church leaders secretly continued to authorize and perform new plural marriages, especially in the church's colonies in Canada and Mexico.[55] The messiness of polygamy's denouement notwithstanding, what mattered most was that with a single short press release, the Mormons had waved the white flag of surrender. In virtually one fell swoop, the pillars of the Mormon kingdom in the West – communitarianism, theodemocracy, and polygamy – were toppled. After decades of unsuccessful attempts, Utah was deemed fit to be granted statehood in 1896. The kingdom of God had crashed and broken up on the shoals of the nation. Mormonism had been coercively, but successfully, "gathered" back into the mainstream of American political, religious, and cultural life.

FIGURE 3.6 Family of Joseph F. Smith, sixth president of the Church of Jesus Christ of Latter-day Saints and nephew of founder Joseph Smith. Despite his personal commitment to plural marriage, with six wives and forty-eight children, Joseph F. Smith was responsible for cementing the LDS Church's prohibition of new polygamous marriages after issuing the "Second Manifesto" in 1904.

Courtesy of the Church History Library, The Church of Jesus Christ of Latter-day Saints, Salt Lake City, Utah

• NOTES

1 Louisa Barnes Pratt, *The History of Louisa Barnes Pratt: Being the Autobiography of a Mormon Missionary Widow and Pioneer*, ed. S. George Ellsworth (Logan: Utah State University Press, 1998), 57–60.

2 Ibid., 60–66.

3 Ibid., 66, 74.

4 Ibid., 70–77.

5 Ibid., 78–79.

6 Ibid., 86–88.

7 Ibid., 88–90.

8 Ibid., 90–93.

9 The fullest history of the Kirtland period is Mark Lyman Staker, *Hearken, O Ye People: The Historical Setting of Joseph Smith's Ohio Revelations* (Salt Lake City: Greg Kofford Books, 2009).

10 See Grant Underwood, *The Millenarian World of Early Mormonism* (Urbana: University of Illinois Press, 1993).

11 Matthew Bowman, *The Mormon People: The Making of an American Faith* (New York: Random House, 2012), 36.

12 Doctrine and Covenants 52:42, 57:1–3.

13 Sidney Rigdon, *Oration Delivered by Mr. S. Rigdon, on the 4th of July, 1838, at Far West, Caldwell County, Missouri* (Far West, MO: Printed at the Journal Office, 1838), 12; reprinted in Peter Crawley, "Two Rare Missouri Documents," *BYU Studies* 14:4 (Summer 1974): 517–527.

14 On the Missouri violence, see Stephen C. LeSueur, *The 1838 Mormon War in Missouri* (Columbia: University of Missouri Press, 1987); Alexander L. Baugh, *A Call to Arms: The 1838 Mormon Defense of Northern Missouri*, Dissertations in Latter-day Saint History (Provo, UT: Joseph Fielding Smith Institute for Latter-day Saint History and BYU Studies, 2000); Leland H. Gentry and Todd M. Compton, *Fire and Sword: A History of the Latter-day Saints in Northern Missouri, 1836–1839* (Salt Lake City: Greg Kofford Books, 2012). For context and analysis of the "nits make lice" comment, see W. Paul Reeve, *Religion of a Different Color: Race and the Mormon Struggle for Whiteness* (New York: Oxford University Press, 2015), 52–55.

15 This section follows the general narrative in Bowman, *The Mormon People*, chap. 3. For divergent interpretations of the Nauvoo period, see Robert Bruce Flanders, *Nauvoo: Kingdom on the Mississippi* (Urbana: University of Illinois Press, 1975); Roger D. Launius and John E. Hallwas, eds., *Kingdom on the Mississippi Revisited: Nauvoo in Mormon History* (Urbana: University of Illinois Press, 1996); and Glen M. Leonard, *Nauvoo: A Place of Peace, a People of Promise* (Salt Lake City and Provo, UT: Deseret Book and Brigham Young University, 2002).

16 Some women did take on more prominent preaching roles in early American churches, but they were exceptions to the rule. See Catherine A. Brekus, *Strangers*

and Pilgrims: Female Preaching in America, 1740–1845 (Chapel Hill: University of North Carolina Press, 1998). A classic work on the construction of gender roles in early America is Nancy F. Cott, *The Bonds of Womanhood: "Women's Sphere" in New England, 1780–1835*, 2nd ed. (New Haven, CT: Yale University Press, 1997).

17 Bowman, *The Mormon People*, 73–74.

18 Richard W. Stewart, ed., *American Military History, Volume 1: The United States Army and the Founding of a Nation, 1775–1917* (Washington, DC: Center of Military History, U.S. Army, 2005), 175.

19 See Patrick Q. Mason, "God and the People: Theodemocracy in Nineteenth-Century Mormonism," *Journal of Church and State* 53:3 (Summer 2011): 349–375.

20 The 1843 revelation, including the language countenancing plural marriage, remains in LDS scripture as Doctrine and Covenants 132.

21 On Emma's feelings about plural marriage and how it affected her relationship to Joseph, see Linda King Newell and Valeen Tippetts Avery, *Mormon Enigma: Emma Hale Smith*, 2nd ed. (Urbana: University of Illinois Press, 1994).

22 Nauvoo polygamy has produced a substantial and hotly contested scholarly literature. For a few examples, see Richard S. Van Wagoner, *Mormon Polygamy: A History* (Salt Lake City: Signature Books, 1986); Todd Compton, *In Sacred Loneliness: The Plural Wives of Joseph Smith* (Salt Lake City: Signature Books, 1997); Kathryn M. Daynes, *More Wives Than One: Transformation of the Mormon Marriage System* (Urbana: University of Illinois Press, 2001); George D. Smith, *Nauvoo Polygamy: ". . . But We Called It Celestial Marriage,"* 2nd ed. (Salt Lake City: Signature Books, 2011); Brian C. Hales, *Joseph Smith's Polygamy*, 3 vols. (Salt Lake City: Greg Kofford Books, 2013).

23 Several friends and associates later reported that Smith had told them that he had been visited by an angel with a drawn sword commanding him to move forward with plural marriage when he was hesitant to do so. See Brian C. Hales, "Encouraging Joseph Smith to Practice Plural Marriage: The Accounts of the Angel with a Drawn Sword," *Mormon Historical Studies* 11:2 (Fall 2010): 55–71. Non-Mormon historian Lawrence Foster argues that whether or not the angel story is true, the evidence suggests that Smith "was, indeed, operating under a sense of intense inner compulsion." Lawrence Foster, "A Little-Known Defense of Polygamy from the Mormon Press in 1842," *Dialogue: A Journal of Mormon Thought* 9:4 (Winter 1974): 32 n. 4.

24 Bushman, *Joseph Smith*, 440.

25 See interview with Kathleen Flake for the PBS special *The Mormons*, transcript available online at http://www.pbs.org/mormons/interviews/flake.html.

26 Quotes in Bowman, *The Mormon People*, 82.

27 Quoted in Bushman, *Joseph Smith*, 492.

28 Cellmate, apostle, and future church president John Taylor's account of the "martyrdom" and his testimony of the prophet Joseph Smith is canonized in LDS scripture as Doctrine and Covenants 135.

29 Ellsworth, *The History of Louisa Barnes Pratt*, 70.

30 Bowman, *The Mormon People*, 92.

31 Wallace Stegner, *The Gathering of Zion: The Story of the Mormon Trail* (Lincoln: University of Nebraska Press, 1992 [1964]), 9–10.

32 Wallace Stegner, "Ordeal by Handcart," *Collier's Weekly*, July 6, 1956, 78.

33 Isaiah 35:1.

34 Brigham Young, "The People of God Disciplined by Trials," *Journal of Discourses* 4:51–52 (September 21, 1856). Another good, brief overview of Mormonism in nineteenth-century Utah is W. Paul Reeve, "The Mormon Church in Utah," in *The Oxford Handbook of Mormonism*, eds. Terryl L. Givens and Philip L. Barlow (New York: Oxford University Press, 2015), 38–54.

35 Leonard J. Arrington, *Great Basin Kingdom: An Economic History of the Latter-day Saints, 1830–1900*, new ed. (Urbana: University of Illinois Press, 2005), 333.

36 Nearly 90% of churchgoing American Mormons voted for George W. Bush and then Mitt Romney in presidential elections from 2000–2012.

37 Quoted in John G. Turner, *Brigham Young: Pioneer Prophet* (Cambridge, MA: Belknap Press of Harvard University Press, 2012), 243–244.

38 Quoted in Bowman, *The Mormon People*, 130.

39 Kathryn M. Daynes, *More Wives Than One: Transformation of the Mormon Marriage System, 1840–1910* (Urbana: University of Illinois Press, 2001), 114.

40 Ibid., chapter 8, quote from 143.

41 Bowman, *The Mormon People*, 134–135.

42 See Bowman, *The Mormon People*, 135–137. See also Judith Rasmussen Dushku, "Feminists," in *Mormon Sisters: Women in Early Utah*, ed. Claudia L. Bushman, new ed. (Logan: Utah State University Press, 1997), 177–197; and Joan Iversen, "Feminist Implications of Mormon Polygyny," *Feminist Studies* 10:3 (Autumn 1984): 505–522; Catherine A. Brekus, "Mormon Women and the Problem of Historical Agency," *Journal of Mormon History* 37:2 (Spring 2011): 59–87.

43 Stegner, *Gathering to Zion*, 6.

44 Quoted in W. Paul Reeve, *Making Space on the Western Frontier: Mormons, Miners, and Southern Paiutes* (Urbana: University of Illinois Press, 2006), 124–125.

45 Jared Farmer, *On Zion's Mount: Mormons, Indians, and the American Landscape* (Cambridge, MA: Harvard University Press, 2008), 61.

46 Ibid., chapter 2, quotes on 71, 87.

47 The best accounts of the massacre are Juanita Brooks, *The Mountain Meadows Massacre* (Norman: University of Oklahoma Press, 1970 [1950]); and Ronald W. Walker, Richard E. Turley Jr., and Glen M. Leonard, *Massacre at Mountain Meadows: An American Tragedy* (New York: Oxford University Press, 2008). For an alternative interpretation, which places blame on Brigham Young, see Will Bagley, *Blood of the Prophets: Brigham Young and the Massacre at Mountain Meadows* (Norman: University of Oklahoma Press, 2002).

48 This section draws on Patrick Q. Mason, *The Mormon Menace: Violence and Anti-Mormonism in the Postbellum South* (New York: Oxford University Press, 2011), 59–62.

49 See Sarah Barringer Gordon, *The Mormon Question: Polygamy and Constitutional Conflict in Nineteenth-Century America* (Chapel Hill: University of North Carolina Press, 2002).

50 See Mason, *The Mormon Menace*.

51 See Terryl L. Givens, *The Viper on the Hearth: Mormons, Myths, and the Construction of Heresy*, updated ed. (New York: Oxford University Press, 2013).

52 Edgar E. Folk, *The Mormon Monster – or, the Story of Mormonism* (Chicago: Fleming H. Revell, 1900), 11.

53 See J. Spencer Fluhman, *"A Peculiar People": Anti-Mormonism and the Making of Religion in Nineteenth-Century America* (Chapel Hill: University of North Carolina Press, 2012).

54 Woodruff's statement is published in the LDS Doctrine and Covenants as Official Declaration-1.

55 See D. Michael Quinn, "LDS Church Authority and New Plural Marriages, 1890–1904," *Dialogue: A Journal of Mormon Thought* 18 (Spring 1985): 9–105; B. Carmon Hardy, *Solemn Covenant: The Mormon Polygamous Passage* (Salt Lake City: University of Utah Press, 1992). In 2014 the LDS Church published an online essay with its most transparent official treatment yet of this complicated era; see "The Manifesto and the End of Plural Marriage," available at https://www.lds.org/topics/the-manifesto-and-the-end-of-plural-marriage?lang=eng.

4

˙Recalibrations

The product of leading Mormon pioneer stock, Ezra Taft Benson, was at the forefront of a generation of twentieth-century Latter-day Saints raised in the spiritual and cultural Mormon heartland but who then reengaged with the nation and the world on new terms. Born in 1899 and living until 1994, Benson's life marked the tensions Mormonism faced as this regional religion sought to shed its provincial reputation while still avoiding being absorbed by the broader culture in the century after the 1890 Manifesto.

Settled by his father and grandfather, Benson's hometown of Whitney, Idaho, was the very picture of homogeneity – white and Mormon, without a single exception. (Though in a college paper, Benson did note that about 13% of the population was "foreign born white.") The church was the center of the community, and Benson's family was at the center of the church. "We never missed going to church," he recalled. "I can't remember even one Sunday when I didn't go to church and to Sunday school." In addition to worship and religious instruction, the church sponsored dances, sports, picnics, concerts, and a genealogical society. It was an idyllic childhood in a Mormon farming community characterized by "neighborliness" and "clean, wholesome amusement."[1]

Ezra Taft Benson's first foray out of the Mormon culture region was as a missionary to England. In just over two years of full-time proselytizing, he had a hand in baptizing ten people into the church – a respectable number for any one missionary, but nothing like the success that Mormon missionaries had enjoyed in the British Isles in the church's first generation. His mission was a formative time for Benson. It deepened his knowledge of and commitment to the faith of his forebears. It steeled his resolve, as much through the opposition he experienced as his evident successes. He loved regaling listeners about the time he and his missionary companion were attacked by a mob outside a train station in 1923. As Benson wrote in his diary, someone from the crowd shouted at him, "You bloody bugger how many wives have you got?" Another answered, "He ain't got any," to which the first replied, "No, and he ain't gonna get any either." The incident lasted only a few moments, with the missionaries getting roughed up a bit before a policeman appeared on the scene and whisked them safely away. But it was just enough for Benson to feel, like so many Mormon missionaries before and after, that he was blessed by God for having been "persecuted for righteousness' sake."[2]

Following his mission and after waiting for her to return from her own mission to Hawaii, Benson married his longtime sweetheart, Flora Amussen – daughter of the third wife of a prosperous Danish convert who died, at age 76, a year after Flora was born. On the day of their wedding, Ezra and Flora packed up all their worldly belongings in an old Ford pickup and started the drive to Ames, Iowa, where he enrolled in graduate studies in agricultural economics at Iowa State College (now University). In so doing Benson was following the same path as many other twentieth-century Latter-day Saints who were raised in the Mormon heartland. They left to acquire education and training from the nation's leading centers of learning, then returned home equipped with newfound skills to benefit their people. Though it was always a risk to send their youth out into "the world," Mormons made the winning calculation that higher education from non-LDS institutions would raise the overall prosperity and talent level of the community. It was part of a general trajectory of twentieth-century Mormon accommodation with the broader culture, seeking to benefit from integration with society without sacrificing their core religious identity.

Back in Idaho, Benson's career flourished, first as a county agricultural official and then in Boise as director of the state's programs in agricultural marketing and economics. The family moved to Washington, DC, when Benson was hired as executive secretary of the National Council of Farm Cooperatives, which represented four thousand major agricultural cooperative associations with some 1.6 million total farmer members. Both in Boise and in Washington, Benson served as a stake president, the highest local priesthood office within Mormonism, with ecclesiastical responsibility over several congregations. He thus tried to balance enormous church responsibilities, professional demands, and raising six children (the burdens of which, he admitted, fell heavily on Flora's shoulders).

In 1943 Benson was called to be a member of the Quorum of Twelve Apostles, the LDS Church's second-highest governing body. When World War II ended two years later, the First Presidency appointed Benson to supervise the church's aid and reconstruction efforts in Europe. He left his family behind and traveled throughout the war-torn continent providing food and other forms of humanitarian relief to starving Europeans, mostly Latter-day Saints but others as well. One German who received cracked wheat from the church recalled eating it "morning noon and night," adding that "the food help literally saved lives."[3] As the LDS Church expanded globally, Benson and other leaders quickly realized that the opportunities attendant to worldwide evangelism also forced them to engage the world's problems in new ways.

Upon his return from Europe, Benson thought he would settle into a lifetime of church leadership. Those plans were unexpectedly interrupted in December 1952 when the newly elected U.S. president Dwight Eisenhower asked Benson to serve as Secretary of Agriculture. This made Benson the highest ranking Mormon in the executive branch of the federal government, before or since. It also landed him on the cover of national publications such as *Time*, *Newsweek*, and *U.S. News and World Report*, and brought network television camera crews into his home to feature his picture-perfect all-American family. Benson's appointment was significant not just for him but for all of Mormonism. It demonstrated how quickly and thoroughly Mormons had gone from being public enemies to ideal Americans. Only sixty-five years earlier, the Republican Party had sponsored federal legislation that aimed to destroy the LDS Church, and now a Mormon apostle held a Cabinet appointment in a Republican administration. In the postwar years, many other Latter-day Saints also assumed prominent positions in an array of American political, business, and cultural institutions. Mormons stand as one of twentieth-century America's great success stories alongside Jews, Catholics, and other "model minority" communities.

As the "culture wars" heated up beginning in the 1960s, most Mormons gravitated toward political and cultural conservatism. Benson went further than most, allying himself with (though never formally joining) a far-right and often conspiratorial

FIGURE 4.1 Ezra Taft Benson, left, Secretary of Agriculture, reaches over to get some papers as he meets with President Dwight D. Eisenhower

anti-communist organization called the John Birch Society. Religion and politics blended so seamlessly for Benson that it was often difficult to tell where one ended and the other began. His political preaching, which rejected an increasingly strict separation between church and state in modern America – recall that just a decade prior Benson was simultaneously a Mormon apostle and Cabinet official – helped galvanize conservative sentiment among the majority of Latter-day Saints while alienating a shrinking minority of self-described moderates and liberals. As much as any other single individual, Benson helped shape the religiously inflected social and political conservatism of modern American Mormonism.[4]

Perhaps Benson's greatest legacy, however, was elevating the status of the Book of Mormon. As will be discussed in more detail in the following chapter, the Book of Mormon was never really invisible within Mormonism, but neither was it particularly prominent for many members and leaders, who were more likely to turn to the Bible when summoning scriptural authority and anecdotes in their sermons. Benson felt passionately about the Book of Mormon from his youth, and his talks as an apostle relied heavily upon it. When he became LDS Church president in 1985, one of his primary messages to the church was to "flood the earth" with the Book of Mormon, which he emphasized (citing Joseph Smith) was the "keystone" of the Mormon religion. President Benson challenged Latter-day Saints to read from the Book of Mormon daily, both as individuals and as families, and made impressive promises about the spiritual blessings they would receive for doing so. Mormons have taken the message to heart, and over the past three decades the Book of Mormon has undoubtedly become the most commonly read, best-known, and most widely cited book of LDS scripture. A cottage industry of Book of Mormon-related art, videos, and even action figures and board games has emerged within popular Mormon culture.[5]

In 1899, the year Ezra Taft Benson was born, the Church of Jesus Christ of Latter-day Saints had some 270,000 members. When he died ninety-five years later, in 1994, the church had just broken the nine million member mark, representing an increase of some 3340% in the course of his lifetime. Two decades later, the church reported an official membership of over fifteen million members. This remarkable growth has meant many things for the development of modern Mormonism. First, Mormonism evolved from a provincial sect into a global church, if not yet a "world religion." Second, the growth of Mormonism meant that by the late twentieth century it could no longer be ignored by scholars and other observers. Whether or not the claim was empirically true, from the 1980s through the 2000s, Mormonism was often given the appellation "the world's fastest growing religion," a label that the church and its members frequently embraced as a sign of their increased influence and respectability.[6] Mormonism began appearing in textbooks, national newspapers, and even on Broadway stages to a degree that would have been unimaginable a few decades earlier. Third, more Mormons has meant a more diverse cast of Mormons, principally via an increasingly international membership but also with growing ideological diversity as well. Maintaining a coherent Mormon identity has become more challenging as the church has successfully expanded beyond the American West.

Though increasingly comfortable in mainstream society, the LDS Church remained conservative on many cultural and political issues. One of Ezra Taft Benson's messages to the membership of the church when he was prophet was that women should stay at home focusing on raising their children rather than going out into the workplace. He was part of a generation of Mormon leaders who actively fought against the passage of the Equal Rights Amendment (ERA) and decried second-wave feminism as a threat to the integrity of homes, families, and divinely ordained gender roles. A generation after his death, debates over family, gender, and sexuality continue to beleaguer the Mormon community, with major battles being waged both internally and externally on issues such as same-sex marriage and women's ordination to priesthood office in the church.

In short, the church that Ezra Taft Benson was born into in 1899 was not the church that he presided over in the late 1980s and early 1990s – nor necessarily the church that has continued to develop in the decades since his death. While twentieth- and twenty-first-century Mormon history may not feature quite the same amount of drama and conflict as did the religion's opening decades, it nevertheless demonstrates the challenges and opportunities attendant to a religion constantly recalibrating in order to gain respectability, navigate modernity, and still maintain its distinctiveness.[7] Rather than a straight chronological overview of Mormon history since 1890, this chapter examines a series of recalibrations that Mormonism has undergone in terms of politics, theology and church governance, growth and racial diversity, and family, gender, and sexuality.

• POLITICS

One of the most significant transitions from nineteenth- to twentieth-century Mormonism was in the religion's relationship to the state. Historians Leonard Arrington and Davis Bitton concluded, "By the end of World War I, if not before, the Mormons were more American than most Americans. Patriotism, respect for the law, love of the Constitution, and obedience to political authority reigned as principles of the faith."[8] To be sure, even in their most critical moments, Latter-day Saints had always thought of themselves as loyal members of the nation, with a special affinity for the religious freedoms guaranteed by the Constitution. But the precise nature of the Mormons' national loyalty underwent a shift in the generation after 1890, setting the tone for a new form of Mormon-American nationalism that has tempered only somewhat as the LDS Church has expanded throughout the globe. This broader shift in political attitudes can be seen in three transitions: the changing Mormon attitude toward participation in national and international wars; the dissolution of the church's own political party and the embrace of national parties and electoral politics; and the depoliticization of the Mormon concept of the kingdom of God, fostered by a decrease in millenarianism and increase in religiously inflected nationalism.

In their early decades Mormons were generally ambivalent about the nation's wars. As the Civil War unleashed its violent fury upon the American nation, the Latter-day Saints sat back in their remote mountain valleys and watched – in their less charitable moments, with smug satisfaction. For one, they saw the war, which began in 1861, as the fulfillment of an 1832 prophecy by Joseph Smith regarding "wars that will shortly come to pass, beginning at the rebellion of South Carolina," in which "the Southern States shall be divided against the Northern States" and "slaves shall rise up against their masters."[9] They were also glad that the Republican Party and the federal government now had more important things consuming their attention other than Mormon polygamy and supposed theocracy. Furthermore, they saw the bloodletting as a divine recompense for the nation's sins against them, and especially as a kind of national atonement for the blood of Joseph Smith. There was a lively sense among the Saints, expressed frequently by Brigham Young, that the North and the South would all but destroy one another, leaving a power vacuum that would be filled when the Mormons heroically rode in from the West to "step in and rescue the constitution."[10] While the Mormons did not take the opportunity to secede from the Union, neither did they marshal troops to support the North's war effort in any material fashion.

Contrast that to the situation in 1898, when Latter-day Saints enthusiastically marshaled their war spirit and patriotism in supporting the Spanish-American War. In so doing Mormons paralleled other minority communities, such as African Americans, who wished to demonstrate their loyalty to the nation by fighting for it. Although some church leaders preached peace, the church's First Presidency wholeheartedly endorsed the war of empire, and Utah became one of the first states to fulfill its quota of volunteers.[11] This would set the tone for the remainder of Mormon history: so thoroughly integrated had Mormons become (or desired to become) in American society that as went the nation so went the Mormons. Latter-day Saints embraced Woodrow Wilson's vision that World War I would be "the war to end all wars." After initial reluctance that echoed a broader American inclination not to get involved in European conflicts, following Pearl Harbor the church leadership openly supported World War II. Even with the reality that Latter-day Saints would be fighting on both sides of the conflict, the First Presidency proclaimed that when "constitutional law . . . calls the manhood of the Church into the armed service of any country to which they owe allegiance, their highest civic duty requires that they meet that call."[12]

This has more or less determined the official LDS view toward war ever since, seeing military participation as a necessary if regrettable aspect of the civic duty affirmed by Mormon scripture.[13] Brigham Young once called conscientious objectors "probably as good a class of men as has ever passed through this country," and the nineteenth-century Mormons' resistance to anti-polygamy laws was a classic case of collective civil disobedience. Yet by the Vietnam era, LDS leaders had all but rejected conscientious objection as a legitimate option for church members.[14] Though Mormonism has never properly been a peace church, the earliest Latter-day Saints did display a strong nonviolent ethic. In response to the violence they experienced in Missouri,

Mormons quickly adopted an ethic of self-defense, which in turn transformed into support for and even willing participation in the wars of the state.[15]

Mormons sought to patch their relationship with the American nation in the 1890s not only by fighting in its wars but also by joining its political parties. In the 1870s and 1880s, Mormons had sought to counter the growing clout of the non-LDS community in Utah by organizing the People's Party, which for all intents and purposes was the church's political organ. When the Manifesto opened the way for a rapprochement with the nation, Mormon leaders set their eyes on the long-denied prize of Utah statehood and knew that they would need support from the two major national political parties. They therefore dissolved the People's Party in 1891 and encouraged their people to align with either the Democrats or Republicans. Many church leaders feared that the membership would become overwhelmingly Democratic, as the Republicans had been the main sponsors of anti-polygamy legislation since the 1860s. Accordingly, folklore has it that in order to maintain parity between the two national parties, some bishops resorted to standing before their congregations and assigning the left half of the chapel to one party and the right half to the other.[16]

For the first half of the twentieth century, the voting patterns of Utah Mormons (which is to say, the vast majority of all Mormons at the time) closely matched national patterns. They even went against their church president's advice in strongly supporting Franklin D. Roosevelt in all four of his elections to the presidency. After World War II, Mormon support for Republican candidates began to grow steadily, with an average thirteen-point gap between them and the national popular vote. That distinction became even more pronounced beginning with the 1980 campaign of Ronald Reagan – since then, Mormons have voted Republican at an average of thirty points above the national average. From 1962 to 1978, half or fewer of Mormons serving in Congress were Republican; in 2012, it was fourteen out of seventeen.[17] A national poll released in 2012 revealed that 74% of Mormons either considered themselves or leaned Republican, while only 17% identified as or leaned Democrat.[18]

Political scientists have attributed American Mormons' gravitation toward the Republican Party as a consequence of the church's conservative entrenchment beginning in the 1960s on "a cluster of issues, including patriotism, gender roles, sex, abortion, marriage . . . and gay rights." Mormons identify so strongly with the GOP not because of official church messaging but in many ways in spite of it. Although the LDS Church has taken conservative positions on a number of particular "moral" issues, as will be detailed below, it is scrupulously non-partisan and sends a letter to be read from the pulpit in every ward during election season affirming its official political neutrality. Studies show that

> Mormons appear to have gotten the message that they are to keep partisan politics out of church. They have the lowest reported rate of politicking at church of all American religious traditions. . . . LDS congregations are also the least likely to have voter registration drives or voter guides at church, or to organize marches or rallies.

Unlike the nineteenth century, when church leaders dictated political preferences with explicit marching orders, American Mormons are swayed today in large part by the conforming pressure of their tightly knit social circles.[19]

Encouraged by their leaders to be engaged in their communities, Mormons have been active in local and national politics throughout the twentieth and twenty-first centuries. Ever since Utah gained statehood, there has been a steady stream of Latter-day Saints prominently placed in Washington, DC, beginning with Reed Smoot, a conservative Republican and member of the LDS Church's Quorum of the Twelve Apostles who was elected to the Senate from Utah in 1903. Though Smoot himself was personally unobjectionable, his status as a Mormon apostle turned his seating into a test case for how much Mormons could be trusted in positions of political leadership. Thousands upon thousands of petitions arrived demanding that Smoot be denied his seat on the grounds that Mormonism was a religious monopoly (this in the era of Progressive trust-busting), and that the church was still secretly sanctioning plural marriages, which in fact it was. The Senate hearings lasted four years, subpoenaing a series of witnesses including church president Joseph F. Smith to testify about all matters of LDS belief and practice from polygamy to temple rituals to prophetic authority and revelation. Apostle Smoot, President Smith, and others vigorously affirmed that Mormons had complete freedom of conscience and that the church leadership did not "shape the belief or control the conduct of those under them in all or any matters, civil or temporal." The hearings publicly embarrassed the church at the very moment when it thought it was regaining respectability. Smith went home and immediately proclaimed a "Second Manifesto" in 1904, which declared that plural marriage would be completely prohibited and that anyone entering into or officiating a new polygamous marriage would be excommunicated. Two apostles who refused to abide by the new order were removed from their ecclesiastical positions. In part thanks to the mediation of Theodore Roosevelt (who wanted another strong Republican ally like Smoot in the Senate), Smoot was finally seated in 1907, and went on to become of one the most powerful figures in the Senate over the first three decades of the century.[20]

A number of other major LDS political figures emerged throughout the mid-twentieth century, including Ezra Taft Benson (Secretary of Agriculture) and George Romney (governor of Michigan, presidential candidate in 1968, and Secretary of Housing and Urban Development). Mormon prominence was on particular display in the 114th Congress, commencing in January 2015, in which Republican Orrin Hatch served as the President pro tempore of the Senate, and Democrat Harry Reid (previously Senate Majority Leader) served as Senate Minority Leader and Democratic Caucus Chair. No doubt the most famous Mormon politician was Mitt Romney, the former governor of Massachusetts who ran for president in 2008 and 2012, the latter time capturing the Republican Party nomination before losing to Barack Obama in the general election. Romney's candidacies once again raised the question of whether a Mormon was acceptable for the highest office in the land. Most observers believe that in the end it was other, more conventional political issues that led to his dual defeats, but Romney's Mormonism was a persistent subtheme in both campaign cycles.[21]

FIGURE 4.2 Mitt Romney (1947–), prominent LDS business leader who ran for president in 2008 and 2012, the second time as the Republican Party nominee

Copyright: Richard Ellis/Alamy

Perhaps the most significant political transition from nineteenth- to twentieth- and twenty-first-century Mormonism was the depoliticization of the LDS concept of the kingdom of God. Certainly by the Nauvoo period, Joseph Smith had come to believe that the kingdom of God often spoken of in the Bible and his own revelations was intended to be not merely a metaphor for God's otherworldly reign but a literal political entity here on earth that the Latter-day Saints were expected to build in anticipation of Christ's Second Coming. This helps explain why in both Nauvoo and then early pioneer Utah, the Mormons essentially sought to construct a state within a state. In Smith's campaign for the presidency in 1844, cut short by his assassination, he spoke of "theodemocracy," in which "God and the people hold the power to conduct the affairs of men in righteousness." Smith believed this political co-participation between humans and the divine would lead to "unadulterated freedom," but skeptics naturally worried that "theodemocracy" would quickly devolve into theocracy, an argument that later Mormon leaders seemed to concede.[22]

The Latter-day Saints' political kingdom of God was always deeply informed by their urgent and sincere millenarianism. While the precise timing of Jesus's return remained speculative, nineteenth-century Mormons took seriously the warning in Smith's revelation that "the great and dreadful day of the Lord is near, even at the doors."[23] Though they argued over how the endtimes would unfold, Latter-day Saints believed that the church was restored by God as a preparation for and bridge to Christ's millennial kingdom. The urgency of establishing the kingdom of God before Christ's return largely inspired the Saints' religious activism and social experimentation. However, as time went on and Jesus still did not return, Mormons – like many other millennialists throughout history – somewhat resignedly settled in for the long haul. As one elderly Latter-day Saint who had been with the church since its earliest years stated in 1903, "we were over seventy years ago taught by our leaders to believe that the coming of Christ and the millennial reign was much nearer than we believe it to be now."[24] America had always enjoyed a special role in Mormon political thought, but before 1890 it was principally honored as a specially prepared nation whose religious liberties made possible the church's establishment. In nineteenth-century Mormon thought, the nation existed to serve the church and kingdom of God, not vice versa.

However, once millennial expectations subsided and the church was forced to abandon its more overtly political ambitions, Latter-day Saints grew more confident that, as scholar Ethan Yorgason has explained, "God would establish his ways as much through the might and influence of the United States as through LDS missionary efforts. No real difference existed between the nation's interests and those of the church and kingdom."[25] Ezra Taft Benson thus spoke confidently of the United States as "the Lord's base of operations in these latter days," promising the Saints in the midst of Cold War anxieties that "God will not permit his base of operations – America – to be destroyed."[26] Naturally, with such rhetoric emanating from the pulpit, many Latter-day Saints nurture a strong sense of American exceptionalism. At the same time, political activity shifted from the church as proto-kingdom to the state as divinely ordained instrument. The LDS Church has embraced what one scholar calls an "apolitical theology of the state," which has served it well in advancing its interests, especially missionary work, in a host of countries around the world, each with its own peculiar political arrangement.[27] Once upon a time enraptured by the idea that "they shall never cease to prevail until the kingdoms of the world are subdued under [God's] feet, and the earth is given unto the saints, to possess it forever and ever," now Latter-day Saints around the world are content to be "subject to kings, presidents, rulers, and magistrates, in obeying, honoring, and sustaining the law."[28]

• THEOLOGY AND CHURCH GOVERNANCE

If politics compelled Mormonism to constantly recalibrate its engagement with the broader culture, shifts in social norms, demographics, and economic organization prompted Mormons to reexamine their theological assumptions and organizational structures in the twentieth and twenty-first centuries. In order to survive and thrive, religions, which typically appeal to the transcendent and transhistorical, nonetheless must adapt to the inevitability of historical change. One of the primary challenges that LDS Church leaders faced in the period after the Manifesto was how to retain the loyalty and faith of the Saints who were forced to abandon so much of what they believed was fundamental to the religion only a few years earlier. President Joseph F. Smith – the nephew of Joseph Smith who had testified in the Reed Smoot hearings and then issued the Second Manifesto – responded to this concern by shifting Mormon identity away from plural marriage, economic communitarianism, and the political kingdom of God and toward "a foundational restoration of Christ's church from apostasy, a base of continuing revelation from heaven, and an assertion of Joseph Smith's revelatory power and divine [priesthood] authority bestowed to those that follow." In a series of sermons, Smith implicitly acknowledged that almost everything had changed while explicitly and confidently proclaiming that in fact the "nonnegotiable core of Mormonism" remained absolutely the same.[29]

Mormon theology, which throughout the nineteenth century had often appeared as an unruly and internally contested set of doctrinal propositions and speculative assertions, underwent a profound systematization in the early decades of the twentieth century. The three men at the helm of this transformation were James E. Talmage, John A. Widtsoe, and B. H. Roberts – all European immigrants and general authorities of the church. As historian Matthew Bowman has indicated, "With a few alterations, the achievement of Talmage, Widtsoe, Roberts, and [Joseph] Smith remains the Mormonism believed by most Latter-day Saints today." The voluminous writings of the three Progressive-era "theologians" (a term used advisedly, since none had formal theological training) essentially developed two basic principles: first, that God is a God of laws derived from the universe that he understands and follows perfectly; and second, that God and humanity share an underlying nature that allows humans to comprehend the nature of God and divine law, and achieve righteousness through faith in Jesus Christ and the development of personal character, discipline, and morality. Talmage's books *Articles of Faith* and *Jesus the Christ* were especially important in clarifying (if not finally resolving) Mormon Christology, in particular establishing Jesus's premortal identity as Jehovah (the God of the Hebrew Bible) and clarifying his distinctive relationship to God the Father, named Elohim in Mormon parlance.[30]

Mormon leaders were not content simply to innovate with their theology. Over the course of a thirty-three-year tenure, church president and former successful businessman Heber J. Grant (1918–1945) remodeled the church's organizational structure after the image of the modern corporation. Indeed, Grant organized the Corporation of the President of the Church to oversee the church's financial interests, and over the decades the ecclesiastical leadership increasingly relied upon a professional and paid bureaucracy to take care of much of the day-to-day operations from church head-quarters in Salt Lake City. Grant and other likeminded leaders applied their exper-tise of business management to church management, which helped stabilize church finances. Under Grant's leadership, the church inaugurated the Church Welfare Pro-gram as an antidote to the Great Depression. The national media widely hailed the program as an outstanding example of private initiative in troubling economic times. As an ardent opponent of Franklin D. Roosevelt and the New Deal, Grant promoted principles of work and personal accountability, thus offering an important corrective in his mind to the "dole" offered by the emergent welfare state.[31] While Mormons often extol the virtues of their internal welfare program over anything offered by the state, church welfare often supplements rather than supplants the safety net of social services provided by the government.

The same impulses that led leaders to manage church finances more carefully also led them to streamline church organization and curriculum – a process eventually known as "correlation." As the church had steadily grown in size, so too had it grown in insti-tutional complexity. Numerous sub-organizations, or "auxiliaries," arose to meet the needs of various groups within the church: the Relief Society for adult women; the Young Men's and Young Women's Mutual Improvement Associations for teenage boys and girls, respectively; the Primary for children under twelve; and the Sun-day School for gospel instruction for adults and teenagers. Originally, each of these auxiliaries had their own budgets, selected their own leadership (other than their presidents, who were appointed by the president of the church), developed their own independent curricula, and published their own periodicals. Beginning in ear-nest in 1960, the church leadership sought to rein in what they saw (and often was) institutional fracture, even chaos. The stated goal was greater coordination between the various auxiliaries and groups, but correlation ultimately went far beyond that, asserting the prerogatives of priesthood leadership, and especially the Quorum of the Twelve Apostles, over every aspect and auxiliary of the church. Independent budgets were now centralized into general church accounts, the panoply of publications were now limited to three monthly magazines (one for adults, a second for teenagers, a third for children), and auxiliary leaders at the general and ward level now answered directly to the priesthood leadership.[32]

The model for LDS correlation was the mid-century American corporation, and in many ways the model was achieved with spectacular success. Standardization, simpli-fication, documentation, and clear lines of authority became the watchwords. Some members complained that in the process of becoming more corporate and efficient, Mormonism had lost something of its soul; indeed, much of the charismatic free-wheeling that often accompanied nineteenth-century Mormon gatherings had now been regulated out of the church, leaving a much more predictable and staid religious experience. Yet it must be admitted that much of the current institutional strength of the LDS Church can be attributed in large part to correlation. The church could now more effectively control the teaching and transmission of doctrine – essential for any religious body that desires some degree of coherence and orthodoxy. With the exception of a temporary crisis in the 1950s due to an overzealous international building campaign, the church's finances were stabilized – and then some, with critics sometimes accusing the LDS Church of being *too* rich. The church curriculum has become standardized to the point that the same Sunday School lesson being given on a particular Sunday in a ward in Salt Lake City is also being given in Sweden and Suriname, all out of official church lesson manuals prepared and translated at headquarters. The church also provides an impressive collection of online and video resources accessible in dozens of languages. This becomes particularly valuable for fledging Mormon congregations in far-flung places around the world that would not have the local resources to develop nearly such a wide array of materials.

In short, correlation produced a leaner, streamlined, somewhat less culturally specific, and more exportable theology, curriculum, and church organization flexible enough to respond to significant LDS Church growth around the world. At the same time, "correlation Mormonism" suffers from many of the same problems as any centralized system, with the sense among many Mormons that it represents a depersonalized and generic religion that aims for the broadest, simplest audience possible. Correlated lesson materials encourage class teachers to ask questions that everyone in the room already knows the "right" answers to. Theological reflection and rigorous discussion of competing ideas are broadly sacrificed for doctrinal unity, encouragement of righteous living, and affirming what people already believe. The recurrent problem for Mormon leadership is how to maintain coherence and stability across the church without producing stagnation and boredom among individual members and congregations.

LDS leaders also felt it necessary, with the advent of the 1960s counterculture, to shore up the church's doctrines and moral authority. In a related process to correlation, church leaders reversed the trajectory toward assimilation that the church had been following since the 1890s in a process of doctrinal and institutional "retrenchment." This retrenchment took multiple forms: 1) increased centralization of ecclesiastical control under the priesthood hierarchy; 2) heightened emphasis on the need to follow the president of the church as a prophet of God; 3) a renewed and expanded resort to the Book of Mormon, generally at the expense of the Bible, in church discourse and instruction; 4) a greatly enhanced proselytizing campaign through the use of young volunteer missionaries, with strategies and evaluation techniques often borrowed from the corporate world; 5) doubling down on policies in support of traditional family values, including discrete gender roles and conservative sexual morality; 6) the expansion and imposition of a daily program of religious instruction, called seminary and Institute, for all Mormon high school and college students; 7) conservative and often literalistic scriptural interpretation, with a corresponding rejection of modern biblical scholarship as an insidious threat to faith; and 8) an increased emphasis on unique LDS doctrines of vicarious baptisms and other temple work (see Chapter 8), with a greatly expanded campaign to build temples around the world. Fearing that an increasingly permissive and secular culture were undermining core values, church leaders hoped that these efforts would retain Mormonism's strictness, separateness, and peculiarity.[33]

Correlation and retrenchment achieved much of what they set out to do, maintaining Mormon distinctiveness and coherence and supporting growth at a time when many other churches in America and Europe were hemorrhaging members. One unintended consequence, however, was that the church's conservative and often selective presentation of its own history created vulnerabilities when the Internet age dawned in the early twenty-first century and a massive amount of information was available to anyone with just a few keystrokes. Suddenly many LDS Church members were finding information online about their religion's past that did not square with what they had learned from an official church curriculum guided in part by the principle, taught by influential apostle Boyd K. Packer, that "some things that are true are not very useful."[34] Challenging aspects of the Mormon past had long been known to scholars and debated in periodicals such as *Dialogue: A Journal of Mormon Thought* and the *Journal of Mormon History*. Yet reading for the first time about issues such as Joseph Smith's participation in folk magic, questions about the historicity and authenticity of Mormon scripture, nineteenth-century Mormon violence against dissenters and "Gentiles" (especially the Mountain Meadows Massacre), and the loss of women's authorization to perform blessings left many Latter-day Saints feeling confused, troubled, and even betrayed. Exact numbers are impossible to gauge, but in the opening years of the twenty-first century, a significant number of Mormons had disassociated from the church as a result of their personal crises of faith connected to these and related issues.

The information revolution, and the wave of disaffiliation that it spawned, has prompted the twenty-first-century LDS Church to reassess its approach to history and adopt a more transparent approach. The first major marker of this new modus operandi was a major church-sponsored research initiative on the Mountain Meadows Massacre, culminating in a highly regarded book fully admitting Mormon culpability for the incident while responsibly denying Brigham Young's direct involvement.[35] An even more ambitious multi-year endeavor underway by the LDS Church History Department is the Joseph Smith Papers Project, which is an exhaustive effort to gather and publish complete, accurate, and annotated transcripts of every document ever produced by Mormonism's founder Joseph Smith.[36] The Church History Department has also made news with the online publication of thirteen essays dealing forthrightly with many of the challenging historical and doctrinal issues that have precipitated doubts among the church membership. Produced in collaboration with many believing but academically trained Latter-day Saint scholars, the "Gospel Topics" essays signaled a new era of transparency and accountability by the church.[37] A generation after the highly publicized and controversial excommunications of a handful of Mormon intellectuals in 1993, the LDS Church leadership now seems more intent on fostering a productive working relationship with scholars and intellectuals rather than disciplining them. Finally, in late 2015 the church opened the doors on a brand new and entirely overhauled Church History Museum across the street from Temple Square in downtown Salt Lake City. The museum not only featured modern interactive exhibits but also highlighted controversial aspects of the religion's founding, including multiple accounts of Joseph Smith's First Vision, his use of a seer stone in the translation of the Book of Mormon, and his clandestine practice of polygamy.[38] All in all, current trajectories suggest that the LDS Church is attempting to maintain a coherent and highly correlated religious culture while softening the sharpest edges of retrenchment and opening the doors for more openness, greater transparency, and a diversity of perspectives within the church.

• GROWTH AND RACIAL DIVERSITY

Mormonism has always been a missionary religion. Several of Joseph Smith's earliest revelations took the form of divine calls to followers to spread the word – "For behold, the field is white already to harvest."[39] Thanks to persistent commitment to its ambitious proselytizing program and slogans such as "every member a missionary," the Church of Jesus Christ of Latter-day Saints has consistently grown at between 3–5% per year, with only a handful of years in its nearly two centuries of history – for instance, during the Missouri persecutions and the Utah War – witnessing net membership losses. The remarkably steady growth trajectory has resulted over time in an exponential increase in total membership (see Figure 4.3). The church took 117 years from its founding to reach one million members, but then reached two million only 16 years later, three million 8 years after that, followed by a pattern of about a million new members added every 3 years or so, culminating in a global membership of over fifteen million in 2015.[40] Another important factor in LDS growth beyond convert baptisms is the Mormon birthrate, which has consistently remained higher than American national averages and has ensured long-term growth and multigenerational stability.[41]

LDS Church growth has lagged somewhat in recent years despite an increase in the number of proselytizing missionaries, suggesting perhaps that the "markets" that Mormon missionaries traditionally operated in over the past half century have reached or are nearing the saturation point for potential converts. Total membership numbers can also be somewhat deceiving, as the church retains a person on its membership lists until s/he dies, is excommunicated, or proactively requests his/her name to be removed from the church rolls. The reality is that in most places the majority of those on LDS membership lists do not regularly attend church, and many no longer even consider themselves to be Mormon. The number of Latter-day Saints who do self-identify and actively participate is probably between a third to a half of the official church membership total. Although this does somewhat deflate the sense

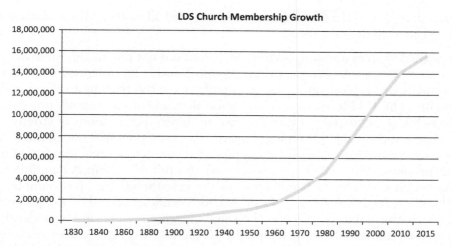

FIGURE 4.3 LDS Church membership growth chart

of Mormonism's size and scope, in this respect the LDS Church is no different from most other religious bodies, for whom the number of listed adherents and active participants is starkly different. For instance, it will come as no surprise to say that not all 1.25 billion Roman Catholics attend mass each week, or even each year.

The steady expansion of Mormonism has created a number of theological and policy-related challenges for the church over the years. Nowhere has this been more evident than in the LDS Church's struggle with racial diversity. To a certain degree Mormonism has simply paralleled the challenges faced by other religions when they expand beyond their initial linguistic, cultural, and ethnic milieu. Indeed, modern Christian notions of enculturation developed only after centuries of more imperialistic and often violent encounters with non-European peoples and races. Yet while Mormonism as a religion has hardly been alone in its often fraught relationship with non-white peoples, the particular history of Mormonism's racial policies does deserve special mention because of the ways in which those policies shaped the tradition and cast a long shadow over current efforts to build a genuinely diverse and global church membership.

From its beginnings, Mormonism was ambivalent about the origins and meanings of racial diversity. Like the Bible, the Book of Mormon included competing passages, some pointing toward a non-racial universalism and others toward ethnoracial chauvinism, with a sense that dark (and especially black) skin color either was a curse from God or at least operated as a marker of a divine cursing.[42] The Book of Abraham, produced by Joseph Smith in 1835, spoke of Noah's son Ham, from whom "sprang that race which preserved the curse in the land," specifically identifying the curse as grounds for members of Ham's lineage being denied "the right of Priesthood."[43] When combined with broader nineteenth-century Euro-American assumptions about Ham being the progenitor of Africans, the dots were all there to connect

Africans, dark skin, and a divine curse that prevented all men of African descent from being ordained to the priesthood.[44]

Their textual sources notwithstanding, Mormons did not pursue discriminatory policies against African Americans during Joseph Smith's lifetime, and even ran into trouble with white Missourians for reportedly being too friendly to slaves and free blacks alike. This led Mormons to adopt ambivalent and often contradictory positions on the political and social questions related to slavery, but in terms of strictly ecclesiastical policy, the early church was consistently cosmopolitan. Though missionaries rarely sought out African Americans as potential converts, a small number of blacks joined the young church and were welcomed into full fellowship. A handful of African American men received ordination to the priesthood. The most famous black priesthood holder, Elijah Abel, had a priesthood certificate signed by Joseph Smith in 1836 which attested to his "zeal for the cause of righteousness" and "confidently recommend[ed] him to all candid & upright people as a worthy member of society."[45] Abel went on to serve multiple missions for the church and was widely hailed as a stalwart member until his death in 1884. Other African American converts similarly earned the praise of early church leaders – Joseph Smith publicly commended the faith of Jane James, and Brigham Young labeled Walker Lewis as "one of the best Elders" the church had.[46]

This relatively open posture changed quickly in the decade following Smith's death. Reports of intermarriage between black male church members and white women were particularly galling to men like Brigham Young who shared the dominant racial views of antebellum white Americans. In 1847, apostle Parley Pratt was the first Mormon leader to make a public statement suggesting that a "Black Man who has got the blood of Ham in him . . . was cursed as regards the Priesthood." Brigham Young followed suit, reversing his previous statement that "of one blood has God made all flesh" and therefore that no distinctions existed between the races when it came to divine approval. In February 1852 Young stood before the Utah territorial legislature and delivered a typically blunt discourse in which he defended slavery (in the form of "servitude") and then proclaimed that "this people that are commonly called Negroes are the children of old Cain," the son of Adam and Eve who killed his brother Abel, and therefore "they cannot bear rule in the Priesthood."[47] Over the ensuing decades, the supporting theological justifications would change – blacks were the seed of Cain, they were the seed of Ham, they were less valiant in choosing Jesus in the premortal life, they were not spiritually prepared for the priesthood, and so forth. Supported by these various explanations, the formal ban on anyone with "black blood" holding the LDS Church's priesthood or entering its temples only calcified over the last half of the nineteenth century and first half of the twentieth.[48]

For most of that time, the priesthood-temple ban sparked little controversy or even mention. Firmly ensconced in their lily-white mountain valleys – recall that Ezra Taft Benson's hometown had exactly zero non-whites – the Latter-day Saints had little to no contact with blacks. Besides, it was America's era of Jim Crow, and most other white churches had discriminatory policies or theologies of some sort. This all changed in the decades after World War II, both because of external pressures resultant from the civil rights movement and internal pressures coming from the LDS Church's international missionary effort. As the church sought to expand in places such as the Caribbean, Brazil, and South Africa, they ran up against the problem of determining who exactly was or was not black. Under direction from church headquarters, mission presidents adopted a functional one-drop rule, and missionaries frequently had to initiate an awkward and frequently offensive conversation of asking potential converts to produce genealogical records proving that their ancestors were not black before they could be baptized or even taught. Despite their efforts to sidestep the issue by limiting black membership growth, a few blacks began joining the church in spite of the priesthood and temple ban. They knew that beyond basic membership their participation in the church was limited, but they felt called by God into the church and hoped that things would change. Central church leadership began receiving letters from people in western Africa who had come across the Book of Mormon and other church literature and were now requesting missionaries to come establish the church in their native lands.[49] At home, the priesthood and temple ban increasingly came under scrutiny by civil rights organizations, college students and administrators, and even many white Mormons. A series of planned protests and marches around Temple Square in Salt Lake City organized by the NAACP in 1963 was called off only after the mediation of U.S. Commissioner of Education Sterling McMurrin, a non-churchgoing Mormon who was himself critical of the church's policy, and a conciliatory statement about civil rights by one of the members of the First Presidency.[50]

As pressure mounted to rescind the ban, the church's First Presidency itself seemed confused on whether the ban was part of the church's official doctrine or not. In 1949 the First Presidency issued a statement saying the priesthood ban "is not a matter of the declaration of a policy but of direct commandment from the Lord," but five years later church president David O. McKay commented that the restriction was "a practice, not a doctrine."[51] In any case, church leaders felt they needed a revelation from God to overturn more than a century of church precedent. Their deliberations were assisted by the 1973 publication of a groundbreaking article called "Mormonism's Negro Doctrine," in which author Lester Bush persuasively demonstrated, contrary to conventional wisdom at the time, that in fact blacks had been ordained to the priesthood during the time of Joseph Smith and that the change in practice had not originally been initiated by any definitive divine command.[52] Finally, in early June 1978 under the direction of church president Spencer W. Kimball, the LDS First Presidency and Quorum of the Twelve Apostles held a meeting in the Salt Lake Temple in which they reported experiencing an overpowering and collective spiritual witness that they all characterized as a clear revelation from God that the time for racial exclusion was past. Without any further explanation or apology, they announced that from that time forward, "every faithful, worthy man in the Church may receive the holy priesthood," and every worthy member could be admitted to enjoy "the blessings of the temple."[53]

On one level, the 1978 revelation changed everything for Mormonism. Nothing stood in its way now for becoming a truly global church. Indeed, church membership in places like Brazil and Ghana began to skyrocket.[54] However, old attitudes die hard. Although there was never any evidence that Mormons were more racist than any other group of white Americans, even after 1978 many Mormons held on to defunct explanations for why the ban had ever existed in the first place. This came to a head in early 2012, in the heat of Mitt Romney's second run for the presidency, when a *Washington Post* article about African Americans in the LDS Church included comments by a highly popular religion professor at Brigham Young University who said that "God has always been discriminatory" in determining who could and couldn't have priesthood authority. The professor suggested that African Americans were not spiritually prepared for the priesthood until 1978, and thus "in reality the blacks not having the priesthood was the greatest blessing God could give them."[55] The LDS Church's official response, appearing the next day, was unequivocal in rejecting the professor's comments, affirming that his claims "absolutely do not represent the teachings and doctrines" of the church. "The Church's position is clear," their statement continued. "We believe all people are God's children and are equal in His eyes and in the Church. We do not tolerate racism in any form."[56] Late the following year, the church published an online essay on "Race and the Priesthood" in which it offered its most comprehensive official narration of the history of the priesthood and temple restriction, concluding with the statement: "Today, the Church disavows the theories advanced in the past that black skin is a sign of divine disfavor or curse, or that it reflects unrighteous actions in a premortal life; that mixed-race marriages are a sin; or that blacks or people of any other race or ethnicity are inferior in any way to anyone else. Church leaders today unequivocally condemn all racism, past and present, in any form."[57]

If anything, the thrust of contemporary Mormonism is to seek out and emphasize diversity. Beginning in 2011 the LDS Church launched a multi-million dollar ad campaign called "I'm a Mormon," featuring prominently placed billboards (including in New York City's Times Square) and extensive television, radio, and Internet ads. The ads and the accompanying website featured highly polished and professionally produced profiles of individual Latter-day Saints from virtually every imaginable background and walk of life. Like all ad campaigns, it was a carefully curated presentation of the Mormon people that was as much aspirational as representative; many Mormons joked internally that as much as they loved the ads, no one in their ward was nearly as diverse or interesting as the Mormons they saw on the sides of buses. Whatever one thinks about how closely ad campaigns should adhere to reality, the fact that the LDS Church even desired to dispel popular notions of itself as a white middle-class American monolith was a significant change for a church that for most of its history had been relatively insular and homogeneous. At the same time that Mormonism's most famous son was being called in the *New York Times* "the whitest white man to run for president in recent memory" and *The Daily Show* was referring to black Mormons as "mythical creatures" and "unicorns," the LDS Church was making every effort to boast of just how non-white it had become.[58]

• FAMILY, GENDER, AND SEXUALITY

Despite the dramatic shift in its racial policies and teachings, no about-face was more dramatic than the transformation of the Mormon family from being a civilizational menace to bastion of traditionalism. Arguably the single greatest recalibration in Mormon history – and indeed, one of the most significant in all of American religious and cultural history – was when the LDS Church abandoned plural marriage in the 1890s and early 1900s. In doing so the church did not jettison its unique family-based theology so much as retool and repurpose it. Whereas "celestial marriage" had once been equated in Mormon parlance with plural marriage, for Latter-day Saints in the twentieth century, the term simply came to describe the marriages (or "sealings") performed in LDS temples for faithful Mormon couples, which they believed would last beyond the grave and into the afterlife. Celestial marriage remains a prerequisite for the highest form of salvation in Mormon theology, called exaltation. Furthermore, it is the vehicle by which families can be sealed together in the eternities rather than being separated at death. The revelation to Joseph Smith that outlined the theology behind this notion of eternal families is the same one that provided the rationale and even command for plural marriage. While the revelation remains enshrined in Mormon scripture, its passages regarding polygamy have been relegated to contingent history while its more generic verses about eternal marriage are interpreted at the level of general principle and divine truth.[59] Mormons still think of temple sealings as ritually binding together the whole human family, but the emphasis has shifted from the dynastic ties associated with polygamy toward the interlocking of multiple generations of nuclear families.

In the decades following the Manifesto, Latter-day Saints recast themselves as the ultimate paragons of a Victorian-style home and hearth. The powerful family theology that had once animated plural marriage was now dedicated entirely to monogamous marriage and a domestic ideal. By the mid-twentieth century, the Mormon family, once an international pariah, was the very icon of household bliss. Mormons identified with and fit comfortably in the Norman Rockwell and "Leave It to Beaver" vision of America that dominated national culture in the 1950s. As the LDS Church continued to grow, and postwar educational and economic opportunities drew its members outside of the Great Basin in a process that scholar Jan Shipps has called "the scattering of the gathering," more and more Americans became acquainted with Mormons and began to admire them for their clean living, devotion to family and faith, work ethic, patriotism, and neighborliness. Titles like "Those Amazing Mormons" replaced screeds against "The Mormon Menace" in national publications. When the 1960s hit, Latter-day Saints cast their lot with the culture rather than the counterculture. As Shipps noted, "it was the dramatic discrepancy between clean-cut Mormons and scruffy hippies that completed the transformation of the Mormon image from the quasi-foreign, somewhat alien likeness that it had in the nineteenth century to the more than 100 percent super-American portrait of the late sixties and early seventies."[60] In a testament to the substantial conflation between domesticity and citizenship in American life, family life had kept Mormons outside the bounds of the national community in the nineteenth century but placed them squarely in the national mainstream in the mid-twentieth.

Just when Mormons were getting comfortable, however, the ground shifted underneath their feet. Opting not to move apace with the culture on issues of feminism and gay rights, by the late 1970s Mormons identified with the cultural and political right in a nation where the center was steadily eroding. When feminist awakenings were happening around the country as women read Betty Friedan's *The Feminine Mystique* (1963), many Mormon women were instead reading Daryl Hoole's *The Art of Homemaking* (1962), which taught women how to thrive while fulfilling their duties at home, and Helen Andelin's *Fascinating Womanhood* (1963), which more controversially encouraged women to please their husbands with obedience and girlish appearance and mannerisms.[61] Although the LDS Church consistently avoided partisan politics, in the late twentieth and twenty-first centuries, it felt justified in speaking out and organizing its members around "moral issues." On a few occasions, the church took unexpected political stances; for instance in opposing the Reagan administration's proposed placement of MX missiles in Nevada and Utah or in openly supporting the widely praised "Utah Compact," proposing a more moderate, family-centric set of national and local immigration policies.[62] Beginning in the 1970s, however, for the most part Latter-day Saints joined coalitions with other socially conservative religious groups such as Roman Catholics, evangelicals, Muslims, and black churches in opposing abortion and protecting religious freedom.[63]

In particular, the LDS Church played a pivotal role in halting the state-by-state ratification of the Equal Rights Amendment, which read, "Equality of rights under the law shall not be denied or abridged by the United States or by any State on account of sex." By 1974 the ERA had passed in thirty-three of the necessary thirty-eight states to be added to the Constitution, and ratification appeared inevitable. Utah seemed poised to add its voice to the chorus of ayes when in 1975 the church leadership, including the Relief Society general president, threw their weight against the amendment. While insisting that they supported full civil rights for women, the church and its allies – such as Phyllis Schlafly's STOP ERA campaign – argued that the amendment threatened the God-given distinctions between men's and women's traditional roles. They suggested that if the ERA passed, motherhood would be devalued and women would be forced to fight in wars. Though most Relief Society women responded en masse to the church's call to actively oppose the amendment, not all marched in lockstep. In 1978 the previously apolitical Sonia Johnson participated in a march in Washington, DC carrying a "Mormons for ERA" banner. Johnson immediately became a media sensation and even testified before a Senate committee. Her public opposition to the church's leadership, which quickly turned into outright criticism and disparagement, finally led to her excommunication late the following year.[64] In the meantime, priesthood leaders spoke of "the honored place of women" in the church and God's plan, often placing women on exalted pedestals of innate spirituality and goodness. As Ezra Taft Benson told LDS women in a 1979 address, "The conventional wisdom of the day would have you be equal with man. We say, we would not have you descend to that level."[65]

The LDS Church applied many of the lessons it had learned in its anti-ERA campaign to its next fight on behalf of the "traditional family." Beginning in the mid-1990s, the church mobilized significant resources to opposing the legalization of same-sex marriage across the United States. The church's most significant efforts came in Hawaii and California, states that contained well-established LDS communities that were called upon to donate significant amounts of both time and money to the cause. During the 2008 battle over California Proposition 8, a ballot initiative to create a state constitutional amendment banning gay marriage, the church's First Presidency sent a letter to every congregation throughout the state outlining the church's doctrinal rationale for its position. In the letter, the church leadership delivered a call to action: "We ask that you do all you can to support the proposed constitutional amendment by donating of your means and time to assure that marriage in California is legally defined as being between a man and a woman. Our best efforts are required to preserve the sacred institution of marriage." Although some Latter-day Saints balked at being given political marching orders by church leaders, most responded with enthusiasm. Campaign leaders estimated that Mormons did 80 to 90% of the early door-to-door canvassing and donated about half of the almost $40 million raised for the narrowly successful pro-Prop 8 campaign.[66] After the U.S. Supreme Court legalized same-sex marriage nationwide in the June 2015 *Obergefell v. Hodges* decision, the LDS Church immediately issued a statement that read in part, "Changes in the civil law do not, indeed cannot, change the moral law that God has established. God expects us to uphold and keep His commandments regardless of divergent opinions or trends in society. His law of chastity is clear: sexual relations are proper only between a man and a woman who are legally and lawfully wedded as husband and wife."[67]

Despite its consistent private and public opposition to same-sex marriage and "same-sex lifestyles" (primarily meaning gay sex), in the late twentieth and especially early twenty-first centuries, the LDS Church nevertheless underwent significant transitions in its understanding of and approach toward homosexuality and LGBT individuals, including members of the church. As the issue gained greater cultural currency beginning in the 1960s, church leaders increasingly spoke out against it. In a widely read 1969 book, apostle Spencer W. Kimball, who would later become president and prophet of the church, referred to homosexuality as "an ugly sin."[68] Twenty-five years later, in a pamphlet circulated to teenaged boys in the church, apostle Boyd K. Packer warned that the notion that some people are simply born "that way" was "a malicious and destructive lie" propagated by the devil. Packer taught instead that boys are divinely programmed to "become men – masculine, manly men – ultimately to become husbands and fathers."[69] Such statements led to the belief that gay and lesbian men and women could be "cured" of their sexual orientation through spiritual counseling, sheer willpower, heterosexual marriage, and in some cases reparative and electro-shock therapy. These approaches were not unique to Mormonism, of course – the American Psychiatric Association's *Diagnostic and Statistical Manual of Mental Disorders* included homosexuality as late as 1986.

By the early twenty-first century, the LDS Church had significantly recalibrated its position on homosexuality. The church released an official website called mormonsandgays.org in 2012, with the headline position statement, "The experience of same-sex attraction is a complex reality for many people. The attraction itself is not a sin, but acting on it is. Even though individuals do not choose to have such attractions, they do choose how to respond to them."[70] Church policy now encourages members who identify as gay or lesbian to remain in the church and participate fully, including attending the church's temples, so long as they remained celibate and unmarried. The church's flagship university, Brigham Young University, now allows gay and lesbian students to profess (but not practice) their sexual orientation publicly without fear of dismissal. Many grassroots Latter-day Saints have joined LGBT alliance groups such as Mormons Building Bridges and have marched in gay pride parades. In short, in the space of only two decades, the church had reversed itself on many previous positions, now accepting homosexuality as an inborn orientation and completely disavowing reparative therapies and marriage to an opposite-sex partner as appropriate "solutions," while maintaining its doctrinal position that the only divinely approved expression of sexuality occurs between a man and a woman in marriage. In the public square, in early 2015 the LDS Church actively supported state laws prohibiting discrimination in housing and employment on the basis of sexual orientation or gender identity.[71]

However, much of the goodwill generated by these developments was undermined when in November 2015 the church added two policies to its official handbook for leaders: 1) same-sex marriage was categorized as apostasy, meaning that anyone in such a marriage, even if legal by civil law, would be subject to church discipline and probably excommunication; and 2) children being raised by same-sex parents were prohibited from receiving naming blessings, being baptized or ordained to the priesthood, or going on missions until they reach the age of eighteen, move out of their parents' house, and completely disavow same-sex marriage.[72] The policy about children in particular generated widespread shock and disapproval even from many orthodox Latter-day Saints, and led to a number of people publicly resigning their membership from the church. Both the short- and long-term effects of that policy are still in question as of this writing. It is safe to say that the church's official views toward and treatment of LGBT members remain in tension, with messages of compassion and condemnation being delivered simultaneously.

The most effective doctrinal tool wielded by the LDS Church in the battles over same-sex marriage did not even exist until 1995. Prior to that, church teachings on family, marriage, gender, and sexuality were gathered piecemeal from scattered scriptural passages and prophetic statements. In the September 1995 General Relief

Society meeting, church president Gordon B. Hinckley read a statement from the First Presidency and Council of the Twelve Apostles called "The Family: A Proclamation to the World."[73] The opening paragraph of the one-page statement, often simply referred to as "The Family Proclamation," made the church's position on marriage clear: "We . . . solemnly proclaim that marriage between a man and a woman is ordained of God and that the family is central to the Creator's plan for the eternal destiny of His children." Later the declaration simply stated, "The family is ordained of God." In concise, straightforward language, the proclamation established a number of related doctrines: all humans are spirit children of "heavenly parents," affirming though not naming the existence of a Heavenly Mother; gender is not culturally constructed but rather an "essential characteristic of individual premortal, mortal, and eternal identity and purpose"; human sexuality should only be fully expressed within the bonds of legal, monogamous, heterosexual marriage; and fathers "preside" and "provide" while mothers "nurture," yet fathers and mothers are "equal partners" in leading the family. The declaration ended with a political admonition, calling upon "responsible citizens and officers of government" to pursue and uphold policies designed to "maintain and strengthen the family as the fundamental unit of society."[74] Through repeated usage in church meetings, talks, lessons, and conferences, the Family Proclamation immediately raced to quasi-canonical status within Mormonism. Many church members framed a copy and hung it on the wall of their home – a practice with little to no precedent in Mormon culture. Though the document's concision means that interpretive gaps are inevitable, over the course of two decades, the proclamation has served as a highly authoritative doctrinal and political tool in the church's internal and external efforts to police, privilege, and preserve monogamous heterosexual marriage as the ecclesiastical and societal norm.

At the same time that it was engaged in political campaigns against gay marriage, internally the church was roiled by a resurgence of feminist activism. Conditioned by changing cultural norms and connected online through blogs, Facebook, and other forms of social media, a new and active generation of Mormon feminists began pushing ecclesiastical and cultural boundaries in calling for greater gender equality and women's participation in the church. On the whole, Mormon feminists have been less radical than their counterparts in other religious traditions, most choosing to remain within the church and work internally for gradual change.[75] Though they are informed by broader secular and religious discourses of women's equality, Mormon feminists are just as likely to look to authentic Mormon sources such as the original Nauvoo Relief Society minutes or the writings of late nineteenth-century Mormon feminists and suffragists. While the male church leadership keeps a wary eye, the most contentious discursive and cultural battles over women's roles in the church, family, and society are often fought out among Mormon women themselves.

The most outspoken feminists have advocated for female ordination to the LDS priesthood. Coalescing in 2013 in a group called Ordain Women, they organized attempts for women (and male supporters) to gain entry to the traditionally male-only

Priesthood Session of LDS General Conference, where they were rebuffed by church employees. Consistent public advocacy, despite appeals from priesthood leaders, led to the excommunication of Ordain Women's founder Kate Kelly in 2014. The quest for female ordination is a distinctly minority position, however, even among self-described Mormon feminists. Polls show that the strong majority of Mormon women do not want the priesthood but do desire to be more involved in the decision-making councils of the church at all levels.[76] The LDS Church has made some small policy changes expanding women's roles within the leadership structures of wards and missions, which suggests that feminist voices within the church are having an effect. As of late 2015, women's ordination is completely off the table for the church leadership, yet it will no doubt remain a contentious issue within Mormonism, particularly as the number of other denominations that ordain women steadily rises.

*

No doubt Joseph Smith could scarcely imagine what would follow from his simple prayer in 1820. Millions of people have responded to the religious message he inaugurated, and in so doing have created Mormonism in all its richness, complexity, and vitality. Mormonism has come a long way from persecution, pioneers, and polygamy, and is about to embark on its third century of history – making it still a mere babe among the world's religions, but a remarkable achievement nevertheless in the panoply of failed religious upstarts over the centuries. In order to survive and thrive, Mormonism has had to constantly adapt so as to achieve stability and attract converts while still retaining its distinctiveness as a theological and socio-cultural system. That historical development and dynamism will continue in the twenty-first century, against the backdrop of a well-developed religious tradition. Having reviewed Mormonism's history, we turn now to outline those distinctive aspects of Mormonism as a religion: its scriptures, authorities, beliefs, and practices.

• NOTES

1 Ezra Taft Benson, "Whitney, Franklin County, Idaho," in Marvin S. Hill Papers, Special Collections, Marriott Library, University of Utah; Benson, "Oral History: Ezra Taft Benson," *Idaho Heritage* 9 (July 1977): 17, 50.

2 Matthew 5:10; Missionary Record of Ezra Taft Benson in the British Mission, LDS Church History Library.

3 Wolfgang Helmut Lother Kelm, personal history, LDS Church Library, 23.

4 See Patrick Q. Mason, "Ezra Taft Benson and (Book of) Mormon Conservatism," in *Out of Obscurity: Mormonism since 1945*, eds. Patrick Q. Mason and John G. Turner (New York: Oxford University Press, 2016), 63–80.

5 Terryl L. Givens, *By the Hand of Mormon: The American Scripture that Launched a New World Religion* (New York: Oxford University Press, 2002); Paul C. Gutjahr, *The "Book of Mormon": A Biography* (Princeton, NJ: Princeton University Press, 2012).

6 The scholar most commonly cited regarding prospects for LDS Church growth is prominent sociologist Rodney Stark, who is himself not a Mormon. See Rodney Stark, *The Rise of Mormonism*, ed. Reid L. Neilson (New York: Columbia University Press, 2012).

7 The standard account of the "transition" period in Mormonism is Thomas G. Alexander, *Mormonism in Transition: A History of the Latter-day Saints, 1890–1930* (Urbana: University of Illinois Press, 1986). For more interpretive accounts of the same period, see Ethan R. Yorgason, *Transformation of the Mormon Culture Region* (Urbana: University of Illinois Press, 2003); and Kathleen Flake, *The Politics of American Religious Identity: The Seating of Senator Reed Smoot, Mormon Apostle* (Chapel Hill: University of North Carolina Press, 2004).

8 Leonard J. Arrington and Davis Bitton, *The Mormon Experience: A History of the Latter-day Saints*, 2nd ed. (Urbana: University of Illinois Press, 1992), 184.

9 Doctrine and Covenants 87:1–4.

10 See John G. Turner, *Brigham Young: Pioneer Prophet* (Cambridge, MA: Belknap Press of Harvard University Press, 2012), 317–329, quote on 320.

11 See D. Michael Quinn, "The Mormon Church and the Spanish-American War: An End to Selective Pacifism," *Pacific Historical Review* 43 (August 1974): 342–366; Ronald W. Walker, "Sheaves, Bucklers, and the State: Mormon Leaders Respond to the Dilemmas of War," in *The New Mormon History: Revisionist Essays on the Past*, ed. D. Michael Quinn (Salt Lake City: Signature Books, 1992), 276–278.

12 "Message of the First Presidency," *Conference Report* 94 (April 1942): 88–97.

13 Latter-day Saints point to many scriptural texts to support their participation in military conflicts, especially Alma 43–63 (Book of Mormon), Doctrine and Covenants 134, and Articles of Faith 12.

14 Walker, "Sheaves, Bucklers, and the State," 276, 287. See also J. David Pulsipher, " 'Prepared to Abide the Penalty': Latter-day Saints and Civil Disobedience," *Journal of Mormon History* 39:3 (Summer 2013): 131–162; Gordon C. Thomasson, ed., *War, Conscription, Conscience, and Mormonism* (Santa Barbara, CA: Mormon Heritage, 1972).

15 See Patrick Q. Mason, " 'The Wars and the Perplexities of the Nations': Reflections on Early Mormonism, Violence, and the State," *Journal of Mormon History* 38:3 (Summer 2012): 72–89.

16 See Arrington and Bitton, *The Mormon Experience*, 247; Matthew Bowman, *The Mormon People: The Making of an American Faith* (New York: Random House, 2012), 155–156.

17 David E. Campbell, John C. Green, and J. Quin Monson, *Seeking the Promised Land: Mormons and American Politics* (New York: Cambridge University Press, 2014), 84–85. For a graphic illustration of these changes, see Brandon S. Plewe, ed., *Mapping Mormonism: An Atlas of Latter-day Saint History* (Provo, UT: Brigham Young University Press, 2012), 188–189.

18 Pew Forum on Religion and Public Life, *Mormons in America: Certain in Their Beliefs, Uncertain of Their Place in Society* (Washington, DC: Pew Research Center, 2012), 57.

19 Campbell, Green, and Monson, *Seeking the Promised Land*, 91–92, 97, 100.

20 See Bowman, *The Mormon People*, 157–160, quote on 158. For a brilliant interpretation of the significance of the Smoot hearings for the transformation of early twentieth-century Mormonism, see Flake, *The Politics of American Religious Identity*.

21 See J.B. Haws, *The Mormon Image in the American Mind: Fifty Years of Public Perception* (New York: Oxford University Press, 2013), chaps. 9–10; Campbell, Green, and Monson, *Seeking the Promised Land*, chap. 9.

22 See Patrick Q. Mason, "God and the People: Theodemocracy in Nineteenth-Century Mormonism," *Journal of Church and State* 55:3 (Summer 2013): 1–27, quotes from 8–9.

23 Doctrine and Covenants 110:16.

24 Quoted in Klaus J. Hansen, "The Metamorphosis of the Kingdom of God: Toward a Reinterpretation of Mormon History," in *The New Mormon History*, ed. Quinn, 232–233.

25 Ethan R. Yorgason, *Transformation of the Mormon Culture Region* (Urbana: University of Illinois Press, 2003), 166.

26 Ezra Taft Benson, "The Lord's Base of Operations," *Conference Report* (April 1962): 103–106.

27 Nathan B. Oman, "International Legal Experience and the Mormon Theology of the State, 1945–2012," in *Out of Obscurity*, eds. Mason and Turner (forthcoming).

28 Doctrine and Covenants 103:7 (see also 65:2–6); Articles of Faith 12.

29 Flake, *The Politics of American Religious Identity*, 115. See also Jan Shipps, *Mormonism: The Story of a New Religious Tradition* (Urbana: University of Illinois Press, 1985), 145.

30 Bowman, *The Mormon People*, 163–167.

31 Ibid., 170–172.

32 This and the following paragraph draw from ibid., 190–197.

33 See Armand L. Mauss, *The Angel and the Beehive: The Mormon Struggle with Assimilation* (Urbana: University of Illinois Press, 1994). See also Mauss's update to his own theory, in "Rethinking Retrenchment: Course Corrections in the Ongoing Campaign for Respectability," *Dialogue: A Journal of Mormon Thought* 44:4 (Winter 2011): 1–42. Scholars have argued that late twentieth-century doctrinal developments amounted to the emergence of a Mormon "neo-orthodoxy." O. Kendall White, *Mormon Neo-Orthodoxy: A Crisis Theology* (Salt Lake City: Signature Books, 1987).

34 Boyd K. Packer, "The Mantle Is Far, Far Greater Than the Intellect," *BYU Studies* 21:3 (1981): 5.

35 Ronald W. Walker, Richard E. Turley Jr., and Glen M. Leonard, *Massacre at Mountain Meadows: An American Tragedy* (New York: Oxford University Press, 2008).

36 See http://josephsmithpapers.org/.

37 The essays are available at https://www.lds.org/topics/essays?lang=eng.

38 See Brady McCombs, "Mormons Acknowledge Early Polygamy Days at Renovated Museum," Associated Press, September 30, 2015, available online at http://bigstory.ap.org/article/bdeafdb234714b82bf8b9dc92f6b9fa9/mormons-acknowledge-early-polygamy-days-renovated-museum.

39 Doctrine and Covenants 4:4.

40 "Growth of the Church," available at http://www.mormonnewsroom.org/topic/church-growth (accessed November 4, 2015). See also "The Church of Jesus Christ of Latter-day Saints Membership History," *Wikipedia*, available at https://en.wikipedia.org/wiki/The_Church_of_Jesus_Christ_of_Latter-day_Saints_membership_history#Table_for_LDS_Church_membership_numbers (accessed November 4, 2015).

41 See Tim B. Heaton, "Vital Statistics," in *Latter-day Saint Social Life: Social Research on the LDS Church and Its Members*, ed. James T. Duke (Provo, UT: Religious Studies Center, Brigham Young University, 1998), 105–132; Tim B. Heaton, "Religious Influences on Mormon Fertility: Cross-National Comparisons," in Duke, ed., *Latter-day Saint Social Life*, 425–440. A 2008 study by the U.S. Census Bureau found that Utah had the highest birthrate in the nation, with 81 children born for every 1,000 women, compared to the national average of 58. "Utah Fertility Rate Tops the U.S. Charts," *Deseret News*, November 7, 2010, available online at http://www.deseretnews.com/article/700079435/Utah-fertility-rate-tops-the-US-charts.html (accessed January 30, 2015).

42 The paradigmatic texts are, respectively, 2 Nephi 26:33 and 2 Nephi 5:20–23.

43 Abraham 1:24, 26, Pearl of Great Price.

44 See Sylvester Johnson, *The Myth of Ham in Nineteenth-Century American Christianity: Race, Heathens, and the People of God* (New York: Palgrave Macmillan, 2004). See also Stephen R. Haynes, *Noah's Curse: The Biblical Justification of American Slavery* (New York: Oxford University Press, 2007).

45 "Elijah Ables's Priesthood Certificate (March 1836)," in *For the Cause of Righteousness: A Global History of Blacks and Mormonism, 1830–2013*, ed. Russell W. Stevenson (Salt Lake City: Greg Kofford Books, 2014), 210–212.

46 Documents quoted in Stevenson, *For the Cause of Righteousness*, 224–225, 241.

47 Quoted in ibid., 247, 241, 262.

48 There are many excellent accounts of the development and then repudiation of the LDS Church's race-based priesthood and temple prohibition. See especially W. Paul Reeve, *Religion of a Different Color: Race and the Mormon Struggle for Whiteness* (New York: Oxford University Press, 2015), chaps. 4–7; Margaret Blair Young and Darius Aidan Gray, "Mormons and Race," in *The Oxford Handbook of Mormonism*, eds. Terryl L. Givens and Philip L. Barlow (New York: Oxford University Press, 2015), 363–385; Stevenson, *For the Cause of Righteousness*; Armand L. Mauss, *All Abraham's Children: Changing Mormon Conceptions of Race and Lineage* (Urbana: University of Illinois Press, 2003), chaps. 8–9.

49 See Stevenson, *For the Cause of Righteousness*, chap. 3; James B. Allen, "Would-Be Saints: West Africa before the 1978 Priesthood Revelation," *Journal of Mormon History* 17 (1991): 207–247. See also Andrew Clark, "The Fading Curse of Cain: Mormonism in South Africa," *Dialogue: A Journal of Mormon Thought* 27:4 (Winter 1994): 41–56.

50 See Haws, *The Mormon Image in the American Mind*, chap. 3; Max Perry Mueller, "The Pageantry of Protest in Temple Square," in *Out of Obscurity*, eds. Mason and Turner (New York: Oxford University Press, 2016), 123–143.

51 Quotes from Stevenson, *For the Cause of Righteousness*, 310, 317. See also Gregory A. Prince and Wm. Robert Wright, *David O. McKay and the Rise of Modern Mormonism* (Salt Lake City: University of Utah Press, 2005), chap. 4.

52 Lester E. Bush, "Mormonism's Negro Doctrine: An Historical Overview," *Dialogue: A Journal of Mormon Thought* 8:1 (Spring 1973): 11–68.

53 Official Declaration 2, Doctrine and Covenants.

54 See Plewe, *Mapping Mormonism*, 222–227; 232–235.

55 Jason Horowitz, "The Genesis of a Church's Stand on Race," *Washington Post*, February 28, 2012.

56 "Church Statement Regarding 'Washington Post' Article on Race and the Church," *Newsroom*, February 29, 2012, available at http://www.mormonnewsroom.org/article/racial-remarks-in-washington-post-article (accessed November 4, 2015).

57 "Race and the Priesthood," available at https://www.lds.org/topics/race-and-the-priesthood?lang=eng (accessed November 4, 2015).

58 Quoted in Reeve, *Religion of a Different Color*, 269, 271–272.

59 See Doctrine and Covenants 132, also 131:1–4. For analysis of this doctrinal development, see Terryl L. Givens, *Wrestling the Angel: The Foundations of Mormon Thought: Cosmos, God, Humanity* (New York: Oxford University Press, 2015), 266–293. A telling example of this shift in consciousness, and a certain embarrassment on the part of the LDS Church regarding its polygamist past, came when the church published a manual of Brigham Young's teachings in which all of his references to "wives" were changed, without any indication, to the singular "wife." *Teachings of the Presidents of the Church: Brigham Young* (Salt Lake City: The Church of Jesus Christ of Latter-day Saints, 1997).

60 Jan Shipps, *Sojourner in the Promised Land: Forty Years among the Mormons* (Urbana: University of Illinois Press, 2000), 98–100.

61 For analysis of these trends, see Julie Debra Neuffer, *Helen Andelin and the Fascinating Womanhood Movement* (Salt Lake City: University of Utah Press, 2014); and Kate Holbrook, "Mormons and Housework during Second Wave Feminism," in *Out of Obscurity*, eds. Mason and Turner (New York: Oxford University Press, 2016), 198–213.

62 See Matthew Glass, *Citizens against the MX: Public Languages in the Nuclear Age* (Urbana: University of Illinois Press, 1993); Steven A. Hildreth, "Mormon Concern over MX: Parochialism or Enduring Moral Theology?," *Journal of Church and State* 26 (Spring 1984): 227–253; www.utahcompact.com; editorial, "The Utah Compact," *New York Times*, December 4, 2010.

63 See Neil J. Young, *We Gather Together: The Religious Right and the Problem of Interfaith Politics* (New York: Oxford University Press, 2015).

64 Sonia Johnson's memoir of her ideological transition and activism is *From Housewife to Heretic* (Garden City, NJ: Doubleday, 1981). See also Haws, *The Mormon*

Image in the American Mind, chap. 4; Martha Sonntag Bradley, *Pedestals and Podiums: Utah Women, Religious Authority, and Equal Rights* (Salt Lake City: Signature Books, 2005).

65 Ezra Taft Benson, "The Honored Place of Women," talk delivered at Los Angeles Temple Visitors Center, August 25, 1979, typescript, Mormons for ERA Papers, Special Collections, Merrill-Cazier Library, Utah State University, 2.

66 Campbell, Green, and Monson, *Seeking the Promised Land*, 144–145; Jesse McKinley and Kirk Johnson, "Mormons Tipped Scale in Ban on Gay Marriage," *New York Times*, November 14, 2008.

67 "Response to the Supreme Court Decision Legalizing Same-Sex Marriage in the United States," June 29, 2015, available online at http://www.mormonnewsroom.org/article/top-church-leaders-counsel-members-after-supreme-court-same-sex-marriage-decision (accessed November 9, 2015).

68 Spencer W. Kimball, *The Miracle of Forgiveness* (Salt Lake City: Bookcraft), 78.

69 Boyd K. Packer, *To Young Men Only* (1994), available online at https://www.lds.org/manual/to-young-men-only/to-young-men-only?lang=eng (accessed November 9, 2015).

70 http://www.mormonsandgays.org/ (accessed November 9, 2015).

71 Dennis Romboy, "LDS Church, LGBT Advocates Back Anti-Discrimination, Religious Rights Bill," *Deseret News*, March 4, 2015.

72 Jennifer Dobner, "New Mormon Policy Makes Apostates of Married Same-Sex Couples, Bars Children from Rites," *Salt Lake Tribune*, November 5, 2015.

73 Ironically, though read in the general Relief Society meeting, the Relief Society leadership had not been consulted in the drafting of the statement nor given advance notice that their meeting would be used for its presentation.

74 "The Family: A Proclamation to the World," available online at https://www.lds.org/topics/family-proclamation?lang=eng.

75 For an articulation of this moderate position, see Neylan McBaine, *Women at Church: Magnifying LDS Women's Local Impact* (Salt Lake City: Greg Kofford Books, 2014). A more diverse collection of LDS feminist voices is Joanna Brooks, Rachel Hunt Steenblik, and Hannah Wheelwright, eds., *Mormon Feminism: Essential Writings* (New York: Oxford University Press, 2015). An important earlier collection is Maxine Hanks, ed., *Women and Authority: Re-Emerging Mormon Feminism* (Salt Lake City: Signature Books, 1992). The most prominent, though hardly the only, Mormon feminist blog is Feminist Mormon Housewives at feministmormonhousewives.org.

76 A 2011 Pew poll showed that 90% of Mormon women did not believe that women should be ordained to the LDS priesthood, compared to 84% of male respondents. See Pew Forum, *Mormons in America*, 54. See also Lynn Matthews Anderson, "Issues in Contemporary Mormon Feminism," in *Mormon Identities in Transition*, ed. Douglas J. Davies (London: Cassell, 1996), 165.

5

·Scriptures

Joseph Smith is no Luther, poring over the scriptures to provide revisionist interpretations of Christian doctrine. . . . He is Moses, bringing down utterly new tablets from the mount.

– Terryl Givens[1]

For I [God] command all men, both in the east and in the west, and in the north, and in the south, and in the islands of the sea, that they shall write the words which I speak unto them. . . .

For behold, I shall speak unto the Jews and they shall write it; and I shall also speak unto the Nephites and they shall write it; and I shall also speak unto the other tribes of the house of Israel, which I have led away, and they shall write it; and I shall also speak unto all nations of the earth and they shall write it.

– 2 Nephi 29:11–12 (Book of Mormon)

The Mormon God speaks. He speaks anciently and modernly. He speaks to Jews and Gentiles, to prophets and laity, to women and men and children. He speaks of past, present, and future. He speaks of the cosmos and where to find food for dinner, of the architecture of heaven and architectural blueprints, of the kingdom of God and frontier urban planning. He speaks, and listens, and responds by speaking some more. In the process, Mormon scriptures are born.

One of the LDS Church's thirteen Articles of Faith begins, "We believe the Bible to be the word of God as far as it is translated correctly."[2] This seems straightforward enough – who wants to believe in a Bible that *isn't* translated correctly? But there's a lot of subtext packed into those seventeen words, especially the last seven.

Mormons insist that they are Bible-believing Christians. But, as Philip Barlow, author of the book *Mormons and the Bible* observes, they are Bible-believing Christians "with a difference."[3] As noted in Chapter 2, Mormonism was born in the milieu of the Second Great Awakening's Bible-centered evangelical Christianity. Joseph Smith went to the grove of trees where he had his first vision in 1820 after reading a passage of scripture from the Epistle of James in the New Testament. Yet even before the Church of Christ was founded in 1830, Joseph Smith had bulldozed the sacred edifice of *sola scriptura* (scripture alone) that Reformation Protestantism and its heirs, especially in nineteenth-century America, worshiped in. First implicitly and then explicitly with the publication of the Book of Mormon and Joseph Smith's own revelations, Mormons declared that the Bible alone was *not* sufficient, and in fact was deficient in serious ways. Nephi, the first narrator in the Book of Mormon, wrote of the Bible that "there are many plain and precious things taken away from the book," which meant that "many parts" of the gospel of Jesus Christ had been lost or corrupted.[4] The Bible still maintained its status as the word of God, but in the Mormon view it was a bit of a fixer-upper, shot through with gaps, holes, and ragged edges. A preeminent aspect of Mormon restorationism, and lying at the heart of Joseph Smith's self-understanding of his prophetic mission, was therefore a restoration and expansion of scriptures in the modern age.

So when Mormons go to church on Sunday, they carry in their hands – or more likely these days, on an app on their smartphones or iPads – a lot more scriptures, amounting to nearly nine hundred more printed pages, than do their neighbors going to the local evangelical or Catholic church. If kids going to Vacation Bible School have a hard enough time memorizing the names of the 66 books in the Bible (73 if they're Catholic), Mormon kids add to that 15 books in the Book of Mormon, 5 books in the Pearl of Great Price, and 138 sections of the Doctrine and Covenants (all technically in 1 book). The official LDS Church "quad," so nicknamed because it contains all four canonized books of Mormon scripture (each divided into smaller books or sections) plus study aids, comes in at the whopping total of more than 3700 small-print pages.

As if that's not enough, the Mormon notion of scripture is even more expansive. In a revelation to Joseph Smith, God declared to the church that

> whatsoever they shall speak when moved upon by the Holy Ghost shall be scripture, shall be the will of the Lord, shall be the mind of the Lord, shall be the word of the Lord, shall be the voice of the Lord, and the power of God unto salvation.[5]

Based on this logic, scripture could proliferate anytime believers speak "when moved upon by the Holy Ghost." Most Mormons would be a little uncomfortable extending the definition quite so far as to say that Sister Johnson's heartfelt testimony from the pulpit in sacrament meeting constitutes scripture. But it's common for Mormons to believe that the talks given by the prophets, apostles, and other general authorities and officers during the church's semiannual General Conference fit this definition of scripture, and should be studied and applied as such. When Mormons say that God is still speaking, they mean that he does so in words, through living prophets and apostles, and that they know exactly what he says.

All this Mormon scripture flying around raises one of the more interesting questions for students of religion – in the words of scholar Laurie Maffly-Kipp, "What is a scripture, and who gets to write one?"[6] Of course, the answer you receive to this question will depend very much on whom you ask, and when. Had you posed this question to virtually any American of Joseph Smith's day, the answer would have been clear and unequivocal: the Bible, consisting of the Old and New Testaments, is the only scripture, and it was written by Israelite prophets and Christian apostles and other designated authors, each of whom was chosen and inspired by God. The common formulation, that *the* Bible is *the* word of God, demonstrated the singularity of the Bible's status and the exclusiveness of its claim to being scripture. By the early twentieth century, however, the category of scripture had become far more pluralistic, inclusive of not only the Jewish and Christian scriptures but also the Muslim Qur'an, the Buddhist sutras, the Bhagavad Gita and other Hindu texts, and so forth. This broader application entailed a transition from regarding scripture as a value-laden category (i.e. scripture as "true" and of heavenly origin) to using it as a descriptive and analytical classification of a particular kind of text. As the preeminent scholar of religion Wilfred Cantwell Smith has observed, there is a stark difference between claiming a text to be divine and understanding a text as something that people have historically thought of as divine. "The former is a metaphysical judgment," he concludes, "the latter a sociological one."[7]

Smith (W.C., not Joseph) also had the essential insight that "no text is a scripture in itself and as such. People – a given community – make a text into scripture, or keep it scripture." Contrary to the normal assumption, then, "scripture is a human activity."[8] This is not (necessarily) to say that God is nowhere to be found in the process. It simply recognizes that a given text only truly becomes and functions as scripture when a community of humans regards it as such. Scripture can be both made and unmade. The Mormon case – which, incidentally, has been almost entirely neglected by scholars of comparative scripture, including Wilfred Cantwell Smith[9] – provides a fascinating study of how scripture originates and develops in the context of a community of believers, a process scholars call "scripturalization."

The proliferation of Mormon scriptures has been a heresy to other Christians from the first day that word of Joseph Smith's "gold Bible" started circulating, but it represents a natural outgrowth in the Mormon mind of a Heavenly Father who is eager to communicate with all his children, regardless of historical or geographical location. "Know ye not that there are more nations than one?," God asks rhetorically in the Book of Mormon. "Know ye not that I, the Lord your God, have created all men, and that I remember those who are upon the isles of the sea . . . and I bring forth my word unto the children of men, yea, even upon all the nations of the earth?" God speaks to all nations, "according to mine own pleasure," and the dispensing of the word of God to one nation does not preclude or invalidate a separate delivery to another nation: "And because that I have spoken one word ye need not suppose that I cannot speak another; for my work is not yet finished."[10] If not exactly chatty, the Mormon God is certainly loquacious.

When pressed on where all these other scriptures are, Mormons will typically say that most are either lost or as yet undiscovered. It is commonly believed that God will reveal additional scriptures only after the Saints have come to fully appreciate those already given to them. But many Mormons will also take a more ecumenical approach, suggesting that the scriptures of the world's religions – the Qur'an, the Gita, the Tao Te Ching – are all instances, or at least echoes, of God speaking to his children all around the world. In February 1978, the LDS First Presidency released a statement affirming that in their view:

> The great religious leaders of the world such as Mohammed, Confucius, and the Reformers, as well as philosophers including Socrates, Plato, and others, received a portion of God's light. Moral truths were given to them by God to enlighten whole nations and to bring a higher level of understanding to individuals.[11]

This statement did not attempt to reconcile the clear differences between LDS doctrine and the writings of the individuals mentioned, but it nevertheless offered a more cosmopolitan approach that is practically and theologically useful to Mormons increasingly aware of and engaged with the religious pluralism of their communities and the world.

In Joseph Smith's world, however, the Bible was the touchstone, and its singular religious and cultural authority meant that it defined in the minds of most Americans what scripture had to look, sound, and feel like. It was therefore no surprise that Joseph Smith, as a product of and operating within "the most Bible-saturated nation on earth," relied significantly on the Bible to fuel his "revelatory creativity," with the language, characters, and stories of the Bible frequently serving as "the vocabulary building blocks of Smith's revelations."[12] In the end, what Smith produced was not a bunch of Bible knock-offs or even commentaries, although some critics have offered such reductive assessments of his revelatory output. Rather, what came from Smith's mouth and pen – regardless of whether it originated in his mind or God's – was a set of genuinely new and distinctive additions to the corpus of world scripture. Smith's scriptural productions substantially differ from one another and from the Bible in content as well as in style, voice, and internal logic. Mormon scriptures take the internal multivocality of the Bible and run with it, thus destabilizing any single concept of what scripture is or how it originates. In so doing, Joseph Smith intuited and modeled what modern scripture scholars have come to appreciate, namely that "scripture emerges out of a set of reading practices and from the sacred purposes a text serves for a community. It does not result from supposed adherence to a set of generic conventions or preconceived rules."[13] There may be a species of writing that we call "scripture," but within that classification exists incredible diversity.

No understanding of Mormonism can be complete without a consideration of the richness of the Mormon scriptural corpus and its utter centrality to the shaping of the Mormon worldview and community. In this chapter, we will review each of the four LDS "standard works," as they are called; we will consider other sources of authority for Mormons in the following chapter. Like the Old Testament prophets, Joseph Smith frequently came down from the mount of revelation with a new word of the Lord for his people – if not exactly inscribed on stone by God's finger, then at least spoken in his voice. These words became scripture when the fledgling community accepted them as such. Mormon scriptures and Mormonism were thus born in tandem.

• THE BIBLE

Brigham Young rarely minced words. His view on the status of the Bible as "the word of God" is indicative of his characteristic bluntness and common-sense approach to knowledge:

> How do we know that the Bible is true? We know that a great deal of it is true, and that in many instances the translation is incorrect. But I cannot say what a minister once said to me. I asked him if he believed the Bible, and he replied, "Yes, every word of it." . . . Well, said I, you can beat me at believing, that's certain. As I read the Bible it contains the words of the Father and Son, angels, good and bad, Lucifer, the devil, of wicked men and of good men, and some are lying and some – the good – are telling the truth; and if you believe it all to be the word of God you can go beyond me. I cannot believe it all to be the word of God, but I believe it as it is.[14]

Not all portions of the Bible were equally valuable, according to Young. He preferred the New Testament to the Old, and was generally more interested in the Good Book's story-based morality than its theology (except insofar as it buttressed Mormon claims). He scorned what he considered to be the "bibliolatry" of other Christians, and many Mormons. Some biblical passages, such as the language that Adam was created "from the dust of the earth," Young rejected completely, saying that he had "banished from my mind all the baby stories my mother taught me when I was a child."[15]

Joseph Smith also acknowledged that the Bible as nineteenth-century Americans had it was full of mistranslations, corruptions, and even errors – hence, the LDS Article of Faith stating that the Bible "is the word of God as far as it is translated correctly." But Smith's mental and theological universe was predicated upon the fact, in his mind, that the Bible was not mere "baby stories" but was in fact a generally trustworthy account of God's interactions and revelations with ancient people, and thus that the figures therein were actual, historical people, not fictional or mythical characters.[16] Smith believed that the prophets and apostles of the Bible had become angels after their deaths, not because he reasoned as much but rather because he reported personal visits from Adam, Moses, Elijah, and others. These episodes often went beyond "mere" visionary experiences to include tactile encounters, such as John the Baptist and Peter, James, and John from the New Testament laying their hands on Smith's head to confer upon him the priesthood. Shaped by repeated recitations of Smith's angelic visits, most Mormons today are closer to his position about the Bible's authority than to Young's. They might implicitly question how literally to take certain stories – for instance, Noah's ark or Jonah spending three days in the belly of a fish – but grassroots Mormon hermeneutics tends strongly toward a literalistic, historical reading of the Bible. They also believe that many of its future-oriented prophecies are referring to the restored church in the current age. When scripture is talking about you, it takes on somewhat greater authority.

The paradox is that Joseph Smith's fidelity to the Bible's basic historicity did not equate to a view of biblical inerrancy – quite the opposite, in fact. Strikingly, Smith considered the words of scripture, including not only the Bible but also his own revelatory productions, to be eminently subject to revision, expansion, and correction. As Barlow observes:

> For the Mormon Prophet, scripture was not the static, final, untouchable, once-and-for-all Word of God that it was for many antebellum Christians. Although his allegiance to it was deep, scripture was for him provisional, progressive, relivable, subject to refinement and addition, spoken as well as written, varied in its inspiration, and subordinate to direct experience with God.

Truth trumped text, and so the latter – no matter how traditionally hallowed – could and should be revised to better reflect the former. New revelation from God would often complement previous revelations and scripture, but it might also supersede it and thus require the older words to be brought into line with God's most recent word.[17]

The audacity of Joseph Smith's translation and publication of the Book of Mormon may be exceeded only by the way he presumed to offer the world a new "translation" of the Holy Bible, easily the most revered and studied book in the history of Western civilization. Indeed, the ink on the Book of Mormon was barely dry and the Church of Christ only two months old when in June 1830 Smith applied his divine calling as a "translator" to the task of revising the Bible. Unlike most professional translators, Smith had no access to early manuscripts, nor did he know any of the Bible's original languages. Instead, he set about translating the Bible the same way that he did the Book of Mormon: by revelation. When Smith went about revising the Bible, he did so not to undermine its authority but rather to enhance it. As biographer Richard Bushman noted:

> Rather than doubting the Bible's inspiration, Joseph believed the original text had been marred in its descent through the ages and proposed to strengthen biblical authority by recovering the original. . . . Unlike the scholarly translators, he went back beyond the existing texts to the minds of the prophets, and through them to the mind of God.[18]

Joseph Smith and his scribes worked in earnest on his Bible translation for about three years from 1830 to 1833, then sporadically until his death in 1844. Mormon periodicals published several excerpts from his revisions, making them accessible to the Saints. Smith worked off an ordinary 1828 King James Version of the Bible, making notes on the pages or dictating to scribes, who filled up hundreds of sheets of paper. Multiple passages were revised more than once, with later revisions sometimes returning the text to its original language or rendering changes to chapters once marked "correct." In all, Smith changed over 3400 verses, about 1300 from the Old Testament and 2100 from the New. Genesis and the four Gospels were worked over the most, with Psalms, Isaiah, Romans, and Revelation also receiving substantial attention. A few verses were deleted, and the entire Song of Solomon (or Song of

Songs) was labeled "uninspired," but overall Joseph Smith's Bible came out longer than the original.[19]

After Smith's death, the manuscripts of the translation remained in possession of his widow Emma, who refused to give them to Brigham Young and his followers when they went west. She finally gave them to the Reorganized Church of Jesus Christ of Latter Day Saints (RLDS), of which her son Joseph Smith III was prophet-president. The RLDS Church published the full text with all completed revisions in 1867 under the name *The Holy Scriptures*. Suspicious of anything related to what they saw as a heretical offshoot, Latter-day Saints more or less neglected Smith's revised Bible until late twentieth-century scholars confirmed that the published RLDS text was true to the original manuscripts produced by Smith and his scribes. The modern LDS edition of the Bible, first published in 1979, remains a standard King James Version, but its uniquely LDS study apparatus includes over six hundred footnotes denoting some of Smith's more doctrinally significant revisions as well as an appendix with selected longer passages from what church members alternately refer to as the "Inspired Version" or "Joseph Smith Translation" (JST).

The JST occupies a somewhat ambiguous place in Mormonism. If asked to look up a Bible verse, church members will invariably go to the standard King James Version. The JST revision, if there is one, will typically be consulted only secondarily, though approvingly. The significance of Smith's translation, then, is really threefold. First, it serves as further confirmation of Smith's prophetic calling to believing members of the church. Second, Smith's revisions serve to Christianize the Old Testament and Mormonize both Old and New Testaments. For instance, Adam and Eve worship Jesus and are baptized in his name, and the structures and functions of priesthood both in Israelite times and the apostolic church is rendered as essentially similar to the priesthood of the latter-day Church of Jesus Christ. This relates to the third significant aspect of the Bible translation, namely that it was a platform for many of Smith's most important doctrinal and ritual innovations. Poring over the Bible with the intent to restore its true meaning, Smith and his associates frequently prayed to God for clarification on various doctrinal questions and in return received new revelation. Some of those inspired words were incorporated into their textual revisions, but others emerged as stand-alone revelations on topics ranging from the nature of salvation to plural marriage to the meaning of the four beasts in the book of Revelation. Just as early Christians had reinterpreted the Hebrew Bible to become an extended prophetic prologue to Jesus's messianic ministry, Joseph Smith reconfigured the Bible into a distinctively Mormon scripture that harmonized with, supported, and even anticipated his ministry of prophetic restoration. The importance of Smith's Bible translation process as foundational for emergent Mormon theology therefore cannot be understated.

In one of Mormon scripture's more ironic twists, at roughly the same time that there was a renaissance of interest in the Joseph Smith Translation, whose very existence spoke to the insufficiency of the seventeenth-century English-language text, senior LDS leaders doubled down on the use of the King James Version as the official Bible of the church. There were many reasons for this, including an appreciation for and familiarity with the Shakespearean quality of the language, a rejection of new scholarly Bible translations as theologically unsound, and the fact that the scriptures produced by Joseph Smith – notably the Book of Mormon – are generally rendered in King James English.[20] Adopting the King James Version, historically the most widely published and commonly used English-language Bible, also became a way for Mormons to build common ground with their Christian neighbors, with missionaries frequently repeating the maxim, "We read the same Bible you do." However, this particular strategy is increasingly outdated, as the King James Version has been eclipsed by more readable and accurate translations – meaning that more and more, Mormons are not in fact reading the same Bible as anyone but the oldest or most conservative Protestants. Alternate translations are occasionally quoted or referenced in LDS churches, but it is often done surreptitiously or with caveats. The King James Bible retains a powerful hold on the scriptural imaginary of Mormonism, with its "archaic tongue" serving as a kind of "special, sacred language" among the faithful[21] – even while they regularly complain about not actually understanding the five-hundred-year-old words.

The way Mormons read the Bible is about as conservative as is their Bible of choice. Though various figures throughout Mormon history have modeled diverse hermeneutical strategies, in the second half of the twentieth century, the field became dominated by a near-complete rejection of higher criticism and a strong posture of functional inerrancy, in which the Bible and all other Mormon scriptures are seen as verbatim dictations from God that are all in harmony with one another and with contemporary LDS teaching. Especially in formal church settings, Mormons typically read even the most fantastic stories straightforwardly as factual, providential history. There are LDS Bible scholars, many of whom have earned doctoral degrees from respected graduate programs and divinity schools. However, upon being employed by the LDS Church in its vast educational system, their scholarly insights become subservient to the teaching authority of the latter-day prophets and apostles, none of whom in recent decades have been formally trained in theology or hermeneutics.

In sum, in spite of acknowledging problems with transmission and translation, Mormons have always considered the Bible to be a faithful and revealed record of God's dealings with humanity. They teach from and study the Bible regularly, dedicating two of the four years in the recurring cycle of Sunday School and seminary lessons to the Old and New Testament, respectively. A 2010 survey showed Mormons to be one of the most biblically literate segments of the American population, excelling even evangelical Protestants.[22] Mormons may have a complicated relationship to the Bible, but the relationship is nevertheless a strong one.

• BOOK OF MORMON

I opened it with eagerness. . . . I read all day; eating was a burden, I had no desire for food; sleep was a burden when the night came, for I preferred reading to sleep. As I read, the spirit of the Lord was upon me, and I knew and comprehended that the book was true, as plainly and manifestly as a man comprehends and knows that he exists.[23]

– Parley Pratt

This prophet Smith, through his stone spectacles, wrote on the plates of Nephi, in his book of Mormon, every error and almost every truth discussed in N[ew] York for the last ten years. He decides all the great controversies – infant baptism, ordination, the trinity, regeneration, repentance, justification, the fall of man, the atonement . . . and even the question of freemasonry, republican government, and the rights of man. . . . [The Book of Mormon] is, without exaggeration, the meanest book in the English language. . . . I would as soon compare a bat to the American eagle, a mouse to a mammoth . . . as to contrast it with a single chapter in all the writings of the Jewish or Christian prophets. It is as certainly Smith's fabrication as Satan is the father of lies.[24]

– Alexander Campbell

All men have heard of the Mormon Bible, but few except the "elect" have seen it, or, at least, taken the trouble to read it. . . . The book is a curiosity to me, it is such a pretentious affair, and yet so "slow," so sleepy; such an insipid mess of inspiration. It is chloroform in print. If Joseph Smith composed this book, the act was a miracle – keeping awake while he did it was, at any rate. If he, according to tradition, merely translated it from certain ancient and mysteriously-engraved plates . . . the work of translating it was equally a miracle, for the same reason.[25]

– Mark Twain

These three quotes represent something of the spectrum of strong opinions that the Book of Mormon elicited in nineteenth-century America and continues to evoke today, with readers variously concluding that it is the word of God (Parley Pratt), a devilish delusion (Alexander Campbell), or simply a colossal bore (Mark Twain). Whatever one thinks of it – or whether one thinks of it at all – the fact is that the Book of Mormon is, by any measure, successful scripture.[26] With over 150 million copies published since it first appeared in 1830, it is the third most widely printed and distributed book in the Western Hemisphere, tied with the Boy Scout Handbook and J.R.R. Tolkien's *The Lord of the Rings* and ranking behind only the Bible and Charles Dickens' *A Tale of Two Cities*. By contrast, *Harry Potter and the Sorcerer's Stone* has only sold a measly 107 million copies.[27] (Admittedly, there is a big difference between selling and giving away that many books.) Millions of people worldwide consider the Book of Mormon to be scripture on par with the Bible, and many of those read it every day as part of their religious devotions. It has inspired art, literature, sermons, pageants, and now even a runaway hit Broadway musical.

So what, exactly, is the Book of Mormon? Is it a harmless romance, epic tragedy, imaginative fiction, damnable heresy, ancient history, American fantasy, theological tract, modern apocrypha, great American novel, or the word of God? In terms of nearly two hundred years of reception, the answer is yes, all of the above, depending on who's speaking. Until recently, the Book of Mormon has eluded serious consideration by non-Mormons. Perhaps the origin story, with gold plates and an angel and a boy prophet in New York, strained credulity to the point that readers and scholars could not take it seriously; Max Weber, the father of modern sociology, referred to the Book of Mormon as "a rank swindle."[28] Or perhaps, if Mark Twain is right, readers simply fell asleep in the middle of it. Whatever the reason for its longtime neglect, both LDS and non-LDS scholars are now paying more attention to the Book of Mormon. Some read it as a new addition to the world's corpus of scripture, others as an artifact of nineteenth-century American culture, and still others as a specimen of early American literature; Mormons generally stand alone in accepting the book as ancient history. In any case, the renewed literary and religious interest in the Book of Mormon, plus a brief synopsis of its narrative features, is perhaps best captured by Pulitzer Prize-winning historian Daniel Walker Howe:

> True or not, the Book of Mormon is a powerful epic written on a grand scale with a host of characters, a narrative of human struggle and conflict, of divine intervention, heroic good and atrocious evil, of prophecy, morality and law. Its narrative structure is complex. The idiom is that of the King James Version, which most Americans assumed to be appropriate for divine revelation. Although it contains elements that suggest the environment of New York in the 1820s . . . the dominant themes are biblical, prophetic, and patriarchal, not democratic or optimistic. It tells a tragic story, of a people who, though possessed of the true faith, fail in the end. Yet it does not convey a message of despair; God's will cannot ultimately be frustrated. The Book of Mormon should rank among the great achievements of American literature, but it has never been accorded the status it deserves, since Mormons deny Joseph Smith's authorship, and non-Mormons, dismissing the book as a fraud, have been more likely to ridicule than to read it.[29]

When Latter-day Saints and others do read the Book of Mormon, what do they find? Structurally, the Book of Mormon appears like the Bible, divided into fifteen books of various length with principal named authors. The earliest versions were printed in paragraph form, but the text was subdivided into chapters and verses beginning with the 1879 edition. The entire text is about 270,000 words long, with the modern LDS edition running at 531 printed pages. The book purports to be primarily the record of people who lived on the American continent from about 600 BCE to 400 CE. There are three primary narrators – Nephi, Mormon, and Moroni – in whose words we are introduced to literally hundreds of characters living in complex premodern societies. The book, as one might expect given its status as scripture, is heavily religious, in a particularly moralistic and often didactic way. Like the Bible, its pages alternate between history, prophecy, sermons, and even poetry. Though the narrative is sometimes complex, often doubling back on itself or pursuing multiple storylines, the Book of Mormon's prose is straightforward and self-consciously "plain." Even though the English is in a King James idiom, most readers find it to be easier to understand than the King James Bible.

First and foremost, however, the Book of Mormon is a narrative.[30] It is an epic tale about familial conflict and the rise and fall of two great civilizations, the Nephites and Lamanites, sprawled out across two continents and a thousand years of history. (This is not counting the narrative-within-a-narrative provided in the Book of Ether, which documents a separate civilization called the Jaredites over the course of some two thousand years.) Its opening phrase – "I, Nephi, having been born of goodly parents"[31] – sets the tone for the rest of the narration, which although it occurs on a grand scale with transoceanic migrations, massive battles, and civilizational holocaust, ultimately is rooted in stories about individuals and families. These stories are recorded on metal plates beginning with Nephi and then passed down from generation to generation.

The narration begins in Jerusalem around 600 BCE with the family of the prophet Lehi, of whom Nephi is the youngest but most faithful son. The people of Jerusalem reject Lehi's message of repentance and impending judgment, and he is warned in a dream to take his family out of the city before they are all killed. Nephi tells us that his two oldest brothers, Laman and Lemuel, are not particularly spiritual and therefore always mumbling and grumbling about something. Resentful of Nephi's prophecies that he is destined to be their leader, they threaten and even attempt to kill their younger brother on multiple occasions, but he is miraculously protected by God. After traveling through the desert (probably in the Arabian Peninsula) for years, they arrive at the shore and, under God's direction, build a boat to sail to the "promised land," presumably somewhere in the Americas.

Lehi dies shortly after their arrival in the promised land, and upon his death the family splits into two factions – those who follow Laman, eventually called the Lamanites, and those who follow Nephi, or the Nephites. The Lamanites are cursed by God for their faithlessness and receive a "skin of blackness" so as to be differentiated from the Nephites.[32] At that point, the book's central storyline and basic terms of conflict are set, with more or less righteous and civilized Nephites always defending against the incursions of the bloodthirsty and depraved Lamanites.[33] For a thousand years the descendants of Lehi engage in seemingly unremitting warfare – some of it documented in great detail – until the Lamanites finally overwhelm the now-degenerate Nephites at the end of the fourth century CE. Despite repeated warnings and insistent calls to repentance from a string of prophets, the Nephites ultimately reject God and thus lose his providential protection. The Book of Mormon thus ends tragically, with a detailed narration of two civilizational holocausts (first the Jaredites and then the Nephites). The closing chapters are written by the lone survivor of the Nephites, the prophet Moroni, who offers some final words of exhortation and farewell before burying the plates around 420 CE.

Although families are central to the narrative, a fair critique of the Book of Mormon is that it is heavily androcentric, far more so than the Bible. Unnamed women pop up throughout the text – such-and-such a person's wife, daughter, or mother – but the book has only six named female characters, three of whom are actually biblical (Eve, Sarah, and Mary), one is a harlot, and none of whom are major characters. To put this in perspective, the Bible – hardly the archetypical feminist text – mentions 188 women by name, compared to the Book of Mormon's six. In the Bible, masculine pronouns ("he" and "his") appear six-and-a-half times more often than female pronouns ("she" and "her"); in the Book of Mormon masculine pronouns appear thirty-five times more frequently.[34]

Despite its androcentrism and intermittent racialism, the essential message of the Book of Mormon, embedded within its narrative content, is the offer of universal salvation through faith in Jesus Christ and obedience to his gospel. The book's universalizing impulse is consistently on display, in striking passages such as Nephi's proclamation that God

> doeth nothing save it be plain unto the children of men; and he inviteth them all to come unto him and partake of his goodness; and he denieth none that come unto him, black and white, bond and free, male and female; and he remembereth the heathen; and all are alike unto God, both Jew and Gentile.[35]

The climactic moment in the Book of Mormon appears about two-thirds of the way through, in the book of 3 Nephi, when shortly after his resurrection and ascension in Jerusalem as recorded in the New Testament, Jesus appears to the people in the promised land (again, presumably somewhere in the American continent). He teaches them his gospel, establishes his church among them, and blesses and heals them. Unlike in the Bible, where only a handful of people are committed to Jesus's message by the time of his death, the Nephites and Lamanites who encounter Jesus are thoroughly transformed, to the point that they create a utopian society predicated upon righteous living, peace, economic and social equality, and human solidarity. This Christian utopia lasts for about two hundred years before pride, materialism, faithlessness, and tribalism tear it apart and ultimately lead to civilizational collapse.

One of the paradoxes of the Book of Mormon is that it juxtaposes its tragic narrative structure with its optimistic message of universally available salvation through Jesus Christ. The Book of Mormon is in fact far more explicitly Christological than is the Bible, a "daring" theological premise for a document purportedly written by New World Israelites.[36] The Book of Mormon's intense, "persistent and exuberant" Christology has served as something of an anchor for Mormonism, keeping it tied to the fundamentals of the Christian gospel when doctrinal innovations within the church and the higher criticism of scripture scholars might otherwise have more fully taken the religion in different directions.[37] In the midst of all its Jesus-talk, the Book of Mormon develops several other themes as well. Various readers have focused on its repeated passages regarding the restoration and gathering of Israel, American Indian origins and Lamanite redemption, social and economic protest, and theo-republican politics, to name a few.[38]

Against a macrohistorical backdrop, the Book of Mormon narrative mostly features close-ups on individuals and families. In the Book of Mormon, God is Lord of all creation but also intensely personal in his relationship with humanity. He communicates with people about all kinds of matters, from the weighty and profound to the personal and quotidian. Prophets and ordinary people alike talk to God, and God responds, often asking questions in the manner of a conversation rather than divine decree. Nephi asks God where to hunt to find food; God tells him. The brother of Jared asks God how to light their boats; God tells him to come up with an idea; the brother of Jared proposes that God touch stones to light them; God obliges.[39] Terryl Givens observes that "these encounters are not monologues in the wilderness but genuine dialogues"; he has coined the phrase "dialogic revelation" for the nature of divine-human communication modeled in the Book of Mormon. Givens suggests that this "insistent message that revelation is the province of everyman" might be the book's "most significant and revolutionary – as well as controversial – contribution to religious thinking." God's revelatory communication with humans sometimes turns into scripture but more often than not is simply the stuff of everyday life.[40]

The question of authenticity has always been central to the spirited debates about the Book of Mormon. The book itself forces readers to appraise its validity as scripture; as Jan Shipps, one of the foremost non-LDS scholars of Mormonism has observed, "Making judgments about whether the book was interesting, informative, or worthwhile was not enough."[41] When LDS missionaries deliver a copy of the Book of Mormon to someone for the first time, they invariably have them read a passage from the last chapter of the book, in which the prophet Moroni (who would later appear as the angel who directed Joseph Smith to the gold plates) offers a challenge and a promise to readers:

> And when ye shall receive these things, I would exhort you that ye would ask God, the Eternal Father, in the name of Christ, if these things are not true; and if ye shall ask with a sincere heart, with real intent, having faith in Christ, he will manifest the truth of it unto you, by the power of the Holy Ghost.[42]

Leading scholars of religion are now coming to terms with the gold plates less in terms of deliberate delusion, deception, or "pious fraud," and more as one remarkable case in a world full of sacred objects, "religious genius," and "abundant events."[43] For their part, orthodox Mormons appreciate but have generally rejected the olive branch. As LDS apostle Jeffrey R. Holland asserted, "*there is no other answer* than the one Joseph gave as its young unlearned translator," namely that the angel was real, the plates were real, and that he translated them "by the gift and power of God."[44]

Indeed, the content of the Book of Mormon is inseparable from its fantastic origin story. At its core, the Book of Mormon is inexplicable.[45] As noted in Chapter 2, naturalistic explanations have come and gone (and sometimes come again).[46] The fact that neither purely naturalistic nor faithful explanations have completely carried the day lends weight to Jan Shipps's assessment that Mormonism's origins, insofar as they are tied to the appearance of the Book of Mormon, are founded upon "a paradoxical event that has proved anomalous enough to sustain the weight of supernatural explanation across a long period of time."[47] In other words, the gold plates operate for Mormonism very much like the resurrection of Jesus does for Christianity – a foundational divine incursion into the material world that transcends known physical laws but carries the weight of multiple independent attestations, and which therefore places an impossible burden of proof on believers and nonbelievers alike. The gold plates are material religion in its most concentrated form.

One of the difficulties that many modern readers have with the Book of Mormon is that it takes its own historicity so seriously. Joseph Smith, no doubt influenced by his visionary experiences with Moroni and other Book of Mormon figures, insisted that the book was a historical record of an actual ancient people, and that Nephi and Mormon were just as real as George Washington and Napoleon. This is both a strength and a weakness for the book's reputation. Because the nature of the book's provenance leaves it strangely impervious to the usual methods of higher criticism – the gold plates are not available for scholars to examine – the Book of Mormon has remained delegitimized in intellectual circles at the same time that it has been somewhat inoculated from academic deconstruction.

Nevertheless, the search for "proof" continues. Since in the orthodox Mormon view the Book of Mormon is ancient history and not "mere" theology, let alone myth, it suggests that there should be corroborating evidence establishing it as a product of the ancient world rather than solely of Joseph Smith's nineteenth-century mind. Apologists and critics alike search for evidence (or the refutation of such) in Mesoamerican archaeological ruins, ancient Near Eastern texts, and DNA studies of indigenous peoples in the Americas. The particular and cumulative results of these studies are very much in the eye of the beholder. Over the decades Mormons have compiled an impressive, if at times idiosyncratic or overly confident, body of scholarship that does raise in compelling ways the question of how a lightly schooled farm boy in upstate New York could have produced a book that contains so many striking correspondences to ancient Semitic, Egyptian, and Mesoamerican cultures, cosmologies, and literary styles. On the other hand, critics are quick to draw attention to what seem to be a number of anachronisms within the Book of Mormon. They also gleefully point out that modern DNA studies show no genealogical link between Middle Eastern populations and indigenous peoples in the Americas, which one would expect if indeed the Book of Mormon's Lamanites were in fact the primary ancestors of modern Native Americans or other indigenous peoples – a claim made by Joseph Smith but which the church has recently backed off from. Furthermore, despite decades of looking, Mormons have not produced a single archaeological finding that has persuaded non-LDS archaeologists to seriously consider, let alone validate, the Book of Mormon's claim to be the translation of an authentically ancient document.[48]

Despite its many critics, the Book of Mormon stubbornly persists as a foundational book of scripture for Latter-day Saints, now perhaps more than ever – this despite the fact that it introduces little to no new doctrine beyond what was available in American Protestantism circa 1830.[49] Indeed, for the first century and a half of Mormonism, the Bible far exceeded the Book of Mormon in actual significance as a source for doctrine and teaching. Curiously, Smith himself rarely referenced the Book of Mormon in his preaching. He was not alone: Book of Mormon passages represented a mere 12% of all scriptural references by LDS general authorities from 1942 to 1986.[50]

Yet from the beginning, the Book of Mormon has been less important for what it teaches than what it represents and enacts. As Terryl Givens observes, "The Book of Mormon is preeminently a concrete manifestation of sacred utterance, and thus an evidence of divine presence, before it is a repository of theological claims."[51] In 1830 and today, the Book of Mormon is offered to the world as the primary proof of Joseph Smith's prophethood and the opening of the heavens. Prospective converts are asked to pray to know whether the Book of Mormon is true, even after having read only a few verses or chapters. If they receive spiritual confirmation of its truth, then, the Mormon logic goes, it must follow that Joseph Smith was a true prophet of God, which in turn means that his other teachings are true and that the Church of Jesus Christ of Latter-day Saints is God's true church on the earth.

Small wonder, then, that Joseph Smith said that the Book of Mormon was the "keystone of our religion," a message reiterated in the 1980s by church president Ezra Taft Benson, who called on Latter-day Saints to repent for their neglect of the book and to incorporate it more fully into their daily devotions and gospel teaching.[52] Members of the church have responded enthusiastically. In recent decades Book of Mormon usage among Latter-day Saints has increased significantly in both volume and intensity, to the point that the book now enjoys a privileged status among Mormon scriptures and functions something as a "first among equals."

• DOCTRINE AND COVENANTS

The Doctrine and Covenants, unlike the Bible and Book of Mormon, is a self-consciously modern book of scripture. It is a collection of recorded and canonized revelations to the church's president-prophets, with the vast majority of its contents being revelations to Joseph Smith. More than any other book, the Doctrine and Covenants underscores the evolving nature of Mormonism. One can trace in it the developing doctrinal and ecclesiastical framework of the church through an analysis of its roughly chronologically arranged revelations, divided into "sections" rather than chapters. Furthermore, the Doctrine and Covenants is an open book of scripture that can be amended when the church receives new revelation. Additions to the LDS edition have been rare, however, with only five new canonized revelations postdating Joseph Smith's death in 1844, and only one since 1918. The Reorganized Church of Jesus Christ of Latter Day Saints, now the Community of Christ, has added new revelations to its Doctrine and Covenants at a much more consistent pace. As of 2015, the Community of Christ's Doctrine and Covenants contained 164 sections compared to the LDS Doctrine and Covenants' 138 (plus 2 "Official Declarations"); the last addition to the Community of Christ canon was in 2010, compared to 1978 for the LDS edition.

Perhaps because it does not take the form of a linear narrative, Mormons have a hard time conceiving of the Doctrine and Covenants as a coherent body of scripture. Though they often cite particular verses in their gospel teaching, Mormons rarely read the Doctrine and Covenants cover to cover as part of their devotional scripture study the way they do the Book of Mormon. To fully appreciate them, the revelations often require historical context, provided in section headings and other extracurricular materials provided by the church rather than embedded in the verses themselves. An individual revelation will often jump from subject to subject, speaking of the cosmos at one moment and paying off debts the next. While much of the content of the revelations in the Doctrine and Covenants can only be described as pedestrian, often telling so-and-so to serve a mission here or there, the book also is a rich source for Mormon theology and practice and contains some of the most poignant passages in all Mormon scripture. The composite result is a "mélange": "unsystematic, concrete, sometimes sweeping, other times pedestrian, both effulgent and spare."[53] Each revelation stands for itself, even as it comprises part of the revelatory expanse of Mormonism.

Joseph Smith felt a kind of ownership for the revelations that appeared in the Doctrine and Covenants, even more so than for the Book of Mormon or his translation of the Bible. And yet, he still insisted that the words were not his. (There are some exceptions, in particular some of the later sections of the Doctrine and Covenants, which consist of canonized letters written by Smith to the Saints, similar to the many Epistles in the New Testament.) Though dictated by Smith, sometimes privately with only a scribe but often with many people in the room observing, the voice and logic of the revelations is external to his mind. They command and occasionally rebuke Smith, just as they command and rebuke others by name. As Smith's biographer Richard Bushman notes, "no one else valued revelations more than Joseph Smith." He believed in them "more than anyone. From the beginning, he was his own best follower." At the same time, he also developed supreme confidence – sometimes bordering on arrogance – in his calling as God's revelator. "Faith in the revelations," Bushman observes, "added to [Smith's] innate personal strength, made him indifferent to rank. . . . Indeed, the Church was built on his confidence."[54] Before they were compiled in books, first in 1833 as the Book of Commandments and then in 1835 as the Doctrine and Covenants, individual revelations would often be published in the church's periodicals, which the Saints would snatch up, hungry for the latest word of the Lord. Many early converts were attracted to the church through the Book of Mormon and its attestation that the heavens were reopened, but they remained in the church in large part because of God's continuing revelations to their prophet.

In addition to the possibility of additional revelation, the Doctrine and Covenants also offers an intriguing case study of the process of decanonization. All nineteenth-century English-language editions of the Doctrine and Covenants included a series of seven lectures, theological in nature and catechistic in style, called the "Lectures on Faith." The lectures were written and delivered in 1834–1835 and have usually been attributed to Joseph Smith, though the consensus of modern scholarship suggests that other church leaders, particularly Sidney Rigdon, were far more directly involved with their authorship. The lectures deal primarily with two themes: the definition, exercise, and fruits of faith; and the nature of the Godhead (God the Father, Jesus Christ, and the Holy Ghost). Nineteenth-century Mormon theologies of the Godhead were varied and often contradictory, sometimes fiercely debated by church leaders. Wanting to systematize the church's core doctrines, in the early 1900s the First Presidency commissioned a document in 1916 called "The Father and the Son: A Doctrinal Exposition." The newly orthodox position – affirming that the Father, Son, and Holy Ghost are all separate beings and that the Father and Son each have physical bodies of flesh and bone – contradicted the language in the Lectures on Faith, which were more traditionally Trinitarian and stated that God is a spirit. Accordingly, when the church printed the next edition of the Doctrine and Covenants in 1921, the Lectures on Faith were unceremoniously dropped – though they are still published independently and are sometimes referenced by members of the church.[55]

• PEARL OF GREAT PRICE

The Pearl of Great Price is Mormonism's curry, with richness and depth belying its seeming simplicity. It packs a lot of layered flavors and sensations into a concentrated form. If some of the individual ingredients seem either unremarkable or unpalatable on their own, or if it's not entirely clear what the various elements have to do with one another, blended together the whole becomes much greater than any of its component parts.[56]

Among the LDS standard works, the Pearl of Great Price is the slimmest, most disparate, and last to arrive. (The Community of Christ does not accept the Pearl of Great Price as scripture.) In the current printed edition, it is a mere sixty-one pages, and can easily be read through in an hour or two. Originally compiled and printed in England by LDS apostle Franklin D. Richards in 1851, the Pearl of Great Price was canonized in 1880. Various changes have been made since then, adding and subtracting material; the current contents have been stable since 1979.

The Pearl of Great Price consists of five parts:

1 The Book of Moses: Joseph Smith's translation of the first seven chapters of Genesis, with an additional "Vision of Moses" not included in the Bible and a lengthy emendation on the ministry of the biblical prophet Enoch.
2 The Book of Abraham: An inspired "translation" of Egyptian papyri purchased by Joseph Smith that he claimed contained hitherto-unknown writings of the ancient patriarch Abraham. The historical accuracy of the translation has largely been rejected by non-LDS Egyptologists, touching off an often-fierce debate about its provenance and authenticity.
3 Joseph Smith – Matthew: Smith's inspired translation of Matthew chapter 24 from the New Testament, containing Jesus's apocalyptic prophecies and judgments about the endtimes.
4 Joseph Smith – History: An excerpt from Smith's official history of the church, containing an account of his First Vision, visitations from Moroni, retrieval and translation of the gold plates, and the restoration of the priesthood.
5 The Articles of Faith, a thirteen-point statement of core beliefs written by Joseph Smith in 1842.

Implicitly, the Pearl of Great Price argues for the continuity of the Christian gospel through the ages, and the Church of Jesus Christ of Latter-day Saints as the modern bearer of the gospel to the world. It frames a "dispensational" Mormon view of history, simultaneously cyclical and progressive in its narrative. In this view, God reveals (dispenses) "the fulness of the gospel" to major prophets, who teach the gospel and call the people to repentance. While some people accept the gospel message, most do not, resulting in wickedness and ultimately apostasy, spiritual darkness, and moral decay. In his mercy, God counters widespread apostasy by granting a new dispensation, with truth and authority restored through newly called prophets. Joseph Smith thus stands as the latest in a string of dispensations heads including Adam, Enoch, Abraham, Moses, and Jesus.

This salvation history is explicitly Christian. Whereas the presence of Jesus Christ must be read either prophetically or allegorically in the Hebrew Bible, in the Pearl of Great Price, Jesus is present explicitly and literally from the beginning. He is identified as the champion of God's plan of salvation in a premortal council of spirits. Jesus, as the Firstborn and specially chosen spirit child of God the Father, works hand in hand with God in creating the earth. The fall of Adam and Eve is portrayed as the result of a conscious if wrenching decision to trigger God's plan of salvation with Jesus at the center. Eve in particular is completely reconfigured from being a scapegoat and pawn in the hands of Satan, as she has been depicted in most of Jewish and Christian history, to being the heroine in what Mormons believe to be a "fortunate fall" or "fall forward." Adam and Eve teach the gospel of faith in Christ, repentance, baptism, and the gift of the Holy Ghost to their descendants, some of whom accept the message but many of whom reject it. Other prophets come to renew the proclamation of the gospel, notably Enoch – a minor figure in the Bible, mentioned in only six verses in Genesis and three verses in the New Testament – who in Joseph Smith's translation becomes the archetypal prophet and founder of a Christian utopia called Zion. In the Pearl of Great Price, the two greatest figures of the Hebrew Bible, Abraham and Moses, do not simply prefigure Christ but offer specific prophecies about him and his gospel. Interestingly, Jesus's mortal ministry is represented in the Pearl of Great Price not through a narrative of his ministry or even his Passion, but rather through a re-rendering of his apocalyptic prophecies. Jesus is thus not only the primary agent of creation and redemption in the plan of salvation, but also the Messiah who will return to earth at the end of days to judge the righteous and the wicked and purify the world. Before his Second Coming, the gospel is to be proclaimed in one final dispensation, initiated in the spring of 1820 when God the Father and Jesus Christ appeared to Joseph Smith and subsequently called to be a prophet in the last days.

Perhaps even more important than its view of salvation history, the Pearl of Great Price is foundational for Mormon cosmology, theodicy, and identity. Passages in Abraham chapter 3 and Moses chapter 4 portray a premortal cosmos of organized "intelligences" or spirits that are co-eternal with God, whose divinity consists in part in being "more intelligent than they all." These spirit-intelligences (the words are used more or less interchangeably in these texts) are posed with a choice: to follow God and his "Beloved Son" (the premortal Jesus Christ), or to follow Satan, who rebelled against God and "sought to destroy the agency of man." The majority of spirits choose Christ, at which point Satan takes the spirits who follow him and becomes the devil, cast out of heaven for seeking to usurp God's power and glory. The spirits who follow Christ in this premortal existence are rewarded by being sent to earth, where they will enjoy a physical body, the promise of continued progression, and ultimately exaltation for those who pursue the path of faith and righteousness.[57]

The Pearl of Great Price also provides a distinctive Mormon theodicy, offering poignant reflections on the goodness of God in light of the existence of evil and the pervasiveness and depth of human suffering. This is not accomplished in systematic fashion, but emerges inductively as the result of several interlocking passages and concepts. The foundation of a Mormon theodicy is the aforementioned notion that human spirits are co-eternal with God, and thus not creations emanating from his will or essence. The precise nature of these eternal spirits (or intelligences) is not fully articulated, though what is clear is that inherent in them is free will, or agency. The improper use of moral agency brings about moral evil. Although the Mormon view presents its own philosophical and theological quandaries – how exactly do spirits have no beginning? – it goes a long way in addressing the age-old question of how evil could exist in a universe created by a good, loving, and sovereign God.

How God feels about and relates to a world of evil and suffering is poignantly depicted in the "Vision of Enoch" (Moses chapters 6–7 in the current Pearl of Great Price), one of Joseph Smith's most remarkable revelatory productions.[58] In the text, the ancient prophet Enoch has a vision of God, Jesus, Satan, and all the inhabitants of the earth – past, present, and future. He sees "their wickedness, and their misery" as a result of forsaking God to follow Satan, who haunts the earth with a "great chain in his hand" and laughs at the wretched condition of humankind. Even the earth, "the mother of men," is "pained" and "weary," asking – in anticipation of an LDS environmental ethic – when will it "rest, and be cleansed from the filthiness which is gone forth out of me?" Enoch spies God also looking down upon the world, and notices something surprising: God is weeping. Shocked to see the Lord of creation displaying vulnerability and emotion, Enoch asks, "How is it that the heavens weep, and shed forth their tears as the rain upon the mountains? . . . How is it that thou canst weep, seeing thou art holy, and from all eternity to all eternity?" God, Enoch assumes, is supposed to be impassive and dispassionate, somehow elevated above the fickleness of human emotion. How can a sovereign God of justice and truth be found in tears? God replies with heartbreaking affection:

> Behold these thy brethren; they are the workmanship of mine own hands, and I gave unto them their knowledge, in the day I created them; and in the Garden of Eden, gave I unto man his agency. And unto thy brethren have I said, and also given commandment, that they should love one another, and that they should choose me, their Father; but behold, they are without affection, and they hate their own blood. . . . Wherefore should not the heavens weep, seeing these shall suffer?

Moved by God's compassion for his own children, who have rejected the gospel of love and accepted the realpolitik of hate, Enoch looks again with new eyes on his fellow humans – "and his heart swelled wide as eternity; and his bowels yearned; and all eternity shook." He begins weeping inconsolably, and refuses to be comforted, until God shows him in vision "the day of the coming of the Son of Man, even in the flesh." Through the atonement of Jesus Christ, humankind – and all creation – will be redeemed, in spite of itself. The wicked will be judged and the righteous vindicated, but all of this will be done under the gaze of a God who weeps for his wayward children, not one who delights to cast his fallen creations down to hell. All God wants, seemingly, is for humans to choose of their own free will to love him and one another, but he literally cannot force them to do so. Though he created the mortal conditions for the exercise of human agency in the Garden of Eden, his only ultimate influence over human free will consists of invitation and persuasion, not coercion.[59]

While the Pearl of Great Price has been a rich source for Mormon theology, one that has really only begun to be tapped, the book is not without controversy, mostly surrounding the translation and authenticity of the Book of Abraham. The book follows the biblical narrative about the prophet and patriarch Abraham, but adds significant details, including an otherwise unknown account of cosmology and the creation. Joseph Smith translated the book via revelation working off Egyptian papyri that he purchased in 1835, producing his text at a time when the scholarly translation of Egyptian hieroglyphics was still in its infancy. Smith's translation was first published in a church periodical in 1842, then was canonized as part of the Pearl of Great Price in 1880. After Smith's death, the papyri and mummies stayed with his family until they sold them to various purchasers in 1856. Tragically, the Great Chicago Fire of 1871 destroyed most of the collection, but a few fragments ended up in the Metropolitan Museum of Art in New York City. When the fragments resurfaced in the mid-twentieth century, professional Egyptologists immediately determined that they contained no mention of Abraham, and were instead standard Egyptian funerary texts used from the third century BCE to first century CE, long after Abraham lived. Many scholars and critics therefore declared Smith's translation of the Book of Abraham, and by extension Smith's claim to prophetic revelation, to be fraudulent.

For their part, most LDS scholars, including professionally trained Egyptologists, have conceded the point that the surviving papyrus fragments do not correspond with Smith's English translation. However, they have generally argued that perhaps Smith translated only part of the papyri in his possession, and that the authentic Abraham texts were lost in the fire; or that the papyri simply acted as a revelatory catalyst for Smith, who produced his English text through a process of inspired dictation similar to how he translated the Book of Mormon. The LDS Church has recently acknowledged but sought to sidestep the academic conversation by concluding on its official website: "The veracity and value of the book of Abraham cannot be settled by scholarly debate concerning the book's translation and historicity. The book's status as scripture lies in the eternal truths it teaches and the powerful spirit it conveys."[60] Most Latter-day Saints are frankly unaware of the controversy surrounding the Book of Abraham, and thus consider it a miraculous and direct translation of an ancient document written by the biblical patriarch. Some people have left the church over the issue, believing that the church has not been transparent about the book's origins and that the controversy sheds real doubt on the legitimacy of Smith's prophethood. There are others, however, who reconcile doubts about the text's actual historicity while still believing its content to be inspired and indeed scriptural.

The Book of Abraham is a pointed example of the challenges that scriptures pose for believers in any tradition. Scriptures are rarely produced through fully rationalistic processes, and they speak to aspects of the human experience that cannot be apprehended solely through logic and empiricism. They are granted power when individuals, communities, and cultures recognize them as sacred and in some way binding. But scriptures are only one source of authority in religious traditions, rarely operating autonomously. In the next chapter we consider several other forms of authority that shape Mormon belief and practice.

● NOTES

1   Terryl L. Givens, *By the Hand of Mormon: The American Scripture that Launched a New World Religion* (New York: Oxford University Press, 2002), 48.

2   Article of Faith 8, Pearl of Great Price.

3 Philip L. Barlow, *Mormons and the Bible: The Place of Latter-day Saints in American Religion*, updated ed. (New York: Oxford University Press, 2013), xxiii. See also Laurie F. Maffly-Kipp, "Mormons and the Bible," in *The Oxford Handbook of Mormonism*, eds. Terryl L. Givens and Philip L. Barlow (New York: Oxford University Press, 2015), 121–133.

4 1 Nephi 13:28, 26, Book of Mormon.

5 Doctrine & Covenants 68:4.

6 Laurie F. Maffly-Kipp, ed., *American Scriptures: An Anthology of Sacred Writings* (New York: Penguin Books, 2010), x.

7 Wilfred Cantwell Smith, *What Is Scripture? A Comparative Approach* (Minneapolis: Fortress Press, 1993), 12.

8 Ibid., 18.

9 In Wilfred Cantwell Smith's seminal study, *What Is Scripture?*, Mormonism receives only passing mention (48, 357 n. 33), and the Book of Mormon is not even listed in the index.

10 2 Nephi 29:7–9.

11 "God's Love for Mankind," First Presidency Statement, February 15, 1978.

12 Maffly-Kipp, *American Scriptures*, xii–xv; Barlow, *Mormons and the Bible*, xxxii–xxxiii.

13 Givens, *By the Hand of Mormon*, 176.

14 Brigham Young, "The Gospel – The Spirit of the Lord – Revelation," *Journal of Discourses* 14:209 (August 13, 1871).

15 Brigham Young, "The Gospel – Growing in Knowledge," *Journal of Discourses* 2:6 (October 23, 1853). On Young's views of the Bible, see Barlow, *Mormons and the Bible*, chap. 3.

16 Barlow, *Mormons and the Bible*, 36.

17 Ibid., 46–47, see also 62, 79.

18 Richard Lyman Bushman, *Joseph Smith: Rough Stone Rolling* (New York: Alfred A. Knopf, 2005), 133.

19 Barlow, *Mormons and the Bible*, 53–55. See also Robert J. Matthews, *"A Plainer Translation": Joseph Smith's Translation of the Bible – A History and Commentary* (Provo, UT: Brigham Young University Press, 1975).

20 For an insightful overview, see Barlow, *Mormons and the Bible*, chap. 5.

21 Ibid., xlix.

22 Pew Research Religion and Public Life Project, "Who Knows What about Religion," September 28, 2010, available at http://www.pewforum.org/2010/09/28/u-s-religious-knowledge-survey-who-knows-what-about-religion/ (accessed January 7, 2015).

23 Parley P. Pratt, *Autobiography of Parley P. Pratt* (Salt Lake City: Deseret Book Company, 1985 [1874]), 20.

24 Alexander Campbell, *Delusions: An Analysis of the Book of Mormon* (Boston: Benjamin H. Greene, 1832), 13, 15.

25 Mark Twain, *Roughing It* (New York: Signet Classics, 2008 [1886]), 127.

26 Grant Hardy, *Understanding the Book of Mormon: A Reader's Guide* (New York: Oxford University Press, 2010), 11.

27 "List of Best-Selling Books," *Wikipedia*, available at https://en.wikipedia.org/ wiki/List_of_best-selling_books (accessed August 11, 2015); Noel L. Griese, "The Bible vs. Mao: A 'Best Guess' of the Top 25 Bestselling Books of All Time," *Publishing Perspectives*, September 7, 2010, available at http://publishingperspec tives.com/2010/09/top-25-bestselling-books-of-all-time/ (accessed August 11, 2015).

28 Weber quickly followed up this negative evaluation by saying that "sociology is not concerned with such value judgments." Max Weber, *Economy and Society: An Outline of Interpretive Sociology*, eds. Guenther Roth and Claus Wittich (New York: Bedminster Press, 1968), 3:1112.

29 Daniel Walker Howe, *What God Hath Wrought: The Transformation of America, 1815–1848* (New York: Oxford University Press, 2007), 314. For an entertaining interpretation by a non-LDS writer extolling the Book of Mormon as American literature, see Avi Steinberg, *The Lost Book of Mormon: A Quest for the Book that Just Might Be the Great American Novel* (New York: Anchor Books, 2015).

30 This is the central argument in Hardy, *Understanding the Book of Mormon*.

31 1 Nephi 1:1, Book of Mormon.

32 2 Nephi 5:21, Book of Mormon.

33 Occasionally the book does complicate its own narrative, presenting stories of righteous Lamanites and wicked Nephites. Overall, however, the Book of Mormon is written from the Nephite perspective, and the narrators carry clear biases against the antagonist Lamanites. For an interesting counterreading, see Richard Bushman, "The Lamanite View of Book of Mormon History," in *Believing History: Latter-day Saint Essays*, eds. Reid L. Neilson and Jed Woodworth (New York: Columbia University Press, 2004), 79–92. See also Jared Hickman, "The Book of Mormon as Amerindian Apocalypse," *American Literature* 86:3 (September 2014): 429–461.

34 See Carol Lynn Pearson, "Could Feminism Have Saved the Nephites?" *Sunstone* (March 1996): 35.

35 2 Nephi 26:33, Book of Mormon.

36 Givens, *By the Hand of Mormon*, 46.

37 Bushman, *Joseph Smith*, 108. For a non-LDS reader's assessment of the Book of Mormon's Christocentrism, see John Turner, "The Book of Mormon in 15 (or so) Days," available at http://www.patheos.com/blogs/anxiousbench/2013/11/the-book-of-mormon-in-15-or-so-days/ (accessed 17 October 2014).

38 For a summary or articulation of these themes, see Grant Underwood, *The Millenarian World of Early Mormonism* (Urbana: University of Illinois Press, 1993); Hickman, "The Book of Mormon as Amerindian Apocalypse"; Nathan O. Hatch, *The Democratization of American Christianity* (New Haven, CT: Yale University Press, 1989), 115–120; Mark Ashurst-McGee, "Zion Rising: Joseph Smith's Early Social and Political Thought" (Ph.D. diss. Arizona State University, 2008), chap. 4.

39 1 Nephi 16:17–31; Ether 2:22–23:6, Book of Mormon.

40 Terryl L. Givens, *The Book of Mormon: A Very Short Introduction* (New York: Oxford University Press, 2009), 22, 37; Givens, *By the Hand of Mormon*, 221.

41 Jan Shipps, *Mormonism: The Story of a New Religious Tradition* (Urbana: University of Illinois Press, 1985), 27.

42 Moroni 10:4, Book of Mormon.

43 For "pious fraud," see Dan Vogel, *Joseph Smith: The Making of a Prophet* (Salt Lake City: Signature Books, 2004). For the gold plates as sacred object, see Ann Taves, "History and the Claims of Revelation: Joseph Smith and the Materialization of the Golden Plates," *Numen* 61:2–3 (2014): 182–207. For "religious genius," see Harold Bloom, *The American Religion: The Emergence of the Post-Christian Nation* (New York: Touchstone, 1992), 80. For "abundant events," see Robert Orsi, "Abundant History: Marian Apparitions as Alternative Modernity," *Historically Speaking* 9:2 (September/October 2008): 12–16, and "Finding the Presence in Mormon History: An Interview with Susanna Morrill, Richard Lyman Bushman, and Robert Orsi," *Dialogue: A Journal of Mormon Thought* 44:3 (Fall 2011): 174–187.

44 Jeffrey R. Holland, "Safety for the Soul," October 2009 LDS General Conference, available at https://www.lds.org/general-conference/2009/10/safety-for-the-soul?lang=eng (accessed August 11, 2015), emphasis in original; Title Page, Book of Mormon.

45 See Givens, *By the Hand of Mormon*, 156.

46 For reviews and critiques of these theories, see Givens, *By the Hand of Mormon*, chap. 6; Bushman, *Joseph Smith*, chap. 4; and Paul C. Gutjahr, *The "Book of Mormon": A Biography* (Princeton, NJ: Princeton University Press, 2012), chap. 2.

47 Shipps, *Mormonism*, 45.

48 The literature on Book of Mormon historicity is voluminous and contentious. For a brief overview, see Gutjahr, *The "Book of Mormon,"* chap. 6; Givens, *The Book of Mormon*, chap. 9. The closest thing to archaeological proof for the Book of Mormon has actually been found in the Arabian peninsula, not in Central America. See Givens, *By the Hand of Mormon*, 120–121.

49 Some evangelical interlocutors have said that they would be more or less content if Latter-Day Saints believed what the Book of Mormon taught and no more. For instance, evangelical New Testament scholar Craig Blomberg, among others, has noted that the Book of Mormon may be more explicitly Trinitarian than is the Bible. Craig L. Blomberg and Stephen E. Robinson, *How Wide the Divide? A Mormon and an Evangelical in Conversation* (Downers Grove, IL: InterVarsity Press, 1997), 124.

50 See Noel B. Reynolds, "The Coming Forth of the Book of Mormon in the Twentieth Century," *BYU Studies* 38:2 (1999): 10; Grant Underwood, "Book of Mormon Usage in Early LDS Theology," *Dialogue: A Journal of Mormon Thought* 17:3 (Autumn 1984): 35–74.

51 Givens, *By the Hand of Mormon*, 64.

52 Quoted in Introduction, Book of Mormon. The original quote was made by Joseph Smith in a meeting with church leaders in 1841 and was recorded in

the journal of Wilford Woodruff, a prominent early Mormon leader and prolific diarist. See also Ezra Taft Benson, "The Book of Mormon – Keystone of Our Religion," *Ensign* (November 1987): 4–7.

53 Bushman, *Joseph Smith*, 172.

54 Ibid., 173. See also Richard Lyman Bushman, "Joseph Smith and His Visions," in *The Oxford Handbook of Mormonism*, eds. Terryl L. Givens and Philip L. Barlow (New York: Oxford University Press, 2015), 109–120.

55 Allen D. Roberts, Richard S. Van Wagoner, and Steven C. Walker, "The 'Lectures on Faith': A Case Study in Decanonization," *Dialogue: A Journal of Mormon Thought* 20 (Fall 1987): 71–77.

56 On the science of curry, see Robert A. Ferdman, "Scientists Have Figured Out What Makes Indian Food So Delicious," *Wonkblog*, available at http://www.washingtonpost.com/news/wonkblog/wp/2015/03/03/a-scientific-explanation-of-what-makes-indian-food-so-delicious/ (accessed August 14, 2015).

57 Abraham 3:18–28; Moses 4:1–4, Pearl of Great Price.

58 Terryl Givens and Fiona Givens, *The God Who Weeps: How Mormonism Makes Sense of Life* (Salt Lake City: Ensign Peak, 2012), 24.

59 Moses 7:24–48, Pearl of Great Price; long quote from 7:32–33, 37. For more on the "weeping God of Mormonism," see Givens and Givens, *The God Who Weeps*, esp. chap. 1; and Eugene England, "The Weeping God of Mormonism," *Dialogue: A Journal of Mormon Thought* 35:1 (Spring 2002): 63–80.

60 "Translation and Historicity of the Book of Abraham," available at https://www.lds.org/topics/translation-and-historicity-of-the-book-of-abraham?lang=eng#33 (accessed August 17, 2015).

6

Authorities

The extraordinary influence of evangelicalism in American religion and culture has meant that Protestant norms and assumptions – not least the centrality and "all-sufficiency" of the Bible – have become a kind of default position when we talk about religion. Yet religion has never been solely reducible to written scriptures, no matter how important those sacred texts are as touchstones, arbiters, and sources of both authority and contestation. Roman Catholics look to church tradition as well as the Bible and Magisterium as sources of authority. In addition to the Qur'an, Muslims consider the Sunna, or teachings and traditions of the Prophet Muhammad, to be authoritative guides for law and moral behavior. Similarly, the rabbinic commentary of the Talmud has played a central role in the ongoing shaping of Judaism. Accordingly, the Protestant Reformation's mantra of *sola scriptura* is clearly the minority view among religious believers, even among the text-based Abrahamic traditions.

For Mormons, written scriptures function as the standard for church doctrine and practice but are nevertheless insufficient in a world of constant change and religious uncertainty. Indeed, Joseph Smith said his earliest vision came as a result of his own despair with the "confusion and strife among the different denominations," all reading and preaching from the same Bible.[1] The lack of centralizing authority structures in nineteenth-century evangelicalism, and the ensuing cacophony of competing religious voices in early America – only to proliferate in the twentieth and twenty-first centuries – was met in Joseph Smith's religious system with an abundance of authorities, with the intention of providing unity and harmony in an age of spiritual fracture and division.

Although not often articulated as such, there are essentially six sources of authority for Latter-day Saints: the canonized scriptures, or standard works; teachings of the modern prophets, especially in General Conference; personal revelation through the Holy Ghost; church organization and leadership; church history, especially from the Joseph Smith and pioneer periods; and, most amorphously, the broad sentiments, moods, and behaviors of the general church membership. The first three are widely acknowledged – though Mormons, as we will see, often debate about which gets priority. The church organization and leadership are usually seen as derivative from the authority of the prophets and apostles, but actually act somewhat autonomously and according to their own logic. Church history is understood as authoritative mostly implicitly, and can be trumped by the preceding four sources. The last – the authority of the general membership – is a somewhat more controversial notion, as Mormons typically think of authority operating from the top-down rather than bottom-up, yet it is nevertheless real and has at times operated as a check-and-balance on the formal leadership.

The LDS Church often appears to be a monolith, precisely because the institution has generally been successful at lining up these various sources of authority. Such unanimity of purpose has frequently come in response to external or internal threats, real or perceived. Yet Mormonism has always been more diverse than most observers have realized. On a macro level, we see this with the proliferation of different churches and other groups all claiming to descend from Joseph Smith's revelations (see Chapter 10). Conflicts have also been endemic within each of the ecclesiastical manifestations of Mormonism, often stemming from a contest over authority – who has it, how it is acquired and employed, and to what end. In short, authority in Mormonism, as in many other institutions, has simultaneously exhibited both centripetal and centrifugal qualities.

Precisely because Mormonism is a religion that takes authority seriously – *very* seriously – it provides an exemplary case study for understanding the internally plural and therefore competing sources of authority within a religious institution. It therefore makes more sense conceptually to speak of *authorities*, plural, within Mormonism. The previous chapter reviewed at length the role of scriptures in Mormonism. Here we will extend that conversation by considering in turn the other authorities in the LDS Church, as well as how they relate to one another.

• LIVING PROPHETS

> Surely the Lord God will do nothing, but he revealeth his secret unto his servants the prophets.
>
> – Amos 3:7

> What I the Lord have spoken, I have spoken, and I excuse not myself; and though the heavens and the earth pass away, my word shall not pass away, but shall all be fulfilled, *whether by mine own voice or by the voice of my servants, it is the same.*[2]
>
> – Doctrine and Covenants 1:38

These two verses, the first from the Hebrew Bible and the other from the preface to the Doctrine and Covenants revealed to Joseph Smith in November 1831, are among the key proof texts that Latter-day Saints employ to establish the necessity and divinely granted authority of living prophets. In the Mormon view, prophets are divinely commissioned servants of God who speak his words and lead his church. Although their words are not infallible, and their teachings can in fact be contested, ignored, or superseded, Mormons pay a tremendous amount of respect and deference toward their prophets, especially the current president of the church. When he speaks, they listen, and they consider his words to be inspired utterances communicated from heaven.

Latter-day Saints typically recognize fifteen men to be "prophets, seers, and revelators" at any given time. (Over history there have been some variations in the number, but fifteen is the norm.) These men – and only men – constitute the First Presidency of the church (the president and his two counselors) and its Quorum of Twelve Apostles. While all fifteen are sustained as "prophets," in normal Mormon parlance "the prophet" refers only to the current president of the church – though in other contexts, "the Prophet," usually capitalized, also refers to Joseph Smith. The three members of the First Presidency are typically referred to as "President" and then their last name, whereas the apostles are called "Elder" and their last name. When any of the fifteen dies, another is chosen to take his place. In the LDS tradition, upon the death of the prophet, the longest-tenured living apostle is appointed as the next president of the church.

Apostles and prophets serve for life, which provides tremendous stability for the institution, especially since the church membership is well familiar with any apostle by the time he reaches the front of the ranks. Yet lifetime terms also create a gerontocracy. This leads to a tendency toward entrenched conservatism in outlook and procedure, and poses the natural challenges of men in their 70s, 80s, and 90s finding the physical and mental strength to lead a massively complex international organization. Some speculate whether the LDS Church will have a "Benedict moment," referring to the retirement of Pope Benedict XVI in February 2013. There is no precedent for the president of the LDS church or an apostle to resign and become "emeritus," though it has occurred in the Community of Christ and, as many observers have pointed out, it wasn't exactly par for the course for the papacy, a much more historic institution than the LDS presidency.

In a global church with millions of members, most rank-and-file Mormons never meet an apostle or prophet in person. This marks a substantial departure from the much smaller and localized world of nineteenth-century Mormonism, in which it was relatively common not only for members to meet apostles in their regular Sunday meetings but also to associate with them personally in business, politics, or other community affairs. With the successive advent of radio, television, satellite, the Internet, and now social media, the prophets' words have reached further throughout the far-flung church even while their physical interaction with the members has proportionately lessened. Mormons hear from their prophets and apostles during the church's semiannual General Conferences, and can read their words in the church's monthly magazines – or anytime online. Furthermore, in church curriculum materials for children and adults alike, quotes from prophets and apostles are sprinkled liberally alongside scriptures.

Perhaps counterintuitively, the increased distance between the top leadership and the membership has served only to enhance the collective status of the prophets and apostles. Perhaps it's harder to idealize a prophet when he smells like the horse you see him riding. In the minds of most contemporary church members, the prophet and apostles exist less as flesh-and-blood (and therefore fallible) human beings and more as idealized icons – even abstractions – of spirituality and divine authority, though church members also love to hear personal stories about the prophets and other gestures that lend a human touch. The possibility of a cult of personality is substantially diffused, however, not only by the fact that there are fifteen instead of only one at a time – though the president of the church, as "the prophet," does receive special attention and deference – but also by what has become a rather staid and corporate public presence, a far cry from the more freewheeling and charismatic days of Joseph Smith and Brigham Young.

Just how much authority does the Mormon prophet have? This was a recurring question during Mitt Romney's candidacies for the U.S. presidency in 2008 and 2012, when he became the Republican nominee. Redeploying a musty old anti-Catholic critique, some observers suggested that Romney would simply be a tool of the Salt Lake City "oligarchy" or that capturing the presidency for Mormonism was a "part of the mission of the church."[3] Damon Linker, the author of a book about how secular American politics and culture were "under siege" by "theocons," wondered what the answers would be to the following questions:

> Does Romney believe that the president of the Mormon Church is a genuine prophet of God? If so, how would he respond to a command from this prophet on matters of public policy? And, if his faith would require him to follow this hypothetical command, would it not be accurate to say that, under a President Romney, the Church of Jesus Christ of Latter-Day Saints would truly be in charge of the country – with its leadership having final say on matters of right and wrong?

Having painted his theocratic picture, Linker concluded:

> As long as the LDS Church continues to insist that its leader serves as a direct conduit from God – a God whose ways are, to a considerable extent, inscrutable to human reason – Mormonism will remain a theologically unstable, and thus politically perilous, religion.[4]

This portrait of a Mormon prophet powerful enough to run the most powerful country in the world through a puppet president – though, ironically, not powerful enough to get said puppet elected – reveals an unsophisticated notion of the authority of the prophet in modern Mormonism. Whether Brigham Young's control over nineteenth-century Utah can properly be considered as theocratic is a legitimate historical question, but to conflate mid-nineteenth-century and early-twenty-first-century Mormonism reveals a shallow understanding of the religion's historical development and contemporary sensibilities. To be sure, many faithful Mormons believe that the prophet's words are dictated straight from heaven and that the current word of the Lord carries greater weight even than canonized scripture. The most prominent modern proponent of this view was Ezra Taft Benson, who served as church president from 1985 to 1994. As the senior apostle next in line to the presidency, in 1980 he delivered an address at Brigham Young University called "Fourteen Fundamentals in Following the Prophet," which the church's monthly magazine *Ensign* subsequently printed and is still cited by Mormons today. Benson's "fourteen fundamentals" included the following statements:

- The prophet is the only man who speaks for the Lord in everything.
- The living prophet is more vital to us than the Standard Works.
- The living prophet is more important to us than a dead prophet.
- The prophet will never lead the Church astray.
- The prophet does not have to say "Thus saith the Lord" to give us scripture.
- The prophet can receive revelation on any matter – temporal or spiritual.
- The prophet may well advise on civic matters.[5]

If Benson's view of virtually absolute prophetic power held true – transcending scripture, unrivaled in its authority, unquestionable by the church membership, and applicable to every sphere of life including business and politics – then Damon Linker's concerns about Mitt Romney's candidacy, and Mormonism in general, would be well justified. Yet Benson felt he had to make such a strong argument precisely because the office of the prophet and president of the LDS Church does *not* in fact operate in the way that he prescribed. While he mustered dozens of scriptures and statements from other prophets and apostles to support his points, he failed to persuade or reflect the view of even his contemporaries among the apostles.

Indeed, Benson may well have been deliberately posturing against the well-established position of Joseph Fielding Smith and Bruce R. McConkie, two of late-twentieth-century Mormonism's most conservative apostles and prolific authors on doctrinal matters (Smith also served as president of the church briefly, from 1970 until his death in 1972). In their writings, widely read during their time and still quoted extensively by Latter-day Saints, both Smith and McConkie took the firm stance that the scriptures – the "standard works" – were indeed the standard by which truth was measured, and that even the teachings of living prophets had to conform to scripture in order to be accepted.

In an address also given at Brigham Young University, delivered less than four months after Benson's "Fourteen Fundamentals," McConkie emphasized to his LDS audience:

> We conform our thinking and our beliefs to what is found in the standard works. We need to be less concerned about the views and opinions that others have expressed and drink directly from the fountain the Lord has given us.[6]

McConkie was even more direct in his book *Mormon Doctrine*, which despite controversy about some of its contents attained status as the virtually essential LDS doctrinal reference work of the late twentieth century. In his entry on "Prophets," McConkie wrote:

> the opinions and views even of prophets may contain error unless those opinions and views are inspired by the Spirit. . . . Whatever is announced by the

presiding brethren as counsel for the Church will be the voice of inspiration. But the truth or error of any uninspired utterance of an individual will have to be judged by the standard works and the spirit of discernment and inspiration that is in those who actually enjoy the gift of the Holy Ghost.

He went on to quote Joseph Fielding Smith – incidentally, his father-in-law – who affirmed:

> My words, and the teachings of any other member of the Church, high or low, if they do not square with the revelations [in the scriptures], we need not accept them. Let us have this matter clear. We have accepted the four standard works as the measuring yardsticks, or balances, by which we measure every man's doctrine.[7]

In short, the prophets and apostles of the church could be trusted as communicating the mind and will of the Lord when all fifteen spoke in unison. When speaking individually, however, their words would have to be measured and weighed by two other preeminent sources of authority: the confirmation of the Holy Spirit, and especially the words of the scriptures.

McConkie deployed his arguments to dispute previous prophets' teachings with which he disagreed. In a private letter to Mormon intellectual Eugene England, who was championing some progressive theological views advanced by Brigham Young that were never fully enshrined in Mormon thought, McConkie wrote with characteristic bluntness:

> Prophets are men and they make mistakes. Sometimes they err in doctrine. This is one of the reasons the Lord has given us the Standard Works. . . . Sometimes even wise and good men fall short in the accurate presentation of what is truth. Sometimes a prophet gives personal views which are not endorsed and approved by the Lord.[8]

There is some irony that McConkie wielded his influence as an apostle to silence England's, and by extension the prophet Brigham Young's, theological conjectures.[9] Yet the very notion that prophets not only make simple mistakes or can be wrong about certain secular matters but that in fact they can and occasionally do "err in doctrine" profoundly challenges the preeminence of prophetic authority articulated by Ezra Taft Benson. This is not a comfortable notion for Mormons. If a person were to say in an LDS Sunday School class, especially without attribution to McConkie, that prophets sometimes "err in doctrine," they may well be rebuked by fellow church members. For the most part, Latter-day Saints have succumbed to what Walter van Beek has called "creeping infallibility," which consists of a somewhat more theologically lazy position rather than robust engagement with what it might mean for God to work through human, and therefore fallible, prophets.[10]

Whether best considered as "creeping infallibility" or the more orthodox phrases "sustaining the brethren" and "following the prophet," Mormons overall do have a high degree of inherent trust in their leaders, especially the church president-prophet and apostles. This is true not merely in matters of church doctrine and policy but also in politics. Recent research by political scientists has demonstrated that "when LDS leaders speak with one voice, operate through official channels, and give specific directions on political issues, Mormons respond – with alacrity." However, when any of those conditions are not met – if church leaders are not publicly unified on an issue, if they do not speak through widely understood official channels, or if they limit their statements to teachings about principles rather than specific directives – then their political influence recedes significantly. Furthermore, Mormon leaders can mobilize their membership so effectively precisely because they do it so infrequently: "The rarity of calls to political action means that when Mormons do receive political direction from Church leaders, it gets their attention."[11] Issue-specific moral influence is a far cry from theocratic puppeteering, as attested by the presence of a small but significant liberal Mormon population – including former Democratic U.S. Senator Harry Reid, a churchgoing Mormon who often took positions contrary to LDS conservative political orthodoxy while serving as Senate Majority and Minority Leader.

Bruce R. McConkie's observation that the particular teachings of individual prophets and apostles might be ignored and even dismissed, but that the unified voice of the entire First Presidency and Quorum of the Twelve Apostles carries special heft, is well displayed in the reverence Mormons give "The Family: A Proclamation to the World." Endorsed by all fifteen members of the First Presidency and the Twelve in 1995, the document is invoked regularly in church discourse at every level. Yet the "Family Proclamation" does not claim to be the word of the Lord, nor does it speak directly in his voice. Church leaders are generally careful not to refer to the proclamation as "scripture" or even "revelation" – which would put it on par with the revelations canonized in the Doctrine and Covenants – but members still widely treat it as such. Simply referring to the proclamation is typically enough, within orthodox Mormon circles and church meetings, to establish a point and foreclose dissenting views. It is conceivable that at some point the proclamation could be incorporated into the Doctrine and Covenants. Yet by keeping the proclamation in a liminal state as quasi-canon, rather than formally installing it in the standard works, church leaders reserve the right to revise its ideas or wording in the future. "The Family" thus signals to the membership that prophets and apostles continue to speak authoritatively for the Lord. Its prominence in contemporary Mormon discourse demonstrates that the words of living prophets are on a level with, and in some ways even exceed in importance and relevance, the words of canonized written scripture.

So to the question, "Which is the primary source of authority in Mormonism, canonized scripture (the standard works) or living prophets?," the answer is: "Both."

• THE HOLY GHOST

One of the signal contributions of Pentecostalism, and charismatic Christianity in general, has been its emphasis on the third member of the Trinity. Christians have been baptized "in the name of the Father, and the Son, and the Holy Ghost" for two millennia now, but with a few exceptions the Father and the Son generally over-whelmed their more ethereal third partner. One would think that the Holy Ghost, declared throughout the New Testament to be "one" with God and Jesus, would be a ranking authority. But the mysterious quality of the Spirit has made it easy to ignore as a source of authority to church hierarchs throughout the centuries who were intent on maintaining internal unity and order.

Decades before the Azusa Street revivals that produced Pentecostalism in America, Mormons were speaking in tongues, prophesying, healing one another, and otherwise exhibiting the "gifts of the Spirit." Indeed, immediately after being baptized in water by immersion, converts are confirmed as members of the Church of Jesus Christ of Latter-day Saints and are told to "receive the gift of the Holy Ghost." This gift is understood as the promise of the "constant companionship" of the third member of the Godhead, dependent upon the individual's personal worthiness for such divine presence. For Mormons, the Holy Ghost plays many roles, but its fundamental mis-sion is to testify of the divinity of Jesus Christ and the truthfulness of his gospel, and to reveal whatever messages God has to deliver to individual believers. Joseph Smith taught, "No man can receive the Holy Ghost without receiving revelations. The Holy Ghost is a revelator."[12] Among the most cited Book of Mormon passages comes from its last chapter, in which the final prophet Moroni urges readers of the book to pray about whether it is truly from God. He promises that God "will manifest the truth of it unto you, by the power of the Holy Ghost. And by the power of the Holy Ghost ye may know the truth of all things."[13] Similarly, even before the church was formally organized, Oliver Cowdery received a revelation through Joseph Smith that when he needed answers to questions, God would "tell you in your mind and in your heart, by the Holy Ghost, which shall come upon you and which shall dwell in your heart. Now, behold, this is the spirit of revelation."[14]

Central to Mormon identity and theology is the belief that God, through the Holy Ghost, continues to communicate with the church and to individuals through revela-tion.[15] Indeed, one of Joseph Smith's core declarations was that the heavens are open and God speaks in modern times just as he did to ancient prophets and believers. Although Mormons believe that the essential truths of the gospel have been revealed to modern prophets (especially Smith), they readily acknowledge that God has much more to teach humans and will do so at his pleasure.

Revelation to and for the entire church will come only through the duly ordained prophets and apostles, Mormons believe, but revelation is not limited to church lead-ers and institutional needs. Indeed, personal revelation is a cornerstone of Mormon devotional life. It typically comes quietly and is "felt" in a person's mind or heart, although Mormons do allow for the reality of other forms of spiritual communi-cation such as dreams and visions. Divine direction may be sought for regarding all kinds of spiritual and secular matters within a person's sphere of responsibility. Thus, parents can receive revelation for the care of their children but not for someone else's; a Sunday School instructor can receive revelation for how best to teach her class but not for how members of the class should specifically live their lives; a bishop can receive revelation for directing the affairs of his ward and even on behalf of individuals who are in spiritual counseling with him, but he has no revelatory authority for anyone outside his ward boundaries.

It is widely understood that revelation is properly received and expressed within the limits of church authority and teachings. Because of strong ecclesiological and cultural constraints, in practice personal revelation through the Holy Ghost typically is not accompanied in modern Mormonism by strong antinomian tendencies – the notion that the reception of God's word and grace frees a person from adhering to law (religious or civil). Nevertheless, the logic of personal revelation contains within it the seeds of interpersonal and institutional conflict. Usually this is relatively minor, as when a man claims to have received revelation that he should marry a certain woman but she says she has received either no such revelation or perhaps a revelation that she should marry someone different. (This happens all the time at Brigham Young University and in singles wards across the church.) Yet the possibility of dueling revelations can also have more serious consequences. The leader of the Ordain Women movement claimed to have been motivated by personal revelation from the Holy Ghost, yet local church authorities excommunicated her in 2014 and in so doing essentially labeled her revelation as invalid. Many (if not most) people who have joined with fundamentalist polygamist groups say that they do so according to personal revelation they have received; they too will be excommunicated by the LDS Church. Claiming to follow the voice of the Spirit wherever it leads has even led some people to commit horrific acts of violence, though mainstream Mormons are quick to denounce such instances as counterfeit or false revelations.[16]

Personal revelation through the Holy Ghost thus carries considerable weight within Mormon communities and discourse, but functionally it operates only in triangulation with scripture and current church teaching (especially from the prophet and apostles) as a source of authority. If a person says the Spirit tells her something that clearly contradicts current prophetic teaching or the church's interpretation of scripture, then the revelation is dismissed as false, misunderstood, or even "from the wrong source" (i.e. the devil). Anything short of violating widely held community norms and beliefs, however, becomes fair game, especially if a person's insights gained from the Holy Ghost are portrayed as merely personal and not binding on anyone else. When a Latter-day Saint says, "the Spirit told me . . ." in regard to an individual or family matter, their fellow church members have little recourse other than to nod and smile, even if they personally disagree.

Those members who are particularly adept in the exercise of certain gifts of the Spirit – to be discussed at greater length in the following chapter – also enjoy a kind of informal spiritual authority within the church. For instance, a certain man might be well known within a ward as giving priesthood blessings of healing that seem to be particularly efficacious, or a particular woman might be respected as an especially gifted and spiritually powerful teacher. The scope of any authority derived merely from spiritual charisma is limited by the overarching ecclesiastical structures of the church, but it nevertheless gives its practitioners a kind of local influence and status.

Perhaps the best example of this came in the nineteenth-century exercise and then suppression of female ritual healing. At one of the original meetings of the Nauvoo Relief Society in 1842, Joseph Smith told the women "respecting the female lay-ing on [of] hands," that "there could be no devil in it if God gave his sanction by healing – that there could be no more sin in any female laying hands on the sick than in wetting the face with water – that it is no sin for any body to do it that has faith."[17] Energized by the prophet's validation, LDS women frequently blessed each other and their children. Since in the nineteenth century Mormons typically laid hands on the afflicted part of the body (now hands are laid only on the head), Vic-torian gender norms prevented men from administering to women in childbirth or otherwise suffering from "female problems." Mormon women frequently reported that an ineffective blessing from church elders was later followed up by a female blessing that resulted in a successful healing. All parties understood that these female administrations were not performed under the authority of the Melchizedek Priest-hood, which only ordained men exercised, but rather by virtue of faith and the gift of healing sent by the Holy Spirit. Women's blessings played a prominent part in frontier Mormonism, but the First Presidency of the church curtailed the practice in the early twentieth century, even while women continued to be extolled by male priesthood leaders as spiritual exemplars. One of the planks of the modern Mormon feminist movement is to reinstate the practice of women's blessings, thus revitalizing a long-practiced but now generally forgotten exercise of female spiritual authority.[18]

• THE CHURCH

According to the influential theory of Max Weber, one of the founders of mod-ern sociology, religious movements typically begin with the charisma of a prophet figure. This prophet gains his authority not from any official appointment or supervisory body, but rather through the self-determined exercise of gifts that are "supernatural," in the sense that they are not given to all and come, at least in the eyes of the believers, from a transcendent sphere. The charismatic prophet "seizes the task for which he is destined and demands that others obey and follow him by virtue of his mission." As powerful as this charismatic authority is, however, it is "naturally unstable." Because the bearer gains legitimacy "solely by proving his pow-ers in practice," he may lose his followers if his prophecies fail or miracles cease. And of course, every charismatic figure will die or otherwise disappear. Thus, every movement that emerges from a charismatic prophet sooner or later faces the same prospect: how to transform the unique and transitory charisma of the founding prophet into a stable and permanent form that can inform mundane daily life and survive across the generations. How does a movement transition from prophet to permanent structure, and what does that do to the movement? Weber refers to this process, wherein "the charismatic message inevitably becomes dogma, doctrine . . . law or petrified tradition," as "the routinization of charisma." The spontaneity of revelation, prophecy, and immediately accessible grace thus transforms into the perennially available structures of institution, bureaucracy, and tradition, which themselves acquire authoritative status as the inheritors and permanent bearers of the charisma originally imparted to and through the prophet.[19]

The broad outlines of Weber's arguments are certainly applicable to the historical and institutional development of Mormonism. Like Moses, Buddha, and Muhammad, Joseph Smith stands as a singular figure in the movement that emerged out of his teachings; even his immediate successor (for Latter-day Saints), Brigham Young, considered the founding prophet's role as unique and essentially irreplaceable.[20] Smith was mindful of the possibility that, without sufficient preparation, the church would not survive without him. Much of his ministry following the publication of the Book of Mormon and organization of the Church of Christ in 1830 can be interpreted as a gradual process of institutionalization and indeed routinization of his prophetic charisma. Richard Bushman astutely observes that

> Mormonism succeeded when other charismatic movements foundered . . . partly because of the governing mechanisms Joseph put in place early in the Church's history. . . . Almost all of his major theological innovations involved the creation of institutions. . . . Joseph thought institutionally more than any other visionary of his time, and the survival of his movement can largely be attributed to this gift.[21]

Step by step, within five years of the church's establishment, Joseph Smith created overlapping layers of priesthood hierarchy, culminating in a system of regular standing councils that would govern the church. A particularly noteworthy development came when the minutes of a February 1834 council meeting were incorporated into the Doctrine and Covenants, positioned alongside Smith's direct revelations from heaven.[22] As Bushman notes, "By putting the work of the councils on the same plane as his own revelations, Joseph set a precedent for inspiration other than his own: revelation through a council." This process continued the following year with the emergence of the Twelve Apostles as a senior governing body – though at the time they did not enjoy the same ecclesiastical status that they do now in the LDS Church. Smith's history after 1835 is increasingly filled with minutes of council meetings (including many he did not personally attend) rather than the direct revelations that were earlier the backbone of his narrative. Having consolidated his prophetic authority, Smith paradoxically diffused it to the councils of the church. He never ceded his unique status as the church's prophet, seer, revelator, and president, yet nevertheless, as Bushman concludes, "At a moment when Joseph's own revelatory powers were at their peak, he divested himself of sole responsibility for revealing the will of God and invested that gift in the councils of the Church, making it a charismatic bureaucracy."[23]

Anyone remotely familiar with the LDS Church's current bureaucracy would be more likely to describe it as "corporate" rather than "charismatic." Yet especially in light of Weber's theory, it is appropriate to speak of the "charismatic bureaucracy" of modern Mormonism. As noted, while Mormons sustain their church president – along with the other apostles – as a "prophet, seer, and revelator," they do not really expect him to pronounce new revelations in the voice of the Lord as did Joseph Smith. It has been nearly a century in the LDS Church since the prophet-president produced a revelation that substantially added to church doctrine.[24] Yet Mormons fully believe that God continues to guide the church through revelation. How do they sustain this faith when their prophets no longer speak so explicitly in the name of the Lord?

Without always articulating it as such, Latter-day Saints believe that more than any single charismatic figure, the leadership councils of the church have become the vehicles of God's revelation. Thus, when the church president presents what outsiders would consider merely a policy change, believers typically consider the statement to be the result of revelation, a sign of God's continuing work within the church. This was on display in October 2012, when church president Thomas S. Monson announced at General Conference that the required age for full-time LDS missionary service would drop from nineteen to eighteen for men and from twenty-one to nineteen for women. Whereas journalists dutifully noted the policy change and speculated what it might mean for the church demographically and sociologically, church members – especially teenagers and their parents – were ecstatic, believing it to be the latest word of God to his people.[25]

The senior church leadership is no doubt aware that the general membership considers policy announcements to be on par with revelation, and they do little to disabuse the masses of the notion. They can follow this course uncynically for two reasons: first, because the leaders themselves believe that their decisions, especially those produced in council together, are inspired by God, even if not resultant from a verbally dictated revelation; and second, because they know that the general membership understands that authority and revelation proceed from church councils, since the membership are themselves participants in such councils on a local level. Part of the sociological genius of Mormonism is that through the creation of many layers of hierarchy, it effectively democratizes the receipt of revelation and thus the exercise of authority to as many members as possible. This revelatory authority is limited to the sphere for which the council has ecclesiastical jurisdiction, but it is authoritative nonetheless. Thus, a ward council can receive inspired guidance for their ward but not the neighboring one, whereas the presiding councils of the church (the First Presidency and Quorum of Twelve Apostles) can receive revelation for the whole. Because of the church's system of lay leadership, most actively engaged church members will at some point in their life be part of a leadership council or presidency on at least the ward level. In the process, they learn implicitly and experientially that church governance is its own form of revelatory authority in Mormonism – and thus, a "charismatic bureaucracy."

Church authority operates in both formal and informal ways.[26] Formal authority is more readily associated with the church's hierarchical organization. The worldwide membership is divided into individual congregations called wards and branches, several of which constitute a stake or a mission. These units are geographically defined

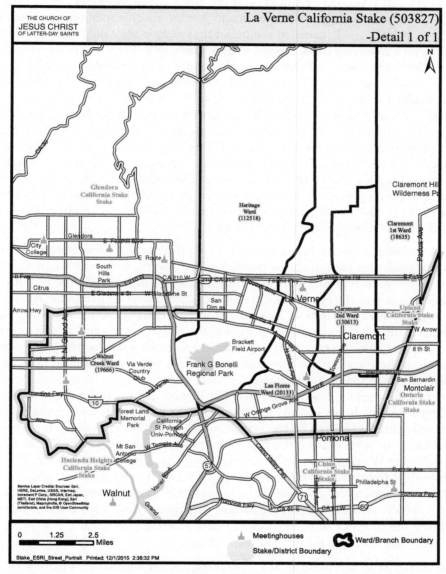

FIGURE 6.1 Map of the LaVerne California Stake of the Church of Jesus Christ of Latter-day Saints. Note that the stake is divided into several wards, each of which is the basic local congregation of the LDS Church.

Used with permission of the LaVerne California Stake

with clear boundaries, and members almost universally attend the ward or branch whose territorial borders they reside within.[27] Wards and stakes constitute the places where the vast majority of church activity occurs.

Except for those at the very highest level of the church, called "general authorities and officers," all positions in the church are filled by lay members who volunteer their time. Beginning at age twelve, men and women receive specific appointments – referred to as "callings" because of the belief that people are called by God to fill the position – on a revolving basis, though a calling may be held by one person for several years. Callings are always received from the leader one step higher in the hierarchy. Every ward contains multiple priesthood quorums and "auxiliaries," each of which operate under the direction of their own president or leader. Most of these quorum and auxiliary heads have two counselors, together constituting a presidency. All told, this means that a fully staffed ward will have upwards of thirty people serving in a leadership position at any given time (see Figure 6.2). When non-leadership callings are added – consisting mostly of teachers for the various church classes – a ward can easily have enough callings for well over a hundred adults and teenagers, producing hundreds of hours per week of voluntary labor in a single congregation. When multiplied by the approximately thirty thousand active LDS wards and branches around the world, the combined effort is staggering.

All these moving parts are regulated and directed by a single leader responsible for everything under his stewardship – the bishop for a ward, and the stake president for a stake. These men typically have full-time employment and families, but also provide upwards of twenty-five hours of volunteer church service per week. At the ward level, in prayerful consultation with his two counselors (constituting a bishopric), the bishop will select individuals to fill various callings; plan and organize Sunday church services and other activities and conferences; set goals for the ward or stake; track church membership and participation; collect tithes and other donations; distribute church welfare assistance; oversee local missionary activities; and coordinate the work of the various quorum and auxiliary heads – all this and more in addition to providing countless hours of spiritual counseling to individuals and families. Bishoprics are substantially assisted by the ward council, which consists of the bishopric and the presidents or leaders from the high priests group, elders quorum, Relief Society, Primary, Young Women's, Young Men's, Sunday School, and ward mission. Insofar as the proverbial trains run on time in any given ward, it is because of this council of lay men and women coordinating the activities of all the other volunteer workers in a ward – which essentially means all active members. Most ward council members would hesitate to speak of their work as being revelatory in nature, but they would affirm that they seek and receive the inspiration of God in their callings.

Formal authority in Mormonism also operates more impersonally, in the classic sense of a bureaucracy. In order to maintain uniformity throughout the globally sprawling and increasingly diverse organization, the church distributes a handbook of regulations and procedures to all priesthood leaders and auxiliary heads, and has recently

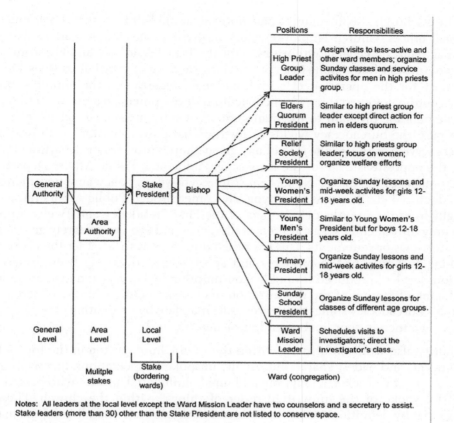

Positions	Responsibilities
High Priest Group Leader	Assign visits to less-active and other ward members; organize Sunday classes and service activites for men in high priests group.
Elders Quorum President	Similar to high priest group leader except direct action for men in elders quorum.
Relief Society President	Similar to high priests group leader; focus on women; organize welfare efforts
Young Women's President	Organize Sunday lessons and mid-week activites for girls 12-18 years old.
Young Men's President	Similar to Young Women's President but for boys 12-18 years old.
Primary President	Organize Sunday lessons and mid-week activites for girls 12-18 years old.
Sunday School President	Organize Sunday lessons for classes of different age groups.
Ward Mission Leader	Schedules visits to investigators; direct the investigator's class.

General Authority — Stake President — Bishop

Area Authority

General Level | Area Level | Local Level

Mulitple stakes | Stake (bordering wards) | Ward (congregation)

Notes: All leaders at the local level except the Ward Mission Leader have two counselors and a secretary to assist. Stake leaders (more than 30) other than the Stake President are not listed to conserve space.

FIGURE 6.2 Ward leadership callings. Every LDS congregation is divided into multiple priesthood quorums and auxiliary organizations, each presided over by male and female lay volunteers.

Graphic designed by and courtesy of Michael McBride

made it publicly available online.[28] Though doctrinally based, much of the handbook deals with administrative minutiae, listing official policies (no open flames allowed in church buildings) alongside official non-policies (birth control is neither encouraged nor discouraged, and is left up to individual couples). The handbook is a valuable coordination tool, creating uniform expectations and experiences for church members worldwide. Although some members complain that the handbook squelches creativity and local initiative, others have been emboldened by its clear directives about the powers and responsibilities associated with their callings. For instance, local male priesthood leaders in India shunned a Relief Society president until she pointed to the handbook's description of her rightful duties, thus carving out a greater space for her voice and leadership.[29]

The LDS Church also maintains a paid bureaucracy in Salt Lake City, Utah, and other regional offices. Church employees work in divisions headed at least titularly, and often actually, by general authorities, with the First Presidency and Quorum of the Twelve Apostles functioning as an overarching (and legal) board of trustees. Deemed necessary for the operation of a multinational organization, the church's bureaucracy coordinates everything from curriculum development to a massive church and temple building program to the management of substantial financial assets. For the most part, the bureaucracy wields its institutional power invisibly, with priesthood leaders serving as the public face of any given church program or department. However, the opposite is true for the increasingly influential Public Affairs Department, which manages the online Newsroom.[30] In recent years, policy announcements and even doctrinal clarifications have typically come through Public Affairs rather than straight from the mouths of members of the First Presidency and Twelve Apostles, who only infrequently speak at press conferences and even more rarely give individual interviews or statements. This has raised questions as to whether the charismatic teaching authority of the prophets and apostles has effectively been replaced by cautious legalese produced for public consumption by lawyers and media handlers – itself a manifestation of the routinization of charisma. Others have wondered if the church's bureaucracy sometimes exceeds its mandate by originating church doctrine rather than merely coordinating and implementing it.[31]

Authority also works informally within the LDS Church, often in the form of cultural norms and widely shared but usually unspoken expectations. In a well-known sermon, Boyd K. Packer, a longtime and highly influential apostle who passed away in 2015, spoke of the "unwritten order of things" within the church. These are things that by definition are not to be found in the church's handbooks, manuals, or even scriptures. Despite being "ordinary," and smacking of micromanagement, these things are – in Packer's view at least – "very important" for maintaining dignity and decorum, which in turn enhances spirituality. A few examples of these unwritten norms include: the highest ranking, or presiding, officer at a meeting should sit near the pulpit facing the congregation; the presiding officer should speak at the end of the meeting, so as to correct any false teachings that came before; people should not turn down callings, nor do they ask to be released; a person should approach their parents or local priesthood leader for counsel or a priesthood blessing before they seek advice from a general authority; funerals should focus on teaching the plan of salvation, not "humorous experiences or jokes"; and church members and especially leaders should be referred to by their full names ("William" not "Bill") in formal church settings.[32]

Unwritten cultural expectations also exercise authority within the church, as we can see with LDS sartorial norms. Men are typically beardless – and are required to be so if they attend a church school, work for the church, or hold a senior priesthood leadership position. Church members are strongly discouraged from receiving tattoos or multiple piercings (men should have none). Both men and women dress conservatively for Sunday church services, with women in long skirts or dresses and men in white shirts and ties (and often suits). A minor scandal ensued when in December 2012 when a group of Mormon women used social media to organize a protest to these informal dress standards by sponsoring a "Wear Pants to Church Day." Although the church responded (via Public Affairs) that there is no formal policy on what people should wear to church, the vitriol expressed in many circles against women who chose to wear pants, or even sympathized with those who did, revealed the pervasiveness and cultural authority of such unofficial norms.[33]

In sum, the LDS Church's official handbook for leaders states, "The Church of Jesus Christ of Latter-day Saints was organized by God to assist in His work to bring to pass the salvation and exaltation of his children."[34] Thus, the very structures of the church are presumed to be not only authoritative but also salvific, and the work of individuals functioning within those structures is exalting both for themselves and those they serve. In Mormonism, particularly as a lived religion, the church is the authoritative and inescapable site where God's voice is heard and his work is done.

• CHURCH HISTORY

Every year, thousands of Mormon teenagers trade T-shirts, shorts, and swimming pools for bonnets, suspenders, and handcarts as they reenact the historic journey of the Mormon pioneers to Utah. These "pioneer treks" – just "trek" to the kids – are elaborate productions that require the construction or purchase of enough working handcarts for the participants, along with hundreds of hours for planning and coordination. This culminates in the actual trek, which usually lasts from three to five days and takes place in a rural or wilderness area where youth pull the handcarts – laden with all necessary food, water, bags, and other supplies – along dirt roads or paths for upwards of twenty miles. Along the way they read scriptures, meet in devotional gatherings, write in personal diaries, cook over a campfire, and enjoy pioneer-era music and dancing. Most come home reporting it to be one of the most powerful and formative experiences they have ever had.

Increasingly popular since the LDS Church celebrated the 150th anniversary of the original pioneer company reaching Utah in 1847, these handcart reenactments have become something of a rite of passage for Mormon youth to do at least once before they graduate from high school. From their origins among stakes in the Mormon heartland in the intermountain American West, pioneer treks have become an unlikely transnational phenomenon, with Mongolian Latter-day Saints donning nineteenth-century American pioneer garb and pulling handcarts across the steppes, and Argentines across the pampas. Pioneer treks have become so popular because they are dramatic, visceral sites for Mormon identity construction and maintenance, all grounded in familiar and authoritative historical narratives and tropes. Originally a grassroots phenomenon, treks have become so popular that in 2015 the LDS Church produced an official thirty-two-page handbook of guidelines, complete with organizational charts, detailed descriptions of assigned roles, patterns for sewing pioneer-era dresses and constructing handcarts, and instructions on what to do in case of insect bites or lightning strikes.[35]

For Latter-day Saints, church history has generally been treated as a repository of faith-promoting stories and characters to be learned from and emulated. History is a platform for presentist moralizing far more than a subject of study for its own sake. For instance, the church's handbook for handcart reenactment instructs: "Treks provide powerful opportunities to strengthen testimonies, build unity, do family history, and learn core gospel principles. Treks can also help youth learn about who they are and what they may become." Through their participation, trekkers are to learn principles of faith, obedience, charity, sacrifice, and persevering through adversity.[36]

Scholar Jan Shipps has persuasively argued that it was the historical experiences of nineteenth-century Latter-day Saints, along with a new prophet and new book of scripture, that set apart Mormonism as a distinctive religion.[37] The very first commandment to the newly formed Church of Christ in April 1830 was to keep a record of its doings, and the opening pages of Joseph Smith's official history are canonized as part of LDS scripture.[38] Those in the founding generations understood themselves to be living in sacred time, recapitulating the travails and triumphs of the biblical Israelites. Early Mormon history thus literally became a sacred text, and has been treated as such by Latter-day Saints in the twentieth and twenty-first centuries. When "Zion and Babylon [came] to terms" in 1890, as Shipps has observed, "the past was filled up. Complete."[39] The LDS capitulation to federal authority thus represents something of Mormonism's "end of history." Contemporary Mormons thus find meaning, inspiration, and cultural authority in ritual re-creations of a sacred past and heroic age, more so than in original statements of their own. This has been echoed in the academy, where scholarly analysis of twentieth- and twenty-first-century Mormonism still lags far behind studies of the religion's founding period.

As large as their collective history looms in the Mormon imagination, Latter-day Saints' relationship to their history is not an uncomplicated one. Especially in the Internet age, when so much information is available with a simple keyword search, it has become increasingly problematic to offer a sanitized and purely heroic narrative of church history. Though exact numbers are difficult to pinpoint, it is clear that in recent decades a substantial number of Latter-day Saints have come to question their faith and even leave the church over discrepancies between what they learned about the church and its history from official sources versus what they discover online.[40] This has led the LDS Church to commission and publish online a series of essays dealing with some of the most traditionally vexatious issues in church history and doctrine, including polygamy, the Book of Mormon translation, the historicity and authenticity of the Book of Abraham, multiple accounts of Joseph Smith's First Vision, women and priesthood, and theosis.[41]

Because of the authority that it holds in the Mormon psyche, church history is deployed both to maintain the status quo and to advocate for change. Feminist historians and theologians in the late twentieth century looked back for inspiration to nineteenth-century precedents, such as female ritual healing and Mormon women's prominent place in the suffragist movement. Their continuing effort to address gender inequities in the contemporary church is considerably bolstered by citing historical teachings by Joseph Smith as well as the practices of faithful Mormon pioneer women.[42] At the same time, the argument for female ordination in the church runs into the problem that in fact Joseph Smith never ordained women to the Melchizedek Priesthood, thus providing a strong historical argument for male-only ordination. Similarly, scholars troubled by the church's racial priesthood and temple ban in the early 1970s published historical research convincingly demonstrating that African American men had in fact been ordained to the Melchizedek Priesthood and even sent on missions for the church during Joseph Smith's time.[43] Yet the ban itself was maintained in the twentieth century in large part because the senior church leadership accepted on face value certain historical sources that (erroneously) placed the ban as originating during Joseph Smith's lifetime. Furthermore, the leadership felt bound by history, deferring to decades of precedent until the 1978 revelation provided the opportunity to break with the past.[44] Mormon fundamentalists, as we will see in Chapter 10, also employ historical arguments to establish the validity of their claims to doctrinal and ecclesiastical continuity with the nineteenth-century church.

In short, church history is an ambivalent but nevertheless authoritative text within Mormonism. Alternately wielded to enforce orthodoxy or in an attempt to recover forgotten alternatives, it offers powerful narrative resources for the construction, maintenance, or disruption of contemporary Mormon identity, belief, and practice.

THE CHURCH MEMBERSHIP

A few years ago, a leading Mormon feminist scholar visited my classroom. When a student asked her why she chose to remain in the church despite her strong objections to some of its patriarchal beliefs and practices, past and present, she responded simply: "Why should I leave? It's my church too."

The typical portrayal of the LDS Church, both within and without, is that it is a top-down hierarchy in which the prophets speak and the members obey. To be sure, church hierarchs hold the cards in any direct ecclesiastical conflict – it is they who can declare what is "doctrinal" and can therefore excommunicate those with whom they disagree, not vice versa. But for most of the LDS Church's history, excommunication has been a blunt tool rarely applied in disputes over orthodoxy, reserved instead primarily for church discipline over moral matters such as adultery. Lay members have frequently and consistently disagreed with their priesthood leaders over a wide variety of issues. In most of those cases, diversity of belief was tolerated, if grudgingly, and in some of those cases the views of the membership prevailed over even strongly worded dictates of the leadership. Though not fully theorized or theologized, in practice the membership wields a significant degree of authority in the LDS Church, especially when there is widespread if unofficial consensus on an issue. Three brief examples illustrate the point.

At a public meeting of the church in August 1843, Joseph Smith accused Sidney Rigdon, his longtime associate and counselor in the First Presidency, of seeking to betray him. Despite Rigdon's protests of innocence, Smith refused to be satisfied and expressed his desire for Rigdon to be removed from the First Presidency and possibly church fellowship. After a conciliatory discourse by Hyrum Smith, the conference attendees showed their continuing confidence in Rigdon by voting for him to retain his place in the First Presidency. In so doing the membership took a clearly contrary position to their prophet. Though frustrated, Smith honored the decision of the conference.[45]

Beginning in the early 1850s and continuing sporadically until his death in 1877, Brigham Young taught both publicly and privately that Adam "is our Father, our God, and the only God we have to do [with]." From the pulpit in General Conference, Young instructed the Saints that it was Adam, as God, who was the father of Jesus Christ, and with his wife Eve the father of all human spirits: "when you see your Father in the Heavens, you will see Adam: when you see your mother that bear[s] your spirit, you will see Mother Eve." While some Latter-day Saints accepted their prophet's novel doctrine, others rejected it wholesale. Young's most prominent adversary on this score – and others – was Orson Pratt, a senior apostle who was also one of the early church's most respected theologians. To a significant degree, the conflict centered on whether ultimate doctrinal authority for the church resided in the scriptures or the prophets – the "living oracles," as Young was fond of saying. The majority of members failed to embrace Young's position. Mostly through their refusal to innovate, the membership of the church expressed greater comfort with Pratt's scriptural traditionalism than Young's speculative theology. The powerful church president – the "Lion of the Lord" as he was known – yielded. Without changing his own views, he grudgingly conceded not to impose his Adam-God doctrine on the church. By failing to follow the prophet, the membership defined church doctrine.[46]

Mormons have also defied their prophets when it comes to politics. In the early twentieth century, the church leadership typically allied itself with the Republican Party while most grassroots Mormons voted Democrat; Utahans even elected a Jewish Democrat as governor in 1916. The public political pronouncements of the church leadership waned somewhat in the 1920s – perhaps because Republicans held the presidency – but heated up again once Franklin D. Roosevelt was on the ticket. Church president Heber J. Grant had been a successful businessman before becoming an apostle, and he despised FDR and all he stood for. Grant frequently used his General Conference addresses as occasions to denounce the evils of government welfare, the importance of private industry, and the necessity of safeguarding the

Constitution. Local and national newspapers quoted Grant and other senior church officials in openly expressing their favor of Roosevelt's various Republican opponents. Yet in all four of FDR's elections, from 1932 through 1944, Mormons overwhelmingly ignored their prophet and voted for the popular Democratic president. Furthermore, during the Roosevelt administration, there were either five or six Mormons elected to Congress or as governors – all Democrats. Frustrated by their inability to corral the Mormon vote, by the middle of the twentieth century, LDS Church leaders stopped offering explicit endorsements of political candidates.[47]

To be sure, these illustrations are the exception to the rule of general harmony between the church's leadership and membership. Most members really do believe that their prophets and apostles speak to and for God, and thus are willing to follow their counsel. At the same time, over the years church leaders have become increasingly savvy about the limits of their authority. It was easier for Brigham Young to act in a theocratic mode when the Latter-day Saints were relatively isolated in frontier Utah. Now Mormons are more able and likely to vote with their feet, and many respond to church teachings with which they disagree with either apathy or disaffiliation. The fact that those high-profile figures – intellectuals, feminists, and dissidents – who have been excommunicated from the LDS Church for "apostasy" in the past three decades can be relatively easily numbered and named suggests that the church is generally more interested in retaining people than purging them.[48]

Like all organizations and subcultures, Mormonism has developed its own set of norms and expectations, particularly in areas where there is a high concentration of church members. (Anecdotally, I find that areas with fewer members adopt more of a "we're just glad you're here" attitude, and thus have somewhat greater tolerance for diverse views.) These group norms exert real cultural authority, with strong tendencies to define who or what beliefs or behaviors are acceptable or not. Those Mormons who for whatever reason do not fit the mold are often uncomfortable; many suffer in silence, others slide away, and a few leave angrily and rage at the church. Public protest has typically been an ineffective means of shifting the views of the leadership or membership, as such oppositional behavior is easily delegitimized as simply "anti-Mormon." With pervasive cultural expectations of top-down authority and obedience to priesthood leaders, it is not always clear how members – especially women – can appropriately voice their concerns and grievances. The Internet and social media have provided platforms for likeminded Latter-day Saints to share their views. There is a lively universe of Mormon blogs known collectively as the "bloggernacle" (a word play on the Mormon Tabernacle) that has galvanized certain subcommunities such as Mormon feminists, ex-Mormons, or "Mormon mommy bloggers," all with the centrifugal tendency of creating echo chambers rather than platforms for dialogue and persuasive discourse.[49] Despite clear precedents and real power, then, the authority of the collective membership remains ill defined, tricky to gauge, and difficult to mobilize, especially when seen as challenging other, better established forms of authority within the church.

A religious tradition, Mormonism or otherwise, can be defined as "a sustained argument, conducted anew by each generation, about the contemporary significance and meaning of the sources of sacred wisdom and revealed truth."[50] All six forms of authority reviewed here – scriptures, prophets, the Holy Ghost, the church, church history, and the church membership – work in balance and tension with one another as a sustained argument about how Mormonism is believed and practiced at any given moment. The precise content of those beliefs and practices, particularly in their dominant forms in contemporary Mormonism, will be examined in the following two chapters.

• NOTES

1 Joseph Smith-History 1:8, Pearl of Great Price.
2 Emphasis added.
3 Harold Bloom, "Will This Election Be the Mormon Breakthrough?" *New York Times*, November 12, 2011; Sally Denton, "Romney and the White Horse Prophecy," *Salon*, January 29, 2012.
4 Damon Linker, "The Big Test," *New Republic*, January 20, 2007; see also Damon Linker, *The Theocons: Secular America Under Siege* (New York: Anchor, 2007).
5 Ezra Taft Benson, "Fourteen Fundamentals in Following the Prophet," *Ensign* (June 1981), available at https://www.lds.org/liahona/1981/06/fourteen-fundamentals-in-following-the-prophet?lang=eng (accessed August 18, 2015).
6 Bruce R. McConkie, "The Seven Deadly Heresies," delivered June 1, 1980, available at https://speeches.byu.edu/talks/bruce-r-mcconkie_seven-deadly-heresies/ (accessed August 18, 2015).
7 Bruce R. McConkie, *Mormon Doctrine*, 2nd ed. (Salt Lake City: Bookcraft), 608–609. For more on Joseph Fielding Smith's strong commitment to the authority of scripture, see Philip L. Barlow, *Mormons and the Bible: The Place of Latter-day Saints in American Religion*, updated ed. (New York: Oxford University Press, 2013), 133–141.
8 Letter from Bruce R. McConkie to Eugene England, February 19, 1981, p. 6; available online at http://www.eugeneengland.org/a-professor-and-apostle-correspond-eugene-england-and-bruce-r-mcconkie-on-the-nature-of-god (accessed August 24, 2015).
9 Brigham Young had his own running feud with apostle Orson Pratt over the relative authority of living prophets versus scriptures. See Barlow, *Mormons and the Bible*, 84–102; Gary J. Bergera, *Conflict in the Quorum: Orson Pratt, Brigham Young, Joseph Smith* (Salt Lake City: Signature Books, 2002).
10 Walter E.A. van Beek, "The Infallibility Trap: The Sacralisation of Religious Authority," *International Journal of Mormon Studies* 4 (2011): 14–44.
11 David E. Campbell, John C. Green, and J. Quin Monson, *Seeking the Promised Land: Mormons and American Politics* (New York: Cambridge University Press, 2014), chap. 6, quotes from 156–157.

12 *Teachings of the Prophet Joseph Smith*, sel. Joseph Fielding Smith (Salt Lake City: Deseret Book Co, 1976), 328.

13 Moroni 10:4–5, Book of Mormon.

14 Doctrine and Covenants 8:2–3.

15 For a detailed ethnographic exploration of this theme, see Tom Mould, *Still, the Small Voice: Narrative, Personal Revelation, and the Mormon Folk Tradition* (Logan: Utah State University Press, 2011).

16 Violence born of personal revelation is a major theme in Jon Krakauer, *Under the Banner of Heaven: A Story of Violent Faith* (New York: Anchor Books, 2004).

17 *A Book of Records: Containing the Proceedings of the Female Relief Society of Nauvoo*, p. 36 (April 28, 1842), available online at http://josephsmithpapers.org/paperSummary/nauvoo-relief-society-minute-book#!/paperSummary/nauvoo-relief-society-minute-book&p=33 (accessed August 24, 2015).

18 See Claudia Lauper Bushman, "Mystics and Healers," in *Mormon Sisters: Women in Early Utah*, ed. Claudia L. Bushman, new ed. (Logan: Utah State University Press, 1997), 1–23; Linda King Newell, "The Historical Relationship of Mormon Women and Priesthood," in *Women and Authority: Re-Emerging Mormon Feminism*, ed. Maxine Hanks (Salt Lake City: Signature Books, 1992), 23–48; Jonathan A. Stapley and Kristine Wright, "Female Ritual Healing in Mormonism," *Journal of Mormon History* 37:1 (Winter 2011): 1–85; Margaret M. Toscano, "Retrieving the Keys: Historical Milestones in LDS Women's Quest for Priesthood Ordination," in *Voices for Equality: Ordain Women and Resurgent Mormon Feminism*, eds. Gordon Shepherd, Lavina Fielding Anderson, and Gary Shepherd (Salt Lake City: Greg Kofford Books, 2015), 137–166.

19 Max Weber, *Economy and Society: An Outline of Interpretive Sociology*, eds. Guenther Roth and Claus Wittich (New York: Bedminster Press, 1968), 3:1111–1123. The routinization of charisma is related to "disenchantment," another dynamic Weber outlined at length, which can be summarized in a few words as the process by which "religion changes from magic to doctrine." Marianne Weber, quoted in Hans G. Kippenberg, "Religious Communities and the Path to Disenchantment: The Origins, Sources, and Theoretical Core of the Religion Section," in *Max Weber's "Economy and Society": A Critical Companion*, eds. Charles Camic, Philip S. Gorski, and David M. Trubek (Stanford, CA: Stanford University Press, 2005), 167. Both the "routinization of charisma" and "disenchantment" also apply in spheres beyond religion.

20 This is a significant theme in John G. Turner, *Brigham Young: Pioneer Prophet* (Cambridge, MA: Belknap Press of Harvard University Press, 2012).

21 Richard Lyman Bushman, *Joseph Smith: Rough Stone Rolling* (New York: Alfred A. Knopf, 2005), 251.

22 See Section 102 of the modern LDS Doctrine and Covenants.

23 Bushman, *Joseph Smith*, 256–258. See also Richard Lyman Bushman, "Joseph Smith and His Visions," in *The Oxford Handbook of Mormonism*, eds. Terryl L. Givens and Philip L. Barlow (New York: Oxford University Press, 2015), 109–120.

24 I refer here to the vision given to President Joseph F. Smith and related to the church in October 1918, which expanded the church's understanding of the

postmortal spirit world. The vision now appears as Section 138 in the LDS Doctrine and Covenants.

25 Thomas S. Monson, "Welcome to Conference," October 2012 General Conference, available at https://www.lds.org/general-conference/2012/10/welcome-to-conference?lang=eng (accessed August 26, 2015). It's worth watching the embedded video to see the brimming excitement of those in the audience upon hearing the announcement.

26 My discussion in this section is influenced by Michael McBride, "Authority in Mormonism: A Rational Choice Analysis," in *Directions for Mormon Studies in the Twenty-First Century*, ed. Patrick Q. Mason (Salt Lake City: University of Utah Press, 2016), 179–203.

27 Exceptions would include wards based on particular demographic characteristics, including singles wards, Polynesian wards, and Spanish-speaking wards. Even so, those wards have a particularly prescribed territory that they cover.

28 *Handbook 2: Administering the Church* (Salt Lake City: The Church of Jesus Christ of Latter-day Saints, 2010), available at https://www.lds.org/handbook/handbook-2-administering-the-church?lang=eng. There are actually two volumes of the Handbook, only the second of which is distributed widely and publicly available. Distribution of the first volume is limited to bishoprics, stake presidencies, and other senior priesthood leaders, and includes information particular to priesthood leadership callings, including procedures for church disciplinary courts.

29 Taunalyn Rutherford, "Indian Mormon Women: Naming the Self, the World, and God," paper delivered at Origins and Destinations: Forty Years of Mormon Women's Histor(ies) conference, Utah Valley University, Orem, Utah, August 9, 2014. See also Neylan McBaine, *Women at Church: Magnifying LDS Women's Local Impact* (Salt Lake City: Greg Kofford Books, 2014).

30 See http://www.mormonnewsroom.org/.

31 See Gregory A. Prince and Wm. Robert Wright, *David O. McKay and the Rise of Modern Mormonism* (Salt Lake City: University of Utah Press, 2005), 158.

32 Boyd K. Packer, "The Unwritten Order of Things," devotional address at Brigham Young University, October 15, 1996, available at http://emp.byui.edu/huffr/The%20Unwritten%20Order%20of%20Things%20—%20Boyd%20K.%20Packer.htm (accessed August 27, 2015).

33 See All Enlisted, "Wear Pants to Church Day," created December 9, 2012, https://www.facebook.com/WearPantsToChurchDay; Peggy Fletcher Stack, "Mormon 'Pants Day': Debate Heats up as Women Prepare to Dress Down," *Salt Lake Tribune*, December 13, 2012 (updated December 19, 2012), http://www.sltrib.com/sltrib/lifestyle/55464305–80/church-women-mormon-pants.html.csp (accessed August 27, 2015).

34 *Handbook 2*, section 2.2, available online at https://www.lds.org/handbook/handbook-2-administering-the-church/priesthood-principles?lang=eng#2.2 (accessed August 26, 2015).

35 *Handcart Trek Reenactments: Guidelines for Leaders* (Salt Lake City: The Church of Jesus Christ of Latter-day Saints, 2015), available online at https://www. lds.org/youth/activities/bc/pdfs/stake/Handcart-Trek-Guidelines-June-2015. pdf?lang=eng. See also Sara M. Patterson, "Everyone Can Be a Pioneer: The Sesquicentennial Celebrations of Mormon Arrival in the Salt Lake Valley," in *Out of Obscurity: Mormonism since 1945*, eds. Patrick Q. Mason and John G. Turner (New York: Oxford University Press, 2016), 302–317.

36 *Handcart Trek Reenactments*, 1.

37 Jan Shipps, *Mormonism: The Story of a New Religious Tradition* (Urbana: University of Illinois Press, 1985), xiii.

38 Doctrine and Covenants 21:1; Joseph Smith-History, Pearl of Great Price.

39 Shipps, *Mormonism*, 63.

40 For surveys and analysis, see whymormonsquestion.org and whymormonsleave.com.

41 "Gospel Topics Essays," available online at https://www.lds.org/topics/essays? lang=eng.

42 See Joanna Brooks, Rachel Hunt Steenblik, and Hannah Wheelwright, eds., *Mormon Feminism: Essential Writings* (New York: Oxford University Press, 2015); Hanks, *Women and Authority*.

43 See Lester E. Bush Jr., "Mormonism's Negro Doctrine: An Historical Overview," *Dialogue: A Journal of Mormon Thought* 8 (Spring 1973): 11–68.

44 See W. Paul Reeve, *Religion of a Different Color: Race and the Mormon Struggle for Whiteness* (New York: Oxford University Press, 2015), chap. 7.

45 Bushman, *Joseph Smith*, 510–511.

46 Turner, *Brigham Young*, 232–236; see also Bergera, *Conflict in the Quorum*.

47 Matthew Bowman, *The Mormon People: The Making of an American Faith* (New York: Random House, 2012), 156–157; Campbell, Green, and Monson, *Seeking the Promised Land*, 85; Brian Q. Cannon, "Mormons and the New Deal: The 1936 Presidential Election in Utah," *Utah Historical Quarterly* (Winter 1999): 4–22.

48 The definition of "apostasy" was expanded by the LDS Church leadership in late 2015 to include married same-sex couples, thus including many more people under that category. See Peggy Fletcher Stack, "New Mormon Edict on Gays Is a 'Policy,' Experts Note, and LDS Policies 'Come and Go,'" *Salt Lake Tribune*, November 11, 2015.

49 See Kristine Haglund, "Blogging the Boundaries: Mormon Mommy Blogs and the Construction of Mormon Identity," in *Out of Obscurity*, eds. Mason and Turner (New York: Oxford University Press, 2016), 234–256.

50 R. Scott Appleby, *The Ambivalence of the Sacred: Religion, Violence, and Reconciliation* (Lanham, MD: Rowman & Littlefield Publishers, 2000), 33.

7

Beliefs

For Joseph Smith, "creed" was a dirty word. In the official account of his First Vision, Smith reported that Jesus called Christianity's creeds "an abomination in his sight."[1] One of Smith's most famous letters, penned while languishing in Liberty Jail in March 1839 and later canonized in the Doctrine and Covenants, suggested that "murder, tyranny, and oppression" were inspired by the same evil spirit as "the creeds of the fathers."[2] In another prison letter written two days later, Smith more positively asserted that

> the first and fundamental principle of our holy religion is, that we believe that we have a right to embrace all, and every item of truth, without limitation or without being circumscribed or prohibited by the creeds of superstitious notions of men.[3]

Indeed, the previous year Smith had declared the difference between Mormonism and "other sects" was that "we believe the bible, and all other sects profess to believe their interpretations of the bible, and their creeds."[4] Summing up his position – and echoing his contemporary Ralph Waldo Emerson – Joseph Smith stated in an 1842 interview with the governor of Illinois, "I have no creed to circumscribe my mind, therefore the people do not like me because I do not, cannot circumscribe my mind to their creeds."[5]

In Smith's mind, one of the chief purposes of the gospel's restoration was to liberate believers from the shackles of theological and confessional creeds that had accumulated over the eighteen centuries of Christian history. Though he would often provide summaries of the Mormon religion in response to inquiries – most famously in thirteen Articles of Faith that have since been canonized[6] – Smith resisted any impulse toward systematic or dogmatic theology. Smith's resistance to creeds had at least three sources. First, he believed that religion was revelatory, open-ended, and unfolding, and thus could not be flash-frozen in a static confession. Second, so long as there were prophets, seers, and revelators on the earth, no council or creed could properly limit what God might say to the world today, tomorrow, or a century from now. The creeds of Christendom, from Nicaea to Westminster, were products of an age of apostasy, not revelation from heaven. Third, although Smith prioritized doctrinal teaching, he did not believe in imposing strict doctrinal litmus tests. When an elderly man was "hauled up for trial before the High Council" for teaching questionable interpretations of the Book of Revelation, Smith denounced the action. "I did not like the old man being called up for erring in doctrine," he told a conference of the church.

> It looks too much like the Methodist[s], and not like the Latter-day Saints. Methodists have creeds which a man must believe or be asked out of their church. I want the liberty of thinking and believing as I please. It feels so good not to be trammelled [*sic*]. It does not prove that a man is not a good man because he errs in doctrine.[7]

Smith's anti-creedalism was its own form of sectarianism, setting the Latter-day Saints apart as the only people truly free to listen to the revealed word of the Lord.

Though Mormonism has produced its fair share of systematic thinkers who have expounded at length on no shortage of distinctive Mormon doctrines, for its first two centuries, Mormonism has more or less remained "atheological." In other words, while Latter-day Saints "subscribe to a few basic doctrines . . . [and] accept general moral teachings, . . . they are without an official or even semi-official philosophy that explains and gives rational support to their beliefs and teachings." This is *not* to say that Mormons are irrational or that their beliefs cannot be defended with logical arguments. What it does mean is that while the church does have a set of core doctrinal beliefs that it would be difficult to imagine changing, the actual number of those absolutely essential propositions is rather short, and furthermore that church members who hold those core beliefs may disagree about their meaning or implications. Because of their belief in revelation, both prophetic and personal, Latter-day Saints have rarely shown much of an inclination for formal theology. Why get a theologian's interpretation, the logic goes, when you can simply get the word of God straight from a prophet or the Holy Ghost? Thus, in contrast to most Catholic and Protestant schools, at LDS Church-owned Brigham Young University, all students are required to take several courses in "Religious Education" but none in theology or philosophy. Operating principally in doctrinal, moralistic, and evangelistic modes, Mormons have typically cared far more about proclaiming and living out the gospel than thinking through the theological, philosophical, and epistemological grounds for it.[8]

The question, "What do Mormons believe?," is thus far more complicated than seems apparent, a fact that can be rather confusing for outsiders and insiders alike. What exactly counts for Mormon doctrine is a moving target, precisely because of the constant negotiations among the various sources of authority explicated in the previous chapter. Of course, Mormons are actually doing theology all the time: every time they teach a class, or give a talk, or agree or disagree with what they hear at General Conference. But in large part because of Joseph Smith's allergy to creeds, the major sources of authority in Mormonism – scriptures, prophets, and the Holy Ghost – are themselves subject to change and open to substantially varying interpretations. As scholar Matthew Bowman observes:

> there is no creed, catechism, or systematic theology to hold Mormonism to any fixed point, and therefore, the cluster of ideas that make up Mormon doctrine, all of which at some time or another seemed the unvarnished truth to some group of saints or another, is in a constant state of evolution.

What is sometimes seen (and experienced) as maddening inconsistency is actually a pragmatic openness to change that recognizes religion as an active construction zone and makes Mormonism, in this sense at least, a quintessentially modern form of religiosity.[9]

In spite of Mormonism's atheological creedlessness, it is possible to sketch out the foundational beliefs which the vast majority of Latter-day Saints would agree upon. While both believers and critics sometimes revel in Mormonism's esoteric doctrinal marginalia – for instance, Kolob as the name of the star closest to where God lives[10] – it is more helpful to focus on the central conceptual pillars of the Mormon belief system. Here we will focus in turn on the LDS concepts of God and humans; Jesus and salvation; agency; the church and priesthood; the Holy Ghost and spiritual gifts; family; the church and the world; and the life of devotion. Though these do not exhaust the range of Mormon belief, these categories will provide a composite window onto the Mormon worldview.

• GOD AND HUMANS

Mormon scripture, teaching, and devotional life are centered on the worship of the God of the Christian Bible. Following the pattern established by Jesus in the New Testament, Mormons frequently refer to God as "Heavenly Father," "Father in Heaven," or simply "Father," and address their prayers to him in those terms. The fatherhood of God is not metaphoric for Mormons. They believe that God is the actual father of their eternal spirits, which reside in and animate their physical bodies. Indeed, the most popular LDS children's song, often sung by adults as well, is called "I Am a Child of God":

> I am a child of God,
>
> And he has sent me here,
>
> Has given me an earthly home
>
> With parents kind and dear.
>
> Lead me, guide me, walk beside me,
>
> Help me find the way.
>
> Teach me all that I must do
>
> To live with him someday.

The Mormon God is not cold, unfeeling, or distant – he is eminently approachable and personal, befitting his identity as the father of human spirits. Mormons revere and worship God as lord over the entire universe, but also consider him to be a loving parent who is a real and intimate part of their personal lives.

Mormons debate the precise meaning of the terms, but for practical and devotional purposes, they consider God to be omniscient and omnipotent. His primary characteristic is love for his children, and his entire existence is oriented toward their eternal salvation and happiness. "For behold," God tells the prophet Moses in a revelation recorded by Joseph Smith, "this is my work and my glory – to bring to pass the immortality and eternal life of man."[11] If this depiction of God sounds rather conventional, especially to anyone even vaguely familiar with the Abrahamic God of Judaism, Christianity, and Islam, it's because it is. When Mormons pray to God, their functional idea of who and what he is differs little from other monotheists.

Yet the story doesn't end there. While Mormons share a similar language of God with other Christians, Jews, and Muslims, perhaps the single greatest doctrinal distinction between Mormonism and other Abrahamic faiths is the doctrine of God taught by Joseph Smith, especially in the final months of his life. In a handful of sermons, most famously the "King Follett Discourse" (preached at a funeral for a man named King Follett), Smith insisted that God and humanity were essentially members of the same species – that humans are not creatures fashioned by God but rather eternal "intelligences" that have always existed independently and can be neither created nor destroyed. Pursuing a radically straightforward reading of certain Bible verses, Smith developed an innovative notion of theosis or deification in which humans are on a path of eternal spiritual progression that follows the pattern set by God himself. This doctrine later found expression in the couplet coined by Lorenzo Snow, an early follower of Smith who later became the fifth president of the LDS Church: "As man now is, God once was; as God now is, man may become."[12]

One of Joseph Smith's most famous, and most controversial, sermons was delivered on April 7, 1844, and is commonly known as the "King Follett Discourse," after the man whose funeral Smith was preaching at. In it, Smith challenged nearly two millennia of Christian orthodoxy about the nature of God and humanity. Here are a few excerpts:

"What sort of a being was God in the beginning? . . . God himself was once as we are now, and is an exalted man, and sits enthroned in yonder heavens! That is the great secret. If the veil were rent today, and the great God who holds this world in its orbit, and who upholds all worlds and all things by his power, was to make himself visible – I say, if you were to see him today you would see him like a man in form – like yourselves in all the person, image, and very form as a man. . . .

"It is the first principle of the Gospel to know for a certainty the Character of God, and to know that we may converse with him as one man converses with another, and that he was once a man like us; yea, that God himself, the Father of us all, dwelt on an earth, the same as Jesus Christ himself did. . . .

"Here, then, is eternal life – to know the only wise and true God; and you have got to learn how to be Gods yourselves, and to be kings and priests to God, the same as all Gods have done before you, namely, by going from one small degree to another, and from a small capacity to a great one; from grace to grace, from exaltation to exaltation, until you attain to the resurrection of the dead, and are able to dwell in everlasting burnings, and to sit in glory, as do those who sit enthroned in everlasting power. . . .

"We say that God himself is a self-existent being. Who told you so? It is correct enough; but how did it get into your heads? Who told you that man did not exist in like manner upon the same principles? Man does exist upon the same principles. . . . The mind or the intelligence which man possesses is co-equal with God himself. . . . The intelligence of spirits had no beginning, neither will it have an end. That is good logic. That which has a beginning may have an end. There never was a time when there were not spirits; for they are co-equal with our Father in heaven. . . .

"The first principles of man are self-existent with God. God himself, finding he was in the midst of spirits and glory, because he was more intelligent, saw proper to institute laws whereby the rest could have a privilege to advance like himself. The relationship we have with God places us in a situation to advance in knowledge. He has power to institute laws to instruct the weaker intelligences, that they may be exalted with himself, so that they might have one glory upon another, and all that knowledge, power, glory, and intelligence, which is requisite in order to save them in the world of spirits."

(Joseph Smith, "Sermon Delivered April 7, 1844," in *American Sermons: The Pilgrims to Martin Luther King, Jr.* [New York: Library Classics of America, 1999], 587–593.)

This teaching of infinite and divine human potential is at the heart of Mormonism's profoundly optimistic orientation toward creation, humanity, and the cosmos. The ultimate goal for Mormons is not merely salvation but rather exaltation – that is, becoming gods themselves, though never supplanting God the Father. Smith was killed before he could fully spell out some of the specific ramifications of this teaching, and some Latter-day Saints have downplayed the centrality of theosis in Mormon theology, adhering instead to Smith's earlier revelations and scriptures (including the Book of Mormon) that portray a God more similar to the one worshiped by traditional Christians. Furthermore, in normal usage and day-to-day conversation, when Mormons talk about who God is and what he has done in their lives, their evident similarity to other believers in Abrahamic traditions is more real than ruse. Nevertheless, by the end of Smith's life, his theology of God had evolved into something new, rich with either cosmic possibility or damnable heresy depending on one's perspective. The King Follett Discourse's conception of the nature of God and his relationship to humanity, while controversial, remains a vital doctrine and pillar of the distinctive prophetic legacy of Joseph Smith.

In addition to a Heavenly Father, Mormons affirm the existence of a Heavenly Mother (or Mother in Heaven), who is the wife of God and the mother of human spirits. She does not formally appear in canonized LDS scripture, but she has been frequently mentioned in LDS sermons and verse.[13] Her most famous foray onto the stage of Mormon consciousness, which both introduced her into popular Mormon thought and keeps her fixed there, comes in an oft-sung hymn somewhat ironically titled "O My Father." The hymn was originally written as a poem by Eliza R. Snow and published in the church's newspaper in 1845, a year after Joseph Smith's death. Snow was one of nineteenth-century Mormonism's most intrepid women, a plural wife of both Smith and Brigham Young, president of the Relief Society in Utah, and the religion's most lauded early poet. When a collection of Snow's poems were published in 1856, this selection appeared first, under the heading "Invocation, or The Eternal Father and Mother" – a title that contemporary Mormon feminists often prefer for its gender inclusiveness.

The third and fourth verses of Eliza R. Snow's 1845 poem "My Father in Heaven," later made into the hymn "O My Father," are among the most popular sources for LDS teaching about Heavenly Mother.

I had learn'd to call thee father,
Through thy spirit from on high,
But until the key of knowledge
Was restor'd, I knew not why.
In the heav'ns are parents single?
No, the thought makes reason stare;
Truth is reason – truth eternal
Tells me I've a mother there.
When I leave this frail existence –
When I lay this mortal by,
Father, mother, may I meet you

In your royal court on high?
Then, at length, when I've completed
All you sent me forth to do,
With your mutual approbation
Let me come and dwell with you.

(Eliza R. Snow, "My Father in Heaven," *Times and Seasons*,
November 15, 1845, 1039)

Despite their frequent affirmation of her existence, LDS leaders have warned church members against speculating about, worshiping, or praying to Heavenly Mother. The church excommunicated a handful of Mormon feminists in the early 1990s for publicly advocating for a more robust role for Heavenly Mother in LDS worship and theology. But she won't go away. In recent years there has been something of a resurgence of discussion about Heavenly Mother, mostly but not exclusively among Mormon women, both in private and public. It is not uncommon to hear her mentioned, if not dwelt upon, in Mormon meetings.

Heavenly Mother's ambiguous place in Mormonism was perfectly encapsulated in the church's 1995 proclamation "The Family: A Proclamation to the World." The document's second paragraph reads: "All human beings – male and female – are created in the image of God. Each is a beloved spirit son or daughter of heavenly parents, and, as such, each has a divine nature and destiny."[14] The traditional formulation "I Am a Child of God" is here replaced by the more precise doctrinal affirmation that human spirits are sons and daughters of heavenly parents, plural – though Heavenly Mother is not explicitly named. The Mother's existence is simultaneously affirmed and obscured. Inasmuch as she is present in the proclamation, however, the character of her existence seems limited to simply giving birth to spirit children. Indeed, the proclamation's next paragraph mentions how God the Father offered a plan of salvation to his children and is in turn worshiped by them, and that the goal of human existence is to "return to the presence of God." The text is entirely silent about the Mother's role in saving her children, being worshiped by them, or reuniting with them upon their exaltation in heaven. In short, the elusive figure of Heavenly Mother offers Mormons a tantalizing but contested resource for discussions regarding the divine feminine and the place of women within the Mormon plan of salvation.

Latter-day Saints teach that God the Father possesses "a body of flesh and bones" that is "as tangible as man's" yet perfected and incorruptible.[15] The materialism of Mormon theology, including the corporeality of God and the rejection of a Triune God consisting of multiple persons sharing one substance, marks one of its most significant departures from creedal Christian orthodoxy. It also opens up Mormons to the charge that they are not monotheists. Strictly speaking, this is true, as Mormons not only acknowledge the existence of innumerable gods in the cosmos but also insist that God, Jesus, and the Holy Spirit, all of whom they worship as members of the Godhead, are three separate persons, wholly united in purpose but distinct in substance and being. If confronted about the issue, Mormons will typically insist that they are in fact monotheists who worship the God of the Bible. This is not so much an evasion on their part as a failure to have any better linguistic options, since "polytheism" and "atheism" – the two other popularly recognized alternatives – are even further from their actual position than is classical monotheism.[16] In short, Mormons are pragmatic monotheists even if their actual theology is rather more complicated than that.

• JESUS AND SALVATION

In conjunction with their belief in God the Father, Mormons emphatically believe in and worship Jesus Christ. Especially since the late twentieth century, much ink has been spilled on the polemical question "Are Mormons Christian?" The ensuing discussion has typically generated more heat than light, but answering the question comes down to a matter of definition: What, precisely, is a Christian? Is a Christian someone who exercises faith in and devotion to Jesus of Nazareth as Son of God and Savior of humanity? Or to be labeled a Christian must a person subscribe to specific beliefs and adhere to certain traditions that descend from a particular historical-theological genealogy – namely the early Christian church councils at Nicaea, Constantinople, Ephesus, and Chalcedon? It suffices to say that Mormons certainly qualify under the first definition, but not under the second, especially given Joseph Smith's rejection of the historic Christian creeds.

The apparent dilemma of which box to put Mormons in may be solved most easily by referencing the LDS Church's official name: The Church of Jesus Christ of Latter-day Saints. In other words, Mormons are sincere followers of Jesus Christ, but they believe that the entire Christian church fell into apostasy shortly after the death of the apostles, thereby necessitating a restoration (not Reformation) of "true" Christianity, of which they are the standard bearers in these "latter days." Scholars debate whether to categorize Mormons as a fourth Abrahamic religion (alongside Judaism, Christianity, and Islam), as an entirely new world religious tradition (along Christianity, Islam, Hinduism, Buddhism, and all the rest), or as a separate branch of Christianity (alongside Roman Catholicism, Orthodoxy, Protestantism, and perhaps Pentecostalism). Though the religion will continue to evolve in the coming centuries, at this juncture it seems that the third option – Mormonism as a distinctive branch of world Christianity – is the most accurate description, precisely because of the centrality of Jesus Christ in Mormon theology, worship, and culture.[17]

Indeed, it is impossible to avoid Jesus Christ in modern Mormonism. In his study of Mormon theology, Catholic philosopher Stephen Webb noted:

> In affirming the divinity of Jesus, Mormons are Christians who do not know where to stop. Mormon rhetoric is guided by the conviction that the only way to say enough about Christ is to say too much. . . . Mormon theology is Christology unbound.[18]

Indeed, Mormons love to quote the Book of Mormon passage:

> And we talk of Christ, we rejoice in Christ, we preach of Christ, we prophesy of Christ, and we write according to our prophecies, that our children may know to what source they may look for a remission of their sins.[19]

Whereas a casual purveyor of Mormon art, music, and sermons from a century ago may have surmised that Mormons primarily revered Joseph Smith and their pioneer ancestors, in recent decades Jesus Christ has taken his place squarely at the center of Mormon spiritual sensibilities, thanks in large part to a renewed emphasis on the highly Christ-centered Book of Mormon.[20] Contemporary Mormons talk about feeling the love of Jesus, and the principal doctrinal touchstone for LDS curriculum and ministry is the atonement of Jesus Christ. Commonly quoted is this statement by Joseph Smith:

> The fundamental principles of our religion is [*sic*] the testimony of the apostles and prophets concerning Jesus Christ, "that he died, was buried, and rose again the third day, and ascended up into heaven"; and all other things are only appendages to these, which pertain to our religion.[21]

Mormons believe that in a premortal existence (or "preexistence") in which humans lived with God as spirits before being born on earth, God anticipated human sinfulness and implemented what Mormons refer to as the "Plan of Salvation" – namely, that Jesus would be sent to earth as a Savior and would atone for the sins of the world. Through his vicarious suffering in the Garden of Gethsemane and on the cross, Jesus repaired the relationship between humanity and God and achieved perfect empathy with the totality of human sin and sorrow. Mormons have typically subscribed to a substitutionary view of atonement, meaning that Jesus mercifully took upon himself the punishment that sinful humans justly deserved, but other interpretations are allowable. Most Mormons spend little time considering the finer theological points of how Christ's atonement works, simply affirming that it does, and that salvation is available to all humanity through Jesus's suffering, death, and resurrection.

Latter-day Saints affirm that Jesus Christ's triumph over death through his bodily resurrection guarantees that all human beings will likewise be resurrected from the grave with a physical but now immortal body. The Book of Mormon is particularly insistent on this point, teaching that "all shall be raised from this temporal death. The spirit and the body shall be reunited again in its perfect form; both limb and joint shall be restored to its proper frame, even as we now are at this time."[22] Mormons believe that the resurrection is a free gift to all humans – the good, the bad, and the ugly – thanks to the grace of Jesus Christ. The universal resurrection reveals both the mercy and justice of God – since individual humans did nothing to deserve their inevitable fate of death, Christ ultimately rescues them from permanent annihilation without requiring any effort of their own.

So we will all live again, according to Mormon theology. The question remains, what will the quality and nature of that life be? When it comes to salvation, Mormonism comes very close to universalism – that is, the notion that all people receive some measure of salvation and none are condemned to never-ending punishment. God's love is extended to all his children, and it is theoretically possible for all people to accept Christ's atonement and thus be cleansed of their sins, reconciled with God, and readmitted into the presence of God to become like him. In one of his most important revelations, Joseph Smith envisioned a multi-tiered division of heaven, an expansion of the traditional Christian heaven-hell dichotomy. The revelation taught that the most righteous people who accept Christ, obey his commandments, and receive necessary priesthood ordinances such as baptism find their place in the "celestial kingdom," which is where God and Jesus reside, families are united for eternity, and eternal progression toward godhood is possible. Reaching the celestial kingdom, which is also referred to as "eternal life" and "exaltation," is the central spiritual goal for Mormons. Good and honorable people who do not accept the full message of the gospel inhabit the "terrestrial kingdom," while the truly wicked (including murders, adulterers, and blasphemers) still receive a "degree of glory" in the "telestial kingdom." Only Satan and his angels are ultimately excluded from God's light and glory, as they are relegated to "outer darkness."[23] A 1918 revelation to church president Joseph F. Smith showed that humans are given additional opportunities even after their death to accept the gospel and thus to inherit a higher glory than they might have merited with their life on earth.[24]

This salvation narrative, including its particular architecture of heaven, is frequently drawn by Mormon missionaries and Sunday School teachers with a series of circles and boxes resembling a horizontal organizational chart (see Figure 7.1). Necessarily oversimplified, the chart seeks to illustrate the progression of human spirits from our premortal existence until, hopefully, our final destiny and reunion with God in the celestial kingdom. Along the way we pass through a "veil of forgetfulness" – explaining why we don't remember our premortal existence – and come to earth to gain a physical body and life experience. After death, our spirits reside for an unspecified time in the "spirit world" as we await our bodily resurrection. At that point, we are judged and assigned to one of the three degrees of glory. Though not often depicted explicitly in this simplified drawing, the role of Jesus Christ is central throughout the entire process, as he is regarded by Mormons to be the creator of the world, the savior and redeemer of our souls, the means by which we are resurrected, and our advocate before God at the final judgment.

THE PLAN OF SALVATION

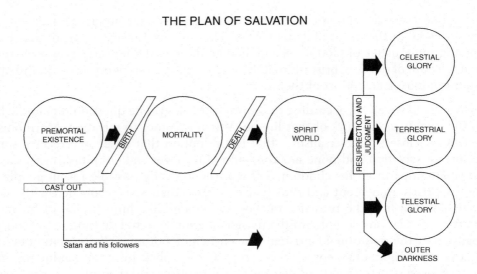

FIGURE 7.1 Graphic depiction of the plan of salvation as taught by the LDS Church. Drawings similar to this, providing a visual representation of LDS cosmology, are frequently used in church lessons and by LDS missionaries in teaching investigators.

• AGENCY

One of the central doctrines of Mormonism is agency, often referred to as "moral agency" or "free agency." Embracing what philosopher Sterling McMurrin called "a life-affirming positive conception of the nature of man," Mormons reject the notion of original sin in which the moral stain of the fall of Adam and Eve is imputed to all humanity from the moment of their conception or birth.[25] The church's second Article of Faith states, "We believe that men will be punished for their own sins, and not for Adam's transgression." All children come into this world sinless and remain pure in the eyes of God until the "age of accountability" (eight years old), at which point they are eligible for baptism. The sad fact is that all humans do sin, meaning that they, of their own free will, separate themselves from the perfect character of God. (The one exception is Jesus, who lived a perfectly righteous life.) Although human behavior is constrained and influenced by a multitude of factors, all humans – excepting young children and the mentally impaired – are accountable for their own actions, according to their capacities and the degree of their moral instruction. The inviolability of moral agency is thoroughly upheld by God, who compels neither humans' choices nor their eternal destiny.[26]

It would be difficult to underestimate the significance of agency in Mormon theology; it is as central as predestination was to sixteenth- and seventeenth-century

Calvinism. Sterling McMurrin captures this fact in observing, "at every turn of Mormon theological discussion the fact of moral freedom and its implied moral responsibility must be met and accounted for." Indeed:

> the assumption that man is characterized essentially by freedom of will is so commonplace in all Mormon thought that arguments defending the attribution of free will to man after the fall are virtually unknown in the literature. Freedom is taken more or less for granted; not simply the freedom to do evil, but the full freedom of alternative action, the power of choice between good and evil.[27]

For Mormons, agency is existential, and inherent in their very being. In Latter-day Saint cosmology, life does not begin at the moment of birth or even conception. Rather, each human is at their core a spiritual being with no beginning and no end, having existed eternally in the premortal existence. The precise nature of this premortal existence remains largely unexplained – though Mormons have frequently imagined what it must have been like, often incorporating campy romantic notions about two premortal beings promising to find one another on earth. The one thing that is doctrinally certain is that our premortal spirits had intelligence and agency, which we used to make a choice to follow God and Christ, who offered to preserve human agency, rather than the devil (Satan or Lucifer), who according to Mormon scripture not only rebelled against God but also "sought to destroy the agency of man."[28] The implications of this foundational theological and ontological commitment to human moral agency are deep and wide. Most substantially, it makes humans active co-participants with Christ in their own salvation and exaltation. Christ's atonement, while utterly necessary not only in offering reconciliation but also in providing the very grounds of moral action, is ultimately insufficient (except for those who are not morally accountable). As a revelation to Joseph Smith stated, the freedom given to humanity in its mortal condition allows "that every man may act in doctrine and principle pertaining to futurity, according to the moral agency which I [God] have given unto him, that every man may be accountable for his own sins in the day of judgment."[29] Agency and accountability are thus two sides of the same coin, which is in many ways the main currency of the Mormon worldview.

● THE CHURCH AND PRIESTHOOD

Although salvation and exaltation are available to all, Mormons believe, there are conditions that must be met to receive the full complement of divine blessings and eternal joy. Many of these conditions are mediated by membership and participation in the Church of Jesus Christ of Latter-day Saints. Faith in and commitment to Jesus Christ is formally expressed in Mormonism through the ordinance of baptism by immersion. Like other Christians, Mormons are baptized in the name of the Father, the Son, and the Holy Ghost. However, because of doctrinal disagreements, most other Christian churches do not recognize Mormon baptisms as legitimate, and Mormons likewise require converts who have previously been baptized in another Christian church to be rebaptized by a Mormon priesthood holder. Baptism is followed in turn by confirmation as a member of the Church of Jesus Christ of Latter-day Saints. Membership in the church is considered essential for entrance into the celestial kingdom, though provisions are made for those who are not baptized and confirmed in this life (see the section on temples in the next chapter). The confirmation ordinance also bestows on the recipient the "gift of the Holy Ghost," understood as promising that the believer can have the "constant companionship" (and thus inspiration) of the Holy Spirit, predicated upon their personal righteousness. Baptism and confirmation are typically performed only once in a person's life. Mormons emphasize the importance of "enduring to the end," which connotes of a lifetime of godly striving and a lasting commitment to "keep the commandments."

Mormonism is a sacramental religion in which the ordinances of the church are administered by an ordained priesthood, which is available to all males age twelve and older. Mormons believe they are following the pattern established by Jesus, who according to the New Testament called his twelve disciples and other followers and then sent them out to do his work. In the Mormon view of history, the priesthood – defined by Mormons as the power and authority of God – was lost with the death of Jesus's apostles and therefore not passed on to new generations of believers, who maintained the church but without legitimate priesthood authority. The lack of proper priesthood authority is one of Mormonism's main claims against other Christian churches. Mormons assert that ordinances such as baptism must be performed by a properly ordained priesthood holder; if conducted by any other person, no matter how sincere, the ordinance is invalid in the eyes of God. One of Joseph Smith's earliest theological insights was that priesthood authority was not to be found on the earth and needed to be restored. About the time that he was completing his Book of Mormon translation and founding the church, Smith and a select group of other early believers reported that they were visited by the New Testament prophet John the Baptist and apostles Peter, James, and John – now angels – who laid their hands on the heads of Smith and his associates and conferred on them the long-lost priesthood authority.

Everyone called to serve in various official church capacities, from the highest echelons of leadership to the pianist for children's singing time in a local ward, are "set apart" as priesthood leaders lay their hands upon the person's head and offer a special prayer – called "the laying on of hands." Because of the bestowal of priesthood authority to all men who comply with church teachings and standards, all leadership positions at the local level are handled by lay volunteers rather than a professional clergy. Mormon priesthood is thus simultaneously highly democratic (for men) and extremely hierarchical, as church callings and ordinations are always received at the hands of supervising priesthood leaders.

Mormonism is a restorationist religion. As indicated above, Mormons believe that Jesus established a church before his death, but that the early Christian church soon fell into apostasy. The LDS narrative of apostasy is more theological than historical, and thus does not point to particular moments or figures that clearly marked the transition from the true church to an apostate form of it. Nevertheless, once the apostasy set in, Mormons believe that centuries passed in which Christianity survived but without proper priesthood authority and with increasingly corrupted doctrines and practices. Reforming the church was not sufficient, as authority was absent and certain truths were lost entirely. In the LDS understanding of salvation history, Joseph Smith technically did not start a new church, but rather restored Christ's ancient church. The emerging Church of Jesus Christ of Latter-day Saints based its organization primarily on an unfolding set of revelations to Smith, rather than on a careful reading and application of the New Testament, as was the case with other nineteenth-century restorationists such as Alexander Campbell. Nevertheless, the basic organization of the LDS Church does include, at least superficially, most of the same offices and titles referred to in the New Testament.

In contrast to the findings of modern biblical scholarship, most Mormons assert that first-century Christians were all part of a unified, hierarchical church presided over by the apostles, Peter at the head. Just like the modern LDS Church, various levels of priesthood hierarchy were organized under the apostles, with local members ordained to discrete offices – pastor, teacher, evangelist, etc. – by their priesthood leaders. In truth, this interpretation of early Christian ecclesiology says far more about modern Mormonism than it does about first-century Christianity, but the reputed parallels in institutional organization between the "primitive" and "latter-day" churches have traditionally been an important part of apologetic Mormon arguments for the authenticity and divine mission of the restored church.[30]

• THE HOLY GHOST AND SPIRITUAL GIFTS

The third member of the Mormon Godhead – not Trinity – is the Holy Ghost or Holy Spirit. Technically Mormons worship the Holy Spirit as a member of the Godhead, but the language and rituals of LDS worship are in practice oriented more toward God the Father and Jesus Christ. The Holy Ghost is the messenger of God who communicates divine truth and comfort to humans. Mormons pray to God the Father in the name of Jesus Christ, then answers to prayers come via the Holy Spirit. They typically speak of "feeling" the influence of the Holy Ghost in either their hearts or minds. In addressing any range of problems, from theological questions to career choices to interpersonal relationships, Mormons will typically advise one another simply to seek personal revelation and "follow the Spirit," truly believing in the power of prayers heard and answered by a personal God through the Holy Ghost. Most of the inspiration received on a day-to-day basis, whether by the church's leaders or ordinary members, concerns relatively mundane matters, though it may seem momentous to the person at the time. Members will often share spiritual experiences with one another, but they will also guard particularly precious moments of inspiration as sacred and private.

Mormons believe in and exercise spiritual gifts. Early Mormons displayed a range of charismatic spiritual gifts that are typically associated more with modern Pentecostalism. They believed that the presence and exercise of such gifts was a sign that God had opened the heavens and restored his true church on the earth again, complete with the same miraculous power that attended the early Christians in the biblical Acts of the Apostles. On one level Joseph Smith encouraged such gifts, as he too saw them as signs of the power of God made manifest through his restored church. However, almost immediately Smith also implemented constraints on the use of certain gifts. For instance, in response to some early followers who claimed that they too were receiving revelations from God for the church, Smith dictated a revelation unequivocally stating that only the president and prophet of the church would speak for God to the whole church. Smith similarly sought to limit what he saw as excesses in the display of some spiritual gifts. Brigham Young, an early speaker in tongues and participant in ritual healings, eventually also worked to quell the ecstatic display of gifts.

Today, Mormons insist that spiritual gifts are real and that God continues to work in the world in miraculous ways. For the most part, however, the enthusiasm of the early Saints has been substantially constrained. The gift of tongues, for instance, is now typically thought of as enabling missionaries who have been called to serve in foreign lands to better learn the native language. Priesthood holders anoint with oil and administer to the sick by the laying on of hands, but Mormons also rely on modern medicine as much or more than on the miraculous power of God. Mormon worship services are the very opposite of ecstatic. Speakers will often become emotional and cry while sharing personal experiences or testimony, but anything more demonstrative would not be deemed culturally appropriate.

When it comes to spiritual gifts, then, Mormons walk a fine line. On the one hand they agree with the Book of Mormon prophet Moroni, who condemns those "who deny the revelations of God, and say that they are done away, that there are no revelations, nor prophecies, nor gifts, nor healing, nor speaking with tongues, and the interpretation of tongues."[31] On the other hand, Mormons would be dubious of anyone whose zeal seems not tempered with middle-class decorum, and particularly suspicious of anyone whose spiritual experiences do not correlate easily with current church teaching and practice. Despite its ecstatic beginnings, within the LDS Church spiritual charisma has been thoroughly domesticated and routinized.

• THE FAMILY

Families are a human universal. Mormons, however, have elevated the family far beyond its terrestrial significance to constitute the basic order of heaven. Early Mormon teaching was similar to contemporaneous Protestantism in emphasizing the relationship of individuals to God, but in the closing years of his life, Joseph Smith gradually developed a theology that correlated salvation and exaltation with the eternal persistence of familial and other social relationships. In Nauvoo, Smith introduced an elaborate temple ceremony (explained in greater detail in the following chapter) that culminated in the "sealing" of husbands and wives "for time and all eternity." These eternal couples would enjoy "eternal increase," meaning not only the permanent binding of earthly parents and their children but also the continued expansion of family relationships into the infinite future. The fatherhood of God is a literal familial connection to be emulated and extended; the destiny of a Mormon man and woman, sealed together in eternal unity, is to become like and do the work of their own Heavenly Father and Mother. Exaltation in Mormonism is thus fundamentally about sociality, kinship, and interdependence – in short, to be exalted is to be a member of and ultimately at the head of an eternal family.

Since the 1840s, then, Latter-day Saints have constructed a theology with family at the heart. The content, form, and meaning of that family-centered theology has changed significantly over the years, with nineteenth-century ideas of familial plurality and spiritual adoption replaced in the twentieth century with a more conventional commitment to the heterosexual, monogamous nuclear family.[32] For most of the twentieth century, the Mormon family tracked well with broader American notions, and Mormonism's family-centeredness became one of its chief vehicles for cultural mainstreaming. When the culture began to shift in the closing decades of the twentieth century, however, Mormons found themselves, along with other religious conservatives, fighting what amounted to a rearguard action to preserve "the traditional family" from the changes associated primarily with feminism and gay rights.[33] What had been a point of continuity between Mormonism and Euro-American culture now emerged as the site of heated conflict.

It was in this context of the "culture wars" that the LDS Church leadership issued "The Family: A Proclamation to the World" in 1995. In it, the church "solemnly proclaim[ed] that marriage between a man and a woman is ordained of God and that the family is central to the Creator's plan for the eternal destiny of His children." The proclamation declared that family relationships were a part of God's plan from the beginning, and that God's commandment to Adam and Eve in the Garden of Eden "for His children to multiply and replenish the earth remains in force." At the same time, the church warned that "the powers of procreation" are sacred, "to be employed only between man and woman, lawfully wedded as husband and wife." Once children were introduced into the family – again, it was emphasized, "within the bonds of matrimony" – fathers and mothers were charged with

> a sacred duty to rear their children in love and righteousness, to provide for their physical and spiritual needs, and to teach them to love and serve one another, observe the commandments of God, and be law-abiding citizens wherever they live.

Fathers and mothers had separate and complementary roles in accomplishing these divinely appointed goals. The proclamation asserted that "By divine design, fathers are to preside over their families in love and righteousness and are responsible to provide the necessities of life and protection for their families." Mothers, on the other hand, "are primarily responsible for the nurture of their children." Both roles were essential and of equal importance, with husbands and wives "obligated to help one another as equal partners." While extenuating circumstances might of necessity force "individual adaptation," the divine pattern and ideal was made clear. The proclamation ended on a stern note, warning that those who are unchaste, abusive, or neglectful of family obligations would "one day stand accountable before God." Furthermore, governments were called upon to do all in their power "to maintain and strengthen the family as the fundamental unit of society," with disastrous consequences – "the calamities foretold by ancient and modern prophets" – waiting in store if they failed to do so.[34]

The Family Proclamation, as it is typically referred to by Latter-day Saints, has been a centerpiece of Mormon teaching and discourse for the two decades since its issuance. Though only one page long, it has proven remarkably useful in speaking to a wide range of LDS doctrines, practices, policies, and ongoing debates, from conservative legal defenses of heterosexual marriage to progressive calls for more egalitarian family arrangements and family leave laws. While doctrinaire in tone and clearly meant to end rather than engender disagreements, the proclamation's brevity has lent itself to ongoing questions and alternative, even competing, interpretations. For instance, many commentators have wondered what exactly it means when the proclamation asserts, "Gender is an essential characteristic of individual premortal, mortal, and eternal identity and purpose." Also widely discussed is the seeming contradiction between the guidance that fathers "preside" while in the same paragraph fathers and mothers are urged to work as "equal partners." A recurring question is whether the proclamation essentialized the particular, in other words taking a model of family life dominant in mid-twentieth-century America and making it the norm for all times, places, and cultures. Some have noted the cursory mention of extended families – they "should lend support when needed" – as either a slight toward or parochial neglect of the centrality of extended kinship networks in many cultures around the world. Others wonder whether idealizing a household dependent solely on a father's income reinforces patriarchy or ignores global economic realities in which dual incomes are a necessity for large swaths of the world's population, increasingly the case even among the working and middle classes in developed nations.

The vast majority of Latter-day Saints are personally committed to the church's stated norms of heterosexual marriage, although a growing minority do not share their leaders' fears about the existential threats posed by homosexuality and gay marriage. Polls suggest a substantial upward trend in the percentage of Latter-day Saints who believe that homosexuality should be socially accepted, at the same time that Mormons are more likely than any other religious group to want their religion to "preserve traditional beliefs and practices" rather than adjust to modern life and culture.[35] These seemingly divergent trends suggest internal contestation within the LDS Church about how to define and apply its family-centered theology in the twenty-first century. One Mormon theologian has controversially sketched out what a "post-heterosexual Mormon theology" might look like, but as of 2015 any substantial institutional change in that regard remains virtually inconceivable.[36] In short, Mormons' deep-seated and theologically informed commitment to family remains one of its most distinctive characteristics, and one that continues to produce both internal and external cohesion and conflict.

• THE CHURCH AND THE WORLD

Mormons are millennialists. They believe in an eschaton in which Jesus Christ will return to earth in a glorious Second Coming that will be preceded by a period of violence and chaos but followed by a thousand-year reign of peace and righteousness (called "the Millennium"). Christ will appear, according to the Book of Mormon and Joseph Smith's revelations, both in the "old" Jerusalem (in Palestine) and in a "New Jerusalem" that will be built on the American continent. Joseph Smith revealed the site of this New Jerusalem to be in Jackson County on the western border of Missouri. Millenarian teaching and speculation figured prominently in the nineteenth-century LDS Church; indeed, the official designation of church members as *Latter-day* Saints denotes the belief that humanity currently lives in the final period before Christ's return to the earth. Though church members will often speak of "preparing for the Second Coming," much of the urgency of this discourse has ebbed as Mormons have eased into the cultural mainstream. Millennialism is a far more useful rhetorical and theological tool for those on the margins of society than those at or near the center.

Declining millenarian fervor notwithstanding, the Church of Jesus Christ of Latter-day Saints considers part of its core mission to be preparing the earth for Christ's return. This preparation is accomplished principally through evangelizing those who have not yet heard the gospel – thus, the massive missionary effort maintained by the church since its early days. Joseph Smith taught that God's ancient covenants with the House of Israel, as recorded in the Old Testament and extended in the Book of Mormon, remain intact but are primarily mediated now through the restored Church of Jesus Christ. Biblical prophecies about the gathering of the lost tribes of Israel are largely fulfilled, in the Mormon worldview, by bringing people into the church.

Mormons believe that they are members of the House of Israel. Mormon rhetoric frequently divides the world between righteous "Israel" (which Mormons primarily equate with the church, and only secondarily with the State of Israel or the Jewish people) and benighted "Gentiles" (which in Mormon parlance means non-members of the church). Jews are honored as a remnant of the tribe of Judah, and Mormons feel a special kinship to their Israelite "cousins." This purported kinship is typically not reciprocated by Jews, who interpret Mormon assertions of Israelite identity as merely amusing, quaint, or mildly offensive. All baptized members of the church are eligible to receive a personalized inspired pronouncement called a "patriarchal blessing" that informs them which of the twelve tribes of Israel they are a member of. Especially in the nineteenth century, this notion of "Israelite" or "believing blood" was an important element of Mormon thought, in many ways related to and inspired by the British Israelism movement.[37] Though patriarchal blessings are still given throughout the church, and often represent a kind of coming-of-age ritual for many Mormon teenagers, internal LDS rhetoric about the House of Israel, like millennialism, has declined precipitously in recent years and is now a minor theme at best.

If millennialism and Israelism have declined somewhat in contemporary Mormonism, the issue of religious freedom has more than taken their place as a dominant theme in the twenty-first century. Strongly conditioned by their own experiences of persecution, especially in Missouri and Illinois in the 1830s and 1840s, as well as by their doctrine of the inviolable agency of each human soul, Mormons have been fierce proponents of religious freedom. For most of the nineteenth century this took the form of self-pleading, most notably in the opposition to federal anti-polygamy legislation, but Mormons also made substantial gestures of religious liberality toward other groups. In July 1843 Joseph Smith stated:

> I am bold to declare before Heaven that I am just as ready to die in defending the rights of a Presbyterian, a Baptist, or a good man of any other denomination; for the same principle which would trample upon the rights of the Latter-day Saints would trample upon the rights of the Roman Catholics, or any other denomination who may be unpopular and too weak to defend themselves.[38]

In recent years Mormon legislators have been among the chief architects and proponents of federal statutes that make the extension and preservation of religious liberty an official plank of U.S. foreign policy. This commitment to religious freedom does not impinge on the church's missionary zeal. To the contrary, it fuels it, as Mormons have always been confident that their ideas will prevail in a free marketplace of religious ideas.

Since the mid-2000s, LDS Church leaders have become increasingly concerned with domestic religious freedom in the United States and Europe, particularly in light of the legalization of same-sex marriage (accomplished nationwide in the United States in the 2015 Supreme Court decision *Obergefell v. Hodges*). Predicated upon their theological commitments to the "traditional" family, Mormons actively opposed marriage-equality initiatives in Hawaii, California, and other states. As it became increasingly clear that the tide of public and judicial opinion was against them, LDS leaders retreated to a position of asserting the church's right not to solemnize or otherwise religiously recognize marriages that it objects to on doctrinal grounds. In its efforts to defend heterosexual marriage, the LDS Church has built coalitions with other likeminded religious groups and leaders, community and legal organizations, scholars, and politicians. Critics have noted the historical irony that Mormons cited religious freedom in advocating for their own right to practice an alternative form of marriage in the nineteenth century, and then used religious freedom arguments to oppose another alternative form of marriage in the twenty-first century.

The deeply felt Mormon commitment to religious freedom does not fully extend to the protection of dissent within the church. In 1999 an apostle declared in General Conference that "in the Lord's Church there is no such thing as a 'loyal opposition.' One is either for the kingdom of God and stands in defense of God's prophets and apostles, or one stands opposed."[39] Strong statements like this contribute to a general ethic of public uniformity among members of the church on matters of doctrine and practice. Nevertheless, there exists a marked degree of ideological and even theological diversity among church members which has flowered especially with the advent of the Internet and social media. Church leaders continue to insist, however, that only the prophets and apostles have the right to define doctrine for the church, and that while no one is compelled to believe or agree with church teachings, those who voluntarily affiliate with the church have a responsibility not to publicly disagree with, let alone disavow, the church's basic teachings and authority structures.

As an Article of Faith, Latter-day Saints "believe in being subject to kings, presidents, rulers, and magistrates in obeying, honoring, and sustaining the law."[40] This typically makes Mormons excellent citizens in whatever country they reside. This loyalty comes not only from the value they place on clean living, thrift, and neighborliness, but also from their healthy respect for government and governments, which translates into civic pride and participation. Mormon teachings about citizenship have frequently included a belief, supported by early revelations to Joseph Smith, that the Constitution of the United States was, to some degree, inspired by God (though no Mormon claims the sanctity of the three-fifths clause). According to LDS scripture, the ideal civil government is broadly democratic in nature, accountable to its own people, and committed to the guarantee of freedom and basic rights (preeminently religious liberty), but the actual form of government matters less than the principles undergirding it. Despite its strong commitment to democratic principles, the church has encouraged is members to be law-abiding citizens even in non-democratic states – a pragmatic practice that has protected the church and its adherents but also sometimes led to ambivalent moral positions such as in Nazi Germany.[41] Although American Mormons have become overwhelming conservative over the course of the past century, finding themselves on the "right" side of the nation's culture wars, in other nations Mormons comfortably fit within socialist and other left-leaning parties, finding complete harmony between their Mormon identity and liberal politics.

There is occasionally tension between Mormons' allegiance to the secular nation-state and the "kingdom of God." This was most pronounced during the nineteenth-century conflict over the Mormons' insistence on their right to practice plural marriage. Since that crisis was resolved (by making church practice conform to the law of the land), Latter-day Saints have rarely engaged in civil disobedience or conscientious objection. Some have predicted an impending crisis for the church if the U.S. or other governments take away the religious exemption when it comes to recognizing same-sex marriages. In the meantime, since the 1890s Mormons have consistently demonstrated their patriotism by participating in the armed forces of whatever nation they live in; in the United States Mormons are disproportionately represented in the military, CIA, FBI, and other national security agencies. The LDS Church tempers its international missionary zeal by proselytizing and maintaining an official presence only in countries that have granted it legal standing.

• THE LIFE OF DEVOTION

The longest LDS Article of Faith is the thirteenth and final one:

> We believe in being honest, true, chaste, benevolent, virtuous, and in doing good to all men; indeed, we may say that we follow the admonition of Paul – We believe all things, we hope all things, we have endured many things, and hope to be able to endure all things. If there is anything virtuous, lovely, or of good report or praiseworthy, we seek after these things.

Mormonism puts a priority on the ethical life of the individual. Although Latter-day Saints prioritize correct doctrine and often use it to set themselves apart from other religions, they believe that the quality of one's devotion to God is demonstrated more by everyday actions than by dramatic professions of faith or precise adherence to certain theological formulations. The life of a committed Latter-day Saint is shaped by the rhythms, patterns, and moral values and teachings of the religion. Mormons sometimes feel overburdened by the weight of all these requirements and expectations, but they value the actively engaged religious and moral life. Cultural capital within the community is best achieved by quiet and consistent devotion to godly living and church participation.

Mormonism is essentially an optimistic, forward-looking religion. To be sure, a Latter-day Saint's characteristic outward cheerfulness can be little more than a veneer covering the whole range of human emotions. (According to one report, Utah, with its majority LDS population, topped the nation in having the most people who report having experienced mental illness, which some attribute to stress and depression caused by the Mormon culture's perfectionist streak.[42]) Nevertheless, one of the most quoted scriptures from the Book of Mormon contains the pithy but powerful phrase: "men are, that they might have joy."[43] Indeed, another common name for the Mormon plan of salvation is the "plan of happiness." I know of no scholarly research to support this claim, but anecdotal evidence suggests that Mormons smile as much or more than other people. (An Eastern European trying to be helpful suggested that Mormon missionaries would relate better with people in his country if they smiled less.) This observation, if true, certainly says more about Mormon cultural norms than actual, measurable psychological wellbeing, but it also is a tangible, embodied reflection of the optimistic theology of Joseph Smith.

While this chapter has emphasized Mormonism's distinctive beliefs, at its best Mormonism is a capacious, curious, encompassing worldview that is constantly open to new knowledge and understanding, regardless of where it comes from. This has always been a paradox within the religion, which can be sectarian, dogmatic, and narrow at one moment and generous, capacious, and (small-c) catholic in the next. In the same July 1843 discourse in which Joseph Smith said he would die to defend the rights of people from other religions, he also considered the question, "Wherein do you differ from others in your religious views?" His response:

> In reality and essence we do not differ so far in our religious views, but that we could all drink into one principle of love. One of the grand fundamental principles of "Mormonism" is to receive truth, let it come from whence it may.[44]

The mix of sectarian triumphalism with ecumenical generosity was similarly on display in another of Smith's sermons ten days later:

> Have the Presbyterians any truth? Yes. Have the Baptists, Methodists, etc., any truth? Yes. They all have a little truth mixed with error. We should gather all the good and true principles in the world and treasure them up, or we shall not come out true "Mormons."[45]

Zeal to police the internal borders of orthodoxy thus coexists with an openness to truth and beauty in all human endeavors. This paradox is perhaps nowhere more evident than at the LDS Church's flagship institution of higher learning, Brigham Young University. The school provides its students with a world-class education in virtually every field of study, taught by professors who have earned their advanced degrees from top universities and are nationally and internationally recognized in their respective fields. At the same time, the school's employment policies make it extremely difficult for non-LDS professors to be hired, a number of leading LDS scholars have been rejected from the faculty for fear that they are not sufficiently orthodox, and all students, faculty, and staff must sign and strictly adhere to an "Honor Code" which not only prohibits alcohol and extramarital sex but also sleeveless shirts and beards. The ongoing tension within Mormonism over how to fully engage the outside world while retaining its distinctive identity is nowhere more fraught than at "the Lord's University."

In short, being Mormon (in the LDS sense) means subscribing to a certain core set of doctrinal claims: faith in God the Father and Jesus Christ, a belief that Joseph Smith was a prophet called by God, that the Book of Mormon is true scripture, that the Church of Jesus Christ of Latter-day Saints is God's true church, and that God continues to lead the church through living prophets and apostles. But in addition to these essential beliefs, being Mormon means living a certain way, disciplining one's behavior to a set of values and standards established by the church. In the day-to-day life of the LDS Church and its members, orthopraxis matters as much (and perhaps more) than orthodoxy. It is to the matter of Mormon practice that we will turn our attention in the next chapter.

• NOTES

1 Joseph Smith-History 1:19, Pearl of Great Price.
2 Doctrine and Covenants 123:7.
3 Letter from Joseph Smith to Isaac Galland, March 22, 1839, reprinted in *Times and Seasons*, February 1840, 54.
4 *Elders' Journal*, July 1838, 42.
5 Joseph Smith Journal, December 31, 1842, in Andrew H. Hedges, Alex D. Smith, and Richard Lloyd Anderson, eds., *The Joseph Smith Papers: Journals, Volume 2: December 1842–April 1843* (Salt Lake City: The Church Historian's Press, 2011), 205, punctuation added for clarity.
6 Articles of Faith, Pearl of Great Price; originally in Joseph Smith, "Church History," *Times and Seasons*, March 1, 1842, 709–710.
7 *History of the Church of Jesus Christ of Latter-day Saints*, 7 vols. (Salt Lake City: Deseret Book Company, 1980), 5:340.
8 James E. Faulconer, "Why a Mormon Won't Drink Coffee but Might Have a Coke: The Atheological Character of the Church of Jesus Christ of Latter-day Saints," *Element* 2:2 (Fall 2006): 21–37, quotes from 21. Notable exceptions to this overall interpretation would be the sophisticated work on display in books such as Sterling M. McMurrin, *The Theological Foundations of the Mormon Religion* (Salt Lake City: Signature Books, 2000 [1965]); Adam S. Miller, *Rube Goldberg Machines: Essays in Mormon Theology* (Salt Lake City: Greg Kofford Books, 2012); and Terryl L. Givens, *Wrestling the Angel: The Foundations of Mormon Thought – Cosmos, God, Humanity* (New York: Oxford University Press, 2015). The scholarly enterprise of Mormon theology seems to be picking up some momentum in the early twenty-first century.
9 Matthew Bowman, "Why Is It So Hard to Figure Out What Mormons Believe?," *Peculiar People*, April 4, 2012, available online at http://www.patheos.com/blogs/peculiarpeople/2012/04/why-is-it-so-hard-to-figure-out-what-mormons-believe/ (accessed December 18, 2015).
10 Abraham 3:3–9, Pearl of Great Price.
11 Moses 1:39, Pearl of Great Price.
12 Eliza R. Snow, *Biography and Family Record of Lorenzo Snow* (Salt Lake City: Deseret Book Company, 1884), 46. The LDS Church provides a concise overview of this doctrine at https://www.lds.org/topics/becoming-like-god?lang=eng#43 (accessed September 21, 2015).
13 See David L. Paulsen and Martin Pulido, "'A Mother There': A Survey of Historical Teachings about Mother in Heaven," *BYU Studies* 50:1 (2011): 70–97.
14 "The Family: A Proclamation to the World," available at https://www.lds.org/topics/family-proclamation?lang=eng.
15 Doctrine and Covenants 130:22.
16 Possible categories to better describe the standard LDS position would be "henotheism," in which a person believes in and worships a single God while accepting the existence of other deities that might also be served; or even better,

"monolatrism" or "monolatry," in which a person recognizes the existence of many gods but consistently worships only one. However, neither of these terms fully captures the subtleties of Mormon theology, and furthermore, their obscurity as technical terms makes them unwieldy in popular usage.

17 This argument is echoed in John G. Turner, *The Mormon Jesus: A Biography* (Cambridge, MA: Harvard University Press, 2016).

18 Stephen H. Webb, "Godbodied: The Matter of the Latter-day Saints," *BYU Studies* 50:3 (2011): 85.

19 2 Nephi 25:26, Book of Mormon.

20 See Stephen Prothero, *American Jesus: How the Son of God Became a National Icon* (New York: Farrar, Straus and Giroux, 2003), chap. 5.

21 (Far West, MO) *Elders' Journal* (July 1838), 44.

22 Alma 11:42–43, Book of Mormon.

23 Doctrine and Covenants, section 76.

24 Ibid., section 138.

25 McMurrin, *The Theological Foundations of the Mormon Religion*, 72.

26 The inviolability of human moral agency is captured in the hymn "Know This, That Every Soul Is Free" (*Hymns* [Salt Lake City: The Church of Jesus Christ of Latter-day Saints, 1985], 240):

> Know this, that ev'ry soul is free
> To choose his life and what he'll be;
> For this eternal truth is giv'n:
> That God will force no man to heav'n.
> He'll call, persuade, direct aright,
> And bless with wisdom, love, and light,
> In nameless ways be good and kind,
> But never force the human mind.

27 McMurrin, *The Theological Foundations of the Mormon Religion*, 77, 81.

28 Moses 4:3, Pearl of Great Price.

29 Doctrine and Covenants 101:78.

30 For a scholarly reconsideration of the Mormon notion of apostasy, see Miranda Wilcox and John D. Young, eds., *Standing Apart: Mormon Historical Consciousness and the Concept of Apostasy* (New York: Oxford University Press, 2014).

31 Mormon 9:7–8, Book of Mormon.

32 For an overview of the development of LDS theology regarding marriage, family, and kinship, see Givens, *Wrestling the Angel*, 266–298.

33 For LDS participation in the conservative religious coalition on various social and cultural issues in late twentieth-century America, see Neil J. Young, *We Gather Together: The Religious Right and the Problem of Interfaith Politics* (New York: Oxford University Press, 2015).

34 "The Family: A Proclamation to the World."

35 Pew Research Center, "U.S. Public Becoming Less Religious," November 3, 2015, available online at http://www.pewforum.org/2015/11/03/u-s-public-becoming-

less-religious/; see also Peggy Fletcher Stack, "Mormons Becoming Even More Republican, More Accepting of Gays, Sweeping Religious Study Shows," *Salt Lake Tribune*, November 2, 2015.

36 Taylor G. Petrey, "Toward a Post-Heterosexual Mormon Theology," *Dialogue: A Journal of Mormon Thought* 44:4 (Winter 2011): 106–141.

37 See Armand L. Mauss, *All Abraham's Children: Changing Mormon Conceptions of Race and Lineage* (Urbana: University of Illinois Press, 2003), esp. chap. 2.

38 *History of the Church*, 5:498. The LDS Church posted this statement and others on its official Newsroom in December 2015 in the context of national and international discussions about refugees, religious pluralism, and religious freedom. See "Church Points to Joseph Smith's Statements on Religious Freedom, Pluralism," *LDS Newsroom*, available online at http://www.mormon newsroom.org/article/church-statement-religious-freedom-pluralism (accessed December 30, 2015).

39 M. Russell Ballard, "Beware of False Prophets and False Teachers," October 1999 General Conference, available online at https://www.lds.org/general-confer ence/1999/10/beware-of-false-prophets-and-false-teachers?lang=eng.

40 Article of Faith 12, Pearl of Great Price.

41 See Blair R. Holmes and Alan F. Keele, comp., trans., and ed., *When Truth Was Treason: German Youth against Hitler* (Urbana: University of Illinois Press, 1995); David Conley Nelson, *Moroni and the Swastika: Mormons in Nazi Germany* (Norman: University of Oklahoma Press, 2015).

42 See SAMHSA, "State Estimates of Adult Mental Illness from the 2011 and 2012 National Surveys on Drug Use and Health," February 28, 2014, available online at http://archive.samhsa.gov/data/2k14/NSDUH170/sr170-mental-illness-state-estimates-2014.htm (accessed December 30, 2015). See also Barbara Christiansen, "Utah Has Highest Rate of Mental Illness in U.S.," *(Provo) Daily Herald*, March 9, 2014; Kristen Moulton, "The Two Faces of Utah: Healthy but Mentally Ill," *Salt Lake Tribune*, March 17, 2014.

43 2 Nephi 2:25, Book of Mormon.

44 *History of the Church*, 5:499.

45 Ibid., 5:517. Brigham Young echoed this sentiment: "I want to say to my friends that we believe in all good. If you can find a truth in heaven, earth or hell, it belongs to our doctrine. We believe it; it is ours; we claim it. Is that right? If you find an error here, I ask you to leave it, pass it by, let it alone; do not embrace it in your faith, do not practice it in your lives." Young, "Truth and Error," *Journal of Discourses* 13:334 (April 24, 1870), available online at http://jod.mrm. org/13/334.

8
Practices

We sometimes forget that religion is not reducible merely to words, ideas, and beliefs. As the prominent scholar of religion Robert Orsi observes:

> The word *belief* bears heavy weight in public talk about religion in contemporary America: to "believe in" a religion means that one has deliberated over and then assented to its propositional truths, has chosen this religion over other available options, a personal choice unfettered by authority, tradition, or society. What matters about religion from this perspective are its ideas and not its things, practices, or presences.

While acknowledging the importance of beliefs, Orsi argues that to fully understand the worlds of religious people, we must go beyond the intellectual, rationalistic, and propositional dimensions of spirituality. We must realize that for most people religion is an integral dimension of the reality of their lives: "The saints, gods, demons, ancestors, and so on are real in experience and practice, in relationships between heaven and earth, in the circumstances of people's live and histories, and in the stories people tell about them."[1] Even in an age of psychological insight, then, we must acknowledge that religion is never merely "in our heads." Religion breathes and bleeds; it can be touched, felt, tasted, and smelled. It is about ideas, yes, but also about personal relationships (human-human and human-divine), shared experiences, communal histories, cultural traditions, and bodily practices. Religion is what we do as much as what we believe.

The Mormon word for someone who is fully engaged in the church is "active"; those who are rarely seen at church or who don't fulfill all their prescribed duties are referred to as "inactive" or "less active." If law is the operative concept for Islam, and ethics for modern Judaism, then "activity" is as good a word as any to describe what it means to be a Mormon. When the Latter-day Saints first settled the Great Basin, they initially called their new home the State of Deseret. The word "deseret" comes from the Book of Mormon, which says it was an ancient word for honeybees.[2] Brigham Young and the other Saints embraced this image – the beehive still adorns the Utah state flag – because it connoted both community and a busy hive of constant activity and industry. The LDS emphasis on righteous human action has led to a steady stream of accusations by evangelical Christians that Mormons seek to save themselves by their works. Mormons – like Catholics, previously the target of evangelical critique – deny the charge, insisting on the theological primacy and saving efficacy of Christ's atonement. Nevertheless, Mormons love the New Testament Epistle of James, which teaches followers of Jesus to be "doers of the word, and not hearers only," and emphasizes that "faith without works is dead."[3] While Latter-day Saints speak of God's grace now more than ever, the underlying impulse behind an active Mormon's religious life is summarized by another of James's statements: "Show me your faith without your works, and I will show you my faith by my works."[4]

This chapter surveys a number of distinctive Mormon practices. Many of these are not unique to Mormons – lots of other people follow particular diets, go to church, and participate in special ceremonies. But what is distinctive about Mormon practices is the way Mormons do them, the reasons they do them, and the cumulative effect of doing them. In other words, there are many stars in the sky of religious praxis, but here we will consider the unique constellation that is Mormon life and practice. This chapter focuses specifically on Mormon lifestyles, missions, meetings, rituals, and finally temples. I have aimed for a portrayal that most Latter-day Saints would recognize as authentically Mormon, even if their own personal practices or experiences vary in some respects. In general, Mormons recognize and tolerate a fairly wide degree of latitude in personal practice on many matters, while insisting on conformity and exactness in others.

• LIFESTYLES

Being Mormon is a way of life. Mormons will often proudly boast that theirs is not a "Sunday-only religion," but that their faith touches upon if not dictates virtually every aspect of their conduct. From their earliest lessons in church (and usually at home), Mormons are taught to "keep the commandments" – and with several thousand pages of scriptures, church manuals and handbooks, and instructions from church leaders, there appears to be no shortage of commandments for Mormons to keep. Though it is not uncommon for Mormons to comply out of either fear of consequences (earthly or heavenly) or iron-willed duty, ideally they would say that they conform their lives to a certain model out of love for God and their fellow humans. Most would also simply say that theirs is a good way to live one's life – a path that leads to stability, purpose, togetherness, virtue, and happiness.

The essentials of a lifestyle we might identify as particularly Mormon have changed considerably over time. In the nineteenth century, as we have seen, to be a Latter-day Saint typically meant uprooting yourself (and ideally your family) and gathering with the Saints; participating in a cooperative if not fully communitarian economic system; pioneering in the Great Basin so as to build the kingdom of God on earth; practicing plural marriage, or at least defending it; and supporting the members of the church hierarchy as political as well as ecclesiastical leaders. Regular church attendance was not required or even fully expected, and if one did go to church it would not have been uncommon to see the bishop's shirt marred with tobacco or coffee stains. Women did not serve as missionaries, and the vast majority of men never did either.

Times have changed. When the LDS Church was forced to give up its defining practices of polygamy, theocracy, and communitarianism, it was left in the early twentieth century without an obvious set of social practices that would define Mormon identity and draw boundaries separating Mormons from the outside world. Church leaders surveyed the situation and drew from the resources already available within the tradition to construct a new set of practices that would come to define twentieth- and now twenty-first-century Mormon orthopraxis. Among these are the Word of Wisdom, law of chastity (and now a correlative defense of the "traditional family"), tithing and other financial offerings, sabbatarianism, church and community service, gospel study, and personal piety and morality.

In place of the far more controversial practice of polygamy, the Word of Wisdom has emerged as arguably the most visible – and effective – boundary separating Latter-day Saints from their non-Mormon friends and neighbors. The Word of Wisdom is, in short, the church's health code. It originated in a February 1833 revelation to Joseph Smith, prompted when Emma Smith complained to her husband of having to clean up after the "disgusting slobbering and spitting" of the men who chewed tobacco and smoked pipes while studying the gospel and being instructed by the prophet.[5] The ensuing revelation offered itself "not by commandment or constraint" but rather as "a word of wisdom" to the church – hence the popular name – given for "the temporal salvation of all saints in the last days." It prohibited the Saints from ingesting "wine or strong drink" (except the wine used for communion in their sacrament meetings), advised against the use of both tobacco and "strong drinks," counseled that meat should be eaten "sparingly" or in times of winter or famine, and recommended a diet consisting mostly of the grains, herbs, and fruits of the earth. Those who follow the revelation's counsel are promised health, wisdom and knowledge, energy, and preservation.[6]

The Word of Wisdom was observed mostly in the breach throughout the nineteenth century. Its importance gradually increased in the early twentieth century before becoming codified by church president Heber J. Grant, a Progressive-era businessman who was strongly influenced by the American temperance movement. Although previous church leaders had on occasion treated adherence to the revelation's advice as a barometer of faithfulness, beginning in 1921 Grant declared that obeying the Word of Wisdom would now be a requirement for entering the church's temples – a rule that has been in place ever since. Grant also clarified the meaning of the revelation's vague prohibition of "hot drinks," labeling coffee and tea as the offenders, but not warm beverages such as hot chocolate and (non-alcoholic) apple cider.[7] On a folk level, Mormons have spent decades debating about what it was in coffee and tea that made them such wicked drinks that God would proscribe them – leading theories have been the presence of tannin or caffeine, the latter of which has led many Mormons to refrain from drinking colas and sometimes look askance at those church members who flaunt their Diet Coke or Mountain Dew habit. The church's official codification of the Word of Wisdom has adapted the wording of the original revelation to now declare that alcohol, tobacco, coffee, tea, and "harmful drugs" are prohibited. The revelation's advice about the limited consumption of meat has never been interpreted as binding, and is often completely ignored.

It would be difficult to overstate the importance of obeying the Word of Wisdom to defining contemporary Mormon identity. Prospective converts must agree to abide by the health code before they are allowed to be baptized. Anyone with a "Word of Wisdom problem" is allowed to attend weekly church services but barred from major leadership callings or the temple (the significance of which will be elaborated below). Church lessons to children, teenagers, and adults regularly either focus or obliquely refer to the importance of keeping the Word of Wisdom. In a 2011 national survey, 81% of Mormon respondents said that not drinking coffee and tea was either "essential" or "important" for being a good Mormon; surely the percentage would have been even higher had the question asked about alcohol, tobacco, or non-prescription drugs.[8]

The reason why the Word of Wisdom is so effective as a boundary marker is precisely because of its conspicuous, physical nature. It's difficult to gauge whether or not someone has love in their heart toward their fellow humans, but pretty easy to tell if they have tobacco smoke on their breath and clothes. Although the arbitrariness of the code provides an easy target for critique – you would not be the first to ask, "So do Mormons really think drinking a cup of coffee will keep a person out of heaven?" – the social effects of the Word of Wisdom are clear. In virtually any social setting, Mormons – who otherwise blend in with the crowd in terms of dress, education, profession, wealth, and other socioeconomic markers – will stand out. When asked why they aren't drinking a beer or smoking pot, they will usually respond (with varying degrees of confidence or meekness), "Because of my religion." At that moment, and in thousands of others over the course of a Latter-day Saint's life, s/he will have asserted his/her religion as a primary identity marker, expressing solidarity more with his/her fellow believers than with her non-LDS social peer group. Thus, while the Word of Wisdom does speak to the willingness of individual Latter-day Saints to "obey the commandments" in order to receive desired spiritual blessings, it perhaps says even more about the power and strength of Mormon community and identity.

Rivaling the Word of Wisdom in cultural importance, and far exceeding it in theological and ecclesiastical weight, is what Latter-day Saints refer to as the law of chastity. The LDS Church's definition of the law of chastity is simple: church members are to have no sexual relations with anyone other than their legally wedded (monogamous, heterosexual) spouse. This means absolutely no premarital or extramarital sex, including oral sex. Masturbation is disapproved of, though without the same vehemence or penalty. In recent years church leaders have also vigorously condemned viewing pornography, the confession and repentance for which many local bishops report dominates their time as spiritual counselors. Church members, especially teenagers but also adults, are also warned against watching R-rated movies, with a special focus on avoiding explicit sexual content in any media. Dating couples can kiss or hold hands – but that's about it, as far as the church is concerned. Teenagers are strongly counseled not to date until they are sixteen, and then to avoid exclusive pairing off until later. The Mormon hierarchy of sin lists violations of the law of chastity as third behind only "denying the Holy Ghost" (a special and somewhat obscure theological category) and murder. Whereas violators of the Word of Wisdom will be stripped of their temple recommends, violators of the law of chastity, especially those who commit adultery, will often (though not always, depending on circumstances) be excommunicated from the church, with the option to be rebaptized later upon sincere repentance.

In recent decades the LDS Church has avoided a major public sex scandal involving any of its top leadership. Nevertheless, local leaders are occasionally found guilty of "succumbing to the flesh" and are immediately removed from their ecclesiastical positions and subjected to church discipline. The church has also taken precautionary measures against sex abuse by imposing stringent guidelines for how and in what ways adult teachers and leaders can interact with children and youth. Naturally, humans being what they are, sexual transgressions will always emerge within any community. But the LDS Church is extraordinarily serious about policing sexual behavior, both in ways that are consonant with the general culture (in preventing sexual violence and abuse) and in other ways that are starkly countercultural (in condemning and even disciplining the sexuality of consenting but unmarried teens and adults).

The demands of Mormon practice resonate in the pocketbook as well as in the bedroom. The communitarian vision of Joseph Smith and Brigham Young has succumbed to free market economics, but Latter-day Saints nevertheless remain financially generous with their church. Faithful Mormons are expected to pay a full tithe – meaning ten percent of their income, before expenses (individuals decide whether that's before or after taxes). Though the principle of tithing is regularly taught in church meetings, the actual collection of tithes is done privately. There is no passing of the plate in Mormon church services, nor televangelists pleading with you to make your donation by calling their 1–800 number. Church members simply place their tithing in a sealed envelope and give it to a member of the ward bishopric – or, more recently, make a direct payment online. Each bishop holds "tithing settlement" once per year, in which individual members review their donations and declare whether or not they indeed pay a full tithe. This matters, because only full tithe payers are allowed into the church's temples – though, like the Word of Wisdom, tithing is not required to attend weekly worship services. Members are also strongly encouraged to donate a "fast offering," which at minimum is the monetary value of two meals that they skip during the church's monthly daylong fast.

In general, tithes are used to pay for church building and temple construction and maintenance, the church's education system (including Brigham Young University, where student tuition is heavily subsidized by the church), the missionary program, and the operating budget of wards, stakes, and the general church. Because Mormonism has a lay clergy, tithing funds are not used for local ministerial and staff salaries – although they do pay for the church's central bureaucracy in Salt Lake City, and provide living stipends for full-time general authorities of the church who are not independently wealthy. Fast offerings, on the other hand, are dedicated for relief of the poor and needy, first at the local level and then around the global church. The system is designed so that the fast offerings collected in affluent wards can assist the poor in less prosperous areas, particularly in the developing world. Members can also donate to various other church funds, including those that support worldwide humanitarian and disaster relief, education for church members in developing countries, and for the support of individual missionaries who cannot afford to pay their own way. All told, it is common for faithful Mormons to donate 12–15% of their income to the church. About four-fifths of self-identified Mormons in the United States in a 2011 survey reported paying tithing, with rates remarkably high (96%) among those with the highest levels of religious commitment and also correlative with education and income, with 91% of college graduates and 83% of those with family incomes over $30,000 reporting that they pay.[9]

Mormons are among the last remaining sabbatarians. Once a religious and cultural fixture, the Sabbath Day has fallen on hard times in the modern United States. Arguably more Americans watch the NFL than attend church on any given Sunday.[10] (To be fair, lots of Mormons watch the NFL too, but only after they go to church.) Faithful Latter-day Saints will avoid shopping or working on Sunday, with the exception of those such as police officers, doctors, and yes, NFL players, whose careers require it. Opinions are divided, with individual members and families making the ultimate call, but it's common for Mormon parents to keep their kids out of sports leagues and competitions that play on Sunday. Brigham Young University will not schedule any sporting events for Sunday, which sometimes limits its competitive opportunities and conference affiliations. Mormons consider Sunday to be a "day of rest," which often translates into a day of church meetings and some extra family time, usually at home. A Mormon friend may or may not attend your birthday party on a Sunday; if they do, they'll probably feel guilty about it, and they almost definitely won't skip church for it. In general, Latter-day Saints aren't as severe in their Sabbath observance as are orthodox Jews or conservative Seventh-Day Adventists – for instance, they will often make pragmatic exceptions especially when traveling – but compared to most of Euro-American Christendom, the Mormon Sabbath remains decidedly holy.

It seems that when Mormons aren't going to church, they're giving service to the church, with any leftover time often dedicated to community service. In this respect Mormons fit into a broader American cultural pattern in which a higher degree of religiosity predicts a higher rate of volunteering for both religious and secular organizations.[11] Because LDS wards are staffed entirely by volunteers, the congregation depends on everybody pitching in. Virtually all active members receive a "calling" of some sort, which gives them not only a specific job to do at church but a divine mandate to do it. Recent surveys show that at least 90% of Mormons who attend church every week hold a calling. More than 70% of survey respondents said they spend five or more hours per week in church service, and more than a quarter reported serving for eleven hours or more per week.[12] A study published in 2013 demonstrated that, excluding full-time missionaries, the average Latter-day Saint provides 336.5 hours of volunteer service annually, or about 28 hours monthly. The vast majority of this service either goes to or is coordinated by the church, usually within the scope of their calling. Still, the number of hours that Mormons spend volunteering for purely secular causes, not including church service, is equivalent to what non-Mormons do. The researchers concluded that "an average active Latter-Day [sic] Saint volunteer provides about nine times more volunteer hours than an average American volunteer."[13]

Nevertheless, the high proportion of service hours dedicated by Latter-day Saints within the bounds of their own wards and stakes suggests an insular focus. Since the doctrine of the gathering was reinterpreted in the twentieth century to take on more of a spiritual rather than strictly physical and geographic meaning, Latter-day Saints have not literally fled from the world and hidden in their own religiously homogenous enclaves – although certain neighborhoods and cities in Utah and Idaho essentially function as such due to the extremely high proportion of Latter-day Saints who live there. Mormons are fully functioning members of society, yet most of their considerable service is performed within their own community. The Mormon welfare system has been praised ever since its inception during the Great Depression, with national and international plaudits such as the extremely favorable 1949 *Reader's Digest* article "They Take Care of Their Own" – a title that the church adopted as something of a tagline.[14] Indeed, LDS wards and stakes are remarkable sites of mobilizing a localized and highly personalized ethic of care. It is a marvel to witness the Mormon machine kick into action when someone has a baby, loses a job, or is diagnosed with cancer. Care for the sick, poor, and needy ranks as one of the preeminent missions of the church, but it has generally taken the form of personal and family welfare rather than as a structural or movement-based approach to social justice.

While highly prosocial, Mormons are also encouraged to spend time in daily personal religious devotions, typically consisting of prayer and scripture study. About two-thirds of Mormons report praying several times per day, with another 19% saying that they pray once daily.[15] Indeed, if members follow the church's counsel, they will pray at least six times daily – personal prayer at morning and night, family prayer at least once a day, and prayers over each meal – not to mention any spontaneous appeals for help with calculus tests or gratitude for avoiding a traffic accident. Mormon prayers are more conversational than formal or meditative, and may be offered silently or vocally. The only prayers that require exact wording are those for baptism and over the sacramental bread and water each Sunday; indeed, most Mormons can't recite standard Christian prayers such as the Our Father. The generic formula for personal prayers is to open by addressing God as "Father in Heaven" or "Heavenly Father," then proceed to thank him for blessings received, ask him for additional blessings, and close in the name of Jesus Christ. Mormons sometimes debate as to whether God should be approached in prayer as a kind, loving, and attentive Dad or more reverentially as the Supreme Being. The church teaches its members to use the old English pronouns of thee, thou, and thine when addressing God, a practice that generally adds a layer of formality. While familiar and spontaneous, Mormon prayers are neither casual and chatty nor loud and exuberant.

The church teaches its members to engage in daily scripture study, ideally both as individuals and as a family. Though there is no prescribed lectionary, especially since Ezra Taft Benson's presidency in the 1980s church members have been told they would receive special blessings by reading daily from the Book of Mormon. How many Mormons actually do this is hard to say. If a 2007 Pew survey is to be believed, over three-quarters of Mormons read their scriptures at least once a week, eclipsing the six-in-ten evangelical and black Protestants who do and more than doubling the rate of the general public.[16] Latter-day Saints' individual gospel study is supplemented by a range of church classes, including two hours of gospel instruction during church each Sunday, hour-long early morning seminary classes each day for high school aged students, required religious education classes at all church-owned universities, optional religious education classes for LDS students at non-church colleges, a religiously based Education Week for adults held every summer at BYU, and a host of other local and churchwide programs. The cumulative effect of all this study and teaching is that Mormons really know at least the basics of their own religion, and often something about other religions as well. On the 2010 Religious Knowledge Survey, Mormons, Jews, and atheists significantly outscored all other groups on a set of thirty-two questions about the core beliefs, history, and leading figures of the world's religions.[17]

All this intentional religious formation among Mormons has a real impact, and at an early age. In a major survey of religious beliefs, practices, and attitudes among American teenagers conducted in 2002–2003, Latter-day Saint youth emerged in many important respects as the most religiously attuned teens in the country. Compared with conservative Protestants, mainline Protestants, black Protestants, Roman Catholics, and Jews, Mormon teenagers polled the highest on the following religious beliefs and behaviors (followed by the percentage): attends church at least once per week (71%); religious faith as extremely important in shaping daily life (43%); belief in angels (80%), life after death (76%), and demons or evil spirits (69%); has had a moving spiritual experience (76%); has received a definite answer to a specific prayer (67%); has taught a Sunday School or religious education class (42%); has fasted (68%); participates in a scripture study or prayer group (50%); has read a religious or devotional book other than scriptures (68%); has spoken publicly about faith in a religious meeting or service (65%); has tried to keep the Sabbath as a day of rest (67%); has shared their religious faith with others not of their faith (72%); has personal daily prayer (57%); their family talks about God or religion and/or prays together at least a few times per week (74%); and openly expresses their faith at school some or a lot (58%).[18]

For teenaged boys and increasingly girls, the goal in the church's eyes – and often in their own – is to get them to serve full-time missions. Indeed, missionary service is in many ways the paradigmatic if somewhat exceptional culmination of Mormon religious life, representing a truly full-time commitment by lay members to serve God, the church, and other people. It is to that quintessential Latter-day Saint rite of passage that we now turn.

• MISSIONS

> *Ding dong.*
> Hello!
> My name is Elder Price
> And I would like to share with you
> The most amazing book.
> *Ding dong.*
> Hello!
> My name is Elder Grant.
> It's a book about America
> A long, long time ago.[19]

So opens *The Book of Mormon*, one of the most successful Broadway musicals in years. Winner of nine Tony Awards (including for Best Musical) and a Grammy (for Best Musical Theater Album), the musical has played to packed houses across the United States and England on multiple tours, and its original Broadway cast recording reached #3 on the *Billboard* charts. Devastatingly brilliant, blasphemous, and crude – and with no shortage of catchy hooks – the musical capitalizes on one of the iconic images of the American (and global) religious landscape: the fresh-faced Mormon missionary with his white shirt and tie, dark slacks, and black nametag, showing up uninvited on your doorstep to share with you a message about Jesus Christ/the Book of Mormon/families/happiness.

The Mormon missionary program is without a doubt one of the most extensive and successful religious evangelization efforts in the modern world. Going on a mission is the ultimate Mormon rite of passage. For decades, getting boys on missions has been one of the primary stated goals of the LDS Church's young men's program. While service for girls has traditionally been seen as optional and is still formally framed that way, the cultural pressure, especially among young women's peers, has grown significantly in recent years. As of late 2015, the LDS Church had over 85,000 full-time

FIGURE 8.1 Perhaps the most visible public face of the Church of Jesus Christ of Latter-day Saints is its global force of volunteer full-time missionaries. Men are referred to as "elders" and women as "sisters."

Copyright: Keith Morris/Alamy

missionaries serving in 406 missions spanning the globe. The vast majority are eighteen- to twenty-five-year-old men and women (since 2012 men can go at age eighteen, women at nineteen), but the total also includes retired married couples and some older single women. The vast majority are on full-time proselytizing missions, though many older couples are assigned primarily to humanitarian service in developing countries. Young men typically serve for twenty-four months, young women for eighteen months, and seniors for anywhere from twelve to thirty-six months. The term "full time" is, if anything, an understatement. Proselytizing missionaries put in sixty-five to seventy hours of work per week, plus an additional two to three hours of study and planning every day. They get one day per week for shopping, laundry, recreation, and writing letters (or e-mails) home. Except in the case of emergencies, they call home only two times per year, on Christmas and Mother's Day.

Missionaries serve on a voluntary basis – though the religious, family, and cultural pressures to go are significant and sometimes overwhelming, especially for young men for whom missionary work is portrayed as a priesthood duty. While they choose whether to go, prospective missionaries have no say in where they will go. Upon passing a series of interviews with local priesthood leaders determining their worthiness and preparation, they submit an application to the Missionary Department in the LDS Church's Salt Lake City headquarters. Within a few weeks, they receive a packet in the mail containing their "call." They are told where they will serve, what language they will speak, and when to report for service. Accompanying materials give detailed instructions on what to bring – and not to bring, including personal electronics of any kind. Before leaving, they customarily give a farewell address in their home ward, often attended by scores of friends and family in addition to regular ward members. On the day of their departure, they say tearful goodbyes to boyfriends/girlfriends, siblings, and parents – who simultaneously couldn't be prouder but also shed tears in buckets at the prospect of sending their child to some unknown corner of the world and not being able to see him/her for eighteen to twenty-four months.

Missionaries receive relatively brief training – only three weeks if they are speaking their native language, up to two months of mostly intensive language training if they are going foreign. The little training they do get focuses on how to teach the core doctrines of the church. The LDS Church has a standardized message and method that all missionaries are expected to follow, though they have considerably more latitude than in the 1960s and 1970s, when missionaries were expected to memorize and then present a series of "discussions" word-for-word. The level of theological sophistication among young missionaries is generally quite low. Though often well versed in the church's basic doctrines and narratives, many have never read the entire Book of Mormon before entering the mission field; the vast majority, even those who attended seminary classes during high school, have never read the entire Bible. What they lack in knowledge they make up for in youthful zeal. In a revelation to the elders of the church in 1831, God said, "Ye are not sent forth to be taught, but to teach the children of men the things which I have put into your hands by the power of my Spirit."[20] Though many missionaries are natively curious and soak up much of the surrounding culture, their prime directive is to teach the gospel, not to act as if they are on an extended study abroad trip.

Life as a missionary is mostly routine and tedious – though in retrospect many returned missionaries romanticize it as "the best two years of my life." The simple fact is that most people don't want to talk to two strangers about religion – especially when those strangers are from another country and are not yet fluent in the language. Missionary work includes a lot of walking around, knocking on unopened doors, conversations on doorsteps and on the street that end practically before they begin, and various other exercises in futility. The often-monotonous reality stands in contrast to the myth of the heroic missionary converting nations by his mere presence.[21] Latter-day Saint children are raised on stories of miraculous conversions and mass baptisms. When missionaries return home and report on their service in sacrament meeting, they invariably speak about all their "success" – usually meaning the people they taught and baptized. Most returned missionaries can easily summon enough faith-promoting stories to fill a twenty-minute church talk.

But the fact is, most Mormon missionaries are not baptizing very many people. The LDS Church's official statistical report for 2014 stated that the church had 85,147 full-time missionaries (not including another 30,404 church service missionaries), which resulted in 296,803 convert baptisms[22] – an impressive number, to be sure, and the envy of many European and American churches who are losing members by the droves. But that averages to just under 3.5 baptisms per missionary per year. This means that if in the space of twelve months a missionary were to bring only one nuclear family of mother, father, and two children into the church, s/he would be batting above average. Put another way, given that a full-time missionary should be logging nearly 3,500 hours of work per year, it equates to about 1,000 hours of missionary labor for every one convert baptism.

So why all the effort? Theologically, the answer is clear: "Remember the worth of souls is great in the sight of God," one of Joseph Smith's earliest revelations declared. "And if it so be that you should labor all your days in crying repentance unto this people, and bring, save it be one soul unto me, how great shall be your joy with him in the kingdom of my Father!"[23] Indeed, the massive LDS missionary effort, as inefficient as may seem, does speak to a fundamental recognition of the inestimable value and dignity of every human soul – that no amount of effort is too great to reclaim and redeem even one of God's children.

But there is another reason the church promotes missionary work so heavily. Arguably, the single greatest purpose and effect of the LDS missionary program is to retain and convert the missionaries themselves. Mormon missions are a brilliant tool in accomplishing the very thing which all institutions (including religions) must do in order to have long-term success but which eludes so many – that is, creating deep and lasting commitment in the next generation, so that they will carry on the institution into the future and bestow it upon their children and grandchildren. When a Mormon mission works the way it is meant to, it takes a young, unseasoned member of the church and turns him/her into a real Mormon. Returned missionaries have acquired a foundational grounding in church doctrine and practice, a store of transformative spiritual experiences and fond memories to draw upon, a wealth of leadership and public speaking opportunities, and the power of religiously and morally disciplined personal habits. The repetitive teaching of the religion – even to those "investigators" who ultimately choose not to accept it – drums it deep within the psyche of the teacher, and every convert gained serves to validate the truth of Mormonism to the missionary.[24]

Perhaps most importantly, young Mormons serve missions at the most crucial, and vulnerable, period of their religious development. Scholars have consistently demonstrated that the period of greatest risk for religious disengagement comes in the late teens and early twenties.[25] A mission not only keeps a young Latter-day Saint in the church but channels his entire being into profound religious commitment at the very time that his old high school buddies have stopped attending their parents' church and thrown themselves into decidedly nonreligious college-age behaviors. Not all returned missionaries stay with the church, but serving a mission, especially when paired with later marrying another Mormon in an LDS temple, is one of the best indicators that a person will remain active in the church throughout his/her life. As former missionaries often quip, the most important convert they made on their mission was him/herself.

Missionary service transforms those members who, as adults, will shoulder many of the leadership responsibilities in their congregations. In particular, the dramatic increase in the number of young women now serving missions proves to have substantial impact both in the short and long term. Greater numbers of sister missionaries means more women who have comparable doctrinal knowledge, church service experience, and leadership skills as the male returned missionaries who have traditionally held an informal edge within any local congregation. It will also mean greater expectations by those women for the wards they return to. After having been on the front lines, so to speak, and entrusted with significant responsibilities and prestige, many female returned missionaries may be dissatisfied if they are not afforded similar opportunities for engagement and leadership back home. By creating opportunities for female empowerment in the mission field, the church might stand to lose some of those once-committed women should they become frustrated with the male-centered structure of their local congregations.[26]

• MEETINGS

Mormons no longer apply the doctrine of gathering in the literal sense of moving to Missouri or Utah. Gathering has become a localized phenomenon, accomplished mostly through a multitude of church meetings. Riffing on the LDS Church's ninth and thirteenth Articles of Faith, Mormons will sometimes joke that they have a fourteenth:

> We believe in meetings – all that have been held, all that are now scheduled – and we believe there will yet be held many great and important meetings. We have endured many meetings and hope to be able to endure all meetings. If there is a meeting, we seek after it.

Mormonism is a social religion – in the sense of the Latin root *religare*, which means to tie or bind together – that can only be fully lived in interaction with other people. Though personal devotions are encouraged, Mormons have no monastic tradition of withdrawal from community or society. It is conceivable for a person to believe in the doctrines of Mormonism by him/herself, far from any church or even human civilization, but it is impossible to be a Mormon in isolation. And so members of the LDS Church heed the counsel of the Book of Mormon to "meet together oft," both on Sundays and throughout the week.[27]

The basic LDS worship service is a three-hour "block" of meetings held on Sundays in local chapels around the world. The first meeting, held in the chapel and typically about seventy minutes long, is called "sacrament meeting." All members of the family attend together, which can make for a fairly raucous experience in wards with lots of babies and young children. Men and women intersperse freely, and there is no assigned seating within the congregation, with the exception of the bishopric and selected speakers for the day who sit at the front of the chapel near the podium. Most people dress conservatively – women in blouses and skirts or dresses, men in suits or at least white shirts and ties.

Sacrament meetings follow a standard format that is generally familiar to those who have attended other Christian churches. The feeling is reverent and subdued but fairly non-liturgical. The meeting opens with a congregational hymn usually accompanied by organ, followed by a prayer offered by a member of the ward. After any announcements and church business, another congregational hymn is sung while two or three young men, ordained as priests in the church's Aaronic Priesthood, prepare the "sacrament," known in other churches as communion or the Lord's Supper. The sacrament, consisting of simple bread and water, is distributed to the congregation, which sits in silent meditation throughout the process. Their reverence throughout the blessing and passing of the sacrament indicates the church members' conviction that receiving the sacrament is the most important and sacred part of the service, as it is a renewal and reminder of the covenants they made at baptism as well as a symbol of the body and blood of Jesus Christ. The remainder of the meeting, typically thirty to forty minutes, is filled by "talks" (not sermons) delivered by two or three speakers from the ward who were selected and invited by the bishopric at least a couple weeks in advance and usually assigned a particular topic. It is common to have one teenager and then an adult man and woman speak, though the format may vary somewhat. There is no regular preacher; even the bishop of a ward typically gives a formal talk only occasionally. Most talks are devotional and doctrinal in nature, liberally peppered with faith-promoting stories and personal experiences; theological treatises are rare. Because of all the opportunities they get, most Mormons are comfortable with the prospect of speaking in church. Even if they are not particularly gifted public speakers – most aren't – they know that expectations and therefore pressure are fairly low. Members of the congregation will listen respectfully or nod off; sometimes they will be genuinely touched or inspired. Children are mostly bored but used to it. The meeting ends with another congregational hymn and prayer.

The thing that many visitors to an LDS sacrament meeting are most surprised at is how utterly unremarkable the experience is. Any anticipation of major weirdness is bound to be disappointed by the prosaic nature of it all. There are lots of handshakes and smiles and hugs before and after the meeting. There is nothing esoteric or ecstatic during the service. Speakers (including men) will often tear up at the podium, but that's about as crazy as things get. In most wards most Sundays, Jesus Christ is the center of attention – it's not uncommon to go an entire meeting with no mention of Joseph Smith.

Perhaps the biggest wild card is if you attend on the first Sunday of the month, which is typically designated as "fast and testimony meeting." Most members will come to church observing their monthly fast. Rather than assigned speakers, after the sacrament is passed the meeting is opened up to anyone who wants to "bear their testimony," including small children (often accompanied by parents). It's Mormonism's version of open mic night, but things rarely get out of hand. Most testimonies are straightforward expressions of gratitude to God or other church members, recounting of special spiritual experiences, or proclamations of religious conviction (i.e. "testimony"). There are certain rhythms and cadences to an LDS testimony which differentiate it from an evangelical testimony, focusing on what the person knows to be true rather than when they came to know they were saved, but it serves much the same function in terms of reinforcing private commitment and affirming the boundaries of communal membership. Testimonies often comprise some variation on a general formula which even children learn quite young:

> "I know Heavenly Father lives and loves me. I know Jesus Christ is my Savior. I know that Joseph Smith was a prophet of God and restored the true church. I know the Book of Mormon is true. I know the church is true. I know we have a living prophet on the earth today. In the name of Jesus Christ, amen."

Many members will report "feeling the Spirit" either while giving their testimony or hearing others', but the feeling is entirely internal, with the possible exception of producing some tears. Mormons collectively say "amen" at the end of a talk or testimony, but will not interject any such affirmations while someone else is speaking.

After sacrament meeting, the next two hours are dedicated to classroom instruction. Children go to Primary for the second and third hours, while teenagers and adults go to Sunday School, divided by age but mixed-gender, for the second hour. During the final hour, members are divided by sex, with adult women attending Relief Society, teenage girls Young Women's, and men and teenage boys a variety of priesthood quorums and groups. At every point, Mormon meetings emphasize lay participation and leadership. Ordinary members provide all the classroom instruction, assisted by centrally produced teacher manuals and other lesson materials that combine scriptures, the teachings of modern LDS prophets and apostles, often stories from church history, and personal application. The curriculum is standardized throughout the church, so that members from Alaska to Zimbabwe are more or less receiving the same lessons on any given week. Classes are meant to be interactive, though the emphasis is on reconfirming received knowledge rather than pushing boundaries or exploring uncharted theological territory. As a result, lessons are for the most part intellectually unstimulating while aiming to be spiritually affirming and inspirational.

Though the three-hour Sunday block is the normative Mormon worship service, it hardly exhausts the limits of LDS meetingdom. Wards or stakes often sponsor Sunday evening "firesides" or devotionals. Those with leadership callings in the ward or stake often have one or more additional meetings before or after church. The young men and women in each ward gather at the church one night a week for activities which can range from serious and spiritual to (more often) casual and fun; the church also relies on Boy Scouts, especially for twelve- to thirteen-year-old boys. The church sponsors regular dances for youth or singles, monthly gatherings for the women of the Relief Society, periodic ward parties and other social activities (often revolving around holidays), monthly or quarterly ward temple trips, and overnight campouts and weeklong summer camps for the youth. Being underscheduled is rarely a problem for an active LDS family.

Meetings also take place in individual members' homes through the home teaching and visiting teaching programs of the church. Every family is assigned two "home teachers" from among the ward's male priesthood holders, and every woman has a pair of "visiting teachers" from the Relief Society. Correspondingly, most men are assigned two to four families to home teach, and most women have two to four sisters they visit teach. Home and visiting teaching visits are for the most part informal and often look more like social calls than ecclesiastical ministry. They are supposed to occur monthly, though observance is often lax and is the subject of many reminders-cum-admonishments from church leaders. Nevertheless, home and visiting teachers are often the first people called when someone in the family gets hospitalized or needs some other kind of special help. In short, home and visiting teaching strengthen social cohesion within a ward and build relational networks that can be mobilized in time of need.

Twice a year, on the first weekends of April and October, no regular sacrament meetings are held as church members tune in to General Conference, held in Salt Lake City and broadcast to the world via satellite TV, internet, and radio. There are six two-hour sessions of General Conference – four general sessions plus a session for women and girls age eight and up and a priesthood session for men and boys age twelve and up. The format resembles a sacrament meeting with music and a parade of several speakers, though the sacrament itself is not administered. Church members look forward to General Conference as the opportunity to hear from their church leaders, especially the prophet-president, his two counselors in the First Presidency, and the members of the Quorum of Twelve Apostles. They consider the messages they hear to be inspired counsel from God. If major policy changes are to be made, they are generally announced in General Conference. The same would be true for the presentation of new revelations or doctrinal proclamations, though in the LDS Church that has been an extraordinarily rare occurrence since the death of Joseph

Smith. For the most part the talks given by the general authorities and officers of the church are pastoral and practical, devotional and doctrinal. They are as scripted now as they were extemporaneous in the nineteenth century. All General Conference talks are published the following month in the church's official magazine, *Ensign*, and become the subject of personal study and lesson materials for the ensuing six months until the next conference. There is a strong feeling in the church that the most recent General Conference talks represent the latest word from the Lord for his church and indeed the world. Nevertheless, almost all conference talks since the 1850s have been archived by the church and are regularly referenced by church members and publications.

• RITUALS

One of the great paradoxes of Mormonism is that although it arose in the age of "the democratization of American Christianity," and historians have interpreted Joseph Smith as a "populist" prophet,[28] by the end of his life Smith had introduced enough priesthood and ritual into the church so as to scandalize Protestants and perhaps make even Catholics blush. In the earliest years of Joseph Smith's restoration, it was entirely conceivable that the movement could have taken a position on the margins of American Christianity, with a fantastic origin story leading to an idiosyncratic but still recognizable restorationist gloss on Protestantism. Yet with every new ritual and layer of priesthood organization he introduced, Smith took a step further away from any other church of this day and more toward the distinctive theological, sacramental, and cosmological system we now recognize as Mormonism.

All this priesthood and ritual – and especially Latter-day Saints' insistence that so much of it was *necessary*, not just additive or symbolic – has acted as a consistent theological wedge between Mormons and other Christians. For *sola scriptura* Protestants, it smacks of the old heresy of "works righteousness," the presumption that human effort is in some way needed to supplement the apparently insufficient power of God's grace. Catholics and Orthodox, on the other hand, agree with Mormons that sacramental rituals make God's grace available in the world, but they would disagree with Mormons' insistence that only rituals conducted by the authority of the LDS priesthood are valid in the sight of God. Thus, Mormons don't formally recognize other Christian baptisms, and in turn other Christians don't recognize Mormon baptisms. Compared to Protestant Christians, it's a matter of *whether* priesthood is necessary; compared to Catholic and Orthodox Christians, a debate over *which* priesthood is authorized by God.

In Mormonism, priesthood "ordinances" (the Mormon term for the rites or sacraments of the church) can be performed only by holders of the priesthood that Joseph Smith said was restored to him and his early associates first by John the Baptist and then by the New Testament apostles Peter, James, and John. Most ordinances are done under the authority of the higher priesthood, known as the Melchizedek

Priesthood, typically conferred on a man at age eighteen. Some ordinances, most notably the blessing and passing of the sacrament, can be conducted by holders of the lesser, or Aaronic Priesthood, which is conferred on boys when they turn twelve (as well as on adult converts as they prepare to receive the Melchizedek Priesthood). Both the Aaronic and Melchizedek Priesthoods are bestowed only on males who profess faith in the basic doctrines of the church and who conform their lives to the church's main behavioral standards (including, most prominently, keeping the Word of Wisdom and law of chastity and paying tithing). There are, however, no other prerequisites in terms of theological or other forms of training – priesthood holders learn on the job, so to speak.

Priesthood ordinances are divided into two categories: those considered essential for salvation or "exaltation" (explained below), and those that bless lives but are not required. The essential ordinances include baptism by immersion, confirmation as a member of the church (with its corresponding bestowal of the gift of the Holy Ghost), ordination to the Aaronic and then Melchizedek Priesthood (available to and required for men only), and the ordinances of the temple. Baptism is considered the gateway to the church and kingdom of God, and in the Mormon plan of salvation is essential for admission into the celestial kingdom. The baptism must be performed by an authorized (LDS) priesthood holder, and must be done by full bodily immersion after the priesthood holder has recited a short prescribed prayer. Baptism is immediately followed by confirmation, which is performed by "the laying on of hands," meaning simply that a group of Melchizedek Priesthood holders stands around a seated individual and lay their hands on her/his head while one acts as voice in speaking for the group and pronouncing the blessing. Confirmation officially makes a person a member of the Church of Jesus Christ of Latter-day Saints. The covenants, or promises, made by a person at the time of baptism and confirmation – namely, to take upon him/herself the name of Jesus Christ and promise to always remember and follow him – are renewed each Sunday as the member takes the sacramental bread and water blessed and passed by priesthood holders in the ward.

In addition to these required ordinances, Mormons also perform other ordinances that are considered vehicles of divine power and grace but which are not essential for a person's path to salvation. These include the blessing of babies (usually when one to three months old); blessings offered by the laying on of hands and given at a person's request for guidance, comfort, or physical healing (the latter accompanied by an anointing with a drop of consecrated olive oil); patriarchal blessings that declare a person's Israelite lineage and typically offer specific guidance for the person's life (see Chapter 7); the dedication of homes and graves, invoking God's spirit and protection upon them; and the formal "setting apart" of members who have been called to serve in various positions within the Church. These blessings are available to all members, male and female, though performed only by men who are ordained to the priesthood. In the nineteenth and the early twentieth century, women commonly performed certain ritual blessings, particularly for healing, but church leaders discouraged and then suspended the practice by the mid-twentieth century.

In short, Mormons believe that priesthood is the means of demonstrating and diffusing divine power in the world – or that, in the words of an 1832 revelation to Joseph Smith, "in the ordinances thereof, the power of godliness is made manifest. And without the ordinances thereof, and the authority of the priesthood, the power of godliness is not manifest unto men in the flesh."[29] The exclusiveness of LDS claims to the priesthood are mitigated, in the Mormon mind at least, by the belief that such ordinances will be made available to all of God's children who ever lived on the earth, not just those who were lucky enough to be in the right time and place and state of mind to hear and accept the Latter-day Saint gospel. This work of extending priesthood ordinances, and thus the promise of salvation and exaltation, to those who are dead is one of the main purposes for Mormon temples.

• TEMPLES

The most distinctive and ceremonial aspects of Latter-day Saint practice are found in temples. A year before his death, Joseph Smith taught that the purpose of the gathering, which the Latter-day Saints had practiced almost since the beginning of the religion, was

> to build unto the Lord a house whereby He could reveal unto His people the ordinances of His house and the glories of His kingdom, and teach the people the way of salvation; for there are certain ordinances and principles that, when they are taught and practiced, must be done in a place or house built for that purpose.[30]

In his 1833 drawing of the Plat for the City of Zion, Smith had placed twenty-four temples at the center of his planned ideal city, with exotic titles such as "House of the Lord for the presidency of the High and most holy priesthood after the order of Melchizedek, which was after the order of the Son of God." As historian Richard Bushman has noted, the centrality of temples in Smith's urban design "transformed a standard plat into a plan for a holy city."[31]

Though envisioned earlier in Smith's prophetic career, the first Latter-day Saint temple was not completed until 1836 in Kirtland, Ohio, with the next constructed in Nauvoo, Illinois, and not finished until more than a year after Smith's death. The Kirtland Temple featured some ceremonial functions – including foot washing, other ritual washings, and holy anointings – but mostly operated as a sacred meetinghouse for the Latter-day Saints. The set of rites grew far more complex in Nauvoo. In May 1842 Smith initiated a small group of faithful followers, whom he would call the Anointed Quorum, into a new ritual that he called the endowment. Much of the ritual had strong resemblances to Masonic ceremonies, and indeed Smith and many other leading Mormons were actively involved in Nauvoo's Masonic Lodge. While some have seen Mormonism's sacred endowment ceremony as simply derivative of Masonic rites, others have argued that "Masonry provided a vehicle for expressing themes Smith had been developing for years." If anything, Smith's newly introduced

FIGURE 8.2 The second temple constructed by the Church of Jesus Christ of Latter-day Saints, the Nauvoo Temple, was where the full elaboration of LDS temple rites was given to church members before they moved west to Utah. The original temple fell into disuse and then was damaged by fire and a tornado before being demolished. A modern temple, which replicates the original exterior, was built on the same site and dedicated by the church in 2002.

Image courtesy of the Church History Department, The Church of Jesus Christ of Latter-day Saints, Salt Lake City, Utah

ritual displayed his innovative eclecticism, as he drew liberally from a number of different sources, including Masonic rites and the priestly ordinances described in the Hebrew Bible, but then imbued them with new character, meaning, and purpose. Through the ceremonies he introduced in Nauvoo and which would then become practiced only in LDS temples, Smith initiated a new type of esoteric Mormonism that guaranteed participants membership in "a sacerdotal kingdom and family."[32] Brigham Young made the preservation, formalization, and extended availability of the temple rites a cornerstone of his claim to being the legitimate successor of Joseph Smith, and the temple has featured centrally in Latter-day Saint cosmology and practice ever since.

If the LDS Sunday worship service is largely prosaic and universally accessible, the temple ceremony is the site of a particular style and form of Mormonism available only to members of the church deemed faithful and "worthy." As opposed to the thousands of LDS chapels and meetinghouses in which regular weekly services are held, as of late 2015 there were 149 operating temples worldwide, with an additional ten under construction and fourteen announced.[33] Except for an open house when a temple is newly constructed but not yet dedicated, LDS temples are not open to the public, nor are they used for regular Sunday worship. They are dedicated instead to the performance of the religion's most sacred ordinances that most robustly fulfill Joseph Smith's vision of uniting heaven and earth and preparing humans for their ultimate destiny to become like God.

In order to enter a dedicated temple, a member of the LDS Church must pass a series of private interviews with members of their local bishopric and stake presidency. In the interviews they are asked if they believe in God the Father, Jesus Christ, and the Holy Ghost; if they believe the Church of Jesus Christ of Latter-day Saints to be true; and if they sustain the president of the church to be God's prophet on earth, and the members of the First Presidency and Quorum of the Twelve Apostles to be prophets, seers, and revelators. They are also asked if they adhere to the Word of Wisdom and law of chastity, if they pay a full tithe, if they are honest in their dealings, if their family relationships are appropriate, and if they associate with or support any apostate groups. The interviewee answers with a simple yes or no to each question, though conversation can ensue if there are any concerns. Though the priesthood leader acts as the formal representative of the church in conducting the interview, for all intents and purposes the person declares his/her own worthiness to enter the temple. Once approved, the person receives a "temple recommend," a small slip of paper that grants him/her access to the temple. The temple recommend interview, conducted every two years, serves as an opportunity for the member to declare his/her own faith and faithfulness – if not exactly in a public confession, in a formal ecclesiastical setting nevertheless. It cements their allegiance and serves as a reward for their devotion. For the church, restricting temple recommends only to those who meet strict standards is an effective means of identifying and maintaining a core group of committed members, and also functions as an incentive and clear bar for "less active" members to strive for. The selective granting of temple recommends – though they are available to anyone who meets the prescribed standards – creates an informal class of Mormonism's spiritual elite, a distinction which is not publicly paraded but nevertheless internally significant. Such selectivity can also create tensions, for instance when a person who does not hold a temple recommend is not allowed inside to witness a family member's or friend's temple marriage.

Temple ordinances and covenants are the most sacred elements of Mormonism and are not discussed in detail outside the temple, even among church members themselves. There is no greater sacrilege in Mormonism than to divulge certain details of the temple ceremonies, and Latter-day Saints ask outsiders to respect what they hold so sacred. It is possible, however, to outline the basic contours of what happens inside LDS temples.[34] When Mormons enter the temple, they show their temple recommend and are granted entry. From there men and women go to separate locker rooms where they change out of street clothes and into all-white temple clothing that symbolizes purity and is suggestive of unity, with no distinctions based on dress or other socioeconomic cues. They then proceed to participate in one or more of three principal sets of ordinances performed exclusively in temples: the endowment, sealings, and baptisms for the dead.

The endowment consists of two distinct rituals conducted in different parts of the temple. The first, called the "initiatory," is patterned on rites conducted in ancient Israel, as documented in the Hebrew Bible, in which Levite priests were washed with water and anointed with consecrated oil to set them apart for their sacred priestly calling. The man or woman performing the initiatory ceremony pronounces blessings on the body of the recipient so that s/he will be able to serve God faithfully. Having undergone the initiatory, women and men then participate in the second element of the endowment ceremony. Participants witness a dramatic performance, now typically portrayed with a video, that reenacts the creation of the world, God placing Adam and Eve in the Garden of Eden, the temptation and then fall of Adam and Eve and their banishment into the fallen world, and then the redemption of Adam and Eve (and by extension all humanity) through the atoning sacrifice of Jesus Christ and obedience to his gospel. The entire ritual is meant to dramatize for participants their place in the grand cosmic salvation narrative. Following the archetypal Adam and Eve, throughout the ceremony participants make a series of covenants with God, including promises of obedience and chastity (meaning sex only within marriage), which will orient them toward a godly life and the inheritance of celestial glory. The ceremony ends with participants moving to the "celestial room" of the temple, a beautifully furnished and impeccably clean room that is meant to symbolize the celestial kingdom and presence of God.

In ritually reenacting this cosmic drama from creation to exaltation, participants are "endowed" with spiritual power and authority. This spiritual power, and the covenants associated with it, becomes tactile through the donning of special priesthood robes worn only in the temple. Members also receive a sacred undergarment to be worn daily, coming in two pieces (top and bottom) and worn under the clothing, which serves as a perpetual reminder of the promises made to and by God in the endowment ceremony. Mormon folklore – and the statements of some church leaders – has sometimes granted special powers of physical protection to these garments, which has led to sniggering comments about Mormons wearing "magic underwear." Though some members do attribute some aspect of tangible sacred power to their garments, most Mormons understand them as a physical reminder of their deepest religious commitments as expressed in the temple. Garments also serve to enforce Mormon sartorial norms of modesty, as the top covers the upper body similar to a short-sleeved T-shirt, and the bottom reaches to just above the knee. Since the outer clothing must cover the garment, endowed Mormons won't wear short skirts or shorts, sleeveless shirts, or other "immodest" clothing – a requirement that places a notably heavier fashion burden on women than men, especially in most Western countries.[35]

The apex of Mormon temple worship, and in many ways of all Mormon theology, is the "sealing" ordinance, which constitutes the eternal binding of a husband and wife and their children. In the sealing ordinance, which is considered essential to attain the highest degree of exaltation, couples are promised that if they are faithful to their covenants they will be united not just until death but for "time and all eternity." In nations such as the United States where the LDS Church is granted authority to marry, the sealing constitutes both the sacred and the civil marriage of a man and a woman. In countries where a non-ecclesiastical civil marriage is required, such as France and

Mexico, couples go to the magistrate first and then enter the temple to be sealed. Any children subsequently born to the couple "in the covenant" will also be sealed to them for eternity. Children born to parents who were not sealed at the time of their birth (usually in the case of adult converts) can be sealed to their parents in what is considered by many to be the most emotionally powerful ritual offered by the church. The belief that families can be sealed together from generation to generation is one of the most compelling doctrines of the church; "Families Are Forever" has become something of a Mormon motto.

The grand hope and design of Mormonism is to unite all of God's children in one extended chain, thus enabling all men and women to return to God in the celestial kingdom as an exalted and ritually sealed human family. Therefore, in temples Mormons perform not only ordinances for living members of the church, but also vicarious ordinances on behalf of the dead who did not receive the ordinances in life but who require them, according to Mormon theology, for their eternal progress and exaltation. This is consistent with the belief that God is both perfectly just and merciful. If he requires certain ordinances for exaltation, then justice requires that the opportunity to receive such ordinances be available to all who have ever lived. The LDS Church thus sponsors a massive genealogical effort to identify the names and basic life information (at the very least, a birth or death date) of the deceased from around the world. Faithful Mormons can then act as proxies in performing the necessary ordinances – including baptisms, confirmation, Melchizedek Priesthood ordination for men, the initiatory and endowment, and sealings – on behalf of the dead in the church's various temples around the world. Mormons find biblical precedent for baptisms for the dead in 1 Corinthians 15:29, but the modern practice actually initiated with a series of revelations to Joseph Smith while in Nauvoo. Proxy endowments became common much later, in the early twentieth century.

While baptism and other ordinances for a deceased man or woman are completed vicariously, Mormon theology posits that the person – as a living, conscious, and agentive spirit living in the postmortal spirit world – ultimately exercises the decision whether to accept or reject the ordinances. This is all part of the Mormon ambition to preach the gospel to the entirety of humanity, living and dead. Indeed, the redemption of the dead stands as one of the church's primary missions alongside proclaiming the gospel, perfecting the church membership, and ministering to the poor and needy. In the late twentieth and early twenty-first centuries, the practice of baptism for the dead attracted some public controversy, particularly when some Jewish groups discovered that Latter-day Saints had been performing baptisms on behalf of Holocaust victims. The LDS Church apologized and suspended the practice, but only for that particular group.

Taken together, the temple ceremonies underscore that the aim of Mormon theology and practice is not simply an ethical life, nor even salvation, but rather exaltation as heirs of God in the celestial kingdom. In one of Joseph Smith's most audacious revelations – and controversial ones, too, as it was the same revelation that legitimated plural marriage – the Lord says that men and women who fulfill their covenants and receive all the ordinances of the temple will

> inherit thrones, kingdoms, principalities, and powers, dominions, all heights and depths . . . and they shall pass by the angels, and the gods, which are set there, to their exaltation and glory in all things. . . . Then shall they be gods, because they have all power, and the angels are subject unto them.[36]

This is, in a nutshell, the Mormon concept of theosis, deification, or exaltation. More than a mere doctrine of the church, this is the sum and substance of all Latter-day Saint theology and praxis. The purpose and function of the religious system introduced by Joseph Smith was to collapse (if not entirely remove) the sacred distance between heaven and earth, God and humanity. A disciplined, consecrated life would allow Smith's followers to develop the characteristics and virtues of God. Priesthood ordinances would allow them to feel and directly exercise God's power. Most of all, the temple is where Latter-day Saints would ritually enter God's presence and be clothed in the priesthood power and authority necessary for them to become gods and goddesses themselves – never to usurp or replace God the Father, but to become "joint-heirs with Christ" in receiving as a celestial inheritance "all that [the] Father hath."[37] It is a bold vision of the divine nature, potential, and destiny of humanity – at once, depending on your perspective, heretical and captivating.

With so much at stake, then, Mormon religious practices start to make more sense – if not necessarily in all the details, then in the passion and seriousness with which Latter-day Saints approach their religion. Becoming like God is hard work.

• NOTES

1 Robert A. Orsi, *Between Heaven and Earth: The Religious Worlds People Make and the Scholars Who Study Them* (Princeton, NJ: Princeton University Press, 2005), 18.
2 Ether 2:3, Book of Mormon.
3 James 1:22, 2:26. Contrast this to Martin Luther, who had a rather dim view of James in light of his theological preference for Paul's doctrine of justification by faith. At one point Luther famously referred to the Epistle of James as "straw." James M. Kittelson, *Luther the Reformer: The Story of the Man and His Career* (Minneapolis: Augsburg, 1986), 178.
4 James 2:18, New King James Version.
5 David Whitmer and Brigham Young, quoted in Linda King Newell and Valeen Tippetts Avery, *Mormon Enigma: Emma Hale Smith*, 2nd ed. (Urbana: University of Illinois Press, 1994), 47.
6 Doctrine and Covenants 89, quotes from verses 1–2, 5, 12.
7 See Matthew Bowman, *The Mormon People: The Making of an American Faith* (New York: Random House, 2012), 170. For a detailed overview of the enhanced

status of the Word of Wisdom in the early twentieth century, see Thomas G. Alexander, *Mormonism in Transition: A History of the Latter-day Saints, 1890–1930* (Urbana: University of Illinois Press, 1996), chap. 13.

8 Pew Forum on Religion and Public Life, *Mormons in America: Certain in Their Beliefs, Uncertain of Their Place in Society* (Washington, DC: Pew Research Center, 2012), 43.

9 Pew Forum, *Mormons in America*, 39.

10 Scholars estimate that about 20% of Americans regularly attend church, somewhere around 60–65 million per week. In 2014, the NFL averaged 17.6 million viewers per game, with five games reaching or exceeding the 29 million viewer mark. The 2014 NFL regular season had 202 million unique viewers, representing about 80% of all American homes. See "Fast Facts about American Religion," Hartford Institute for Religion Research, http://hirr.hartsem.edu/research/fast facts/fast_facts.html#attend (accessed September 22, 2015); Sara Bibel, "NFL 2014 TV Recap," TV by the Numbers, January 9, 2015, http://tvbythenum bers.zap2it.com/2015/01/09/nfl-2014-tv-recap-202-million-viewers-game-view ership-nearly-triples-broadcast-primetime/348433/ (accessed September 22, 2015). For the rise and fall of religious observance on Sunday, see Craig Harline, *Sunday: A History of the First Day from Babylonia to the Super Bowl* (New York: Doubleday, 2007).

11 See Robert D. Putnam and David E. Campbell, *American Grace: How Religion Divides and Unites Us* (New York: Simon & Schuster, 2010), 444–446.

12 David E. Campbell, John C. Green, and J. Quin Monson, *Seeking the Promised Land: Mormons and American Politics* (New York: Cambridge University Press, 2014), 53.

13 Van Evans, Daniel W. Curtis, and Ram A. Cnaan, "Volunteering among Latter-Day Saints," *Journal for the Scientific Study of Religion* 52:4 (December 2013): 827–841, quote from 838.

14 Katherine Best and Katherine Hillyer, "They Take Care of Their Own," *Reader's Digest* 54 (March 1949): 73–76.

15 Pew Forum, *Mormons in America*, 36.

16 Pew U.S. Religious Landscape Survey 2007, cited in Campbell, Green, and Monson, *Seeking the Promised Land*, 51.

17 Pew Research Center, "U.S. Religious Knowledge Survey," September 28, 2010, available at http://www.pewforum.org/2010/09/28/u-s-religious-knowledge-survey/ (accessed September 23, 2015). For a dire assessment of religious knowledge among Americans, see Stephen Prothero, *Religious Literacy: What Every American Needs to Know – and Doesn't* (San Francisco: HarperSanFrancisco, 2007).

18 Christian Smith, *Soul Searching: The Religious and Spiritual Lives of American Teenagers* (New York: Oxford University Press, 2005), chap. 2.

19 "Hello!," *The Book of Mormon* (Ghostlight Records, 2011).

20 Doctrine and Covenants 43:15.

21 For a memoirist's account, see Craig Harline, *Way Below the Angels: The Pretty Clearly Troubled but Not Even Close to Tragic Confessions of a Real Live Mormon Missionary* (Grand Rapids, MI: William B. Eerdmans Publishing Co., 2014).

22 "2014 Statistical Report for 2015 April General Conference," *Newsroom*, http://www.mormonnewsroom.org/article/2014-statistical-report-for-2015-april-general-conference (accessed September 24, 2015).

23 Doctrine and Covenants 18:10, 15.

24 See Rodney Stark, "The Basis of Mormon Success: A Theoretical Application," in *Latter-day Saint Social Life: Social Research on the LDS Church and Its Members*, ed. James T. Duke (Provo, UT: Religious Studies Center, Brigham Young University, 1998), 57.

25 See Stan L. Albrecht, "The Consequential Dimension of Mormon Religiosity," in *Latter-day Saint Social Life*, 263–265; Putnam and Campbell, *American Grace*, 78–79.

26 See Courtney Rabada, "A Swelling Tide: Nineteen-Year-Old Sister Missionaries in the Twenty-First Century," *Dialogue: A Journal of Mormon Thought* 47:4 (Winter 2014): 19–46.

27 Moroni 6:6, Book of Mormon.

28 See Nathan O. Hatch, *The Democratization of American Christianity* (New Haven, CT: Yale University Press, 1989), esp. 113–122.

29 Doctrine and Covenants 84:20–21.

30 *History of the Church of Jesus Christ of Latter-day Saints* (Salt Lake City: Deseret Book Co., 1980), 5:423.

31 Richard Lyman Bushman, *Joseph Smith: Rough Stone Rolling* (New York: Alfred A. Knopf, 2005), 220.

32 Samuel Morris Brown, *In Heaven as It Is on Earth: Joseph Smith and the Early Mormon Conquest of Death* (New York: Oxford University Press, 2012), chaps. 6–7, quotes from 178, 188.

33 See https://www.lds.org/church/temples/find-a-temple?lang=eng.

34 For a quasi-official explanation of the temple by a Mormon apostle, see Boyd K. Packer, *The Holy Temple* (Salt Lake City: Bookcraft, 1980).

35 In an effort to defuse rumors and satisfy public curiosity, the LDS Church posted a webpage with explanations and video footage of temple garments. See http://www.mormonnewsroom.org/article/temple-garments.

36 Doctrine and Covenants 132:19–20.

37 Romans 8:17; Doctrine & Covenants 84:38.

9

Globalization

Though made in the United States, Mormonism has always had global aspirations. Mormon scripture addresses both local and universal themes, but generally favors the latter. From its very beginnings, the religion was not content to be simply another American denomination. Joseph Smith and his followers understood themselves to be establishing the kingdom of God on earth, destined to revolutionize and fill the entire world. This expansionist impulse can itself be identified as distinctly American, particularly as it originated in an era of the United States' growing territorial ambitions. Yet while Mormonism's global impulse has no doubt partaken of the American spirit of Manifest Destiny, it owes more to a sincere commitment to Christianity's Great Commission, in which Jesus urged his disciples, "Go ye therefore, and teach all nations, baptizing them in the name of the Father, and of the Son, and of the Holy Ghost."[1] A year before he published the Book of Mormon and organized the church, Joseph Smith recorded revelations in which God called his latter-day disciples to engage in the "marvelous work" of taking the restored gospel to all who would listen, with the message intended for all "the inhabitants of the earth."[2]

Mormonism transcended national boundaries almost immediately. Less than six months after the church was founded, Joseph Smith's father and brother traveled from upstate New York to Canada to tell friends about the Book of Mormon. The church's first formal international mission commenced at the same time, when a pair of revelations sent a group of four missionaries to preach the gospel to "the Lamanites" (Native Americans) in the Indian Territory beyond the western frontier of the United States.[3] During Joseph Smith's lifetime, missionaries traveled from the church's headquarters in Ohio, Missouri, and Illinois to increasingly far-flung destinations including the British Isles, Australia, Prussia, Germany, and Palestine. Addison Pratt, whom we met in Chapter 2, led the church's first foreign-language mission to French Polynesia, which resulted in the baptism of some two thousand people; on his journey to and from his mission field, Pratt earned the distinction of becoming the first Mormon to circumnavigate the globe.[4] Brigham Young was a committed missionary, having served ten missions himself (including to Canada and England) by the time he became president of the church. In the early years of his presidency, he expanded the church's global proselytization campaign, sending missionaries to the Sandwich Islands (Hawaii), Samoa, Jamaica, Chile, South Africa, Malta, India, Siam, Hong Kong, and most European countries.[5]

Most of these early missionary efforts were fairly haphazard and enjoyed mixed results; the British Mission was by far the most successful, and vital to Mormonism's early growth. A series of setbacks at home including the Utah War, Civil War, and national anti-Mormon campaign of the 1870s and 1880s forced the church to constrict its international outreach; by 1869 the church's only significant international mission field was northern Europe.[6] Furthermore, because of its doctrine of the gathering, which called all able converts to relocate to Zion, the LDS Church never built communities of substantial size anywhere outside the American Intermountain West until the second half of the twentieth century. In short, from the very beginning Mormonism has had its eyes on the entire world, but its global vision has always outpaced its actual reach.

The establishment of permanent LDS communities outside the American West began in earnest only after World War II. In 1955, 92% of Latter-day Saints lived in the United States, but outmigration from Utah and especially a reenergized missionary program led to sustained church growth throughout the United States and other parts of the world. In 1996 the LDS Church announced that for the first time it had more members living outside the United States than within it. The vast majority of this international growth has occurred south of the U.S. border: over 70% of the church's non-U.S. membership now resides in Latin America. Indeed, while in recent decades the LDS Church has become less American in the sense of no longer being an exclusively United States-based institution, it remains a dominantly "American" church in the broader sense, as approximately 85% of its current membership lives in North, Central, and South America.[7]

Numerical growth and the establishment of church institutions tell only a small part of the story of global Mormonism. Statistics and official organizational history can obscure the lived experience of Mormonism outside the United States. How does a religion that originated, is headquartered, and still retains its strongest membership base in one particular country attract adherents in other nations and cultures? How do those members experience Mormonism? What does the religion mean to them? What challenges does the religion face in indigenizing in diverse cultures? To what degree does the LDS Church retain and promote a particular American identity even in foreign countries? How is a sense of collective unity maintained in an increasingly demographically diverse church? What prospects are there for the continued expansion of Mormonism both in terms of numbers and influence worldwide? Much more research needs to be done to fully answer those questions.[8] Here we will get a glimpse of Mormonism in one particular country, Romania, before moving on to consider more broadly the opportunities and challenges attendant to modern Mormonism's internationalization.

• CASE STUDY: MORMONISM IN ROMANIA

My family and I lived in Romania for five months in early 2015 under the auspices of the U.S. State Department's Fulbright Scholars program. I taught at a local university and conducted research on Mormonism in this eastern European nation through participant-observation in an LDS branch in Timişoara and formal interviews with Romanian Latter-day Saints throughout the western part of the country. I chose Romania as my field site because the LDS Church is still young in the country – it celebrated its twenty-fifth anniversary the week we arrived. Because of that, Mormonism is very much a converts' religion in Romania, with as yet no substantial adult second generation raised in the church. Furthermore, most Romanian branches are still heavily reliant on American missionaries. The LDS Church in Romania is quite small, with approximately 15 small-to-medium-sized branches scattered throughout the country that collectively see about 300–500 members attending services on any given Sunday. Furthermore, the context in which Mormonism operates in Romania is rather different than in western Europe and the Americas, where Protestantism, Catholicism, and secular liberalism dominate. By contrast, Romania is a traditionally Orthodox country shaped dramatically in the modern period by several decades of communism and religious repression until the revolution that overthrew dictator Nicolae Ceauşescu in 1989. The country is now undergoing a historical and cultural transition from its traditional past to its future as an aspirationally modern European nation, a process that gained momentum when Romania joined the European Union in 2007.

Mormonism had a brief appearance in Romania at the turn of the twentieth century, but its real beginnings in the country date to early 1990. Only six weeks after the 1989 revolution ended, a group of LDS general authorities traveled to Bucharest to meet with the new government. The church received permission to establish an official presence in the country, and immediately sent four adult couples who worked on humanitarian projects, primarily providing supplies and service to the nation's teeming and desperately underfunded orphanages. Proselytizing missionaries appeared later that year, and the first converts were baptized in the spring of 1991. From its beachhead in the capital Bucharest, the church then spread gradually to other cities; missionaries arrived in the major western cities, where I conducted my research, in 1996 and 1997. As with every new language culture that it encounters, the church had to quickly ramp up its translation services to provide scriptures, hymns, curricula, and other materials in Romanian. In each new city they arrived in, missionaries had to secure meeting spaces, which ranged from unheated high school classrooms to leased villas. The church didn't have its own freestanding chapels in the country until 2000, and even now most branches meet in rented spaces rather than actual church buildings.[9]

Numerically speaking, the fortunes of Mormonism in Romania over the past quarter century could be illustrated with a bell curve. As one of my interviewees noted, "It's been a hard twenty-five years for the church here. There were some good years at the beginning in the 1990s and early 2000s. The nation was extremely open to new influences. . . . There was high curiosity." But in the past decade, he said, "People have become more reluctant." He identifies the traditionalism of Romanian society as Mormonism's greatest obstacle: "The church brings new things to the table, new scripture. This is a hard one for the nation because it's a pretty conservative nation."

Another interviewee named Pavel reminisced that when he was baptized in 1997, he was one of only about five church members in Arad, a fairly large industrial city. Within a few years, when he served as branch president, they had about sixty people attending church. Now the same branch is down to about twenty people per week. Ioan, a member from the nearby city of Oradea, paints a similar portrait, saying that his branch has declined from about sixty to sixty-five attendees on Sunday to around twenty-five.[10]

Indeed, almost all of the active church members I met or interviewed were baptized in the late 1990s or early 2000s, and the pattern of a decade of rapid growth followed by a decade of decline is consistent in virtually every branch throughout the country. It may be that the history of initial growth followed by stagnation or decline is typical. In his study of Mormonism in England, Matthew Rasmussen argues that "much of the history of global Mormonism is characterized by a simple pattern: an initial advance, a subsequent retreat, and an eventual regrouping and reassertion."[11] Even if it conforms to broader trends, however, each situation will have its own particularities. In this case, we must take into account the rapidly changing social, cultural, economic, and political landscape in post-revolution Romania. The country reveled in its newfound freedom in the years immediately after the revolution, and oriented itself toward the West and especially America. Mormons were just one of a welter of American churches and businesses that rushed in to fill the post-communist vacuum, and for the most part they were embraced with open arms. (One telling example of American cultural influence during the 1990s is that most of my students at the university, who were born in this period, learned English by watching Cartoon Network on television.) For several years Mormonism thrived along with Jehovah's Witnesses, Adventists, and various evangelical churches who all took advantage of the newly opened religious market.

So what changed? At least three factors contributed to Mormonism's reversal of fortunes in Romania. First, the novelty of all things American simply wore off, as Romanians became more confident and wanted to maintain their own culture and not simply imitate America's. (Cartoon Network is now dubbed in Romanian.) Second, when Romania joined the European Union in 2007, droves of its citizens took advantage of open borders and moved to other EU countries for higher wages, quality education, and increased opportunities. This was true of a large number of the young Latter-day Saints who had joined the church in their teens and twenties and were looking for a better life. There are lots of Romanian Mormons – but outmigration means that most of them live in Germany, Italy, England, or the United States.

The third factor that has stymied Mormonism's prospects in the country is that after being sublimated under communist rule, the Romanian Orthodox Church has reemerged from decades of repression and reasserted itself as a core part of national identity. In a way that most Americans (including Mormon missionaries) find difficult to grasp, religion is integrally related to what it means to be nationally and ethnically Romanian. There is no native tradition of proselytization or notion of a truly free religious marketplace. An Orthodox priest I spoke to recalled his idyllic child-hood growing up on a street with Orthodox, Catholics, and Protestants, all of whom got along and attended one another's baptisms and weddings – precisely because no one ever expected that their neighbors would switch religions. Many of my stu-dents at the university literally could not grasp the concept of approaching someone to change religious affiliation. Proselytizing churches including Jehovah's Witnesses, Adventists, Mormons, and some Pentecostals are known collectively as the *pocaiesc*, or "repenters" – not a term of endearment. There are no legal penalties imposed on a Romanian who becomes a Mormon, but the cultural pressure not to do so is signifi-cant. A convert is often seen as turning his or her back on not just a particular church or theology but an entire matrix of history, culture, heritage, family, and nationhood. For most citizens, to be Romanian is to be Orthodox, maybe Catholic. To be Mormon is to be, well, not quite Romanian.

Other than the relative handful of children born in recent years to families in the church, the one thing that unites Romanian Latter-day Saints is that they are all converts. There is no single profile of a Romanian convert to Mormonism. Those I interviewed came from a spectrum of (generally Christian) religious backgrounds. Prior to being baptized Mormon they were, respectively, Orthodox, Catholic, Bap-tist, Reformed, Pentecostal, and Jehovah's Witness. Some were what we would call religious seekers – none more so than Weronika, who was born to a Catholic mother and atheist father, got involved in Buddhist meditation, then became a Jehovah's Witness, then studied with a Hindu guru, then converted to Mormonism when she read the Book of Mormon that her future husband gave her. Some interviewees were religiously observant in their previous tradition, others identified with their tradition but were not active participants, whereas a few were essentially nonreligious (usually because of communism).

Just as they came from multiple backgrounds, the members each had different stories of how they became Mormon, though some general trends emerge. Several encoun-tered Mormonism through the free English language classes offered by missionaries. These classes were especially popular in the 1990s and early 2000s, when studying English with native speakers – and doing so for free – was highly attractive particularly to young people looking to enhance their career prospects. The classes themselves were nonreligious, except a "spiritual thought" delivered at the end of the lesson, and there was no obligation to attend or join the church. Indeed, only a relatively small percentage of students inquired about the church, but that still resulted in a substantial number of baptisms nationwide. English classes remain one of the LDS missionaries' main tools for meeting new people, though the classes have become less distinctive; now it is common for Romanians to learn English in school or online. Many converts were drawn to the missionaries' persona, sometimes in near-mystical fashion. As Eva recalled, "the purity of those two missionary boys who came to me that day impressed me profoundly. I would have liked to have children like them. Their eyes reflected such purity, and a certain light."[12]

The converts I interviewed gave several reasons for why they were interested in learning more about the missionaries' religion. Izabela said she had several religious questions that the pastor of her Reformed church couldn't answer; she was also troubled by the bad behavior of some of the religious leaders in her congregation.[13] Levi remembered feeling "cold" in other churches – even though he was an observant Catholic – and having "this nice and good feeling" when he met with the missionaries and came to their church.[14] Rodica and Colina enjoyed studying the scriptures with the missionaries, as opposed to what they perceived as the lack of religious education they received in Catholic and Orthodox services.[15] Cristina was drawn to the social fellowship, particularly the excitement of all the young people who were taking English classes and coming to church activities together.[16] Another interviewee said his father "was just interested in the American culture," and thus happily invited the American missionaries into his home.[17]

Once they started taking lessons from the missionaries, several people reported that it was the Book of Mormon that clinched their decision to be baptized. Weronika said that upon reading the book, "my heart opened and I realized this is the truth."[18] Florin's family had converted to Mormonism four years earlier but he resisted until he prayed about the truthfulness of the Book of Mormon and felt he received an answer from God that he would "never be able to deny."[19] Many of my interviewees had similar dramatic spiritual experiences that precipitated their conversion. After taking English classes and starting to read the Book of Mormon, Monica "heard a voice in my mind saying you have to keep seeing and keep listening to the missionaries, they really are telling you the truth."[20] Pavel responded to a dream in which he saw the missionary he was meeting with dressed in white and say, "You must come and be a part of this church."[21] Experiences like these correlate strongly with those recorded by converts throughout the history of Mormonism, thus reflecting a continuity in the centrality of personal spiritual experience as an authenticator of the validity of their newfound religion for many individuals.

It is one thing for people to join the LDS Church, but quite another for them to stay long term. Indeed, low retention of converts is a major issue throughout the modern church, particularly in areas where the church is young and experiences high rates of initial growth. One published estimate of the "active membership" in Romania – that is, those baptized members who attend church services with some regularity – is 30%.[22] Based on my experience in the country, however, I would say that estimate is quite high and should perhaps be halved. There are any number of reasons why people struggle to maintain their original commitment to the church. More so now than in the heady days of early growth in Romania, many look around at the perpetually low numbers of people meeting in rented halls and wonder, "Is this a church?"[23] For those involved in leadership, burnout is a real factor. Precisely because the church is so small in many areas, new converts often receive major leadership callings relatively early in their membership, and those who are active usually have to take on multiple callings and extra responsibilities. Levi is a branch president as a single man in his late twenties. In only a decade, Florin went from being a new convert to being called as a district president, in which he supervises several branches over the entire western third of the country. Since joining in 1997, Pavel has served almost constantly in branch and district presidencies. While affirming that it is all worth it, Izabela did admit that "it takes a lot" to carry the load in a small branch, and that the many hours of largely unappreciated and unacknowledged work do lead to frustration and burnout.[24] This is an issue with the LDS Church's lay leadership everywhere, but Monica suggests that it might be even more of an issue in Romania where the culture is not predicated on voluntary associations as it is in America and people are used to having priests take care of everything in religious congregations.[25] Weronika echoed the theme that other observers of European Mormonism have made, namely that Mormonism has a high cost of membership – socially, emotionally, culturally, and financially – meaning that a person has to have very strong internal motivations in order to remain committed over the long haul.[26]

The architectural and geographical realities of Mormonism in Romania are strikingly different than in the Mormon heartland. Branches are territorially huge, often taking in entire counties (the equivalent of American states). As mentioned, most branches do not have their own dedicated chapel. The lack of their own buildings is a constant refrain repeated by Romanian Mormons when asked what obstacles the church faces in their country. As Ioan said, "A chapel is the answer. If we had a chapel, I'm sure there would be more members. . . . When [investigators] are coming here they don't see this place as a church." This is probably even more true in Romania and other European countries where churches are historically large and ornate, than in America with its low church tradition that fosters storefront churches and megachurches that spatially have more in common with sports arenas than cathedrals. Because the LDS Church has pursued a missionary strategy of building "centers of strength" in urban areas, there are large swaths of Romania's small villages and countryside that have still never seen a Mormon missionary – let alone a Mormon convert, who would have a very hard time traveling to church in one of the approximately fifteen cities where Sunday services are held. Another major difference is the significant distance to the nearest LDS temple in Freiburg, Germany. Because of low wages and even lower government pensions, most Romanian church members simply cannot afford to make the long trip to the temple, thus making it difficult to access the religion's most sacred rites. Many save up for years to make the journey, which takes twenty hours or more by bus. A number of devout elderly women I knew in the Timişoara branch had been unable to afford a trip to the temple for several years until an American missionary couple subsidized their journey. Whereas American Mormons are often encouraged to attend the temple monthly, Ioan flatly stated, "I cannot afford going every year to the temple, that's for sure."[27] The temple remains central to Romanian Mormons' religious imagination, but more as an ideal than an actuality.

Part of the psychological and social cost of being a Mormon is dealing with popular anti-Mormonism. While this remains an issue in America, it is even more dramatic in countries where Mormonism is new and there are relatively few Mormons to counter misinformation or negative stereotypes. Izabela complained that the Romanian public is "extremely misinformed" about Mormonism. At times it borders on the absurd, she said, such as the time that a young man came to the church "just to see if it's true what he read on the internet that we sacrifice little babies and drink their blood for sacraments."[28] Romanian-language websites lag far behind the abundance of anti-Mormon material available in English, but with a few exceptions the information about Mormonism that Romanians can access in their own tongue is highly critical. One article, for instance, warned against Mormon missionaries "invading" the country. Another sarcastically asked whether Romanians were interested in joining a community "which eats up to 10% of your income on a monthly basis and teaches that you must constantly wear some magic underwear without which you will never ever reach heaven." A 2012 article on a website hosted by the Romanian Orthodox Church called Mormonism "a sect of the Antichrist and a recruitment pool for the CIA and FBI."[29] Furthermore, Mormonism continues to be associated with polygamy in the popular mind. While some church members simply make a joke out of it with their friends, other converts have left the church after learning about its polygamist past. Sara reported that her son-in-law prohibited his wife (her daughter) from attending church with her for fear that his own daughters would be sucked in to the polygamist cult.[30] A segment about Mormonism that aired on a religious radio station called it a "modern heresy" that trafficked not only in polygamy but also in witchcraft, exploitation, and delusion.[31]

Mormonism is commonly referred to with the Romanian word for "sect," which clearly affords it lesser status than respectable, established "religions" like Orthodoxy and Catholicism. At other times it is even more derogatorily called a "cult," with accusations that the church brainwashes its members and steals them from their families. In short, Monica lamented, the majority of Romanians think that Mormonism is a "weird church," characterized by fanaticism, too many strict rules, and anti-social behaviors (such as the prohibition on drinking alcohol).[32] Knowing this, local church leaders have stressed the importance of public relations work to improve the nation's image of Mormonism. They believe this will not only ease some of the social and cultural frictions that church members face in Romanian culture but also smooth the way for greater proselytizing success. As Izabela said bluntly, "It's very important for people to see that we are not weird. We are not freaks."[33]

Given Mormonism's origins and history in the United States, the fact that the vast majority of the church's general leadership is American, and the heavy dependence of the Romanian church on American missionaries and leadership, I wondered to what degree the religion was perceived in Romania as being an American church. A few interviewees said that the notion of Mormonism as inherently American had never even occurred to them until I asked. Others acknowledged that it was a common perception that even they had to work through when they joined the church. One respondent frankly admitted that American values pervaded the culture, if not doctrines, of the church – the "first layer," but not the core. In particular he noted the church's pragmatism, goal-oriented leadership, and "constant drive for efficiency."[34]

Most interviewees, however, engaged the question of Mormonism's Americanness only to dismiss it. Their reasoning generally followed one or more of three arguments, which were given consistently enough that I wondered if it had been a topic of conversation either at church or informally among church members. The first response was that Mormonism originated in America so it was only natural that's where the membership would be the largest and strongest. As Weronika said straightforwardly, "It had to start somewhere." A second response, which echoed the language of many church leaders who have spoken on the special mission of America in the world, is that America was the only nation at the time with sufficient religious freedom that could allow the establishment of the church, its early difficulties notwithstanding. The third, and by far most common response, was to deny any national particularity about the church or the religion. Florin emphasized that "Jesus Christ doesn't have any nationality," and neither does his church. Eva argued by way of historical parallel, saying that just because Jesus came from Palestine didn't mean that Christianity was a Palestinian church. Pavel summarized the prevailing logic: "God is not American, nor Romanian, nor Russian. God is God. We are serving God and not the Romanian state, or the American state, or the Greek one. The church belongs to God, no matter where it is located on earth."[35] In my conversations with them, most of the church members seemed generally unaware of Mormonism's cultural engagement with contemporary America, from California Proposition 8 to the *Book of Mormon* musical. Indeed, the putative Americentrism of Mormonism seemed more salient for outsiders than for the Romanian church members themselves. From an inside perspective, the Romanians' religion really was local, and the prevailing attitude toward American missionaries and church leaders was one of appreciation and gratitude for their assistance, not resentment of foreign control. As Weronika noted, "I appreciate the Americans that they do so much work for us."[36]

What is the future of Mormonism in Romania? Outside observers and local members disagree. A recent study of the international LDS Church concludes that Romania has

> limit[ed] prospects for greater long-term growth due to low member activity and convert retention rates in addition to few convert baptisms. Most cities remain highly dependent on full-time foreign missionaries for Church administration and missionary activity, creating challenges for future self-sustaining growth.[37]

To a person, my interviewees disputed this dire assessment. When I asked what they envisioned for the church in Romania in the next twenty-five years, all of them projected growth. Eva speculated that the church would be "ten times larger." Sara simply exclaimed, "Big!" More measured responses included anticipation that negative public stereotypes would "gradually disappear," and that reverse migration would bring many of the early Romanian converts currently in diaspora back to the country. Almost every person expressed their hope for chapels in their cities and around the country, again underscoring the importance of sacred architecture. As Florin noted, "When [Romanians] think and talk about church, the first thing they have in mind is a building." Many pined for a temple in the country, or at least in neighboring Hungary.[38]

In short, Romanian Mormons' vision for the church in their country very much parallels the Mormon experience in twentieth-century America, characterized as it was by stability, growth, and increased respectability. Whether that particular religious model is truly exportable remains to be seen.

• GLOBAL ISSUES

We cannot take the Romanian experience as typical for all of "global Mormonism," but many of the themes that emerge there appear more broadly in the LDS Church's international expansion efforts of recent decades. In particular, globalizing Mormonism faces recurrent questions of public image, growth and retention, the nature of conversion, and indigenization and enculturation, among others. These issues confront any religious group that seeks to gain an international membership and cultivate a transnational community of believers. Mormonism's relative youth prevented it from taking part in the complex and often coercive connections between religion and empire that were so prominent in Christianity's and Islam's global expansions. Yet whether the modern LDS Church operates in an essentially colonial mode, with the American (really, Utah) center exercising control over the global periphery, remains a matter of discussion and debate. Also at stake is the question of whether Mormonism constitutes a world religion, with authentically indigenized and native expressions of the tradition in local cultures around the globe, or whether it remains an essentially American church with tendrils reaching out into foreign mission fields.

Public image

Mormonism remains relatively unknown and consistently unpopular in almost every country around the world, even more so than in the United States. Debunking stereotypes thus becomes a major job for Mormon converts, public affairs officials, and missionaries – even as the very presence of missionaries often fuels suspicion. An anthropologist conducting fieldwork in Haiti, for instance, found a widespread belief that the LDS Church and the CIA are one and the same, or that the church is there to advance the interests of the CIA, with missionaries as American agents. When asked whether he had heard of such a connection, one Haitian exclaimed, "Oh, yes. Those people are spreading all over my country. Damn CIA!" A Haitian grandfather discouraged his grandson from attending LDS services, saying, "Mormonism is a bad religion. . . . Mormons don't serve God, they serve the CIA."[39]

If Mormons are not being confused with the CIA, they are often being mistaken for other religions. The most common conflation is between Mormons and Jehovah's Witnesses – an honest enough mistake, since the main way that many people have encountered representatives of the two religions is through their similar door-to-door proselytizing techniques. In addition, many Europeans confuse Mormons with the Amish, thanks in large part to the 1985 film *Witness*, starring Harrison Ford and taking place mostly in an Amish community in Pennsylvania. Apparently because "Amish" would not have meant anything to most European viewers, the movie's sub-titles in many languages simply used the name of a better-known offbeat American religion and thus identified the Amish characters as "Mormons."[40] Europeans are thus sometimes surprised when they meet a Mormon who dresses in modern attire, uses electricity, and drives a car.

By far the most persistent albatross for Mormonism's public image around the world is the lingering association with polygamy. Long after the LDS Church gave up the practice, dime novels and other sensationalistic accounts continued to be published in many languages that connected Mormonism and polygamy. These popular sources did far more to shape the public mind around the world than any official statements of denial or clarification from Utah. Furthermore, there were and continue to be so few Mormons in most places around the globe that there is little opportunity for a persuasive corrective. Popular media in many countries continue to perpetrate the ste-reotype, knowingly or not. For instance, while the American version of the popular tel-evision show *Big Love* included a disclaimer that the LDS Church no longer endorses polygamy and is opposed to the practice, the Italian version of the first season did not. Professional journalists are often little better. One study examined 991 articles in Italian newspapers and periodicals during Mitt Romney's 2008 presidential cam-paign that mentioned he was a Mormon. Of those 991 articles, 473 indicated that his religion was associated with polygamy, but only 115 explained that Romney's church no longer actually practices polygamy.[41] Even in America, where there are far more Mormons around to dispel such notions, polygamy remains one of the most common one-word associations with Mormonism in public polls, trailing only "cult," "family/family values," and "different."[42] Though perpetually frustrating to Mormons, who feel they can only disclaim the association so many times and in so many ways, the legacy of polygamy exercises a powerful influence on the public imagination worldwide.

Growth and retention

The twentieth century was a period of geometric growth for the worldwide Church of Jesus Christ of Latter-day Saints. For reasons stated above, the eye-popping num-bers and rates of membership increase belied rather poor long-term retention of new converts, often hovering around 20%. Nevertheless, real growth did occur throughout the globe. Perhaps the best indicator of this is the multiplication of LDS stakes, the creation and maintenance of such requires meeting certain minimal requirements of total members, active priesthood holders, and tithe payers. Stakes thus represent a concentration of local leadership, strength, and organizational maturity, whereas areas without those things are constituted as missions. For instance, due to its relatively low number of active members and local priesthood leaders, Romania remains a mission of the church rather than a stake; since the church's organization there in 1990, the Romania-Moldova Mission has been presided over by a series of American leaders. Before 1923, all of the LDS Church's stakes were in the American Intermountain West. New Zealand became home to the first non-American stake in 1958. Since then the number of stakes worldwide has skyrocketed, reaching nearly 3200 by late 2015, with just over half of those outside the United States.[43] In short, by any measure Mormonism has grown substantially in recent decades, and much of that expansion has been genuinely global.

In the second half of the twentieth century, Mormons became smitten with their own growth. In some cases this led to practices – some unsavory and others merely absurd – to perpetuate an ever-steeper upward growth curve. A number of mission presidents instituted competitions within their missions, offering rewards of various kinds for those missionaries who could baptize the most people. Encouraged by their leaders to create sports clubs to attract youth, some missionaries in Europe went further and made baptism – without any kind of religious instruction or explanation – a kind of entrance requirement for participation on the baseball or basketball team. In the fever pitch to report high numbers, some missionaries baptized boys without permission of their parents, while others falsified records after baptizing boys who were under the church-prescribed age of eight. This brief "baseball baptism era" went forward despite the misgivings of many senior church leaders, mission presidents, and missionaries themselves. After only a few years, the excesses of the program became clear and it was brought to a halt.[44]

Baseball baptisms were the tactical exception, but the general strategy of maximizing international church growth through rapid "conversions" was a churchwide phenomenon in the late twentieth century. Several factors contributed to this approach. In the decades after World War II an increasing number of mission presidents and other senior church leaders came from careers in corporate America. It was only natural for them to apply the lessons and skills they had learned from their professional training to their ecclesiastical callings. They believed that religiosity, like any other human endeavor, could be quantified. Just as the success of an employee, manager, or corporation could be charted by output, the success of a missionary, mission president, or mission could be most easily measured by the number of baptisms they achieved. LDS proselytizing methods increasingly borrowed directly from sales techniques popular in corporate America. The internal language of Mormon missionary life became one of "goals, quotas, comparative charts, incentives, material rewards, and deadlines."[45]

With baptisms an increasingly important measure of successful missions – in some cases, the only important measure – the hard work of religious instruction and socialization of investigators and new converts was often attenuated. In many areas it was church policy that a person could be baptized after attending church only once. The regular rotation of missionaries, with an elder sometimes staying in a particular locale as short as a month or two, meant that missionaries frequently pressured their investigators to get baptized before they left the area. The result was large numbers of people who got baptized often for no better reason than they liked a particular missionary. When he was transferred, the new convert was left with only a shallow connection to the local branch or ward. This is compounded by the fact, still true today, that the sole authority to determine who can get baptized and when resides with the young missionaries themselves, under direction of the mission president. This means that local wards become responsible for newly baptized members despite in many cases the bishop and other local leaders not having more than a brief introduction to the recent convert. In general, the international Mormon missionary system in the second half of the twentieth century emphasized baptisms at the cost of in-depth religious formation, socialization, and long-term convert retention.

One of the challenges that Mormonism faces is that most of the people willing to join the LDS church are almost by definition not already heavily involved in another church. As scholars of Mormon conversion and retention have observed:

> Most converts come from backgrounds where they had not previously been regularly participating believers in any religious tradition. This transition from little to no religious activity to the intense levels of participation demanded by the Mormon faith is a challenge for many.

The attrition of newly baptized members is especially high in the first two months after their baptism, "suggesting that many of those who leave never made the necessary life changes to become committed life-long Mormons."[46]

These dynamics hold true in most LDS mission fields across the world, but have been particularly acute in Latin America – the site of modern Mormonism's most spectacular and in many ways most dubious growth. Chile is in many ways the poster child for the complicated story of international LDS growth and retention. According to official statistics, 3.3% of Chile's total population as of 2007 was Latter-day Saint – far outstripping the United States' 1.9%. Yet the inactivity rate in Chile hovers around 80%, even higher than the Latin American norm. This high rate of inactivity resulted in the contraction of numerous LDS stakes in the country, from 116 in 1999 to 74 in 2005, a decrease of some 36%. Such trends have not gone without notice among senior church leaders, who took the unusual step of sending one of the twelve apostles to supervise the church in Chile from 2002–2004 (a similar intervention was pursued in the Philippines, another high-baptism, low-retention area). While in Chile, the apostle took a number of steps to *slow down* the baptism rate, including increasing (to three) the number of successive weeks an investigator had to attend church before being baptized. Missionaries were also told to spend half of their time identifying and reactivating lapsed members.[47]

This new approach was championed by church president and prophet Gordon B. Hinckley in 1999 when he said:

> There is absolutely no point in doing missionary work unless we hold on to the fruits of that effort. . . . To the missionaries, I repeat, it will do no good for you to baptize someone and have that individual fall away from the Church shortly thereafter. What have you accomplished?[48]

Hinckley's admonition was institutionalized in a new missionary program published in 2005 called *Preach My Gospel*, which has "increased missionary focus on preparing converts not merely to accept baptism, but to become active and participating Mormons."[49] Partly as a result of this renewed emphasis on convert preparation and retention, the LDS average annual growth rate in Chile declined precipitously from 23.5% from 1976–1985 to 3.5% from 1990–2008.[50]

This slowdown may also be attributed, both in Chile and more broadly, to market saturation – that "most people who might be interested in joining the Church had probably heard the Mormon message by now."[51] This theory is supported by the fact, as noted in Chapter 8, that the dramatic increase in LDS missionaries worldwide since 2012 has not been matched by a proportionate rise in convert baptisms.

Conversion

The previous section demonstrated that the LDS Church has had much more success finding people willing to be baptized than those who make a lifelong commitment to full activity in the church. In short, it is far easier to make a convert than it is to make a Mormon. Putting it that way, however, begs the question: what exactly is conversion? And is being a Mormon the same regardless of a person's location, background, and culture?

Finding an exact definition for conversion that applies in all cases has eluded scholars, precisely because the phenomenon involves complex spiritual, cultural, psychological, familial, and sometimes political calculations. Switching religions is not like switching a light bulb on and off – people rarely go from being completely one thing to entirely another. The very concept of "switching," which is common in sociological literature, does not fully account for the ways in which people blend religious ideas and identities. For many people, their personal religiosity looks more like a patchwork quilt with lots of stitched-together parts, or an Impressionist painting in which the distinct colors and images blur into one another especially when viewed at close range.

These complicated negotiations hold just as true for Mormon conversions as for other religions. American converts to Mormonism have their spiritual mélanges too, but the phenomenon is put in starker relief when Mormonism travels beyond its native shores. Conversion always takes on local qualities. For some illiterate Haitians, for instance, conversion to Mormonism does not follow the standard script of reading the Book of Mormon and praying about it, since they cannot read the text. Many Haitian converts connect more viscerally with stories about the visionary experiences of Joseph Smith, who was similarly poor and uneducated in their eyes. Their inquiry is thus less rationalistic and more rooted in their own religious culture, which remains open to visions and other supernatural experiences. A missionary who served in Haiti reported that when he taught people about Joseph Smith's First Vision, their response would often be, "That's good. My friends just saw God and Jesus Christ last night." When Haitians are baptized Mormon, that does not mean they have made a clean break with their native religious traditions and cultures. Many Haitian Mormons have no problem testifying that the LDS Church is the only true church and then going to a *houngan* or Vodou priest for guidance. When pressed, some will admit that "all Haitians practice Vodou, even Mormons." Simultaneously subscribing to multiple cosmologies is seen by many Haitians as natural and complementary, which frustrates American missionaries who have more of an either-or mentality.[52]

Complex religious hybridity is not simply a function of new converts who don't yet "get" it. Several native Hawaiian students at Brigham Young University reported that although their families have been LDS for generations, they still believe in the reality of the old Polynesian gods – they just don't worship them. As folklorists have documented:

> Whereas once when a baby was born to a female ancestor, she would have offered her placenta to the waves as part of an old Polynesian religious ritual, today family elders at each birth would tell the story of how the placenta used to be offered, all in a manner that suggested that in no way were the old gods forgotten yet scrupulously avoiding any hint of worshiping them in a way counter to LDS Christianity.[53]

This narrative can be read as an example of how converts retain cherished native cultural traditions even after generations of committed dedication to Mormonism. Yet it also speaks to Mormonism's impulse toward a spiritual monopoly, as native practices can only be retained if relegated to the sphere of harmless nostalgia.

Church president Gordon B. Hinckley regularly invited non-Mormons to "bring with you all that you have of good and truth which you have received from whatever source, and come and let us see if we may add to it."[54] President Hinckley's gentle and seemingly ecumenical invitation notwithstanding, Mormonism has not typically understood itself as simply adding a cherry on top of a person's prior religious experience and understanding. The spirit of Mormon conversion is captured by Jesus in his major sermon in the Book of Mormon: "Old things are done away, and all things have become new."[55] In practice, the Mormon God is a fairly jealous god.

Indigenization and enculturation

The LDS Church's persistent sectarianism – its belief that it is the one true church and that all others, including all other Christian churches, are in some ways false, deluded, or corrupted – has contributed to a highly protective and insular ecclesiastical culture in which loyalty and conformity are chief values. The correlation program of the late twentieth- and twenty-first-century church, with its doctrinal conservatism and hyper-emphasis on centralization and proper authority, should thus be seen as a continuity rather than departure from longstanding Mormon norms.[56] When applied to globalization, the church hierarchy's deep concern with maintaining the integrity and unity of the institution has led to a highly conservative approach to indigenization (local control of institutions) and enculturation (the absorption of local customs, styles, and norms). The LDS Church has typically been resistant to many forms of local variation and adaptation. When Mormonism comes into a country, it brings (in translation) a ready-made set of doctrines, church programs, formalized rituals, periodicals and other literature, and behavioral expectations. Worship style is prescribed, the content of lesson materials predetermined. In reality, locals become Mormon far more than Mormonism becomes local.

Examples could proliferate, ranging from the relatively trivial to significant. For instance, white shirts have become the semi-official uniform of the LDS priesthood, with many suggestions (bordering on instructions) from church leaders that men performing priesthood ordinances, and especially young men passing the sacrament, should wear white shirts as a symbol of purity. However, white connotes purity primarily in Atlantic culture; in much of East Asia white is the color for mourning, whereas in Africa it symbolizes fertility (perhaps a less-than-desirable association for twelve-year-old boys).[57] In another example, official LDS Church policy states that "organs and pianos, or their electronic equivalents, are the standard instruments used in Church meetings. . . . Instruments with a prominent or less worshipful sounds, such as most brass and percussion, are not appropriate for sacrament meeting."[58] Yet in West Africa, drumming has been a vital dimension of sacred worship for generations, and pianos are popularly associated with bars and brothels.[59] To date, particular Anglo-American Victorian notions of hymnody and "worshipful" instrumentation have prevailed in the global church, at the expense of native sacred musical expressions.

The LDS Church as an institution shows relatively little capacity to adapt especially in areas where the church is still organized as a mission and Americans exercise most leadership; oftentimes non-local missionaries and mission presidents simply don't possess the local knowledge necessary to make culture-specific adaptations, even when they are inclined to. When locals are in charge, however, they have often taken the initiative to make Mormonism their own, even in ways that contravene Salt Lake City. In the midst of the LDS Church's fight against same-sex marriage in the United States beginning in the mid-1990s, an apostle traveled to Europe and instructed stake presidents there also to marshal their members to oppose same-sex marriage in their countries. As the European anthropologist (and former stake president) Walter van Beek noted, "All stake presidents listened dutifully and then conveniently forgot the advice." At the same time that many church leaders in America (and especially California) were pressuring members to canvass neighborhoods and donate money to the cause, their European counterparts – presumably including some who were personally disagreed with same-sex marriage – essentially shrugged off an apostle's directions. What explains the different approach? Van Beek suggests at least two factors. First, Europe was so far ahead of the United States in legalizing same-sex marriage that by the time the LDS Church got serious about the issue, responding to American domestic politics, the die had been cast in Europe. (A truly global church, the reasoning goes, should have been just as active in the European debates, not fixated only on the American scene.) Second, local leaders knew that taking a strong public stance against legalized same-sex unions "would be a public relations disaster for the Church in Europe." It was no use joining a battle that had already been decided, much less on the losing side, especially when European public opinion of Mormonism was so low to begin with.[60]

In some contexts, converts have not had to navigate the choice of Mormonism or their local culture because they see one as the extension of the other. This was the case among the New Zealand Maori, who converted to Mormonism en masse in the late nineteenth century. At one point nearly one-tenth of all Maori were baptized Mormon, providing the basis for a multigenerational and stable base of Maori Mormons on the island ever since. Grant Underwood, a historian who has studied the Maori conversion, argues that "there was a clear sense that in becoming Mormon one was not abandoning Maori culture" but rather enhancing it. Maori converts could feel that way for at least two reasons. First, sources indicate that several of their *rangatira* (chiefs or leaders) had spoken prophecies that were said to predict the coming of the Mormon missionaries. Thus, when the missionaries came and people responded to their message, they felt that it was the white elders fulfilling their own leaders' prophecies – thus placing Mormons in the Maori story rather than vice versa. Second, Maori immediately latched onto the Book of Mormon "as supplying forgotten but traditionally compatible details in their collective consciousness of the past." Specifically, the Maori read as their own the story of Hagoth, an otherwise obscure Book of Mormon character who recruited a number of people to build ships and sail away, and "were never heard of more." The Maori, along with other Pacific Islanders, thus embrace the Book of Mormon as their own origin story. As Underwood notes, "The American missionaries may have carried it to them and the American Pakeha [white man] Joseph Smith may have translated it, but for well over a century [the Book of Mormon] has been read as the story of their ancestors."[61] In this view, Mormon scripture is even more Maori than it is American.

Indeed, Mormonism's demographic success, proportionally speaking, has been greatest in the South Pacific, where "nearly half of Tongans are LDS, and almost all [Polynesian] island groups have a higher proportion LDS than the United States does." However, those percentages can be deceptive for many reasons, including low activity rates, religious hybridity, and the small population on most islands. For instance, although the entire country of Niue is 20% LDS, that represents only about 300 members.

Still, Mormonism has had a significant impact on Polynesian culture, and there are many substantial enclaves of Polynesian Latter-day Saints who have relocated to the western United States and thus exerted influence on "mainland Mormonism."[62] The LDS Church's continuing commitment to the South Pacific is institutionalized at Brigham Young University-Hawaii, with a student population that is heavily Asian and Pacific Islander, and the Polynesian Cultural Center, one of the most popular tourist destinations on the island of Oahu.

If we turn our gaze to Africa, however, we see that the LDS Church has done a relatively poor job of indigenization and enculturation, resulting in prospects for growth that are modest at best and which pale in comparison to other churches on the continent. Mormonism's performance in Africa has been helpfully analyzed and contextualized by two friendly non-LDS experts in global Christianity. Philip Jenkins acknowledges that the LDS Church has experienced significant growth in certain areas in Africa, most notably the western African nations of Nigeria and Ghana, where there are now LDS temples (a third West African temple has been announced in Ivory Coast). Indeed, as Jenkins notes, "Mormonism should be as at home in Africa as a fish in water," due to shared Mormon and African beliefs in prophecy, angelic messengers, visions and revelations, healing and spiritual gifts, a strong connection to ancestors, traditional family values, and affinity for Old Testament religious forms such as temples. However, simply in terms of numbers, "the Mormon experience in Africa has actually been disappointing," with growth that is "moderate at best and limited to some small areas."[63]

Jenkins offers several explanations for this relatively tepid performance. First, of course, is the longtime ban on blacks holding the priesthood or attending the temple. Although Mormons sent missionaries to Africa as early as 1853, they only worked among the continent's minority white populations until after 1978. Even when a number of West Africans got a hold of Mormon printed materials beginning in the 1940s and pled with church leaders to send missionaries or additional literature, even starting their own non-official Mormon affiliates that claimed thousands of members, the leadership in Salt Lake was hamstrung by its own policy. This led to Jenkins' second explanation, namely that Mormons simply got into the game too late in Africa, decades (or centuries) after other Christian churches. The explosive growth in Christianity on the continent proceeded with Mormonism mostly sitting on the sidelines. At this point, the LDS Church will always be playing catchup, and projections are that its continued growth in Africa will nevertheless lag behind other religions and even total population growth. Third, Jenkins argues, the LDS Church hierarchy simply can't let go and allow local members, especially in areas where the church is young, to fully take charge. The institution makes "strikingly few concessions to local tastes or customs. . . . It is one of the very last churches of Western origin that still enforces Euro-American norms so strictly and that [it] refuses to make any accommodation to local customs." In doing so, Mormon leaders and missionaries "have resolutely refused to draw on the historical lessons offered by any other church." The

LDS Church suffers from "a classic example of over-control of the kind that most churches weaned themselves from a half-century before."[64] Strong centralizing tendencies raise the question of whether the institution can empower its local leaders and members to act autonomously to grow the church in culturally appropriate ways.

Another scholar, Jehu Hanciles, puts a finer point on the impact of the LDS Church's racially restrictive policies, which meant that "well into the twentieth century, the face of Mormonism remained racially distinctive and its presence geographically concentrated." This legacy stretches well beyond 1978, as 86% of American Mormons remain white compared to 62% of the national population. Furthermore, in an age of global migration, when diaspora populations in the United States are important sites of religious exchange with communities back home, only 7% of American Mormons are foreign born, compared to 13% of the total population. Despite what he sees as some genuine efforts to increase local capacity in LDS communities around the world, Hanciles remains dubious about the LDS Church's commitment and capacity to the significant changes that must take place for it to become a more authentically globalized institution, in Africa and beyond:

> An inbuilt or programmatic resistance to enculturation puts Mormonism out of step with other major Christian traditions that are flourishing on the African continent and, indeed, with the African Christian experience itself. The centralized control of form and content that marks Mormonism means that the Church takes on a decidedly American image in non-Western contexts at the expense of local creativity and rootedness. To some extent, this pattern reflects the strong power differential between Utah and indigenous communities worldwide. It also denotes inherent limitations in Mormonism's capacity to globalize.[65]

It seems that a robust, locally driven process of indigenization and enculturation is the only way to ensure substantial long-term Mormon success in Africa and elsewhere around the world. What remains to be seen is the degree of local autonomy that the LDS Church hierarchy could tolerate. Modest decentralization efforts have thus far been centrally directed from Salt Lake City. It is difficult to imagine how the LDS Church can enjoy both authentic globalization and a fully coherent, universal Mormon identity and culture. Local empowerment will necessarily proliferate many ways of being Mormon. Whether such a thing is conceptually possible is in far less doubt than whether the American LDS Church leadership will deem it truly desirable.

• NEO-COLONIALISM OR WORLD RELIGION?

How are we to assess global Mormonism? Whether one judges the LDS Church's global expansion in the past half century as stunningly successful or as underachieving and problematic is in the eye of the beholder. The growth curve continues to shoot upward, but as we have seen, interpreting the meaning of that upward trajectory is not entirely self-evident. The more academically interesting question is how to think about the forms and processes attendant to LDS globalization. What is the best model for understanding the LDS encounter with global populations in the late twentieth and twenty-first centuries?

One way to conceptualize Mormonism's internationalization is as a form of neo-colonialism. A handful of scholars have adopted this critical view, with one of the most prominent being Walter van Beek – a Dutch anthropologist who has spent most of his career working in sub-Saharan Africa. Van Beek argues that "the Utah-based modern Church has replicated the same colonization process on its membership abroad to which it was once subjected" by the U.S. government. Drawing on *dependencia* theory used to describe the relationship between the United States and Latin America, van Beek observes that, from their establishment, international units of the church have been heavily dependent on church headquarters for "ideology, leadership, mission personnel, and finances." While many local areas have developed to the point of having stakes and even become financially self-supporting, the fact remains that all church policies are made in Salt Lake, as well as decisions about buildings and temples, missionaries, stake formation and reorganization, humanitarian aid, and public affairs initiatives. In order to facilitate the management of this sprawling international church, Salt Lake City's "administrative apparatus has mushroomed; what used to be a tribal council now is a multinational board of directors" supervising a professionalized, specialized, and multi-tiered bureaucracy. The American church, particularly in Utah, constitutes the "metropolis" while even well-developed non-American units remain mere "satellites." Information – in the form of policies, doctrinal interpretations, official curricula and church literature, and even moral politics – "flows only one way: from the center to the satellite Church, and not vice versa."[66] While questions can arise from the periphery, answers originate in the center. Satellites are answerable to the metropolis for the exact performance of their prescribed duties, but they never expect or receive a full and transparent accounting from the center. Humanitarian and development initiatives, including the church-sponsored Perpetual Education Fund which provides low-interest loans to (mostly) returned missionaries in developing nations so that they can receive the education to become competitive in the job market, are all centrally administered. On many levels, to be a Mormon anywhere in the world is to be dependent on church headquarters.

While illuminating, this neo-colonial model is not fully satisfactory for several reasons. Much of what was said above about international church units also holds true for a ward in downtown Salt Lake City. Since its beginning, the LDS Church was structured hierarchically, with ecclesiastical and spiritual authority residing in the prophet and apostles of the church. Correlation has exacerbated the church's administrative and doctrinal centralization, to be sure, but that affects American church units and members just as much as it does Argentines. Furthermore, the Mormon "metropolis" actually benefits relatively little, materially speaking, from the "satellites." Financial resources in particular flow from the center to the periphery, not vice versa. The temples built in most developing nations have been paid for, essentially, by tithe payers in prosperous wards in Utah and California; Ghanaians are not subsidizing temple building in Utah. Members in the church's international missions, such as the Romanians I interviewed, know full well that they are dependent on American missionaries and leadership, but they see the unequal relationship as benefiting them far more than it does the Americans themselves or even the American church. This speaks to the non-coercive nature of Mormon adherence, which belies the logic of colonialism in which people are subjected to forces entirely out of their control which they also cannot escape. Membership in the LDS Church is entirely voluntary – in fact, arguably more so in international settings than in Utah, where cultural pressures sometimes make disaffiliation from the LDS Church psychologically and socially difficult. There is virtually no cost, and often plenty of social incentives, for a Peruvian or Nigerian or Filipino Mormon to simply walk away. It minimizes the agency of those who choose active devotion to Mormonism if we reduce them to mere colonial subjects, even while recognizing the unequal power dynamics between church headquarters and local church units.[67]

A second model for understanding Mormonism's internationalization has been to argue for its emergence as a new world religion. The term "world religion" is a marker of status and longevity as much as size or dispersion. For instance, few people would argue against categorizing Judaism as a world religion, though its combined branches have fewer adherents than the LDS Church (approximately 14 million and 15 million, respectively) and it is heavily concentrated in Israel and America. On the other hand, size and dispersion do seem to matter somewhat: Zoroastrianism, which is older than Judaism and arguably just as influential, hardly registers on anyone's radar, with reportedly less than three million modern adherents mostly in Iran and India. University courses on world religions typically cover Christianity, Islam, Judaism, Buddhism, and Hinduism, possibly also branching out into the likes of Confucianism, Daoism, Sikhism, Jainism, and Yoruba religion.

The question is, should Mormonism make the list? Many people, including some non-LDS scholars, have answered yes. Jan Shipps argued persuasively that Mormonism is "a new religious tradition" standing in relationship to Christianity as Christianity did to Judaism; Rodney Stark declared that Mormonism "stands on the threshold of becoming the first major faith to appear on earth since the prophet Muhammad rode out of the desert"; and Eric Eliason proposed that Mormonism could be considered "America's fledgling contribution to the great world faiths."[68] Other observers are not so sure. Douglas Davies suggests that "if a world religion is one that becomes established in many different cultures and adapts itself to local patterns of ritual and of thought as have Buddhism, Christianity and Islam, then Mormonism is unlikely to follow that path."[69] Matthew Bowman similarly concludes that "While Mormonism may be a global religion . . . it is not yet a world religion, one that, like Islam or Catholicism, has found a way to adapt its forms to share its meaning in a panoply of cultures."[70]

"World religion" is a subjective category, to be sure, but as long as Mormonism struggles so mightily with indigenization and enculturation, it does not deserve the honorific. The Community of Christ has been far more successful than the LDS Church in adapting to local cultures worldwide, but it remains a small minority within the broader Mormon family of churches. Mormonism (here speaking again more narrowly of the LDS Church) successfully applied its considerable resources to global expansion over the past half century, but outside the United States Mormonism remains an imported product. The passage of time and the rise of third-, fourth-, and fifth-generation Mormons in a variety of local contexts around the globe will do much to help the religion "go native," but only insofar as the institution allows. Mormonism, then, is best understood neither as a neo-colonial imposition nor as a thoroughly indigenized and enculturated world religion, but rather as a young but genuinely global church with strong and powerful roots in the United States. It has been proven that you can take Mormonism out of America; the question persists whether you can truly take America out of Mormonism.

• NOTES

1 Matthew 28:19.
2 Doctrine and Covenants 4:1; 5:5.
3 Doctrine and Covenants 28:8; 32:2.
4 David J. Whittaker, "Early Missions," in *Mapping Mormonism: An Atlas of Latter-day Saint History*, ed. Brandon S. Plewe (Provo, UT: Brigham Young University Press, 2012), 40–42.
5 David J. Whittaker, "Missions of the 19th Century," in *Mapping Mormonism*, ed. Plewe, 94–95.
6 "The Church in 1870," in *Mapping Mormonism*, ed. Plewe, 121.
7 Samuel M. Otterstrom, "Membership Distribution," in *Mapping Mormonism*, ed. Plewe, 174. As of September 2016, official LDS Church statistics reported that North, Central, and South America contain 12,963, 273 church members and 23,623 congregations out of global totals of 15,634,199 members and 30,016 congregations; see http://www.mormonnewsroom.org/facts-and-statistics# (accessed September 5, 2016).
8 Wilfried Decoo has set much of this research agenda in his essay, "Expanding Research for the Expanding International Church," in *Directions for Mormon Studies in the Twenty-First Century*, ed. Patrick Q. Mason (Salt Lake City: University of Utah Press, 2016), 99–131.
9 See Carmin Clifton, *Come Lord, Come: A History of the Church of Jesus Christ of Latter-day Saints in Romania* (San Jose: Writers Club Press, 2002).
10 Interviews with anonymous, Cluj-Napoca, Romania, 10 March 2015; Pavel Piper, Arad, Romania, 12 March 2015; Ioan Filip, Oradea, Romania, 11 March 2015.
11 Matthew Lyman Rasmussen, *Mormonism and the Making of a British Zion* (Salt Lake City: University of Utah Press, 2016), 191.

12 Interview with Eva Costea, Oradea, Romania, 11 March 2015.

13 Interview with Izabela Geambasu, Oradea, Romania, 11 March 2015.

14 Interview with Levente Toth, Oradea, Romania, 11 March 2015.

15 Interview with Rodica Constantin and Calina Hundabut, Cluj-Napoca, Romania, 10 March 2015.

16 Interview with Cristina Marin, Arad, Romania, 12 March 2015.

17 Interview with anonymous.

18 Interview with Weronika Iepure-Gorska, Cluj-Napoca, Romania, 10 March 2015.

19 Interview with Florian Geambasu, Oradea, Romania, 11 March 2015.

20 Interview with Monica Simona Kiss, Floreşti, Romania, 10 March 2015.

21 Interview with Pavel Piper.

22 David G. Stewart and Matthew Martinich, *Reaching the Nations: International LDS Church Growth Almanac*, 2 vols. (Henderson, NV: Cumorah Foundation, 2013), 1:915. Stewart and Martinich's volumes offer an impressive compendium of LDS Church membership in every country throughout the world where the church has a presence. For a critical overview of the merits and shortfalls of Stewart and Martinich's analysis, see the review panel in *Mormon Studies Review* 3 (2016): 147–162.

23 Interview with Florin Geambasu.

24 Interview with Izabela Geambasu.

25 Interview with Monica Kiss.

26 Interview with Weronika Iepure-Gorska. See also Armand L. Mauss, "Can There Be a 'Second Harvest'? Controlling the Costs of Latter-day Saint Membership in Europe," *International Journal of Mormon Studies* 1 (2008): 1–59.

27 Interview with Ioan Filip.

28 Interview with Izabela Geambasu.

29 All sources quoted in Sorin Ahagioaei, Miruna Batineanu, Alexandru Oravitan, and Alexandru Szollo, "What's in a 'Sect'? Revealing Prejudice towards the Church of Jesus Christ of Latter-day Saints in Romanian Media," unpublished paper in author's possession.

30 Interview with Sara Emilia Fodor, Oradea, Romania, 11 March 2015.

31 Andreea Goldea, Iulia Nan, and Mihaela Toma, "Mormonism in Romanian Media: Television and Radio," unpublished paper in author's possession.

32 Interview with Monica Kiss.

33 Interview with Izabela Geambasu.

34 Interviews with Izabela Geambasu; anonymous.

35 Interviews with Florin Geambasu, Eva Costea, and Pavel Piper.

36 Interview with Weronika Iepure-Gorska.

37 Stewart and Martinich, *Reaching the Nations*, 1:919.

38 Interviews with Eva Costea, Sara Fodor, Pavel Piper, Monica Kiss, Florin Geambasu, Izabela Geambasu.

39 Jennifer Huss Basquiat, "Embodied Mormonism: Performance, Vodou and the LDS Faith in Haiti," *Dialogue: A Journal of Mormon Thought* 37:3 (Winter 2004): 4–5.

40 See Michael W. Homer, "LDS Prospects in Italy for the Twenty-First Century," *Dialogue: A Journal of Mormon Thought* 29:1 (Spring 1996): 145. I also had this confirmed in conversations with people who had seen the movie subtitled in Russian and Romanian, respectively.

41 Massimo Introvigne, "The Mormon Factor in the Romney Presidential Campaign: European Perspectives," *International Journal of Mormon Studies* 2 (2009): 103.

42 "Views of the Mormon Religion," Pew Research Center, 23 November 2011, available at http://www.pewforum.org/2011/11/23/romneys-mormon-faith-views-of-the-mormon-religion/#oneword (accessed 10 December 2015).

43 Richard O. Cowan, "Stakes," in *Mapping Mormonism*, ed. Plewe, 184–185; "Statistics: Church Units," Temples of the Church of Jesus Christ of Latter-day Saints, available online at http://www.ldschurchtemples.com/statistics/units/ (accessed 10 December 2015).

44 D. Michael Quinn, "I-Thou vs. I-It Conversions: The Mormon 'Baseball Baptism' Era," *Sunstone* (December 1993): 30–44.

45 Ibid., 32.

46 Seth L. Bryant, Henri Gooren, Rick Phillips, and David G. Stewart Jr., "Conversion and Retention in Mormonism," in *The Oxford Handbook of Religious Conversion*, eds. Lewis R. Rambo and Charles E. Farhadian (New York: Oxford University Press, 2014), 771.

47 Henri Gooren, "Comparing Mormon and Adventist Growth Patterns in Latin America: The Chilean Case," *Dialogue: A Journal of Mormon Thought* 46:3 (Fall 2013): 50–51.

48 Gordon B. Hinckley, "Find the Lambs, Feed the Sheep," satellite broadcast, 21 February 1999, available online at https://www.lds.org/general-conference/1999/04/find-the-lambs-feed-the-sheep?lang=eng (accessed on 10 December 2015).

49 Bryant, Gooren, Phillips, and Stewart, "Conversion and Retention in Mormonism," 766.

50 Gooren, "Comparing Mormon and Adventist Growth Patterns in Latin America," 66. See also Mark L. Grover, "Mormons in Latin America," in *The Oxford Handbook of Mormonism*, eds. Terryl L. Givens and Philip L. Barlow (New York: Oxford University Press, 2015), 515–528.

51 Gooren, "Comparing Mormon and Adventist Growth Patterns in Latin America," 49.

52 Basquiat, "Embodied Mormonism," 14–15, 25–26.

53 Eric A. Eliason and Tom Mould, eds., *Latter-day Lore: Mormon Folklore Studies* (Salt Lake City: University of Utah Press, 2013), 407.

54 Gordon B. Hinckley, "The Marvelous Foundation of Our Faith," October 2002 General Conference.

55 3 Nephi 12:46–47, Book of Mormon.

56 This echoes the argument in Matthew Bowman, "Zion: The Progressive Roots of Mormon Correlation," in *Directions for Mormon Studies in the 21st Century*, ed. Mason, 15–34.

57 See Walter E.A. van Beek, "Mormon Europeans or European Mormons? An 'Afro-European' View on Religious Colonization," *Dialogue: A Journal of Mormon Thought* 38:4 (Winter 2005): 23.

58 *Handbook 2: Administering the Church*, section 14.4.2, available online at https://www.lds.org/handbook/handbook-2-administering-the-church/music?lang=eng#144 (accessed December 11, 2015).

59 Eliason and Mould, *Latter-day Lore*, 407.

60 Van Beek, "Mormon Europeans or European Mormons?," 31.

61 Grant Underwood, "Mormonism, the Maori, and Cultural Authenticity," in *Latter-day Lore*, eds. Eliason and Mould, 482, 476. The Book of Mormon story of Hagoth is found in Alma 63:5–8.

62 Reid L. Neilson, "Australia and the Pacific," in *Mapping Mormonism*, ed. Plewe, 238–239. Church records suggest that Tonga is 45% LDS, but the rate of Tongans who self-identify as Mormon is much lower. See "The Church in 2012," in ed. Plewe, *Mapping Mormonism*, 172.

63 Philip Jenkins, "Letting Go: Understanding Mormon Growth in Africa," in *From the Outside Looking In: Essays on Mormon History, Theology, and Culture – The Tanner Lectures on Mormon History*, eds. Reid L. Neilson and Matthew J. Grow (New York: Oxford University Press, 2015), 339, 344.

64 Jenkins, "Letting Go," 347–348. For a similar critique by an LDS scholar, see Walter E.A. van Beek, "Church Unity and the Challenge of Cultural Diversity: A View from across the Sahara," in *Directions for Mormon Studies in the Twenty-First Century*, ed. Mason, 72–98.

65 Jehu J. Hanciles, "'Would That All God's People Were Prophets': Mormonism and the New Shape of Global Christianity," in *From the Outside Looking In*, eds. Neilson and Grow, 361, 369–370, 365.

66 Van Beek, "Mormon Europeans or European Mormons?," quotes from 3, 15, 17–18, 20.

67 Similar dynamics are seen among the church's Spanish-speaking membership in the United States. For a memoirist's account, see Ignacio M. Garcia, *Chicano While Mormon: Activism, War, and Keeping the Faith* (Madison, NJ: Fairleigh Dickinson University Press, 2015).

68 Jan Shipps, *Mormonism: The Story of a New Religious Tradition* (Urbana: University of Illinois Press, 1985); Rodney Stark, *The Rise of Mormonism*, ed. Reid L. Neilson (New York: Columbia University Press, 2005), 139; Eric Eliason, ed., *Mormons and Mormonism: An Introduction to an American World Religion* (Urbana: University of Illinois Press, 2001), 15.

69 Douglas J. Davies, *An Introduction to Mormonism* (New York: Cambridge University Press, 2003), 248.

70 Matthew Bowman, *The Mormon People: The Making of an American Faith* (New York: Random House, 2012), 221–222.

Mormonisms

Most of this book has operated under an interpretive fiction – though I believe a useful and defensible one. Both the title of the book and most of its content suggest that there is a single thing that we can label and understand as Mormonism, even while acknowledging persistent internal diversity and contestation. But in fact, if we take "Mormonism" as a general category for any religious movement descending from the visions and teachings of Joseph Smith, then in fact there have been over four hundred organized "Mormonisms" since the Church of Christ's initial organization in April 1830, with approximately eighty still operating as of 2007.[1] The previous chapters have focused on just one of those institutional manifestations: the Salt Lake City-based Church of Jesus Christ of Latter-day Saints. If all this attention on just one of four hundred groups seems a bit lopsided, consider that this one group's membership comprises between 96 and 98% of all current "Mormons" (speaking broadly).[2] Furthermore, many if not most of those 2–4% who are not members of the LDS Church would reject the term "Mormon" as a label. In other words, if you ever meet a self-described Mormon, the overwhelming likelihood is that s/he is a member of the Church of Jesus Christ of Latter-day Saints.

Because the term "Mormon" has been very nearly monopolized by the LDS Church and its members, scholars and other observers have struggled to find a suitable term to capture all of the groups who trace their religious genealogy to Joseph Smith. A frequently used term is "Restorationist," but it has the problem of also applying to other early nineteenth-century churches that were also seeking to "restore" Christianity to its pure New Testament form yet had nothing to do with Joseph Smith, and in fact were often vocally opposed to him and his followers. Another option is "Latter Day Saint," which is useful because almost all of the four hundred groups share the history of the movement from 1834–1838 when it was called the "Church of the Latter Day Saints." (Note that the LDS Church uses a small-d for "day" and hyphenates "Latter-day," whereas most other groups capitalize all the words and do not use a hyphen.) Nevertheless, that moniker has fallen out of favor with many, including the second-largest denomination, once named the Reorganized Church of Jesus Christ of Latter Day Saints but since 2000 has been known as the Community of Christ. We will probably never settle on a universally agreeable umbrella term that satisfactorily covers all four hundred-plus groups, so "Mormon," "Restorationist," and "Latter Day Saint" continue to be employed, each with caveats and qualifiers. Unlike previous chapters, where I used "Mormon" and "Mormonism" as synonyms for the LDS Church, in this chapter I will use "Mormon" in its more capacious sense, referring to the Church of Jesus Christ of Latter-day Saints with the shorthand designators Latter-day Saint and LDS.

Dissent, schism, and sectarian proliferation were not late developments in the history of the Mormon movement; they were present from the very beginning. Joseph Smith had to fend off rival prophets within the church in the very first year of its existence, and the earliest schismatic sect broke off from the Church of Christ in 1831. Several more groups emerged during the lifetime of Joseph Smith, though none survived long. The most notable was the True Church of Jesus Christ of Latter Day Saints, which published a newspaper in Nauvoo exposing plural marriage and other reported abuses by Smith, setting off a chain of events resulting in the prophet's arrest and finally murder in June 1844. Joseph Smith was exaggerating when he claimed to be "the only man that has ever been able to keep a whole church together since the days of Adam," yet he nevertheless had been the glue holding together disparate elements and personalities within the church.[3] Without a clear plan for succession following his death, the Mormon movement went into a period of fragmentation from 1844–1860. There were eight possible succession options and at least fifteen significant groups that emerged during these years, all of which claimed to be the true inheritors and carriers of Smith's legacy. Many of those groups flamed out within a few years, and others coalesced into what became the Reorganized Church of Jesus Christ of Latter Day Saints, formed in 1860 under the leadership of Joseph and Emma Smith's oldest surviving son, Joseph Smith III. While a number of other, smaller groups persisted and even proliferated, the RLDS Church constituted the largest and most significant counterweight to the much larger LDS Church, led by Brigham Young and firmly ensconced in the Intermountain West.[4]

The LDS Church's stress on authority and obedience – a clear legacy of Brigham Young's leadership – has exerted a powerful centripetal force on its membership, offering one explanation for the church's multigenerational success. Yet a strong centrifugal logic has also always been inherent to Mormonism, due to its dual emphasis on prophetic authority at the top and personal revelation among the grassroots. An openness to continuing revelation from heaven, coupled with the necessity of responding to changing circumstances and historical development, has necessarily created a dynamic, fluid religious movement. Empowered to seek their own revelation, Mormons have reacted to new doctrines, policies, and other forms of institutional change in a variety of ways, ranging from full acceptance to outright rejection. Joseph Smith left behind a complex, often contradictory, and not fully worked out religious system, which was ripe for successors, both at the time and ever since, to interpret and reinterpret. Furthermore, at the time of Smith's death most Mormons lived in the outlying branches of the church scattered throughout America and Great Britain, and were therefore completely unaware of some of the more esoteric theological and ritual developments introduced in Nauvoo by the prophet during the last two years of his life (notably temple ordinances, plural marriage, and the doctrine of theosis). Disparate groups have thus been able to declare with singular authority that they carried Smith's mantle by virtue of 1) returning to an earlier, "pure" form of the religion; 2) preserving his teachings as they existed at the time of his death; or 3) continuing his prophetic trajectory by revealing new doctrines and claiming them as faithful extensions of his original visions.[5] All this means that schism and dissent have been more the rule than the exception in Mormonism. While individual churches may go to great lengths to police their internal borders of orthodoxy and orthopraxis, inheritors of the legacy of Joseph Smith will always find at least some among them who move in different spiritual directions.

The end result of all this proliferation is a religious family tree with branches stretching in almost every conceivable direction. As noted by historian Steven Shields, the various Latter Day Saint groups

> are theologically diverse, roaring across the entire spectrum of issues, ideas, verbiage, and practice. Some have been conservative in their outlook, others liberal. . . . Some of these expressions have been fiercely monogamous, many polygamous, several embracing the gay and lesbian community fully, others denouncing such relationships.[6]

If we were to chart these various groups in terms of their theological, political, and cultural positions, the LDS Church would appear as a center-right party. We can better appreciate the fuller spectrum of Mormonisms by expanding our horizon to consider the Community of Christ, which occupies a position to the left of the LDS Church, as well as the group of self-described "fundamentalist" churches that remain dedicated to polygamy and other nineteenth-century LDS distinctives, thus placing them to the right of current LDS orthodoxy. Elaborating the history, basic beliefs and practices, and authority structures of the Community of Christ and fundamentalist Mormons will demonstrate just how far the various branches of the Latter Day Saint religious family have diverged since their point of common origin from 1830–1844.

• COMMUNITY OF CHRIST

History

The Community of Christ, formerly the Reorganized Church of Jesus Christ of Latter Day Saints, shares the same history as the Church of Jesus Christ of Latter-day Saints from Joseph Smith's earliest vision in 1820 until his death in 1844. In a testament to the malleability of history, however, the two churches' respective interpretations and presentations of that history often differs. In recent decades this has became less true among historians from the two churches who adhere to similar professional standards. Indeed, beginning in the 1960s, the Mormon History

Association, John Whitmer Historical Association, and other scholarly organizations provided important venues for rapprochement and dialogue between members of the two communities. Yet when church history is viewed through a theological lens, as is often done within a religious tradition, then the content and meaning of that history naturally changes. The Nauvoo period was a point of contention between RLDS and LDS historians and church leaders for decades, as the RLDS generally denied, rejected, or minimized many of the doctrinal and ritual innovations made there by Joseph Smith, and which Brigham Young and the LDS Church preserved and extended.

It would not be correct to say that the RLDS Church emerged merely as an opposition faction to Brigham Young. Yet is true that the early leaders and members who constituted the Reorganization in 1860 predominantly drew from the approximately one-third of Mormons at the time of Smith's death who chose not to follow Young and the Twelve Apostles to the West. Their disagreements with the "Brighamites," as they called the Utah church, were multiple, but primarily and most publicly centered on three issues: succession, polygamy, and theocracy.

As mentioned above, Joseph Smith failed to leave an unambiguous plan for succession, resulting in multiple claimants resting their case on various forms of authority. Brigham Young and the Twelve argued that Smith had given them the "keys of the priesthood," which allowed them to authorize and perform the all-important priesthood ordinances of the church, from baptism to the newly introduced temple endowment and sealings. Young did not, however, claim the prophetic mantle, arguing that all the necessarily priesthood authority resided with the Twelve as a body (his position, as the senior apostle, was as president of the Twelve). The Latter-day Saints would not reorganize the First Presidency, with Young as the sole president of the church, until three-and-a-half years after Smith's death. The Twelve's claims carried the day with the majority of Mormons. However, a substantial minority believed that the restored church should be led by a living prophet, not a dead one. Many looked to the Smith family itself, but that was problematic. Joseph's clear would-be successor, his brother Hyrum, had been murdered along with him in Carthage Jail. Another brother, Samuel, died of natural causes shortly thereafter. A fourth Smith brother, William, was seen by many as controversial and erratic. Joseph Smith III, who had a clear claim, was only eleven years old at the time of his father's death. That left space for non-members of the Smith family to step forward as the movement's new prophet. The most prominent was James Strang, who for a time held the allegiance of more Mormons, including several surviving members of the Smith family, than anyone other than Brigham Young and the apostles. Strang's prophetic style and career in many ways echoed that of Joseph Smith, with visions, revelations, and translated metal plates. Strang also alienated many followers due to a theocratic leadership style and rumors (which proved to be true) of polygamy. In 1856 Strang, like Smith before him, was killed by gunfire, once again leaving the non-Brighamite Mormons without a prophet.

What came to be known as the Reorganization was spearheaded by Jason Briggs and Zenos Gurley, two men who after Joseph Smith's death held leadership positions in various of the Midwestern Mormon churches, including Strang's, but were ultimately dissatisfied with what they experienced there. Their efforts rallying together small communities of Mormons in northern Illinois and southern Wisconsin paid off in April 1860 when Joseph Smith III, at the age of 27, felt inspired to take up his father's prophetic mantle and accepted ordination as president of what came to be known as the Reorganized Church. Over the course of the next decade, many of those Mormons who had followed other leaders during the period of fragmentation gathered together under the banner of the Reorganization. They believed that the right of prophethood was patrilineal, and that Joseph Smith III was therefore the rightful spiritual heir of his father. Initially reluctant, the new church president quickly grew into his role and confidently led the RLDS Church for over five decades until his death in 1914.

The issues of polygamy and theocracy were interrelated in the nation's opposition to the LDS Church from the 1850s through the 1880s, and the same held true for Joseph Smith III and the Reorganization. Smith's biographer notes that "from the 1850s onward the destruction of all vestiges of plural marriage within the Mormon movement was perhaps the greatest passion of the Reorganization." Having failed to convince the majority of the Latter-day Saints to submit to his leadership during four missions to Utah in the 1870s and 1880s, Joseph Smith III turned instead to politics as a means of thwarting what he saw as a corrupted church under the leadership of Brigham Young and his successors. While the Latter-day Saints took shelter in their mountain retreats during the Civil War and awaited the nation's implosion, in 1863 Smith submitted a "Declaration of Loyalty" to Congress. He actively advocated for the string of anti-polygamy measures that Congress passed from the 1860s through the 1880s. As the son of the dead Mormon prophet and as the most viable option for Mormon leadership besides Brigham Young, Smith was welcomed into the offices of numerous Congressmen and Senators in Washington. He advised a strong but temperate response, supporting measures that would destroy polygamy and the political power of the LDS Church while nevertheless protecting individual Latter-day Saints' freedom of worship (which, of course, in his mind did not extend so far as to include plural marriage). Smith was gratified, and the RLDS movement was in many ways validated, when Congress finally succeeded in forcing the Utah church to submit. As his biographer concluded, "Although Joseph Smith had mixed feelings about the suffering of the Utah Saints at the hands of federal officials, he took great pride in the elimination of plural marriage as a tenet of the religion."[7]

When Joseph Smith III died in 1914, the reins of the RLDS Church passed to his son Frederick (Fred) M. Smith. Fred was the first graduate of the church's new college, called Graceland, located in the RLDS town and then-headquarters of Lamoni, Iowa, due north of the 1830s Mormon settlements in western Missouri. With an MA in

FIGURE 10.1 Joseph Smith III, the son of Joseph Smith Jr. and Emma Hale Smith, became the first president-prophet of the Reorganized Church of Jesus Christ of Latter Day Saints, which rejected polygamy, temple rites, and the leadership of Brigham Young.

Image courtesy of the Church History Department, The Church of Jesus Christ of Latter-day Saints, Salt Lake City, Utah

sociology and Ph.D. in psychology, Fred partook fully of the Progressive Era spirit of moral perfectionism, social reform, and centralized social engineering led by trained experts. In the early twentieth century, RLDS Church members spoke "incessantly" of Zion, applying the adjective "Zionic" to various fledgling business, educational, and agricultural enterprises. They found ideological allies and shared language in the writings of contemporaneous Social Gospel Protestants such as Walter Rauschenbusch.

In the Progressive vision, social reform and moral progress were often accomplished through the careful guidance of powerful experts. Accordingly, in an effort that would anticipate the later LDS correlation movement, Fred M. Smith won a costly power struggle within the RLDS Church – called the Supreme Directional Control crisis – to centralize and streamline administrative policies, finances, and thus control. Smith felt that such centralization "was necessary to coordinate the Church's experiments in Zionic living." But his victory came at a price, including the disaffection of many members and leaders who were put off by Smith's use of prophetic revelation to give a divine stamp to his own positions and remove opponents (including his brother Israel A. Smith) from leadership positions.[8]

Fred and Israel Smith reconciled shortly after the Supreme Directional Control controversy, and Israel served as a counselor to his brother and then became president of the church when Fred died in 1946. Israel oversaw the church's international expansion through missions in the South Pacific and Europe in the wake of World War II. Upon his death in a car accident in 1958, church leadership passed to yet another son of Joseph Smith III, W. Wallace Smith, who served until he retired and became "president emeritus" in 1978. W. Wallace Smith's tenure coincided with a wave of modernization that swept the RLDS Church along with many other Christian bodies, most notably the Roman Catholic Church during the Second Vatican Council. During W. Wallace's presidency, the church began to edge away from some of its more distinctively Latter Day Saint roots and toward a broader liberal Protestant ecumenism. He called Roy Cheville to be the church's presiding evangelist, a post that up until that point had been exclusively reserved for a member of the Smith family. Cheville, who earned a Ph.D. in religion from the University of Chicago, had already been influential in reshaping the theological direction of the RLDS Church (discussed in the next section). Furthermore, the church's international mission program both accelerated and changed dramatically, emphasizing indigenization and the basic concepts of biblical Christianity rather than the particular features of Latter Day Saint doctrine and history.

The seeds of modern reform within the RLDS Church flowered during the successive presidencies of Wallace B. Smith (W. Wallace's son), W. Grant McMurray, and Stephen M. Veazey. Wallace B. Smith presented one of the most important revelations in RLDS history to the church in its April 1984 World Conference. Canonized as Section 156 of the RLDS/Community of Christ's Doctrine and Covenants, the revelation proclaimed that the church's new temple, which members and leaders had been talking about building for years, would be "dedicated to the pursuit of peace" and would stand as a "place in which the essential meaning of the Restoration as healing and redeeming agent is given new life and understanding." (The church dedicated the distinctively shaped temple in Independence, Missouri, in 1990.) The revelation went on to speak of priesthood, lamenting the "loss of spiritual power" in the church due to priesthood holders who had been neglectful of their duties. As part of a call to renew the power of the priesthood among "those who have an abiding faith and desire to serve me with all their hearts," the revelation declared that "all are called according to the gifts which have been given them" – including women.[9] Wallace B. Smith further broke with RLDS tradition by appointing as his successor W. Grant McMurray, the first prophet-president of the church not to be a direct descendant of Joseph Smith. Extending priesthood ordination to women and abandoning the once-foundational principle of patrilineal prophetic succession alienated many members and led to the disaffection of approximately one-quarter of total church membership. Believing Wallace B. Smith to be a "fallen prophet," these dissenters continued in independent RLDS or Restoration branches, reconstituted in more conservative groups such as the Restoration Church of Jesus Christ of Latter Day Saints or Remnant Church of Jesus Christ of Latter Day Saints (headed by Frederick Larsen, a descendent of Joseph Smith through Frederick M. Smith), or left the movement altogether.

The church continued its evolution under Grant McMurray, a progressive-thinking historian who led the church from 1996 until his resignation in 2004. After much debate, in 2000 the church changed its official name to Community of Christ. The name change culminated a decades-long process in which the church had been gradually moving away from its history and identity as a Latter Day Saint sect and toward a more ecumenical position as a small but nevertheless distinctive member of the worldwide body of Christians. Recalling the movement's original name in 1830 as the Church of Christ, the Community of Christ affirms that its new name "honors our heritage, reflects our core value of building community, and proclaims the gospel of Christ."[10] McMurray counseled that the Community of Christ should think of itself less as a "people with a prophet" and more as a "prophetic people," being "respectful of tradition" but not "unduly bound by interpretations and procedures that no longer fit the needs of a worldwide church."[11]

One of McMurray's own departures from church tradition was in not naming a successor upon his resignation. The church selected Stephen M. Veazey in 2005, whose administration has been marked by a deepening commitment to the church's Zionic vision of building "communities of generosity, justice, and peacefulness."[12] During Veazey's presidency, women have assumed senior leadership positions at every level within the church, with the church presidency itself as the only office that a woman has yet to hold. The Community of Christ has also become more inclusive of the LGBT community, with the U.S. Conference recommending that the church marry same-sex couples and ordain LGBT members to the priesthood. Such progressive stances have taken the Community of Christ even further from its LDS cousins, and in so doing has attracted some disaffected Latter-day Saints who have struggled with the Utah-based church's more conservative positions on women's ordination, LGBT inclusion, and social justice.[13] At the same time, in recent decades the Community of Christ has sometimes struggled to identify and communicate a vision and identity that is positively distinctive from any other liberal ecumenical Christian church.

FIGURE 10.2 The Community of Christ Temple in Independence, Missouri, dedicated in 1994 to worship and the pursuit of peace. Unlike dedicated LDS temples, the Community of Christ Temple is open for public worship and tours.

Beliefs, practices, and leadership

The Community of Christ, which now counts about 250,000 members worldwide, has undergone a substantial evolution in beliefs and practices over the past half century. In its early years the Reorganized Church discarded Joseph Smith's Nauvoo-era innovations including the plurality of gods, baptisms for the dead, temple rituals, and of course polygamy. The church settled instead on a "Kirtland theology," or in other words the state of Mormon belief and practice in about 1838, which remained intact for about a century. However, this led to two different types of struggles for the RLDS Church, one external and the other internal. Historian William Russell observes that throughout the late nineteenth and early twentieth centuries, members of the Reorganization

> never wanted to be confused with the "mountain Mormons" so they rebelled at being called "Mormon," constantly working to educate inquirers about what they saw as "abominable doctrines" that they attributed to Brigham Young in Utah. Few of them realized that Joseph Smith Jr. had actually developed them in Nauvoo. The vast majority of RLDS members really believed that Brigham Young introduced polygamy and the plurality of gods in Utah, the two most offensive Utah doctrines.[14]

When change came, and historical scholarship convincingly demonstrated that many of the traditional RLDS historical claims about Brigham Young's supposed innovations were invalid, the church moved further away from Utah Mormonism, not closer to it. W. Wallace Smith appointed a number of highly educated and liberally minded men to key positions in the church and at Graceland University beginning in the late 1950s. Many of these leaders engaged in sustained (though often confidential) dialogue with nearby liberal Protestant theologians, which in turn influenced their thinking and their counsel to the church. As a result, the RLDS Church gradually started to back away from many of the more sectarian claims of early Latter Day Saint belief. In particular, traditional claims that it was "the one true church" were replaced by more ecumenical language such as, "we [are] a tributary to a stream that was and is the church universal. . . . We [are] called to a marvelous work and a wonder that extends beyond ourselves and embraces all people of faith."[15] The church also began to distance itself from its founder. By the 1960s, RLDS historians had begun to cautiously admit that Joseph Smith, not Brigham Young, had introduced polygamy and other Nauvoo doctrines. For many RLDS members, their founding prophet went from being a hero and icon to an "embarrassment" and "a skeleton in the closet."[16] In many official church materials, Joseph Smith has been rendered entirely invisible.[17]

Changes in church polity and governance were just as significant as theological and historical developments. When Wallace B. Smith announced in 1984 that women would be ordained, and then a decade later the First Presidency expressed support for open communion (allowing people with non-RLDS Christian baptisms to participate in the celebration of the Lord's Supper), it demonstrated that the leadership had decisively cast its lot with mainline Protestant theological liberalism rather than Latter Day Saint tradition. Abandoning the tradition of the church presidency being held by a Joseph Smith descendant also troubled many. These developments led to fierce critiques by traditionalist members of the church, and precipitated the schisms of the 1980s and 1990s. Pointing to the key moment of transition in the 1960s, historian William Russell concludes that "Wallace B. Smith's leadership clearly ended the Church's history as a 'Mormon' church, aligning it more closely with mainstream, ecumenical Protestantism."[18] Indeed, in 2010 the Community of Christ was admitted into the National Council of Churches, an ecumenical consortium of mostly liberal and mainline churches.

"Today," the Community of Christ curriculum teaches, "we embrace a generous Christian orthodoxy, relying on our Restoration heritage for our grounding, while being broadly informed by all of Christian history, doctrine, and practice."[19] "Generous Christian orthodoxy" basically means that Community of Christ beliefs are broadly consonant with modern mainline Protestantism. Foundationally, the church affirms the classical Christian formulation of the Trinity. Its view of salvation focuses more on reconciliation and healing in this life than eternal rewards in the next; LDS notions of exaltation are completely absent. Indeed, virtually anything resembling a distinctive Latter Day Saint doctrine has generally been excised in recent decades, though some Christian themes remain seasoned with a recognizable Restoration flavor. For instance, the church declares that the Bible is "the foundational scripture for the church," but adds that it "uses the Book of Mormon and the Doctrine and Covenants – not to replace the witness of the Bible or improve on it, but because they confirm its message that Jesus Christ is the Living Word of God." In practice, however, many church members use the Bible exclusively, and the Book of Mormon in particular has diminished in importance substantially in recent decades. Zion remains the church's social ideal, but it receives somewhat less explicit attention than it did in the early twentieth-century RLDS Church. In general, the church is wary of anything that resembles doctrinal imposition or exclusiveness; even the church's statement of basic beliefs is prefaced by the caveat that the listed doctrines are offered "not as the last word, but as an open invitation to all to embark on the adventure of discipleship."[20]

Both the Community of Christ and LDS Church believe that God still speaks to and through them, but the Independence-based church has been far more willing to canonize divine pronouncements that have come since the death of Joseph Smith Jr. As of 2016, the Community of Christ Doctrine and Covenants has 164 sections, whereas the LDS edition has 138. Fifty-one sections in the Community of Christ's edition postdate Joseph Smith's death, as opposed to only three, plus two additional "Official Declarations," in the LDS version. Counterintuitively, the church that has retained a stronger sense of prophetic authority has canonized far less scripture emanating from the prophet than has the church that has moved toward a more deliberative, grassroots-led system of governance. (The LDS Church does have one more book of scripture than the Community of Christ, in the form of the Pearl of Great Price, but it is entirely the product of Joseph Smith's revelations and translations.) For many decades the RLDS Church placed greater value on Joseph Smith's Bible translation, also known as the Inspired Version, while the LDS Church remained wary (since the manuscripts and copyrights remained in RLDS possession). However, in recent decades, LDS views of the Bible have remained fairly conservative, with the church officially yoked to the King James Version, while the Community of Christ's openness to modern biblical scholarship has led it to embrace updated translations such as the New Revised Standard Version. The Community of Christ's scriptural hermeneutic has become increasingly liberal, as it sees "scripture as an indispensable witness to the Word of God (Jesus Christ), rather than God's literal words."[21]

The spiritual vision of the Community of Christ in many ways finds symbolic expression in its two temples – in Kirtland, Ohio (the first Mormon temple, which the RLDS Church gained legal possession of in a late nineteenth-century court battle),[22] and in Independence, Missouri (the site of current church headquarters). Unlike LDS temples, these temples are open to the public and are not home to any esoteric rituals. The Independence temple in particular is designed as a "sacred center of worship, education, community building, and discipleship preparation."[23] Dedicated as it is to the pursuit of peace, the temple's architecture reflects the church's ethos of peace-building, reconciliation, spiritual journey, ecumenism, and interfaith relationships. Church members who worship in the temple, often in conjunction with the church's World Conferences, often report a sense of spiritual inspiration and transformation, but there is no sacramental or other form of obligation to visit the temple.

The organizational structure of the Community of Christ remains largely recognizable from the Restorationist church that Joseph Smith established in the 1830s. The church is led by a prophet/president supported by two counselors, who together comprise the First Presidency. The Council of Twelve Apostles, now including women and men, oversees the work of the church around the world, while the three-person Presiding Bishopric supervises church finances. The Seventy report to the Apostles as specially designated missionaries around the world, while the Standing High Council, a body that has receded in importance over time, operates in a largely advisory capacity. Locally, congregations (parallel to an LDS ward or branch) are grouped together in mission centers (parallel to an LDS stake). A congregation is led by a pastor or presiding elder, while each mission center has a president. Other priesthood offices, such as teachers and deacons, also participate in the local ministry, and all are open to both women and men. Most local offices are filled on a volunteer basis, though some congregations are able to hire a paid full-time pastor. Priesthood office is not universally bestowed on teenagers and adults, but is available to those who feel called and prepare themselves for the ministry.

A World Conference is held every three years and attended by delegates from missions and congregations around the globe. The Community of Christ retains the structure of a top-down hierarchy as introduced by Joseph Smith, but decision-making on church policy and doctrine has become far more democratic and bottom-up than in the nineteenth and early twentieth centuries. At World Conference, delegates discuss, debate, and vote upon resolutions to govern the church, including whether to accept or reject new sections in the Doctrine and Covenants. Whereas General Conference in the LDS Church functions as "a mechanism for instructing the Saints," the Community of Christ World Conference operates as "a deliberate and legislative body." This is one of the chief reflections of the differences in principal values between the two religious communities, with the LDS Church emphasizing authority, harmony, and obedience, while the Community of Christ prizes democracy, deliberation, and broad-based participative decision-making.[24] Latter-day Saints talk about "following the prophet" and "sustaining the brethren," whereas Community of Christ members "trust that individual members are guided by the Holy Spirit and together can collectively discern God's calling for the church in our present moment."[25]

• FUNDAMENTALIST MORMONISM

History

In a curious twist of history, the now-liberal and always anti-polygamous Reorganized Church may have helped inspire Mormon fundamentalism, committed in large part to the preservation of the doctrine and practice of plural marriage. From her husband Joseph's death in 1844 until she passed in 1879, Emma Smith adamantly denied her husband's association with polygamy. Late in life she was visited by a prominent member of the LDS Church and responded to a series of his questions about early church history. When asked if her husband had "any more wives than you," she replied, "Not to my knowledge." She also denied that Joseph had received the revelation on plural marriage.[26] It was a willful act of misremembering, since she was in fact fully aware of at least some of Joseph's plural marriages and except for a brief period of acquiescence virulently opposed them, putting a major strain on their marriage. However, trusting his mother's testimony and believing that Brigham Young and the Utah Saints were knowingly sullying his father's name and reputation, Joseph Smith III repeatedly and insistently denounced any notion that polygamy originated with Mormonism's founding prophet. Even before he assumed the presidency of the Reorganization, Joseph III declared that "the Mormons of Salt Lake City are not the Mormons of my father's faith. They teach doctrines which are bound to carry those believing [in them] and practicing them to eventual destruction, but my father never taught or believed them."[27]

Often in direct response to Emma and Joseph III's denials, Brigham Young and the LDS leadership took every opportunity to demonstrate that the religion's founder had in fact revealed and practiced plural marriage. Beginning with the 1852 public announcement of the doctrine, LDS leaders frequently interpreted Smith's 1843 revelation on marriage as meaning that polygamy's practice, or at the very least a firm belief in the principle, was required for exaltation in the celestial kingdom. The religious centrality of plural marriage became even more significant in the 1870s and 1880s as Latter-day Saints attempted to preserve it from federal attacks by arguing it was a core religious belief and practice protected by the First Amendment.[28] Church president John Taylor, who spent much of his administration on the "Mormon Underground" evading federal marshals, articulated the Latter-day Saints' no-surrender position by stating, "There never can be any hope of our yielding up, under any circumstances, a principle of conscientious or religious conviction."[29]

By the 1880s, then, the combination of RLDS claims and the national anti-polygamy crusade had forced the Latter-day Saints into a corner, where they adopted a siege mentality and doubled down on the belief and practice of polygamy as a fundamental principle of the gospel. When Wilford Woodruff did capitulate in 1890, followed up by later and increasingly strict "manifestos" by succeeding church presidents Joseph F. Smith and Heber J. Grant, the faith of many Latter-day Saints was shaken. It was inevitable that such a dramatic reversal in church policy and doctrine would lead to disenchantment among a certain percentage of true believers. Many of them had gone to prison for their practice of polygamy. They sincerely believed John Taylor and other leaders who proclaimed that God would preserve the church if it held fast and never relented on fulfilling his command to practice plural marriage. Even the leadership was not united. In 1906 apostles John W. Taylor (son of the former prophet) and Matthias Cowley were forced to resign their positions in the Quorum of Twelve, and Taylor was excommunicated five years later for his continued resistance to the church's abandonment of plural marriage.

Beginning in the 1920s, a group of those who believed that the church had fallen into error beginning in 1890 coalesced around the leadership of Lorin C. Woolley, constituting the beginnings of what would come to be known as fundamentalist Mormonism (or Mormon fundamentalism). Woolley claimed that church president and prophet John Taylor had received a revelation in September 1886 in which God told him, "All commandments that I give must be obeyed by those calling themselves by my name, unless they are revoked by me or by my authority, and how can I revoke an everlasting covenant[?]"[30] According to fundamentalist claims – strongly disputed by the LDS Church, as is the 1886 revelation – John Taylor prophesied that the church would be forced by the government to give up polygamy, so he secretly called a few faithful men to a special "Priesthood Council" that would exist in parallel to the regularly organized church and retain priesthood authority even once the church lost its way. By 1928, Lorin Woolley was the only surviving member of the Priesthood Council, so he reconstituted it with six new members (plus himself). Most fundamentalists trace their authority to Woolley, and by extension to John Taylor, although one group claims their authority straight from Joseph Smith through one of his contemporaries and trusted associates, Benjamin Johnson, and others broke off from the

LDS Church much later in the twentieth century. Fundamentalist Mormonism is therefore not one single thing, but rather an umbrella term for a bewilderingly complex and diverse set of groups and individuals, many of whom fiercely disagree with one another and have even resorted to violence and other forms of intimidation to destabilize competing sects.

It is not possible here to document in detail all the numerous iterations of fundamentalist Mormonism, especially because it is often practiced by "independent fundamentalists" who do not recognize the authority of any group beyond their own family. However, the majority of fundamentalists gathered together under the leadership of the Priesthood Council in the 1930s. They established a colony called Short Creek (now Colorado City, Arizona, and Hildale, Utah) in an isolated region on the Utah-Arizona border. In addition to practicing polygamy, the group attempted to preserve the cooperative economic system of the early church, calling their system the United Effort Plan. In 1944, state and federal law enforcement officials raided Short Creek, arresting about fifty people and breaking up polygamous families, sending husbands to jail and children to foster homes. An even larger raid in 1953 led to a public backlash when the media portrayed it as heavy-handed state repression of a peaceful and harmless, if idiosyncratic, community.[31] The Colorado City fundamentalists experienced a major schism in the 1950s which ultimately led to the creation of two separate groups, the Fundamentalist Church of Jesus Christ of Latter-Day Saints (FLDS) and the Apostolic United Brethren (AUB), each of which claim some eight to ten thousand members. The FLDS branch in particular has endured several power struggles and schisms in recent decades. In the 1980s the movement transitioned from joint leadership under the Priesthood Council toward the unique authority of a single man, supported by an emergent doctrine called the "One Man Rule."[32] Rulon Jeffs led the group until his death in 2002, at which point his son Warren Jeffs was ordained prophet and president of the church.

Warren Jeffs's tenure as FLDS prophet-president has been marked by constant controversy and legal troubles. In 2003, he directed many of his followers to establish a new colony outside of Eldorado, Texas, where they built a large three-story temple in the center of what they called the Yearning for Zion (YFZ) ranch. In April 2008, law enforcement officials raided the YFZ compound in response to what turned out to be fraudulent phone calls reporting child abuse. State officials removed over four hundred children from the ranch and made several arrests. The raid generated widespread national and international media attention, which focused largely on images of girls and women wearing old-fashioned "prairie dresses," no makeup, and distinctive hairstyles. Legal proceedings stemming from the raid resulted in the conviction of six FLDS men on child sexual assault charges, mostly related to underage marriages performed in the temple on the YFZ ranch. All of this came on the heels of the arrest and conviction of the FLDS prophet-president Warren Jeffs, who was convicted in 2007 and then again in 2011 of two counts of child sexual assault and is now serving a life sentence in prison.[33]

Other polygamous communities have generated far less drama. A group in Centennial Park, Arizona, which split off from the Colorado City fundamentalists in the mid-1980s, has about 1500 people, a large meetinghouse, a public charter school and private high school, a medical clinic, and a number of small businesses. Another group in southeast British Columbia lives unmolested by the Canadian government, which has adopted a laissez-faire approach so long as the polygamists do not engage in any illegal activity (other than polygamy) or otherwise cause any trouble. The Apostolic United Brethren (AUB) are headquartered in Bluffdale, Utah, at the southern end of Salt Lake Valley, though they also have satellite communities in Montana, central Utah, and southern Utah. Their brush with controversy came when their leader, Rulon Allred, was assassinated in 1977 on the order of a rival fundamentalist faction headquartered in Mexico. Otherwise they have generally avoided the spotlight, and meet regularly in buildings they have constructed for church services, schooling, and social gatherings. The largest segment of fundamentalist Mormons are "independents," numbering perhaps as many as fifteen thousand. They may loosely associate with other families or even groups, but they are primarily organized around the immediate family without adhering to any formal organization. Some independents are active members of the LDS Church while secretly believing in or practicing plural marriage. Most independent fundamentalists are well integrated into society, as depicted in the popular television series *Big Love* and *Sister Wives*. A radical fringe, however, have sometimes adopted abusive and even violent practices, as made famous in Jon Krakauer's bestselling book *Under the Banner of Heaven*.[34]

Beliefs, practices, and leadership

The sheer diversity of fundamentalist Mormonism makes it impossible to offer a systematic and coherent body of beliefs and practices that they all share. However, historian D. Michael Quinn has identified "three pillars of Mormon fundamentalism" that are common to nearly all groups:

> Mormon fundamentalists believe that the LDS church is "out of order" – in other words, it has strayed off its divinely instituted path by abandoning or changing various practices and beliefs. They are also convinced that plural marriage is a divine revelation and commandment that should be practiced today by those who are willing and worthy. Finally, Mormon fundamentalists accept priesthood authority and officiators not sanctioned by the LDS church.[35]

While organizing outside the LDS Church and practicing polygamy are their most apparent features, many fundamentalists also retain a number of distinctive doctrines from nineteenth-century Mormonism that have been discarded by the LDS Church. (Most of these doctrines were never promulgated by the Reorganized Church.) For instance, one independent fundamentalist published a book of "ninety-five theses" (echoing Martin Luther) in which he critiqued not only the abandonment of plural marriage but also the cessation of the United Order and other cooperative economic endeavors, the repudiation of Brigham Young's Adam-God doctrine, changes in the temple garments and ordinances, a shift away from pursuing missionary work "without purse or scrip," an end of the physical gathering to Zion, and the reversal of the race-based priesthood-temple ban.[36]

Fundamentalist Mormons use all four books of LDS scripture – the Bible, Book of Mormon, Doctrine and Covenants, and Pearl of Great Price. Their interpretation of scripture often parallels late nineteenth-century LDS usage, with heavy emphasis on millenarianism, obedience to authority, religious and cultural distinctiveness, and of course polygamy. Considering themselves the rightful spiritual heirs of Joseph Smith and Brigham Young, some fundamentalist prophets have produced their own additional books of scripture. For instance, in 2012 the FLDS Church published an 854-page tome entitled *Jesus Christ Message to All Nations*. While it includes a long section of early Mormon revelations and history, the majority of the book consists of revelations received by the incarcerated FLDS prophet-president Warren Jeffs from 2010–2012. (Warren Jeffs is listed as the book's copyright holder, Jesus Christ as the author.) The revelations repeatedly declare Jeffs's innocence and purity, demand his release from prison, predict the imminent return of Jesus Christ and end of the world, and call upon all nations to repent and stop persecuting the FLDS Church.[37]

Most fundamentalist Mormons are highly doctrinaire in their religious instruction. Indeed, one researcher found that "a major appeal of fundamentalism is the intensity of its doctrinal emphasis compared with the primarily social emphasis of the LDS church." Many of those who convert from the LDS Church to fundamentalism report a desire to explore "deep doctrine," which is often discussed in fundamentalist settings but increasingly rarely in LDS meetings. These converts typically gravitate toward groups such as the AUB, with a much smaller percentage seeking out the more restrictive and authoritarian FLDS. For many of these converts, the practice of polygamy is secondary, and often comes much later – if at all.[38] Fundamentalist worship styles typically parallel LDS practice, with similar priesthood ordinances and weekly meeting formats. They will often sing from the LDS hymnal, approvingly cite LDS prophets (even those that have come since 1890), and speak in a distinguishably Mormon vernacular. Most meetings are comfortable and familiar, like LDS Sunday services.[39] Independent fundamentalists will generally conduct meetings in their homes, while the larger organized groups have constructed chapels or other meeting spaces. As a rule, fundamentalists have an all-male priesthood, and most retain even stronger and more conservative gender distinctions than the contemporary LDS Church. Indeed, while allowing for technological advances, most fundamentalist Mormons look to 1880s Mormonism as the golden age that they endeavor to preserve or re-create.

As in pioneer Utah, simple demographics dictate that not all fundamentalists can actually practice plural marriage, though it is often seen as the ideal form of matrimony and family life. Marriage practices vary, with the FLDS Church generally the most conservative, having developed the notion of "placement marriages" in which priesthood leaders assigned brides, often as young girls, to prospective husbands.[40] (This practice is largely what led to the conviction of Warren Jeffs and others for child sexual assault, both as perpetrators and accomplices.) Other groups and families allow considerably more freedom, encouraging but not requiring children to pursue polygamous marriages. Since the 1953 Short Creek raid, law enforcement officials in the United States, Canada, and Mexico have mostly opted not to prosecute polygamous marriages among consenting adults, intruding in fundamentalist communities only to investigate routine crimes as well as more serious allegations of child abuse and sexual assault, tax and welfare fraud, and other felonies not related to plural marriage per se.

While there have been a number of harrowing exposés written by both women and men who have "escaped" the movement, most women in fundamentalist communities report being satisfied and freely opting for a polygamous lifestyle. Perhaps counterintuitively, far more women than men convert to polygamous groups. One study demonstrated that a full 70% of converts over a forty-year period (1953–1993) were female, with the majority of them being single women of childbearing age. Research suggests that women who are drawn to polygamous groups as converts are "marginalized in the mainstream church and the larger society" and are seeking

> tight-knit religious and economic solidarity with other women who have the same standards and desires. . . . They want to be connected to, though not dependent on, a man who honors his "priesthoods" and can enable them to bear many children.[41]

Just as LDS women staged large public demonstrations in support of plural marriage in the late nineteenth century, fundamentalist Mormon women in the twenty-first century have created advocacy groups and published books and magazines promoting plural marriage as a legitimate option for consenting adults. They have worked closely with state attorney generals to build bridges of understanding between law enforcement and polygamous communities, and have lobbied state legislatures and in other ways sought to forge a path toward the decriminalization of polygamy.[42]

Mormon fundamentalists have generally not preserved the ecclesiastical structure shared by the LDS Church and Community of Christ. While retaining many of the priesthood offices laid out in Mormon scripture, in most cases fundamentalist leadership follows either the oligarchic governance model of the 1930s Priesthood Council or the more authoritarian model of a single prophet ruling the church (or, for independents, a single patriarch ruling over his family). Many throughout the history of the fundamentalist movement have seen themselves in a cryptic passage in an 1832 revelation to Joseph Smith which prophesied that God would send "one mighty and strong" to "set in order the house of God."[43] Competing revelations and interests have inspired many individuals and groups to disclaim the authority of established leaders or to proclaim their own unique calling and divine message from heaven. The swirl of personal, doctrinal, and legal conflicts characterizing fundamentalist Mormonism since the 1930s has led to a movement that, while it has produced spiritual meaning and social community for tens of thousands of people, on the whole has been institutionally unstable, deeply fractious, and in high tension both with other Mormon churches (fundamentalist and LDS) and the outside world.

• MORMONISM AS MICROCOSM

From the Community of Christ to the Church of Jesus Christ of Latter-day Saints to the Fundamentalist Church of Jesus Christ of Latter-day Saints, we see the array of religious options that can be developed from a common origin in less than two centuries. These are highly distinctive groups which in many ways have more differences than similarities at this point, and arguably increasingly so with each passing year. This has led to battles over who gets to, or even wants to, use the term "Mormon."[44] Setting aside the contested politics of legitimacy, understanding Mormonism in its broader sense allows us to examine with greater depth a number of trends in modern religious history. The Community of Christ represents a liberal ecumenical church that has achieved cultural inclusion and respectability but nevertheless struggles to define and maintain a distinctive identity. The modern LDS Church has enjoyed remarkable growth and relative influence, yet it faces the constant challenge of "maintaining indefinitely an optimum tension" between the impulses to accommodate to culture on the one hand and resist it on the other.[45] Fundamentalist Mormonism demonstrates the appeal to a small but devoted minority of absolute doctrinal certainty, together with a sense of chosenness and persecution, that marks the persistent attractiveness of fundamentalist remnants in many traditions.[46]

Though the vast majority of self-identified Mormons affiliate with the Church of Jesus Christ of Latter-day Saints, taken together the diversity of Mormon expressions reveals a movement characterized by substantial internal pluralism, both ideologically and institutionally. The inheritors of Joseph Smith's legacy have defined their primary religious commitments in a range of ways, from peace to polygamy. This speaks to the deep and wide theological, social, and cultural reservoirs available to draw upon within the Mormon tradition, which in turn have generated tremendous religious energy and innovation among believers and the organizations they create.

The Mormon solar system thus displays many of the same features as the broader galaxies of Christianity and American religion, which themselves are fixtures in the all-encompassing religious universe. We see multiple bodies of various shapes, compositions, and orbits all held together, however loosely and with varying degrees of strength, by a common gravitational field – in Mormonism's case, the religious legacy of Joseph Smith and the early Latter Day Saints. Each orbiting body, whether the size of a large planet or a small asteroid, has its own integrity and distinctive qualities, while at the same time existing in a dynamic, organic, yet often invisible relationship with all the other orbiting bodies in the system. The original energy and raw materials came from the Big Bang of Smith's revelations, but in a constantly evolving system those materials are always being reshaped and reimagined, sometimes taking surprising forms. In short, Mormonism is a living, expanding, and diverse system.

• NOTES

1 Newell G. Bringhurst and John C. Hamer, eds., *Scattering of the Saints: Schism within Mormonism* (Independence, MO: John Whitmer Books, 2007), 9.

2 This calculation is based on the various church's reported or estimated memberships. The 98% figure is based off reported numbers for all churches, including the LDS Church's 15 million members, whereas the more conservative 96% figure is calculated by maximizing the possible number of adherents within the non-LDS "Mormon" churches while halving the number of "actual" members of the LDS Church to 7.5 million. For a convenient overview of the various churches and their membership totals, see https://en.wikipedia.org/wiki/Latter_Day_Saint_movement and https://en.wikipedia.org/wiki/List_of_sects_in_the_Latter_Day_Saint_movement (accessed January 6, 2016).

3 *History of the Church of Jesus Christ of Latter-day Saints*, 7 vols. (Salt Lake City: Deseret Book Company, 1980), 6:408–409.

4 See Bringhurst and Hamer, *Scattering of the Saints*, 1–6. On the various succession options after Smith's death, see D. Michael Quinn, "The Mormon Succession Crisis of 1844," *Brigham Young University Studies* 16 (Winter 1976): 187–233. See also Steven L. Shields, *Divergent Paths of the Restoration*, 4th ed., rev. and enl. (Los Angeles: Restoration Research, 1990); Roger D. Launius and Linda Thatcher, eds., *Differing Visions: Dissenters in Mormon History* (Urbana: University of Illinois Press, 1994); and William D. Russell, "Understanding Multiple Mormonisms," in *The Oxford Handbook of Mormonism*, eds. Terryl L. Givens and Philip L. Barlow (New York: Oxford University Press, 2015), 81–91.

5 See Bringhurst and Hamer, *Scattering of the Saints*, 9.

6 Steven L. Shields, "Foreword," in *Scattering of the Saints*, eds. Bringhurst and Hamer, 6.

7 Roger D. Launius, *Joseph Smith III: Pragmatic Prophet* (Urbana: University of Illinois Press, 1988), chap. 11, quotes from 247, 266.

8 David J. Howlett, " 'The Making of a Steward': Zion, Ecclesiastical Power, and RLDS Bodies, 1923–1931," *Journal of Mormon History* 32:2 (Summer 2006): 1–37, quotes from 11, 17. On the LDS parallel, see Matthew Bowman, "Zion: The Progressive Roots of Mormon Correlation," in *Directions for Mormon Studies in the Twenty-First Century*, ed. Patrick Q. Mason (Salt Lake City: University of Utah Press, 2016), 15–34.

9 [Community of Christ,] *Book of Doctrine and Covenants* (Independence, MO: Herald Publishing House, 2007), 206–208 [Section 156:5, 7–9].

10 David J. Howlett, Barbara B. Walden, and John C. Hamer, *Community of Christ: An Illustrated History* (Independence, MO: Herald Publishing House, 2010), 68. See also Mark A. Scherer, " 'Called by a New Name': Mission, Identity, and the Reorganized

Church," *Journal of Mormon History* 27:2 (Fall 2001): 40–63; W. Grant McMurray, "A 'Goodly Heritage' in a Time of Transformation: History and Identity in the Community of Christ," *Journal of Mormon History* 30:1 (Spring 2004): 59–75.

11 Community of Christ Doctrine and Covenants 162:2.

12 Community of Christ Doctrine and Covenants 163:3.

13 See Garnet Henderson, "Dissatisfied Liberal Mormons Find Refuge in the Community of Christ," *The Guardian*, October 1, 2015, online at http://www.theguardian.com/us-news/2015/oct/01/women-lgbt-mormons-community-of-christ (accessed January 7, 2016).

14 William D. Russell, "The Last Smith Presidents and the Transformation of the RLDS Church," *Journal of Mormon History* 35:3 (Summer 2008): 51–52, 54.

15 Howlett, Walden, and Hamer, *Community of Christ*, 56.

16 "After all, he was a cult leader who preached doctrines anathema to many Christians, engaged in sexual hijinks of the worst order, sought to take over the United States and make it into a theocracy with him in charge, and, failing that, allowed himself to be martyred as a rallying point for his followers." Roger D. Launius, "Is Joseph Smith Relevant to the Community of Christ?," *Dialogue: A Journal of Mormon Thought* 39:4 (Winter 2006): 62.

17 Joseph Smith Jr. is never mentioned in the booklet *Sharing in Community of Christ: Exploring Identity, Mission, Message, and Beliefs*, 3rd ed. (Independence, MO: Herald Publishing House, 2012), a foundational internal document developed to outline the church's core beliefs and principles. The three-page section on church history (pp. 30–32) mentions and has a picture of Joseph Smith III, but not his father. By contrast, the church's brief illustrated history (Howlett, Walden, and Hamer, *Community of Christ*) dedicates ten pages out of seventy to Joseph Smith Jr. and his period of church history.

18 Russell, "The Last Smith Presidents," 83.

19 Howlett, Walden, and Hamer, *Community of Christ*, 57.

20 *Sharing in Community of Christ*, 14–15.

21 Howlett, Walden, and Hamer, *Community of Christ*, 56.

22 For the importance and multiple functions of the Kirtland Temple throughout history, see David J. Howlett, *Kirtland Temple: The Biography of a Shared Mormon Sacred Space* (Urbana: University of Illinois Press, 2014).

23 Community of Christ Doctrine and Covenants 163:8.

24 O. Kendall White Jr. and Daryl White, "Ecclesiastical Polity and the Challenge of Homosexuality: Two Cases of Divergence within the Mormon Tradition," *Dialogue: A Journal of Mormon Thought* 37:4 (Winter 2004): 71.

25 Howlett, Walden, and Hamer, *Community of Christ*, 50–51.

26 Linda King Newell and Valeen Tippetts Avery, *Mormon Enigma: Emma Hale Smith*, 2nd ed. (Urbana: University of Illinois Press, 1994), 298.

27 Quoted in Stephen C. Taysom, "A Uniform and Common Recollection: Joseph Smith's Legacy, Polygamy, and Public Memory, 1852–2002," in *Dimensions of Faith: A Mormon Studies Reader*, ed. Stephen C. Taysom (Salt Lake City: Signature Books, 2011), 184.

28 The LDS Doctrine and Covenants included Smith's 1843 revelation justifying plural marriage beginning in 1876. It replaced an 1835 declaration by the church endorsing monogamy, which has been included in RLDS/Community of Christ editions until today. For the legal conflict over polygamy, see Sarah Barringer Gordon, *The Mormon Question: Polygamy and Constitutional Conflict in Nineteenth-Century America* (Chapel Hill: University of North Carolina Press, 2002).

29 Quoted in Anne Wilde, "Fundamentalist Mormonism: Its History, Diversity and Stereotypes, 1886–Present," in *Scattering of the Saints*, eds. Bringhurst and Hamer, 261.

30 Quoted in Wilde, "Fundamentalist Mormonism," 261.

31 See Martha Sonntag Bradley, *Kidnapped from that Land: The Government Raids on the Short Creek Polygamists* (Salt Lake City: University of Utah Press, 1993).

32 See Marianne T. Watson, "The 1948 Secret Marriage of Louis J. Barlow: Origins of FLDS Placement Marriage," *Dialogue: A Journal of Mormon Thought* 40:1 (Spring 2007): 83–136.

33 The best analysis of the YFZ raid, and the broader context of the contemporary FLDS Church, is Cardell K. Jacobson and Lara Burton, eds., *Modern Polygamy in the United States: Historical, Cultural, and Legal Issues* (New York: Oxford University Press, 2011).

34 Jon Krakauer, *Under the Banner of Heaven: A Story of Violent Faith* (New York: Anchor Books, 2004). Krakauer's book has been the bestselling book about Mormonism for over a decade, speaking to not only his powerful storytelling abilities but also the public fascination with polygamy and violence. For a helpful overview of the various fundamentalist groups, see Wilde, "Fundamentalist Mormonism."

35 D. Michael Quinn, "Plural Marriage and Mormon Fundamentalism," in *Fundamentalisms and Society: Reclaiming the Sciences, the Family, and Education*, eds. Martin E. Marty and R. Scott Appleby, vol. 2 in *The Fundamentalism Project* (Chicago: University of Chicago Press, 1993), 244.

36 Ogden Kraut, *Nine-Five Theses*, as summarized in J. Max Anderson, "Fundamentalists," in *Encyclopedia of Mormonism*, available online at http://eom.byu.edu/index.php/%22Fundamentalists%22 (accessed January 11, 2016). See also Wilde, "Fundamentalist Mormonism," 258–259.

37 *Jesus Christ Message to All Nations* (Colorado City, AZ: Fundamentalist Church of Jesus Christ of Latter-day Saints, 2012).

38 Quinn, "Plural Marriage and Fundamentalist Mormonism," 252; Janet Bennion, "The Many Faces of Polygamy: An Analysis of the Variability in Modern Mormon Fundamentalism in the Intermountain West," in *Modern Polygamy in the United States*, eds. Jacobson and Burton, 168.

39 Ken Driggs, "Twentieth-Century Polygamy and Fundamentalist Mormons in Southern Utah," *Dialogue: A Journal of Mormon Thought* 24:4 (Winter 1991): 55.

40 See Watson, "The 1948 Secret Marriage of Louis J. Barlow." For more in-depth analysis of fundamentalist marriage practices, and comparisons to nineteenth-century practice in Utah, see Quinn, "Plural Marriage and Mormon Fundamentalism," and the essays in Jacobson and Burton, *Modern Polygamy in the United States*.

41 Janet Bennion, *Women of Principle: Female Networking in Contemporary Mormon Polygyny* (New York: Oxford University Press, 1998), 5.

42 See Wilde, "Fundamentalist Mormonism," 287–288.

43 LDS Doctrine and Covenants 85:7.

44 See Ryan T. Cragun and Michael Neilson, "Fighting over 'Mormon': Media Coverage of the FLDS and LDS Churches," *Dialogue: A Journal of Mormon Thought* 42:1 (Spring 2009): 65–104.

45 Armand L. Mauss, *The Angel and the Beehive: The Mormon Struggle with Assimilation* (Urbana: University of Illinois Press, 1994), 5.

46 See Gabriel A. Almond, R. Scott Appleby, and Emmanuel Sivan, *Strong Religion: The Rise of Fundamentalisms around the World* (Chicago: University of Chicago Press, 2003).

A century is a long time. One hundred years ago, in 1917, there was no such thing as fundamentalist Mormonism. The RLDS Church was still largely preoccupied with being not-LDS. And the LDS Church was struggling to navigate its transition from polygamy to monogamy, political kingdom to accommodationist church. Joseph Smith's nephew was the Latter-day Saints' president and prophet, providing a tangible link to Mormonism's founding generation while also signaling that the church had to be prepared to move into the future. Mormon women enjoyed substantial autonomy in their Relief Societies, engaging in activities such as storing and selling grain, providing needed social services in local communities, publishing their own periodical, and holding meetings calling for the international abolition of war. Racial exclusion was settled policy, and same-sex marriage was literally inconceivable. The global LDS membership – consisting of less than half a million people – was almost entirely confined to the American Intermountain West, and the leadership, in part inspired by the difficulties of immigration attendant to the Great War in Europe, had only just begun encouraging converts to remain and build the church in their homelands.

The rapidity of change in the modern era makes it foolhardy to offer long-term prognostications with any degree of confidence. Systemic threats to contemporary social organization, ranging from climate change to economic inequality to nuclear proliferation, make it impossible to predict what kind of world Mormons (and everyone else) will inhabit in 2117. Attempts to forecast Mormon growth or decline are wild guesses at best, since past performance is no indicator of future achievement.

So what can be said of Mormonism's prospects in the twenty-first century? In the near term, the first fact we must take into consideration is simple demographics: real Mormon growth is occurring almost entirely in the global South, not in the United States and Europe. Given broader trends of secularization, especially among "millennials," it is difficult to conceive how Mormonism might become more attractive to North Atlantic populations. To be sure, there are still plenty of converts coming in as a result of the LDS Church's impressive missionary program. But as we have seen, long-term retention of those converts is a major challenge, meaning that the bucket has a hole that is leaking out members on the other side about as fast as they come in. If the claim that Mormonism was the "world's fastest growing religion" was ever true, it isn't anymore. Both internally and externally, those with a vested interest in Mormonism will have to come up with a new narrative of the religion's significance that doesn't center on simple numerical growth.[1]

In the near future, the LDS Church's engagement in the public square will continue to be dominated by three themes: humanitarian assistance, in which the church has become a globally respected player despite its relatively modest size; religious freedom, largely connected to self-interested questions of not being forced to sanction same-sex marriages; and gender and sexuality, mostly concerned with the place of LGBT individuals in the church and the question of women's ordination to the priesthood. While the Community of Christ will continue become more LGBT-affirming and inclusive, we should not expect to see any substantial changes in the LDS Church's official policies on same-sex marriage or women's ordination anytime soon. The church may conceivably budge somewhat on the exercise of female priestly power, perhaps returning to the nineteenth-century precedents in which Mormon women gave blessings by the laying on of hands to their children and to other women. The Relief Society may also have restored to it some of the autonomy that was largely stripped away over the course of the twentieth century.

The resignation of Pope Benedict XVI in 2013 has led many Latter-day Saints to look again at their own gerontocracy, which has become both more entrenched and problematic in an era when medical science makes it possible to keep bodies functioning much longer than minds. The inherent organizational conservatism of a seniority-based leadership provides the church with tremendous stability, but in recent decades a fully active church president has become more the exception than the norm. With so much authority vested in them, when even a handful of the fifteen members of the First Presidency and Quorum of the Twelve Apostles are incapacitated or substantially slowed by age-related symptoms, it has serious consequences for the governance of the church and, increasingly, the confidence of its members.[2]

Questions about the gerontocracy are arising at the same time that Mormonism is experiencing similar dynamics of generational change that affect all other religions and institutions. Whereas an older generation of Mormons was characteristically doctrinaire and inward-oriented, the younger generation is more activist and socially engaged. Many younger Mormons are experiencing discontent and anomie with a church that typically offers a strong internal culture but relatively little connection to local non-Mormon communities. Furthermore, the messages they hear at church, especially about marriage and sexuality, are nearly the polar opposite from what has become normative in the general culture. The short-term approach of church leaders has been to retrench and draw sharp distinctions between the church's revealed doctrines and what they characterize as moral drift in the broader culture. A century ago, the LDS Church was willing to give up its core teachings about family in order to remain culturally relevant, which in turn allowed for its success as a missionary religion. It remains to be seen whether and to what degree the church will have to adjust its policies and doctrines in order to avoid marginalization and perhaps even prosecution in countries that are increasingly committed to full rights and protection for LGBT individuals and families. Even if it remains uninhibited by legal action, the question arises of whether a church with strong anti-LGBT policies will have broad appeal in twenty or thirty years or simply appear in the popular mind as a reactionary sect. On the other hand, holding the traditional line on gender and sexuality may enhance Mormonism's appeal in the global South, where many societies remain morally conservative and religious believers are critical of what they see as most American and European churches' willingness to cave to liberal culture and moral relativism.

Independent of its position on gender and sexuality issues, Mormonism will have a limited appeal to major segments of the U.S. and global population so long as its image continues to be that of a white, suburban, middle-class, conservative church. The LDS Church will have to advance its pace of indigenization and enculturation if it is to have a robust long-term global presence. Mormon culture will have to not only tolerate but authentically embrace genuine diversity in terms of political ideology, socioeconomic status, and ethnic and racial identity. To reach historically marginalized populations, the church's near-exclusive focus on doctrinal purity and individual morality will need to be complemented by structural analysis and a greater commitment to social justice, including a recognition of its past and present short-comings. Missionaries and church members will need to become more comfortable with the world's staggering religious diversity, and to develop less sectarian strategies for operating in pluralistic and especially non-Christian environments.

These challenges notwithstanding, Mormonism will continue to thrive as one of America's most prominent and successful religious minority communities. As an amazing self-replicating system, Mormonism will continue to make Mormons. The strength and commitment of the core membership of any LDS congregation would be the envy of virtually any other religious denomination.

The question ultimately facing Mormonism in the twenty-first century is not whether it will thrive, but what it will contribute. Not everyone will accept the offer of its particular doctrines and rituals of salvation. Will Mormonism be relevant only for Mormons, or can it apply its unique insights and communal gifts to addressing the variegated social, cultural, political, economic, and ecological challenges that will vex humanity in the new millennium? There are many possible paths ahead, but it is not inconceivable that Mormons in the twenty-first century might become like Jews in the twentieth century – concentrated in numbers but disproportionately influen-tial because of a core set of values that fosters an ethic of serving and transforming that transcends their own internal religious community. If the story of nineteenth-century Mormonism was about origins and survival, and twentieth-century Mormon-ism was focused on growth and stabilization, then perhaps in the twenty-first century, Mormonism will be characterized by a mature reflection on what the religion and its adherents can accomplish not just in but for the world.

Mormonism has succeeded as one of modernity's original contributions to the world's rich mosaic of religious thought and devotion. Drawing on the legacy of Joseph Smith's revelations and his prophetic vision of Zion, Mormons seek neither to escape nor withdraw from the world but rather to inhabit and transform it. The cumulative result of all their shared history, beliefs, practices, and culture is the production of nothing less than an internally plural yet nevertheless distinctive and coherent Mormon way of being modern. What Mormons and Mormonism will look like in a hundred or thousand years is anyone's guess – but that they're in for the long haul is a sure bet.

• NOTES

1 This and the following paragraphs are adapted from Patrick Q. Mason, "Mormonism's Future: Influential Beyond the Numbers," *Patheos*, August 5, 2015, available online at http://www.patheos.com/Topics/Future-of-Faith-in-America/Mormon ism/Mormonisms-Future-Patrick-Mason-08-05-2015 (accessed January 22, 2016).

2 See Gregory A. Prince, Lester E. Bush Jr., and Brent N. Rushforth, "Gerontocracy and the Future of Mormonism," *Dialogue: A Journal of Mormon Thought* 49:3 (Fall 2016): 89–108.

Index

Note: Page numbers in italic indicate illustrations.

Farmer, Jared 66
fast and testimony meeting 195
fasting 185
fast offering 185–6
feminism 64, 96, 99–100, 149
First Presidency 133, 146, 150, 235
First Vision 29–32, *31*, 221
Folk, Edgar 70
Ford, Thomas 58
Friedan, Betty 96
fundamentalism 139, 149, 244–50;
    beliefs, practices, and leadership
    247–50; history 244–7
Fundamentalist Church of Jesus Christ
    of Latter-Day Saints 246, 248–9

garments *see* temple garments
gathering 43, 47, 208, 248
gay marriage *see* same-sex marriage
gender norms and roles 23–4, 95–100,
    117, 171–2, 256–7
genealogy 203
general authorities 144, 186, 197
General Conference 107, 133, 142,
    196–7
Gentiles 173
gifts of the Spirit *see* spiritual gifts
Givens, Terryl 106, 118, 120
God 29, 106, 108, 124–5, 138,
    158–63, 167, 169, 171, 188
Godhead 122, 138, 163, 169
gold plates 33–8, 118–19
gospel culture 4
Gospel Topics essays 89, 148
Graceland University 236, 241
Grant, Heber J. 86–7, 150–1, 183, 245
growth of LDS Church 79, 90, *91*,
    217–20, 223–4, 255–6
Gurley, Zenos 236

Haight, Isaac 67
Hanciles, Jehu 225
Handbook of Instructions 144–5
Harris, Martin 28, 34–5

Hatch, Orrin 83
Hawn's Mill Massacre 51
Hayes, Rutherford B. 68
Heavenly Father *see* God
Heavenly Mother 99, 161–2, 171
hermeneutics 88, 110–13, 243
Hill Cumorah 33
Hinckley, Gordon B. 99, 220, 221
history, LDS approach to 89–90,
    147–9, 235
Holy Ghost 107, 137–40, 168,
    169–70, 195, 244
Holy Spirit *see* Holy Ghost
home teaching 24, 196
homosexuality 97–9, 172, 256–7;
    see also gay marriage
Hoole, Daryl 96
House of Israel 173–4
Howe, Daniel Walker 115
Howe, Eber 48
hymns *see* music

"I Am a Child of God" 158
independent fundamentalists 246, 247
indigenization 221–5, 257
initiatory 201–2
Institute 88
intelligences 124, 159–60; *see also*
    premortal existence

James, Jane 92
Jaredites 116, 117
Jeffs, Rulon 246
Jeffs, Warren 246, 248, 249
Jenkins, Philip 224
Jesus Christ 29, 117–18, 123–4, 156,
    163–7, 169, 173, 195, 221
Jesus Christ Message to All Nations 248
John Birch Society 79
Johnson, Benjamin 245
Johnson, Sonia 96
John the Baptist 39, 110, 168, 197
John Whitmer Historical
    Association 235